KV-637-869

Gender, Economy and Culture in the European Union

Gender, Economy and Culture in the European Union provides a comprehensive analysis of comparative gender difference in Europe. In addressing a range of empirical issues – from employment and households to the state, migration, male violence and values and attitudes – the book transcends the conventional 'economy/culture' divide. This wide coverage is contextualised within an overall view of structuring 'gender cultures' which vary historically and spatially, also allowing the recognition of important regional differences, as well as national contrasts.

The contributors, all of whom are experts in their field, are drawn from a variety of intellectual, disciplinary and national backgrounds. Each contribution is written to a common structure, allowing the reader to compare between chapters and to read across them. It is an important contribution to cultural studies, gender studies and sociology, and will be essential reading to students and researchers of related disciplines, such as politics and social policy.

Simon Duncan is Professor in Comparative Social Policy at the University of Bradford and was previously Associate Director of the Gender Institute at the London School of Economics. From 1994 to 1998, he was chair of the European Foundation network 'Gender inequality and the European regions'. His most recent publication is *Lone Mothers, Paid Work and Gendered Moral Rationalities*.

Birgit Pfau-Effinger is Professor of Sociology at the Berlin School of Economics. She has published widely in comparative sociology and social policy; the sociology of inequality and labour markets; family sociology and gender studies. She is a member of the EU Action Programme 'Changing Labour Makets, Welfare Policies and Citizenship'.

Routledge Research in Gender and Society

1 **Economics of the Family and Family Policies**
Edited by Inga Persson and Christina Jonung

2 **Women's Work and Wages**
Edited by Inga Persson and Christina Jonung

3 **Rethinking Households**
An Atomistic Perspective on European Living Arrangements
Michael Verdon

4 **Gender, Welfare State and the Market**
Thomas P. Boje and Arnlaug Leira

5 **Gender, Economy and Culture in the European Union**
Simon Duncan and Birgit Pfau-Effinger

Gender, Economy and Culture in the European Union

Edited by
Simon Duncan
and
Birgit Pfau-Effinger

London and New York

First published 2000 by Routledge
11 New Fetter Lane, London EC4P 4EE

Simultaneously published in the USA and Canada
by Routledge
29 West 35th Street, New York, NY 10001

Routledge is an imprint of the Taylor & Francis Group

Typeset in Baskerville by
Prepress Projects Ltd, Perth, Scotland
Printed and bound in Great Britain by
University Press, Cambridge.

British Library Cataloguing in Publication Data
A catalogue record for this book is available
from the British Library

Library of Congress Cataloging in Publication Data
Gender, economy, and culture in the European Union/edited by
Simon Duncan and Birgit Pfau-Effinger
      p. cm. – (Routledge research in gender and society)
   Includes bibliographical references and index.
   1. Sex discrimination against women – European Union
   countries. 2. Sex role – European Union countries. 3. Sexual
   division of labour – European Union countries.
   I. Duncan, Simon. II. Pfau-Effinger, Birgit. III. Series.
   HQ1237.5E85 G45 2000
   305.4′094–dc21   00-062570
ISBN 0-415-23911-7

Contents

List of figures   viii
List of tables   x
List of contributors   xi
Preface   xiv
Acknowledgement   xvi

1 Introduction: theorising comparative gender inequality   1
SIMON DUNCAN

1.1 Issues: the spatiality of gender 1
1.2 Theorising gender spatiality at the national level – from gendered
*   welfare regimes to local gender cultures 4*
1.3 Theorising gender spatiality at the local level – from spatial
*   divisions of labour to local gender cultures 16*
1.4 Afterword 20

PART I
Gender divisions of labour – paid and unpaid work   25

2 Paid work: participation, inclusion and liberation   27
GUNNEL FORSBERG, LENA GONÄS AND DIANE PERRONS

2.1 Issues: mapping the inequality – an explanatory approach 27
2.2 Patterns: gender inequality in paid employment 28
2.3 Explanations: gender regimes, cultures and contracts 41
2.4 Afterword 46

3 Households and families: changing living arrangements
and gender relations   49
MARÍA JOSÉ GONZÁLEZ LÓPEZ AND MONTSERRAT SOLSONA PAIRÓ

3.1 Issues: changing gender relations and living arrangements 49

3.2   Patterns: new and old households across European states 52
3.3   Explanations: the role of women in inducing family change 62
3.4   Afterword 79

4   Reconciling divisions of labour   87
EILEEN P. DREW

4.1   Issues: patriarchy, paid work and the household 87
4.2   Patterns: gendered divisions of labour in markets and households 88
4.3   Explanations 101
4.4   Afterword 108

PART II
**Gender divisions of power – citizenship, rights
and control**   113

**5   Gender and European welfare states: context, structure
and agency**   115
HENRIK P. BANG, PER H. JENSEN AND BIRGIT PFAU-EFFINGER

5.1   Issues: the need to contextualise welfare state policies 115
*5.2   Patterns: variations in the gender policies of welfare states and
        problems of interpretation 116*
*5.3   Explanations: welfare state policies in the context of gender
        arrangements 123*
*5.4   Afterword: from essentialism to anti-essentialism in gender
        analysis 130*

**6   Gender, migration and social inequalities: the
dilemmas of European citizenship**   143
MARINA CALLONI AND HELMA LUTZ

6.1   Issues: gender, contracts and citizenship 143
6.2   Patterns: migration in post-war Europe 149
*6.3   Explanations: feminised migration – the case of female domestic
        workers 158*
*6.4   Afterword: multiculturalism, globalisation and cosmopolitanism:
        towards a negotiated citizenship 161*

**7   Male violence and control: constructing a comparative
European perspective**   171
CAROL HAGEMANN-WHITE

7.1 Issues 171

7.2 *Patterns 181*
7.3 *Explanations 191*
7.4 *Afterword: heterosexuality, violence and culture 202*

PART III
Gendered understandings – cultures and values   209

8 **Challenging and negotiating the myths: gender divisions**
    in the situation comedy   211
    LIZA TSALIKI

    8.1 *Issues: differentiated gender cultures and the sitcom 211*
    8.2 *Patterns: the sitcom and gender representations 215*
    8.3 *Explanations: gender cultures and sitcom representation 223*
    8.4 *Afterword 229*

9 **Living through the myths: gender, values, attitudes and**
    practices   233
    ROSEMARIE SACKMANN

    9.1 *Issues: the relation between values and practices 233*
    9.2 *Patterns: gender values and practices in the European Union 237*
    9.3 *Explanations: connecting values and practices 251*
    9.4 *Afterword: gender difference and equality 254*

10 **Conclusion: gender cultures, gender arrangements**
     and social change in the European context   262
     BIRGIT PFAU-EFFINGER

     10.1 *Introduction 262*
     10.2 *Main changes in Western European gender structures 263*
     10.3 *The integration of 'culture' into cross-national analysis of change 264*
     10.4 *'Gender equality' as a relational concept 271*
     10.5 *Afterword 273*

     Index   277

Figures

1.1 Allocating countries to gender systems: feminist social policy models   7

1.2 Allocating countries to gender systems: feminist sociology models   11

2.1 Change in the female/male activity rate ratio (15–24 years) in the European Union, 1987–96   30

2.2 Change in the female/male activity rate ratio (25–54 years) in the European Union, 1987–96   31

2.3 Female/male activity rate ratio (25–54 years) in the European Union, 1996   33

2.4 Total female/male employment rate ratio in the European Union, 1996   34

2.5 Female/male unemployment rate ratio in the European Union, 1996   35

2.6 Weighted female/male activity rate ratio (15–24 years) in the European Union, 1996   37

2.7 Weighted female/male activity rate ratio (25–54 years) in the European Union, 1996   38

2.8 Women employed in market services in the European Union, 1996   39

2.9 Men employed in market services in the European Union, 1996   40

3.1 Types of living arrangements in the European Union, 1994   53

3.2 Women's partnership status at birth of first child; age group interviewed 25–29, selected European countries   58

3.3 Average size of households (number of persons), selected European countries, 1991   59

3.4 Time allocated to household work: women and men aged 25–64, selected European countries   60

3.5 Average age of women at first marriage, selected European countries, 1980 and 1996   64

3.6 Cumulative percentage of married women by educational level: 1955–59 cohort (aged 32–36 in 1991), Spain   65

3.7 Cumulative percentage of women aged 30–34 who have left the parental home by birth cohorts, selected European countries   67

3.8   Average duration in three conjugal states (single, cohabiting
        and married) for women (aged 15–49), selected European
        countries, mid-1980s   68
3.9   Cohabiting women in Portuguese regions, 1991   74
3.10   Births outside marriage in Portuguese regions, 1991   74
4.1   Male activity rates, European Union, 1975–97   89
4.2   Female activity rates, European Union, 1975–97   90
4.3   Percentage of employed women working part-time,
        European Union, 1975–97   91
4.4   Percentage of employed men working part-time, European
        Union, 1975–97   91
4.5   Percentage of women aged 25–59 who were 'inactive',
        European Union, 1975–97   98
7.1   The triangle of forces making male violence visible   172
8.1   Sitcoms and gender myths   230
10.1   Culture, institutions, social structures and social action
        within the gender arrangement   267

Tables

1.1	Genderfare in developed countries	16
3.1	Cohabitees according to age group and sex (%), selected European countries, 1996	69
3.2	Proportion of marriages ending in divorce by marriage cohorts and total divorce rate in 1995, selected European countries	72
3.3	Births outside marriage (per 100 births), selected European countries, 1970–97	77
3.4	Reformulation of gender relationships: new and old living arrangements	80
5.1	Women's labour force participation: case study countries, 1993	118
5.2	The labour force participation of mothers, ratio of female to male earnings, publicly funded services for children, and maternity/paternity leave arrangements: case study countries, around 1990	120
6.1	Participation and unemployment rates in selected OECD countries by sex, place of birth and nationality, 1995	156
7.1	Overview of representative prevalence data on physical violence by partner or member of household in European countries	183
9.1	The equality model in the European Union: ideal and reality	241
9.2	Ideal and actual divisions of labour, EU 12	242
9.3	Attitudes to women's roles in the European Union, 1990, percentage of full agreement with the six statements	243

Contributors

Henrik P. Bang researches and teaches in comparative politics and political theory, with a particular interest in constructivism, democracy between government and governances and new modes of civic engagement. Recent work includes *Hverdagsmageren* (*The Everyday Maker*, Akademisk Forlag, Copenhagen); *Demokrati franeden* (*Democracy from Below*) (co-editor, Akademisk Forlag, Copenhagen) and *Governance, Governmentality and Democracy* (editor, Manchester University Press).

Marina Calloni is Professor for the Philosophy of Social Sciences at the University of Milan – Bicocca and co-ordinator of the International Network for Research on Gender based at the London School of Economics Gender Institute. Her main research interests are social philosophy, gender studies and critical theory. Recent co-authored books include *Migration, Biographie, Geschlecht* (Universität Bremen Verlag, 2000) and *Pensare la Societa: Idea di Filosofia Sociale* (Carocci, 2000). She is also co-editor of *Research and Networks Across the Boundaries: a Different Approach to Globalisation* (Nordic Council of Ministries, 2001).

Eileen P. Drew is a senior lecturer in the Department of Statistics and Centre for Gender and Women's Studies at Trinity College, Dublin. Her research has focused on flexible employment, demographic change and gender and leadership, and she has recently completed projects on gender equality in the Irish civil service and on women and management in the millennium.

Simon Duncan is Professor in Comparative Social Policy at the University of Bradford and was previously Associate Director of the Gender Institute at the London School of Economics. From 1994 to 1998, he was chair of the European Foundation network 'Gender inequality and the European regions'. His most recent publication is *Lone Mothers, Paid Work and Gendered Moral Rationalities*.

Gunnel Forsberg is Professor in Human Geography and Urban and Regional Planning at Stockholm University. Her research interests are in gender and the labour market, the restructuring of the countryside and regional gender contracts. Her most resent research deals with integrating rural and urban policies for dynamic planning and with understanding how gender discourses are performed and represented in specific places.

Lena Gonäs took her PhD in economic geography from the University of Uppsala, and has subsequently researched on labour market processes and policies, labour relations, the restructuring of the welfare state and changing gender relations. She is currently head of a reseach programme on gender, work and health at the National Institute of Working Life in Stockholm, and is also professor of Work Life Science at the University of Karlstad.

María José Gonzáles Lópes works at the Centre of Demographic Studies in Barcelona. She was previously visiting researcher at the El Colegio de la Frontera Norte (Tijuana, Mexico), research fellow at the European Gender Reseach Laboratory (London School of Economics) and subsequently at the European University Institute in Florence. She is co-editor of *Gender Inequalities in Southern Europe* (Frank Cass, 2000).

Carol Hagemann-White studied history at Harvard University and later took a PhD in philosophy, and a higher research degree in sociology, from the Free University of Berlin. She was appointed Professor in Educational Theory and Women's Studies at Osnabrück University in 1988. She has researched widely on gender inequality, especially violence against women, and was recently awarded a prize for research excellence by the Swedish Tercentenary Foundation, spending 12 months at Uppsala University.

Per H. Jensen is a sociologist and currently Associate Professor in Comparative Welfare State Studies at Aalborg University. Since 1981, he has conducted several research projects on labour markets and welfare states in comparative perspective. He is chair of an EU network on 'Changing labour markets, welfare policies, and citizenship'.

Helma Lutz is reader in sociology and educational sciences at the University of Münster. She researches on women, ethnicity and migration in Europe. She has recently co-edited *Women in Transit: Between Tradition and Transformation* (special issue of the *European Journal of Women's Studies* 2000), *The New Migration in Europe* (Macmillan, 1998) and *Unterschiedlich Verschieden. Differenz in der Erziehungswissenschaft* (Leske und Budrich, 2000).

Montserrat Solsona Pairó is a lecturer in Demography and Gender at the Autonomous University of Barcelona and a researcher at the Centre of Demographic Studies. She studied economics at the University of Barcelona and demography with the United Nations in Chile. She was guest scholar at the European Gender Research Laboratory (London School of Economics), and subsequently worked at the Centro de Desenvolvimento e Planejamento Regional (Belo Horizonte, Brazil). She is co-author of *Estructuras Familiares en Espana* (Instituto de la Mujer, 1990).

Diane Perrons is senior lecturer in the Department of Geography and Environment and Associate Fellow of the Gender Institute at the London School of Economics. In her spare time she is a member of the UK's Women's Budget Group. Recently she co-ordinated a project on flexible working and the reconciliation of paid work and family life for the European Union and she is currently researching the new economy and the work–life balance.

Birgit Pfau-Effinger is Professor of Sociology at the Berlin School of Economics. She has published widely in comparative sociology and social policy, the sociology of inequality and labour markets and family sociology and gender studies. She is a member of the EU Action Programme 'Changing Labour Makets, Welfare Policies and Citizenship'.

Rosemarie Sackmann is assistant professor in the Institute for Intercultural and International Studies at the University of Bremen. Educated as a social scientist, she has researched widely in comparative gender studies and in urban and regional sociology. She is currently researching on the collective identities of Turkish migrants in Germany.

Liza Tsaliki is Marie Curie Research Fellow in the Department of Communication at the University of Nijmegen. After obtaining her PhD on the relationship between television and national identity at the University of Sussex, she taught media studies at the University of Sunderland. She is currently writing a book on globalisation, power and identity.

Preface

Purpose of the book

The terrain of this book is the field of comparative gender studies, in the particular context of Western Europe. The European Union, national and local governments, and researchers have all become increasingly concerned with gender issues, such as the reconciliation of home and family with paid work, women's political representation and employment, domestic violence and sexual harassment, and with how these vary between different countries and regions. Yet this flurry of activity remains fragmented on all levels – conceptually, by subject matter and in terms of role. Thus the aim of this book is to cover the field in an empirically and conceptually coherent way.

First, the book addresses a spectrum of gender issues, from employment and households to culture and attitudes, taking in the state, migration and male violence along the way. This wide coverage is then placed within an overall conceptual view of gender inequality as being both structured, and partly produced, by deep and long-lasting 'gender cultures', which nevertheless also vary spatially, and are subject to change historically. This approach necessitates attention to the various spatial levels on which gender cultures operate, including regions and labour markets as well as national states, and also allows the book to transcend the 'economy/culture' divide.

Structure of the book

The variability of gender inequality in Europe, in terms of the outcomes for the lives of women and men, and the ways in which these variations are produced and changed are the book's key concerns. This subject matter is organised into three major thematic parts:

1 *Gender divisions of labour – paid and unpaid work.* This includes chapters about the universality of, and differences in, gender inequality in employment (Chapter 2), changing gender relations in households and families – do new forms of family mean more egalitarian gender relations, and is this to 'blame' for new patterns of fertility and parenting? (Chapter 3), and reconciling paid and unpaid work – how can gender equality in divisions of labour be achieved? (Chapter 4).

2 *Gender divisions of power – citizenship, rights and control.* This part consists of chapters dealing with the role of the welfare state in the reproduction – and alteration – of gender inequality (Chapter 5), changes in gender relations and inequalities caused by increasing inter-European mobility and new forms of migration (Chapter 6), and variations in levels of male violence and what this may say about gender relations (Chapter 7).

3 *Gendered understandings – cultures and values.* The chapters in this part deal with gender stereotyping and challenge in soap opera (Chapter 8) and the connections between gendered values and practices (Chapter 9).

In moving through this structure the subject matter describes an 'empirical circle' where the concerns of the later chapters re-address those of the earlier chapters, although from a different angle. An introduction (Chapter 1) reviews theoretical perspectives on comparing gender inequality, while the conclusion (Chapter 10) tries to integrate the comparative analyses of gender inequality with the way these could be theoretically conceptualised.

Each chapter (apart from the introduction and conclusion) has the same structure of four sections:

1 an introductory 'issues' section which outlines theoretical and empirical issues in the subject area, and sets out problems for analysis;

2 an empirical 'patterns' section which comparatively describes salient features for Western Europe, paying particular attention to the spatial levels on which these processes operate;

3 a synthetic 'explanations' section which draws together the patterns discovered in (2) with causal explanations; and

4 an 'afterword' outlining theoretical and empirical issues yet to be resolved.

This structure will allow readers both to compare between chapters and to read across them along the four levels.

Acknowledgement

This book records the work of the 'Gender Inequality in the European Regions' network supported by the European Science Foundation (ESF) between 1994 and 1997. The editors and authors thank the European Science Foundation for making this publication possible.

The European Science Foundation is an association of fifty-nine major national funding agencies devoted to basic scientific research in twenty-one countries, representing all scientific disciplines. The Foundation acts as a catalyst for the development of science by bringing together leading scientists and funding agencies, in its programmes, networks and research conferences, to debate, plan and implement pan-scientific and science policy initiatives.

1 Introduction

Theorising comparative gender inequality

Simon Duncan

1.1 Issues: the spatiality of gender

Gender inequality is widespread in human history. At the same time, however, women and men in different social circumstances, in different places, show an immense divergence in their experiences and in their relations to one another. How inequality takes place, to what degree, in what areas of life, and with what effects – all can differ substantially in different places. Similarly, both women and men possess different opportunities in different places for altering, or coping with, their position and experiences. Even among the relatively small group of Western European countries, just looking at the present and recent past, there are substantial differences in gender inequalities and gender relations. Men and women, in different European countries, lead different lives and possess different expectations of what their lives should be – even though all live within gender inequality. Nor is this difference just a matter of cross-national differences alone: there are also significant variations at the levels of different regions, local labour markets and neighbourhoods – both across and within countries.

These variations in gender inequality can be surprising, especially as both lay people and researchers alike often assume that their own experience, in the place in which they live or research, is normal or even universal. This is actually most unlikely to be the case and because of this comparative research (which is not only cross-national research) can be illuminating, even shocking or liberating. Social norms are not necessarily normal somewhere else, and things can happen differently. Gender is no exception. At the same time comparative research becomes pivotal in building up an explanatory account of how gender relations work, and how gender inequalities are formed and change. For now the issue becomes one of *how* processes can vary, what the various outcomes are and how they are differentially caused. This is the focus of this book.

Unfortunately, much of social science has traditionally neglected the spatiality of society, implicitly assuming that social actions and objects can exist on the head of a pin, and are not affected by where they take place. In this view gender relations would be more or less the same everywhere. Even if there are spatial differences these are assumed to be trivial – certainly at the causal level where such differences are regarded as idiosyncratic fluctuations around an invariant and non-spatial social process. But space does make a difference. Social (and natural) processes do not take place in some ethereal location above the real world. As social scientists, we may *think about* gender (or class, discourse, or whatever) in a spaceless way but such phenomena are always constituted in particular places. And places are never a 'clean slate'. Other natural and social phenomena are already unevenly distributed spatially. We can conceptualise the effects this has in three ways:

1   *Space as a contingent effect on outcomes.* Natural and social processes have already created uneven spatial distributions and relations, and in this sense we can talk of a pre-existing spatial landscape. Any social process will then interact contingently with other spatially varying phenomena. So, for example, welfare states or gender relations may have certain inherent features, logics or properties, but they will always be in interaction with other spatially constituted phenomena – inheritance systems, economic conditions, religious beliefs, or soil types, for instance. Welfare states and gender relations will then be different in different places.

2   *Space as a contingent effect on process.* It is not just that the same social processes contingently produce different outcomes in different conditions (places). In addition the same processes will work differently in different conditions (places). For example, what it means to be a man or a woman, or to be a member of a certain class, will be different in different places. This is why, for example, women's part-time work can be seen as generally reinforcing women's domestic role in Britain, but is more likely to be supportive of their 'worker-citizen' role in Sweden. How gender relations work, and hence gendered experiences and consequences, are also different in different places.

3   *Space as a scale effect.* These contingent effects also mean that different social processes will take place at different spatial scales. For example, national states may allocate resources through social policy, and as this will be gendered then this allocation will also differentially affect men and women, in different ways, in different welfare states. But the market allocation of jobs and investment takes place through spatial divisions of labour which link the global market with local labour markets. Different sorts of jobs and occupations, which are also gendered, are then differentially allocated on a regional or local labour market scale. Similarly, resources from social networks (such as informal childcare or moral support) are often allocated at a neighbourhood scale. Again, these local allocations are deeply gendered – for example they may depend on ideas of good motherhood formed in local discourse and practices.

The 'spatial amnesia' of much of social research has periodically been opposed by some varieties of geography and sociology which have recognised the difference that space makes. All too often, however, these reactions have swung to the other extreme of 'spatial determinism' – social processes are seen to be almost completely dominated by where they take place. Research has swung from one extreme to the other as the inadequacies of each become apparent (see Gregory and Urry 1985). How, then, can we research the marked differences in gender inequality over space without swinging on the pendulum once more, and without falling into either of the two traps of spatial amnesia or spatial determinism?

Some post-modernists might react to this dilemma by simply rejecting it. As there are any number of overlapping and temporary discourses of femininity and masculinity, and because these are historically and culturally viable, it would be futile to look for coherent, stable and repeated spatial effects. This encourages a tendency to downplay the influence of structures, spatial or otherwise. There is however another resolution, inspired by realist versions of explanation in social science (Sayer 2000). In this view spatial differences are indeed socially constituted (and also constituted by processes in the 'natural' world). There is no pre-given natural or absolute space which structures society. This is why it is wrong to look for invariable spatial relations, as so often assumed in the spatial determinist view. At the same time, however, as spatial differences *have been* constituted, then all social objects and relations will be spatially variant. What they are like, and how they relate, will be contingent upon where they take place, for this influences how they interact with other social and natural forms. Social processes do not float around in some ethereal dimension located somewhere above the real world. Theorising at an abstract level might need to assume this in order to make our mental models clearer, but as soon as we apply these ideas empirically then we must re-admit spatial contingency one way or another (see Duncan 1989 for development). This view also implies that while the post-structuralist critique is correct to attack structural*ism* it is incorrect in downplaying the effect of socio-spatial structures. This is equivalent to throwing out the baby with the bathwater.

What we must do is to hold two propositions simultaneously. There are no general social processes because of space, but there are also no general spatial processes because of society. How social processes work, however, will vary spatially. Hence, our attention needs to be drawn to the particular spatial effects of the specific social process we are examining, and the scale at which it operates. This was one resolution of the 'locality debate' of the late 1980s (see Duncan and Savage 1991). Comparative research then becomes prioritised in this view of difference, both in describing variations and in building up an explanatory account of how social structures differentially operate. This provides the overall theme for the chapters that follow.

1.2 Theorising gender spatiality at the national level – from gendered welfare regimes to local gender cultures

Much of social science remained gender blind long into the 1970s, when if at all gender was usually represented in terms of academically peripheral 'women's issues' such as 'the family' or 'women's employment'. However, it soon became clear that these issues had quite different profiles in different European countries. Thus researchers in Britain and Germany were forcibly struck by the development of public childcare and other 'family-friendly' welfare arrangements, like parental leave or leave to look after sick children, in the Scandinavian countries. In contrast with their own countries, these developments allowed women to be both mothers and full-time workers, and to have both a family life and a public life. Scandinavia became something of a model, therefore, for 'women-friendly' welfare state reforms. And as gender became more central as a theoretical concept in explaining social forms, rather than just an empirical add-on, so researchers began to ask how these differences could be socially explained, over and above as just resulting from the presence – or absence – of women-friendly social policies. Why were different welfare states more or less women friendly?

Gendering the three worlds of welfare capitalism

A first answer was provided by the influential work of Gøsta Esping-Andersen, especially in *The Three Worlds of Welfare Capitalism* (1990). Esping-Andersen was not particularly concerned with differences in gender inequality between countries, but he was interested in explaining how social policies differed between countries, and what effects this had. His starting point was to ask how far different welfare states erode the commodity status of labour in a capitalist system (how far people are independent from selling their labour) and, as a consequence, how far welfare states intervene in the class system. Empirically, relative levels of this 'decommodification' were measured with reference to the level and nature of income transfers for sickness, unemployment and old age, and this resulted in the identification of the three worlds of welfare capitalism into which different states fell.

In the *Liberal Welfare Regime* social policy is used to uphold the market and traditional work-ethic norms, with modest and means tested benefits aimed at a residualised and stigmatised group of welfare recipients. While no one country presents a pure case of any regime, and countries may straddle or move between them, the USA is a type case – with Britain moving in this direction. In the *Social Democratic Welfare Regime* social policy reforms based on decommodification are extended to all classes, with equality at the highest standards rather than minimal needs. Typically, the labour movement has high levels of access to state power. The market is de-emphasised but the high taxation necessary to finance universal welfare means that the emphasis is on avoiding problems in the first place, where every adult should be able to participate in the labour market. Sweden is archetypical. In the *Conservative Welfare Regime* states also intervene in a highly regulatory way, but this intervention is essentially concerned with the preservation of status differences. Social rights are connected to status and class, guided by the Catholic-inspired principle of subsidiarity where states should only support – not replace – existing social institutions such as families or firms in providing welfare. The 'social market' is therefore presented as a third way between the excesses of both liberalism and socialism. West Germany is the type case. Finally, we should add the 'fourth world' of the *Mediterranean Welfare State Regime* of southern Europe, not included by Esping-Andersen, to this scheme. Here, there is little right to welfare or any history of full employment, and a recent history of authoritarian politics has prevented their development. While residualism and forced entry to the labour market remind us of the liberal model, the state can rely on surviving elements of the household subsistence economy, a large informal sector, and church-inspired charities to provide both welfare and top-up employment. This is bolstered by moral and practical expectations of support from family and kin (in contrast to expectations of state support in social democratic countries). Nonetheless, the state does intervene in a small number of 'first order' social risks, where families are generally unable to provide support, and some restricted but favoured groups (for example civil servants) may receive high levels of benefit (Ferrera 1996; Trifiletti 1999). It may be possible to extend these categorisations further, where there may be 'non-Western' welfare regimes, such as the authoritarian populism emerging in parts of Eastern Europe or the 'East Asian' model (Deacon *et al*. 1992). Similarly, Ito Peng (1997) shows how a concept of the 'Japanese style welfare state', stressing the work ethic within traditional norms, has been promoted in overt opposition to both Liberal and Social Democratic regime types.

Crucially, this classification is not merely ad hoc and descriptive, but is based on analytical distinctions about what the welfare state does, how this can differ and, hence, why we would expect different outcomes in terms of social policy. Hence any particular policy, and comparisons between them, could be related to an explanatory account of the structure of the welfare state. This allowed a first explanation of why some states were more 'women friendly' than others, for these different welfare regimes would have different implications for women and men, and hence for the level and nature of gender inequality. As Barbara Hobson puts it, 'Both women and men are more and less poor in certain welfare states because of the fact that welfare regimes are systems of stratification' (1994: 175).

It soon became clear that this resolution was inadequate, however, for the three (or four) worlds did not seem particularly accurate for gender issues (Sainsbury 1994). For example, the position of women in France – with high levels of full-time work and public childcare – seemed similar to the Social Democratic regime type, although the Esping-Andersen model placed France in the Conservative Welfare State regime along with Germany, where married women were institutionally situated as housewives and with one of the lowest levels of women's full-time work. Nor did the regimes work that well for explaining particular policy differences. Thus for lone mothers, for example, Austria and Germany, in the Conservative regime, resembled the USA in the Liberal regime group, while Australia, Britain and Ireland split off from this regime to form a group of their own (Duncan and Edwards 1999). It is not only that there were exceptions and transitional cases (something to be expected in any categorisation), but that there appeared to be complete category splits.

The source of this problem is that the Esping-Andersen model is largely gender blind. As Jane Lewis (1992) puts it, women disappear from the analysis as soon as they disappear from the labour market. Even in terms of the original model, this has major implications. Thus, Esping-Andersen sees the social democratic countries as the most decommodifying welfare state regime but it is here that women are in fact most commodified. They predominantly sell their labour – and it is the development of the social democratic welfare state that facilitates this. Similarly, women are perhaps least commodified in the Conservative regime, again not surprisingly as it is here that the housewife role is most supported institutionally. Esping-Andersen also neglects the fundamental role played by unpaid domestic and caring work, and by families as institutions, in mediating individual levels of commodification. These omissions are, of course, heavily gendered. As Mary Langan and Ilona Ostner (1991) point out, women are different 'gendered commodities' from the outset; they already have different positions vis-à-vis markets and welfare states because of their gender.

Some followers of Esping-Andersen have therefore paid more attention to the gender-specific outcomes of welfare state regimes. Indeed, Stephan Leibfried (1993) sees gender as central to the concept of social citizenship established in the Conservative regime (renamed 'Bismarckian institutional welfare states') where public policy is used to consolidate traditional male citizenship. This is opposed to the gender neutral citizenship of 'Scandinavian modern welfare states'. (In 'Anglo-Saxon' residual welfare states social citizenship is being progressively reduced while on the 'Latin Rim' of rudimentary welfare states social citizenship remains weakly developed.) Langan and Ostner (1991) use Leibfried's variant to place the socio-economic position of women at the centre of the welfare regime classification. Figure 1.1a represents this cartographically.[1] Alan Siaroff (1994) has produced another 'gender sensitive' reworking of Esping-Andersen's typologies. Siaroff uses indices of family welfare orientation, which parent is in receipt of benefits, and female work desirability. Relative rankings on these indices produce country groups not unlike the four groups produced by Esping-Andersen and Leibfried. The only major difference is that Switzerland and Ireland join a 'Late female mobilisation welfare state' cluster that otherwise includes the 'Latin Rim' countries.

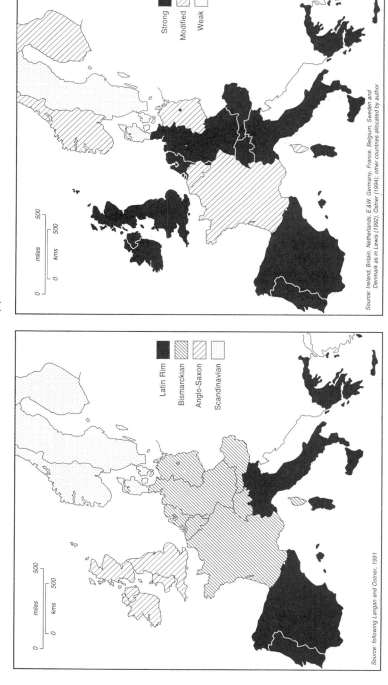

(b)

Strong
Modified
Weak

Source: Ireland, Britain, Netherlands, E.&W. Germany, France, Belgium, Sweden and Denmark as in Lewis (1992); Ostner (1994); other countries allocated by author

(a)

Latin Rim
Bismarckian
Anglo-Saxon
Scandinavian

Source: following Langan and Ostner, 1991

Figure 1.1 Allocating countries to gender systems: feminist social policy models. (a) Gender welfare state regimes; (b) strong, modified and weak breadwinner states. *Sources:* (a) After Langan and Ostner (1991). (b) Ireland, Britain, the Netherlands, East and West Germany, France, Belgium, Sweden and Denmark as in Lewis (1992) and Ostner (1994); other countries allocated by the present author.

Adding in the socio-economic position of women in these ways improves the descriptive value of the welfare state regime model as far as gender is concerned, even though the grouping of countries remains virtually unchanged. However, this 'gendering' of the worlds of welfare capitalism does not help us very much in extending the understanding of the relative positions of women and men in different welfare states. However gendered, the categories are the same as in the original and therefore just as inaccurate. Indeed, the whole exercise of gendering welfare state regimes has been criticised as not going far enough (Sainsbury 1994; Duncan 1995). This is for two major reasons. First, in terms of content, the model does not say enough about unpaid work, largely carried out by women and fundamental to gendered public–private divides, nor about the consequent salience of service provision in enabling or constraining women. Similarly, the role of familial and gender ideologies in structuring welfare policies is underplayed. The second criticism focuses more on explanatory dynamic where gender remains an optional add-on. The theoretical core of Esping-Andersen-derived models is firmly rooted in capital–labour divisions in a capitalist system, based around the relationship of (male, standard) workers to markets as modified by the welfare state. This is how the welfare state typologies are differentiated and where they come from. The explanatory dynamic remains gender blind however much gender description is added on.

Differentiated patriarchy

Simply gendering Esping-Andersen's welfare regimes seems to bring us to a dead end. The implication is that, in order to understand gender differences over space, we need to start with theoretical traditions which place gender in a central position. Jane Lewis (1992) made a first stab at this in her categorisations of 'strong', 'modified' and 'weak' 'breadwinner' states (see also Ostner 1994). This shifted attention to unpaid work and family relations. Ireland, France and Sweden are type cases of each category. This model is represented cartographically in Figure 1.1b.

This solves the problem of some of the welfare state regime model misallocations, although it does seem to create others. Thus most countries fall into the 'strong' group, where cases like Britain, Germany and Greece are quite different in the form that 'strong breadwinning' takes. The weakness of this solution is that it remains a descriptive model (Sainsbury 1994). How and why are these breadwinner states strong, modified or weak? Similarly, 'weak' and 'modified' are both characterised in terms of what they are not. In essence 'breadwinning' is an implicit, if less politicised, empirical pseudonym for 'patriarchy' – but without an overt theory of how this form of patriarchy works we cannot explain where differences come from and how categories develop.

Although introducing an implicit idea of patriarchy, Lewis's work was still set within the tradition of comparative social policy focusing on the welfare state. But to understand comparative gender inequality we need more socially comprehensive approaches. There are, indeed, a number of wider alternatives, which developed in parallel with, but apparently without reference to, the more limited social policy approach. Taking their inspiration from feminist sociology and feminist political history, these alternatives are more synthesising, but at the same time differ in the way in which they include, and variably stress, the importance of culture and agency.

The concept of patriarchy provided one starting point for the comparative categorisation of gender inequality, as developed by Sylvia Walby. Working in a sociological tradition, her *Theorising Patriarchy* (1990) is partly a defence of the concept of patriarchy against charges that it is essentialist, structuralist and ahistorical. To mount this defence, however, Walby develops the concept so that it can embody difference. This, then, provides the seeds for comparative analysis. There are two crucial steps to the development. First, Walby draws upon realist reactions to structuralism (see Sayer 1992). Earlier grand theories of patriarchy do have problems in dealing with historical and cultural variations, but this is because they use simple base-superstructure models of causal relations. One causal element (for example male violence or motherhood) is seen as determinant; not surprisingly there are problems in explaining variation and change in multifaceted gender inequality. In addition, the attempt to explain specific circumstances by using concepts developed at an abstract level is almost bound to be determinist and inaccurate. In other words, it is not the *substantive* notion of patriarchy, as a structured system of gender relations, which is essentialist, ahistorical and structuralist. Rather, these are faults of the *way* the concept has been used in constructing explanation. Critics have confused their (correct) criticism of method with a criticism of content – the baby has been thrown out with the bathwater.

Walby's second step is to define the content, naming six patriarchal structures through which men dominate and exploit women. These are the patriarchal mode of production (in households), patriarchal relations in paid work, the patriarchal state, male violence, patriarchal relations in sexuality, and patriarchal relations in cultural institutions. These are empirically substantiated by reference to previous research. Following the realist model of explanation, these structures can now be used to develop a structural – but non-structuralist – explanatory theory which can allow both determination and variation. The six structures will be differentially developed as they interact with pre-existing situations, changes in other social structures (like capitalism) and each other. While at an abstract level each outcome will be patriarchal, at the specific level there will be considerable variation. This reformulation of a differentiated patriarchy neatly deals with most of the criticisms raised against patriarchy as a concept of gender inequality (see Duncan 1994 for discussion). And unlike the gender welfare models discussed earlier, this formulation has the substantial advantage that gender relations are centrally positioned in the explanatory account. Gender is not just an empirical, almost optional, add-on. It provides the central causal dynamic – and it necessarily varies over space and time.

Walby (1994) later develops an explicit explanation for geographical differences in patriarchy. To do this she distinguishes between the form of patriarchy and the degree of patriarchy. The *form* of patriarchy refers to the relationship between the different elements of patriarchy, for instance whether or not women have widespread access to full-time paid work over their adult lives. Public and private patriarchy represent two overall forms. The *degree* of patriarchy refers to the intensity or extent by which women are subordinated to men, for instance the level of wage inequality between women and men. This distinction, according to Walby, 'creates the theoretical space to avoid ethnocentrism in comparative analysis, since a particular form is no longer necessarily associated with a particular degree of inequality' (1994: 1340). It is possible to have specific instances of public patriarchy with high degrees of patriarchal inequality or, alternatively, public patriarchy with lower degrees of patriarchal inequality. Similarly, private patriarchy may be combined both with high degrees of patriarchal inequality or with lower degrees of patriarchal inequality. For example, Walby discusses how Britain and Sweden both tend towards public patriarchy with high degrees of female labour market participation. However, Sweden – with a low wage gap – has a lower degree of patriarchal inequality. The wage gap is much higher in Britain, so that while the *form* of patriarchy is similar in the two countries the *degree* of inequality produced is substantially different. Figure 1.2a presents a possible mapping using this model.

On the face of it, this resolution was an attractive one in combining a theorised account of gender differences with empirical classification. But in application, two problems emerged. First, classifying by the form and degree of patriarchy for each of the six patriarchal structures resulted in considerable complexities where the same country could be located at different positions for different structures. Second, and more fundamentally, the concept of patriarchy overemphasises the power of men, and underemphasises that of women. Women too have power; they are not merely passive victims but active social agents who change things too. But the various geographical combinations of the degree and form of patriarchy can be said to simply describe the varied outcomes of male domination and exploitation of women. But how have these differences arisen in the first place and, in particular, what about the actions of women in changing their circumstances? In the climate of the late 1990s, with a strong reaction against structuralist explanation, this objection seemed damning and Walby's notions never became popular. Instead, a body of work developed in feminist political history and cultural sociology, particularly in Germany and Sweden, seemed to better provide the 'missing link' between structure and action in explaining different forms of gender inequality.

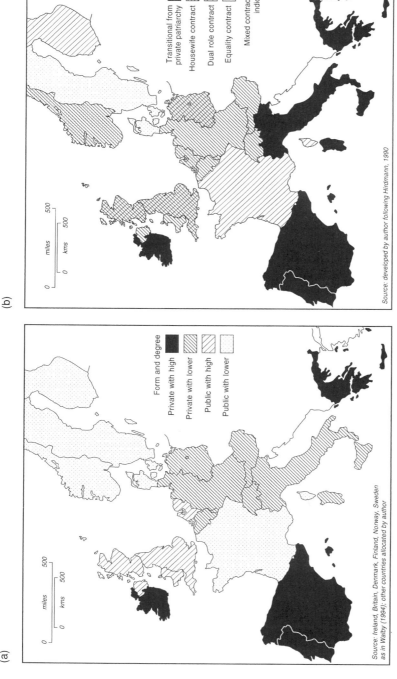

(a)

(b)

Source: Ireland, Britain, Denmark, Finland, Norway, Sweden
as in Walby (1994); other countries allocated by author

Source: developed by author following Hirdmann, 1990

Form and degree

Private with high

Private with lower

Public with high

Public with lower

Transitional from
private patriarchy

Housewife contract

Dual role contract

Equality contract

Mixed contracts as
indicated

Figure 1.2 Allocating countries to gender systems: feminist sociology models. (a) Differential patriarchy; (b) national gender contracts. *Sources:* (a) Ireland, Britain, Finland, Denmark, Norway and Sweden as in Walby (1994); other countries allocated by the present author. (b) Developed by the present author following Hirdman (1990).

The three worlds of gender culture

The starting point is the Scandinavian idea of the 'gender contract'. This developed in a situation where welfare states had an expressed commitment to gender equality, with explicit sex equality programmes and substantial 'women-friendly' reforms, such as comprehensive public day care. Thus women can be both mothers and full-time workers. The meaning of motherhood also changes, becoming less of a defining division of labour and more of a private social role. However, the overall effect of these changes was to alter women's lives rather than men's. Women could act in a male role, although inevitably less efficiently than men could. Activities, tasks and objects all remained resolutely gendered; the gender coding of society and its equipment had not been removed – it was merely that women's space was enlarged.

Theories of the 'gender contract' developed in this context of both substantial change in women's roles and the maintenance of gender divisions. According to Yvonne Hirdman (1988, 1990) the gender system (*genussystemet*) arranges people according to two overall rules: (1) virtually all areas of life are divided into male and female categories, and (2) this distinction is hierarchical – the male is the norm, the female is ascribed lower value. This again resembles a theory of patriarchy in different name. However, it is the 'gender contract' (*genuskontrakt*) which operationalises the gender system in specific circumstances. Each society, at any time, develops a contract between the genders, which sets up any particular gender coding – what people of different genders should do, think and be.

Note that the notion of a contract does not imply equality; men and women are not equals and so the contract is an unequal one. Rather, the notion was developed in ironic analogy with the idea of the social democratic contract, or 'historical compromise', between capital and labour so beloved of political theorists, where Sweden is seen as the archetypical case. (It was in this tradition that Esping-Andersen's work developed.) However, these political theories are gender blind, and Hirdman shows how a compromise between men and women was just as important to the development of Swedish society as the capital–labour compromise. The gender compromise also set rules and expectations for divisions of labour and power. It was just that the capitalist compromise – being carried out in a dominant male discourse of the economy and public politics – completely overshadowed the parallel compromise over gender divisions of labour and power, where the discourse about families, children and women was politically peripheral. However, as with labour in capitalism, although women in the gender system may be structurally subordinate, nevertheless they have substantial influence and room for action. For example, by the early twentieth century in Sweden women had gained the vote, were increasingly entering the formal labour market and were relatively well organised politically, as well as retaining more traditional bases of social power in families and households. So, too, any given contract will leave numerous less defined, grey areas which become the site of new conflict and, possibly, the origin of transition to another overall contract. The gender system will therefore show major variations in space and time, with regard both to the nature of the gender contract and to its rigidity.

Hirdman develops this notion historically for Sweden since the turn of the century, describing how different gender contracts emerged and transformed through social conflict and compromise. A *housewife contract* emerged in the 1930s and lasted into the 1960s as a response to an inter-war crisis between the sexes. While traditional, agrarian family forms had been eroded, the position of women vis-à-vis marriage, domestic life and paid work was not established and was if anything less secure. The housewife contract was one attempt to resolve the competing demands for time, resources and roles made by men, married women and unmarried women. These conflicts, and the compromise – or gender contract – they led to, were pursued in 'political' institutions, pre-eminently political parties, the institutional expressions of labour (such as the union movement) and capital (such as the employers' federation), and the 'people's movements' in general (for example the cooperative movement). This housewife contract was in turn challenged by the circumstances of the 1950s and 1960s, leading to a transitional phase where women and men again voiced competing demands. A reinforced housewife contract (rather like the 'Bismarckian model' in West Germany) was not possible given the position and demands of Swedish women, and eventually an *equality contract* emerged from the late 1960s onwards. While this allows women substantial gains, it too has its unsolved problems, heightened by the economic recession of the 1990s and the new political power of neo-liberalism. Another transitional phase may now be emerging. (See Duncan 1994 for a detailed review.)

Hirdman does not develop her analysis with reference to geographical differences at one time. However, it is clearly possible to use it in this way; for example, judging from the positions of women vis-à-vis men (Duncan 1996) former West Germany shows a continuing housewife contract, Britain may be in a transitional phase from this contract, the former GDR may be returning to a housewife contract, and so on. Unlike the other models reviewed so far, it is more possible to conceptualise transitional forms, where these are an explicit part of the explanatory account; see Figure 1.2b (this replaces Hirdman's 'transitional' contract by a 'dual role' contract, in recognising that the situation where women are formally positioned as different to men, in combining both mother and worker roles, can be less transitional than was the case for Sweden).

Nonetheless, the problem of origins reimposes itself. How do these different gender contracts arise, and why do they differ between different countries? This is not so much a problem for Hirdman's work on Sweden, where she follows a specific historical evolution and concentrates on outcomes which can be more easily 'traded off' in political systems, such as labour market participation and day care. It is not clear, however, how this can be generalised for other, less institutionalised, countries – especially for gender issues which are harder to 'trade', such as domestic responsibility or control through male violence. It is to this problem that Birgit Pfau-Effinger (1994, 1998) turns in explaining national variations in female labour market participation.

In developing the concept of gender contract (which she renames *gender arrangement*) in order to explain comparative differences in women's participation in paid work, Pfau-Effinger places considerable emphasis on dominant social norms and values about the nature of families and gender relations within them, which she calls the *gender culture*. She identifies three long-standing 'family/gender models' in Western Europe, rather than assuming a single 'traditional' or 'breadwinner' or 'patriarchal' family (see also Chapter 5).

In the *family economic* model, men and women cooperate in a family economy in farm holdings or small businesses. This model can be seen to correspond, historically and geographically, to petty commodity production where women were involved both in production and in the public sphere (although gender relations were unequal and sometimes deeply exploitative). Children were also socialised as members of the family economic unit and the notion of childhood, as an institutionalised period, hardly existed. The *male breadwinner/ female home carer* model 'is based on the ideal of the separation of male public and female private, subordinate, spheres. This corresponds to Jane Lewis' 'strong' breadwinner regime, sometimes called the 'bourgeois' family, and to the widespread, but in fact historically inaccurate, understanding of the 'traditional' family. Children and childhood belong in this private sphere and 'motherhood' emerges as a specific, unpaid gender role. This model is fundamentally self-contradictory, where male and female citizens are equal in theory but unequal in practice as men and women. Historically, this family form developed with mercantalism and the industrial/capitalist trans- formation. Currently, modernised versions – the *male breadwinner/female part- time carer* model – give more scope for women's paid work, but only supplementary to their caring and homemaker role as defined by motherhood and partnering. However, partly because of the contradictions between such 'breadwinner' models and democratisation and individualisation processes, more *egalitarian* family/gender models have emerged during the twentieth century. These are based on the idea of men and women as individual breadwinners, although childhood is also constructed as a long phase of life with its own worth. The way this 'role separation' between caring and paid work is achieved produces different forms of this model. In one form, now culturally dominant in Scandinavia (and in a slightly different way in France), caring for children is both supported by, and partly provided by, the welfare state. Other forms, less culturally dominant, are emerging in Britain and the USA, where the market is seen as providing care, and in the Netherlands, where both paid work and caring is shared by both partners. Throughout,

Pfau-Effinger places emphasis on the notions of childhood inherent in each form rather than, as in the other models reviewed in this chapter, considering only the relations between men and women. This is important where, arguably, much feminist research has neglected parenting, and in particular mothering, or merely seen this one-dimensionally as just part of a patriarchal exploitation.

One important conclusion is that 'the state' is not the single determinant actor – in contrast to the assumptions of most social policy research, including the theories of welfare state regimes and breadwinner states. Rather, different welfare state systems will reflect pre-existing gender cultures. For example, a pervasive day care system has been developed in Finland, but this works to support the pre-existing norm of women as full-time workers in both the agrarian family model and the succeeding equality model – it was not the development of day care that created the norm. Similarly in West Germany, part-time childcare is most common, and this developed in support of a pre-existing dependent motherhood role where the ideal of the bourgeois family remains institutionally dominant. Overall, the notion of gender contracts/ cultures is particularly useful in directing attention to where alternative ideas about male and female roles come from, how they are put in place, and how they are maintained. This concept, then, can more successfully place differential gender into welfare state regimes.

The discussion so far points to a fundamental conclusion about gender variations in welfare states – they reflect variations in *both* the capital–labour contract and the gender contract (or gender arrangement). The former is represented by Esping-Andersen-type models, including the various feminist-inspired critiques and developments, the latter by the work of Hirdman and Pfau-Effinger. Elsewhere I have named this combination the 'genderfare' model (Duncan and Edwards 1999). Naturally, one 'contract' will affect the other. For example, the nature of capital–labour relations in particular welfare state regimes will substantially influence the position of women vis-à-vis men – for example women's wages are closer to men's in states with corporatist labour markets. Much less appreciated, however, is that the process also works the other way round. The 'equality contract' between men and women in Sweden not only requires particular welfare state provisions (so despite some retrenchment in welfare benefits in the 1990s, as a response to economic stagnation, the provision of day care has expanded) but also acts against the peripheralisation of women in the labour force and hence also affects the strategies that can be followed by employers and unions. Similarly, West Germany's housewife contract has necessitated the widespread use of 'guest worker' labour (where women are less available) and hence eases both peripheralisation as a management strategy and the maintenance of a status-driven social policy where 'standard', German, male workers can be treated as the core. In the terms of critical realism, the position of women in welfare states is a concrete outcome of two 'necessary relations', not just one – the state welfare regime and the gender contract (see Table 1.1).

Table 1.1 Genderfare in developed countries

Gender contract	Welfare state regime			
	Southern	*Liberal*	*Conservative*	*Social Democratic*
Traditional	*Greece* *Spain*	*Ireland*	*Japan*	
	– – – – – – – – *Italy* – – – – – – – – – – – *Switzerland* – – – – – – – –			
Housewife		*New Zealand* *Australia*	*Germany* *Austria*	
	UK		*Belgium*	
	– *Netherlands* – – – – – –			
Dual	*Portugal*	*USA*	*France*	
	– *Norway* – – – – –			
Equality				*Denmark* *Sweden* *Finland*

Source: Adapted from Duncan and Edwards (1999).

1.3 Theorising gender spatiality at the local level – from spatial divisions of labour to local gender cultures

The discussion so far has exhibited one effect of 'spatial amnesia' in social science – the equation of spatial differences with national differences alone. Commonly, social scientists who remain indifferent to or unaware of the effects of space nonetheless find they have to recognise differences in their empirical work. Lacking adequate theorisations of how space makes a difference, they simply equate different 'societies' ('German society', etc.) with the nation state. The theories of differentiated patriarchy and gender contracts discussed above are examples. Presumably, this identification of spatial difference and 'societies' with nation state reflects the fact that modern social and political discourse is heavily infused by national assumptions (see Williams 1995). This infusion is particularly strong in social policy, with its Fabian origins, where the state is enthroned as dominant social actor as well as the only spatial container. But as mentioned in section 1.1, while the nation state is both an important actor and scale for action, this neglects other spatial scales which may be of central importance to how social processes operate, and there is no reason to think that gender relations are an exception.

The various theorisations of welfare state regimes are one obvious example of this 'state fetishism'. Indeed, because of the theoretical dominance of the state, these theorisations are unable to deal with, or even recognise, regional or local gender differences. For the same reason, it is theories of gender contracts or gender cultures, which place the nation state in a secondary and contingent position, that offer the greatest scope for development in this respect. However, it is theorisations within geography, in the political economy of space tradition, which have most explicitly addressed the issue of spatial variations in gender roles and relations.

The essential starting point for this work is that uneven development is a structural feature of capitalist economies. People are not, however, simply left passive as 'capitalism' creates and destroys geographies around them. It is people who create, run and adapt to these processes even if they do not do so in freedom from others, or in conditions of their own choosing, where Marx's 'nightmare of the past' (and, we may add, space) is always bearing down upon them. Some may move in line with the direction of investment and job opportunities, while others jointly create 'spatial fixes' to secure investment in their area, and the infrastructure and social life that accompany them; these spatial fixes often overlap with the 'spatial coherences' of interacting and self-reinforcing local economic and social conditions that are necessary for economic development in the first place. Regional and local concentrations of economic activity can remain relatively fixed over time, therefore, although always subject to sudden dislocation or restructuring as the profitability surface is altered.

The upshot of all this is that, to use Doreen Massey's memorable and now classic title, the division of labour in capitalism is also a 'spatial division of labour' (Massey 1984; see 1995 for retrospect). Particular jobs, skills and occupations are differentially distributed to different labour markets – and hence job opportunities, the development of human capital and income levels will also vary widely on a local level. The development of any one area can then be understood in terms of a 'geological metaphor' – the current economic and social landscape will preserve relics of past spatial divisions of labour, overlain and reformed by newer socio-economic accretions. This local differentiation of development, jobs and incomes will also interact, if in a complex way, with social, political and cultural differences, as amply documented by the British 'localities projects' of the 1980s (Cooke 1989; Bagguley *et al.* 1990). This is not simply an economic process, where local labour markets reflect the forces of supply, demand and profitability. Rather spatial divisions of labour are complex social processes, conditioned by historical patterns and mediated by cultural understandings and negotiations.

These spatial divisions of labour are also gendered. The jobs, skills and occupations which are distributed to different labour markets are usually coded – by both employers and job-takers – as women's or men's jobs. Once jobs are gendered these divisions seem remarkably rigid and enduring; only relatively rarely do jobs change 'gender' (Walby 1986). Indeed, this gendering of jobs in itself can be an important factor affecting investment decisions (Massey 1984). The economic and social geographies created and influenced by spatial divisions of labour are also gender geographies, therefore, where women's roles, possibilities and expectations will vary.

Mapping this geography of gender (e.g. McDowell and Massey 1984; Duncan 1991a,b; Jarvis 1999) produced a surprising result, however – the geography of women's work roles was different to those better known geographies of economic performance and prosperity. Regions and local labour market areas which were economically expansive could also be areas with low levels of paid work for women, where mothers in particular concentrated on a domestic and caring role. Conversely, areas of economic decline or stagnation could be areas where women, including mothers, were highly oriented to the labour market and showed high levels of paid work. These patterns also seemed enduring. For example, Rosemarie Sackmann and Hartmut Haüssermann (1994) have compared the relative propensity of German women to take up paid work, by region, for 1890 and 1990. Despite fundamental shifts in regional economies over the last 100 years (with the south replacing the north as economic leader), two World Wars, the Depression and the rise and fall of Nazism, and all those other changes over the century in which Germany was often the fulcrum, the regional pattern of women's labour force participation remained the same.

How can this apparent paradox between the more familiar geography of economic growth and the less familiar, but strikingly different, geography of women's work roles be explained? In part this disjuncture reflects a general criticism of the spatial divisions of labour approach that – whatever claims are made for the cultural mediation of economic process – it remains an economically determinist theory. In this sense the theory of spatial divisions of labour is the sub-regional equivalent of gendered welfare regimes at the national level.

A first solution to this apparent paradox was to prolong historically economic determinism. Current gender divisions of labour were seen as a hangover from traditions set up by earlier spatial divisions of labour. These established traditions would then set conditions in which later divisions of labour would develop. For example, in areas where women had long been exploited as a casual and ill-paid labour force in agriculture (as in the Fenland and East Anglia in Britain) women would remain in similar status jobs even when, as in this example, the areas entered a boom based on services and high-tech manufacturing. Similarly, but obversely, women's high orientation to paid work in areas of past economic growth (such as industrial Lancashire in Britain) would be maintained even when these areas went into decline (McDowell and Massey 1984; see Sundin 1996 for similar arguments for Sweden). In other areas immigration and the concentrated residence of different ethnic groups may bring different traditions about women's work to particular localities (for example in parts of Inner London Black mothers expect to be in full-time paid work; Duncan and Edwards 1999). In this way the geography of women's work roles would combine with, and transcend, current economic structures.

This first solution to the paradox of the non-correspondence between economic structure and women's paid work is a little too simple, however.

This is for two reasons. First, divisions of labour are intimately bound up with other social changes. It was in industrial Lancashire, for example, that women gained greater power both within households and in public life. Women in Lancashire often have greater control over male income, and 'joint marriages' (that is, when partners share the same social network) first became a norm in this area. Similarly, Lancashire women joined trade unions on a scale unknown elsewhere in the country and became a potent force in local politics. Local welfare services were sometimes highly developed as a result. This renegotiation of gendered power does not result simply from women taking up paid work and contributing more to the household wage. Empirical studies generally show that this has little effect on the definition of gender roles within households. Rather, gender role renegotiation seems to follow cultural redefinitions. Thus within Lancashire towns it was the type of work undertaken by women compared with men, their relative wage levels and above all the dissolution of gendered relations of authority and subordination in the workplace that appeared to be important in explaining the local level of women's political influence (Mark-Lawson *et al.* 1985; Mark-Lawson 1988). Similar processes can be discerned in other areas, for example in west Inner London where more career-oriented women have gained some measure of institutional and political independence (Duncan 1991b). At the other extreme, social institutions and gender relations in family farming areas combine to minimise women's independent role. 'Farmers' wives' may be crucially important in the production economy of the farm, as well as to reproduction tasks – but socially they remain just that: farmers' wives (Whatmore 1991). It seems that the ideology of the 'rural idyll', where the wife plays a central symbolic function at its domestic core, contributes as much to women's continuing domestic role in rural commuting areas as the long commuting times undertaken by breadwinning men (Little 1987).

This parallels the conclusion made by Sackmann and Haüssermann (1994) in their research on long-standing regional variations in women's propensity to take up paid work in Germany. This was not just a function of local economic structures, rather these variations reflected the different ways that household work and paid work were integrated, and specifically women's position in this integration – whether this was dominated by the labour market or by the family (domestic work and caring). According to Sackmann and Haüssermann, different regional traditions of women's social integration were established in the breakdown of household-based production (where women's work was integral) in the Industrial Revolution. Partly, these traditions were influenced by emergent labour market structures of the time. However, once established these different systems of integrating household and paid work 'become independent of economic structure and tend[s] to determine women's attitudes towards employment outside the home' (ibid.: 1386). Similarly, by the early twentieth century in industrial Lancashire, 'economic factors had become further reinforced by three generations of social conventions. It had become almost unthinkable for women *not* to work' (Liddington 1978: 98–

99). In other words gender divisions of labour are culturally reproduced – even when the economic conditions that may have produced them in the first place are long gone.

These examples bring us to the second simplification in this 'economic hangover' solution. It is not just spatial divisions of labour that define women's role, it is also people's own gendered expectations, negotiations and demands about what being a women or a man is, and what they should do in consequence. These understandings are informed not only by economic conditions in local labour markets but also by other social relations in households, neighbourhoods and community networks. This conclusion returns us to the theorisation of gender contracts and gender cultures – although now expressed at the sub-national scale.

Gunnel Forsberg (1998) has applied this insight to Sweden and finds substantial regional variations within that country's national equality gender contract (see also Bühler 1998 for Switzerland). 'Traditional' gender contracts were still strong in rural and small town forestry and industrial areas. Here labour market segregation was high, women played a minor role in political life, and social infrastructure (such as caring) was largely provided in families. In contrast, in the 'modernised' gender contract of the metropolitan areas, especially in the Stockholm region, labour market segregation was less and women were well integrated in public life. These regions are dominated by the service sector. Young women often migrated from the traditional to the modernised regions, not just for job opportunities (as traditionally assumed) but to find a place which better allowed them to be the sort of person they wanted to be. Finally, in some peripheral and rural areas the gender contract was 'non-traditional'. The economic base was traditional but gender relations were more equal than in the traditional contract regions. These were also regions with somewhat unconventional social and cultural histories which were also undergoing economic and social transformation.

Starting with spatial divisions of labour also brings us back, as with the discussion of cross-national differences in section 1.2, to gender cultures – but this time at the regional level. Putting these two processes together produces a sub-national analogy with the concept of 'genderfare' which ended that section. In explaining sub-national differences in gender inequality and the lives of women and men, we need to combine analyses of both economic and cultural relations.

1.4 Afterword

The comparative study of differences in gender inequality and gender relations demands an ambitious programme of research. A first task is to describe these differences. This is no easy task, partly because of the scarcity of coherent information in many areas of concern. There is little useful cross-national information of any sort, for instance on male violence or cultural (re)production of gender stereotypes, even though we know both to be crucial elements in the creation of gender inequality. Even where there is good cross-national information, little may be available at sub-national levels where many of the crucial processes of gender inequality operate and take effect. Even then researchers still face the task of integrating different spatial scales. And even supposing that this descriptive problem is solved, then there remains the problem of explaining how these differences have come about and how they change. I have tried to delineate some avenues of analysis in the preceding sections, but it is difficult to see how we can integrate these frameworks with the thematic, but non-spatial, explanations usually advanced in social science. We may have particular theoretical understandings about gendered values, for example, but how do these apply differentially in different places? How is this understanding filtered through the lived experience of different gender contracts, both locally and nationally?

This ambitious agenda became that of the European Science Foundation's 'Gender Inequality in the European Regions' network, and the chapters that follow represent the work of the network (see also the special editions of *Innovation*² and *European Urban and Regional Studies*³, both published in 1998). This is why the chapters that follow must be seen as both innovative and path-breaking.

Notes

1 In each case I have allocated countries to different categories following the authors involved as far as is possible. As these authors do not designate the position of every country in their published accounts (and in fact Hirdman does not attempt any geographical designation) I have allocated the remainder as indicated in Figures 1.1 and 1.2, guided by empirical information on gender divisions of labour, the provision of public childcare, and the nature of the family (see Siaroff 1994; Duncan 1996).

2 *Innovation: the European Journal of the Social Sciences*, 11, 2 (1998), Special issue 'The Spatiality of Gender', contains articles on 'Women's employment and state policies' (Rosemary Crompton), 'Gender cultures and the gender arrangement' (Birgit Pfau-Effinger), 'European gender roles' (Rosemarie Sackmann), 'Regional variations in the gender contract' (Gunnel Forsberg), 'The second demographic transition from a gender perspective' (Montserrat Solsona), and 'Analysing patriarchy, capitalism and women's employment in Europe' (John MacInnes).

3 *European Urban and Regional Studies*, 5, 1 (1998), Special issue 'Gender Inequality in the European Regions', contains articles on 'Mapping gender inequality in Europe' (Diane Perrons), 'Explaining regional differences in gender inequality in Swiss employment' (Elisabeth Bühler), 'Equality, labour market regimes and new employment patterns in Sweden' (Lena Gonäs), 'Homeworking in rural Spain' (Mireia Baylina and Dolors Garcia-Ramon), and 'Women's employment and gender relations in Greece' (Nota Kyriazis).

References

Bagguley, P., Mark-Lawson, J., Shapiro, D., Urry, J., Walby, S. and Warde, A. 1990. *Restructuring: Place, Class and Gender*. Sage, London.

Bühler, E. 1998. Economy, state or culture? Explaining regional differences in gender inequality in Swiss employment. *European Urban and Regional Studies*, 5, 27–39.

22   Introduction

Cooke, P. (ed.) 1989. *Localities: the Changing Face of Urban Britain*. Unwin Hyman, London.
Deacon, B., Castle-Kanovera, M., Manning, N., Millard, F., Orosz, E., Szalai, J. and Vidinova, A. (eds) 1992. *The New Eastern Europe. Social Policy: Past, Present and Future*. Sage, London.
Duncan, S. 1989. Uneven development and the difference that space makes. *Geoforum*, 20, 2, 131–140.
Duncan, S. 1991a. The geography of gender divisions of labour in Britain. *Transactions of the Institute of British Geographers*, 16, 420–439.
Duncan, S. 1991b. Gender divisions of labour. In Green, D. and Hoggart, K. (eds) *London: a New Metropolitan Geography*, pp. 95–122. Unwin Hyman, London.
Duncan, S. 1994. Theorising differences in patriarchy. *Environment and Planning A*, 26, 1177–1194.
Duncan, S. 1995. Theorizing European gender systems. *Journal of European Social Policy*, 5, 4, 263–284.
Duncan, S. 1996. The diverse worlds of European patriarchy. In Garcia-Ramon, D. and Monk, J. (eds) *Women of the European Union: the Politics of Work and Daily Life*, pp. 74–110. Routledge, London.
Duncan, S. and Edwards, R. 1999. *Lone Mothers, Paid Work and Gendered Moral Rationalities*. Macmillan, London.
Duncan, S. and Savage, M. 1991. New perspectives on the locality debate. *Environment and Planning A*, Special issue, 155–308.
Esping-Andersen, G. 1990. *The Three Worlds of Welfare Capitalism*. Polity Press, London.
Ferrera, M. 1996. The "southern" model of welfare in social Europe. *Journal of European Social Policy*, 6, 17–36.
Forsberg, G. 1998. Regional variations in the gender contract: gendered relations in labour markets, local politics and everyday life in Swedish regions. *Innovation*, 11, 2, 191–210.
Gregory, D. and Urry, J. (eds) 1985. *Spatial Structures and Social Process*. Macmillan, London.
Hirdman, Y. 1988. Genussystemet – reflexioner kring kvinnors sociala underordning. *Kvinnovetenskaplig Tidskrift*, 3, 49–63.
Hirdman, Y. 1990. *Att Lägga Livet till Rätta: Studier i Svensk Folkhemspolitik*. Carlssons, Stockholm.
Hobson, B. 1994. Solo mothers, social policy regimes and the logics of gender. In Sainsbury, D. (ed.) *Gendering Welfare States*, pp. 170–187. Sage, London.
Jarvis, H. 1999. The tangled webs we weave: household strategies to coordinate work and home. *Work, Employment and Society*, 13, 225–247.
Langan, M. and Ostner, I. 1991. Gender and welfare: towards a comparative framework. In Room, G. (ed.) *Towards a European Welfare State?*, pp. 127–150. School for Advanced Urban Studies, University of Bristol, Bristol.
Leibfried, S. 1993. Towards a European welfare state? In Jones, C. (ed.) *New Perspectives on the Welfare State in Europe*, pp. 133–150. Routledge, London.
Lewis, J. 1992. Gender and the development of welfare regimes. *Journal of European Social Policy*, 2, 3, 159–173.
Liddington, J. 1979. *One Hand Tied Behind us: the Rise of the Women's Suffrage Movement*. Virago, London.
Little, J. 1987. Gender relations in rural areas: the importance of women's domestic role. *Journal of Rural Studies*, 3, 335–342.

McDowell, L. and Massey, D. 1984. A woman's place? In Massey, D. and Allen, J. (eds) *Geography Matters!*, pp. 128–147. Cambridge University Press, Cambridge.

Mark-Lawson, J. 1988. Occupational segregation and women's politics. In Walby, S. (ed.) *Gender Segregation at Work*, pp. 157–173. Open University Press, Milton Keynes.

Mark-Lawson, J., Savage, M. and Warde, A. 1985. Gender and local politics: struggles over welfare 1918–1934. In Murgatroyd, D., Savage, M., Shapiro, D., Urry, J., Walby, S. and Warde, A. (eds) *Localities, Class and Gender*, pp. 195–215. Pion, London.

Massey, D. 1984. *Spatial Divisions of Labour*. Macmillan, London.

Massey, D. 1995. *Spatial Divisions of Labour*, 2nd edn. Macmillan, London.

Ostner, I. 1994. The women and welfare debate. In Hantrais, L. and Morgan, S. (eds) *Family Policy and the Welfare of Women*. Cross-National Research Papers, Third Series, 3. European Research Centre, University of Loughborough.

Peng, I. 1997. Single mothers in Japan: unsupported mothers who work. In Duncan, S. and Edwards, R. (eds) *Single Mothers in an International Context: Mothers or Workers?*, pp. 115–148. UCL Press, London.

Pfau-Effinger, B. 1994. The 'gender contract' and part-time work by women: Finland and West Germany compared. *Environment and Planning A*, 27, 1355–1376.

Pfau-Effinger, B. 1998. Gender cultures and the gender arrangement – a theoretical framework for cross-national gender research. *Innovation*, 11, 2, 147–166.

Sackmann, R. and Haüssermann, H. 1994. Do regions matter? Regional differences in female labour market participation in Germany. *Environment and Planning A*, 27, 1377–1397.

Sainsbury, D. (ed.) 1994. *Gendering Welfare States*. Sage, London.

Sayer, A. 1992. *Method in Social Science: a Realist Approach*. Hutchinson, London.

Sayer, A. 2000. *Realism and Social Science*. Sage, London.

Siaroff, A. 1994. Work, welfare and gender equality: a new typology. In Sainsbury, D. (ed.) *Gendering Welfare States*, pp. 82–100. Sage, London.

Sundin, E. 1996. Gender, technology and local culture: tradition and transition in a Swedish municipality. *Gender, Place and Culture*, 3, 61–76.

Trifiletti, R. 1999. Southern European welfare regimes and the worsening position of women. *Journal of European Social Policy*, 9, 49–64.

Walby, S. 1986. *Patriarchy at Work: Patriarchal and Capitalist Relations in Employment*. Polity Press, Cambridge.

Walby, S. 1990. *Theorising Patriarchy*. Basil Blackwell, Oxford.

Walby, S. 1994. Methodological and theoretical issues in the comparative analysis of gender relations in western Europe. *Environment and Planning A*, 27, 1339–1354.

Whatmore, S. 1991. *Farming Women: Gender, Work and Family Enterprise*. Macmillan, London.

Williams, F. 1995. Race, ethnicity, gender and class in welfare states: a framework for comparative analysis. *Social Politics*, 2, 2, 127–139.

Part I

Gender divisions of labour – paid and unpaid work

2   Paid work

Participation, inclusion and liberation

*Gunnel Forsberg, Lena Gonäs
and Diane Perrons*

2.1 Issues: mapping the inequality – an explanatory approach

In a global perspective women in the European Union have a comparatively advantageous position. Equal opportunities policies, which provide a framework for working conditions and wage negotiations, exist in all countries and the overall material level of well being is high. However, significant cross-national differences in the living and working conditions of women and men remain. These differences are more noticeable at the regional level and are perhaps greater still at the level of households and workplaces.

In this chapter we will illustrate the universality of, and differences in the extent of, gender inequality in employment across the regions of the European Union. More specifically, maps are used to illustrate different aspects of gender inequality. By providing empirical detail we hope to cast light on some of the theoretical debates that have taken place in recent years in relation to the factors influencing the differential involvement of women in paid work, such as the gender welfare regimes approach (Lewis 1992; Sainsbury 1994), differentiated patriarchy (Walby 1994) and gender contracts (Hirdman 1990; Pfau-Effinger 1998). See also Forsberg (1998) and Perrons and Gonäs (1998) for a brief review of these debates.

This chapter therefore seeks to analyse national and regional differences in the gender structure of the labour market and relate them to other regional and/or national characteristics such as state support (tax/benefit structure and social infrastructure), cultural norms and economic transformation. It is also necessary to stress what the aim of the chapter *is not*. It does not aim to explain why the labour market is segregated by gender, nor the subordination of the female labour force. The interest here is why and in what ways this subordination and segregation varies between states and regions and also to consider the way gender relations have changed over time at the regional level. Space makes a difference, and the spatial dimensions of gender inequality illustrated by simple choropleth maps can help to highlight the processes that construct and deconstruct gender asymmetries even though statistical mapping can never tell the whole story (see also Perrons 1998a).

Different spatial scales suggest different stories. As Susan Hanson and Geraldine Pratt (1995) have argued, you get a quite different picture by 'gazing from the skyscraper' than from 'walking through the street'. Gender studies have had a tendency to favour analyses of the welfare state and the way different welfare regimes have support systems that are beneficial to women or not. The national level is important because it is here that the framework for gender negotiations is set. Without underestimating the national level, the following analysis also tries to develop a regional and sub-national way of illustrating and understanding the similarities and differences in gender inequality, which, in some instances, transcend national borders. Furthermore, the use of different indicators or measures of gender relations can also paint different pictures.

In the following section we explore regional differences in the gendered division of paid employment through a set of maps based on labour force survey data from Eurostat. Regional analysis shows that gender relations differ not only by class, ethnicity and age but also according to place, and thus suggests that the welfare regimes (Esping-Andersen 1990) or gendered welfare regimes approaches (Sainsbury 1994) can provide only a partial explanation for gender differences. The importance of historical factors, culture, tradition and the specificity of the economy in the place where the individual lives and works is highlighted in a regional analysis and adds further to the explanation of gender differences. Eurostat provides data disaggregated by gender and by region but the data relate only to the quantitative aspects of employment. In order to provide information on the quality of employment, surveys of working conditions made by the European Foundation are used but these provide data only at the national level.

2.2 Patterns: gender inequality in paid employment

Overview of gender differences in paid employment

Participation in paid employment influences and almost governs the everyday life of women and men in many ways. For many people it provides the main source of income, absorbs a significant amount of time and takes people away from other activities, including care work, thus necessitating that substitute care is found. Participation is, however, highly differentiated by gender at both national and regional levels. Participation can be measured by the activity rate or by the employment rate. Activity rates are defined as the proportion of the population in the active age range (15–64 years of age in most countries) which is either employed or unemployed.[1] Other people of working age are counted as inactive. The employment rate measures the proportion of the potentially active population currently employed. Both measures are very crude, and the way in which the active are distinguished from the inactive has been debated for several years (Rubery *et al.* 1998) because this official categorisation seldom represents an accurate portrayal of actual working lifestyles.

The demarcation line between being active and inactive is formed by different institutional factors, such as regulations for pensions and the educational system. In countries with well-developed day care for children and the elderly, and also parental leave systems, conditions are set for a high female activity rate. For example, a parent at home taking care of the child and using parental leave insurance is registered as employed, but absent from work. The Scandinavian countries are an example. In countries without these conditions, as in southern Europe and Britain, women do the care work unpaid and statistically they are registered as inactive, but in practice are actively occupied with care work. Many individuals also work in the informal economy, for example as homeworkers for manufacturing companies, or in family enterprises. In such cases they may or may not be formally recorded (see Stratigaki and Vaiou 1994; Baylina and Garcia-Ramon 1998).

There are further limitations with the use of activity rates as a measure of participation in the labour force. Not only do they underestimate the total amount of work performed, but they also take no account of the differences in actual hours of paid work between women and men. Consequently use of these statistics alone can give a misleading impression of the extent of participation in the labour market (Jonung and Persson 1993; Gonäs and Spånt 1997) and the inferred degree of financial autonomy. Part-time workers may work a wide range of hours, people may hold a number of jobs simultaneously and furthermore women may be registered as active but in some countries may in reality be on parental leave. Labour force surveys are beginning to include more sophisticated measures of participation, but these are not yet available at the regional level. In general the surveys are still premised on the assumption that participation is equivalent to being in paid work in one full-time or part-time job, yet with the increasingly flexible nature of employment reality is much more complex. Even so it is still the best source for international comparison and these definitions are used in the maps below.

Regional activity rates by gender and age

In the following analysis the data have been divided into three age groups, for those aged 15–24, 25–54 and 55–64. This is because the labour market situation for the young and old, relative to those in the middle group, is very different. Most emphasis is placed on the middle age range as it is here where the gender differences are most marked, presumably reflecting the gender-differentiated response to the presence of children within the household.

Figures 2.1 and 2.2 (note 2) illustrate the dramatic increase in women's participation in the last ten years especially in Spain, Germany, southern France and Ireland. There has, however, been a generational shift. Throughout most of Italy, in many regions of France, in the eastern part of Spain, in Ireland and in northern Germany the activity rate of young women (aged 15–24) has decreased during the last ten years. Conversely, that of women

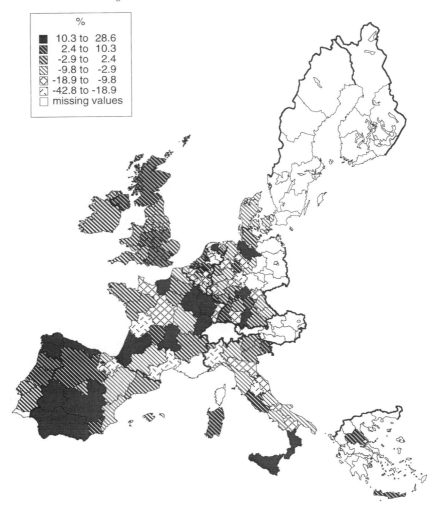

%
■ 10.3 to 28.6
▨ 2.4 to 10.3
� -2.9 to   2.4
▨ -9.8 to -2.9
� -18.9 to -9.8
� -42.8 to -18.9
□ missing values

Figure 2.1 Change in the female/male activity rate ratio (15–24 years) in the European
Union, 1987–96. *Source*: Eurostat Labour Force Survey.

between 25 and 54 has generally increased with the exceptions of Denmark
and regions in southern Italy where the female activity rates for this age
group have also decreased. On the other hand male activity rates have
declined throughout the European Union (EU). This decrease is as widespread
as the increase in the female activity rate, but not as profound.

The change for the younger age group in part corresponds to the gender
structure in education. In France, Spain, eastern Germany and Scandinavia,
women constitute the majority of university students. Young women are
turning their backs on the tradition of having a low-paid job as a temporary
situation before marriage and family. Instead they turn to the universities

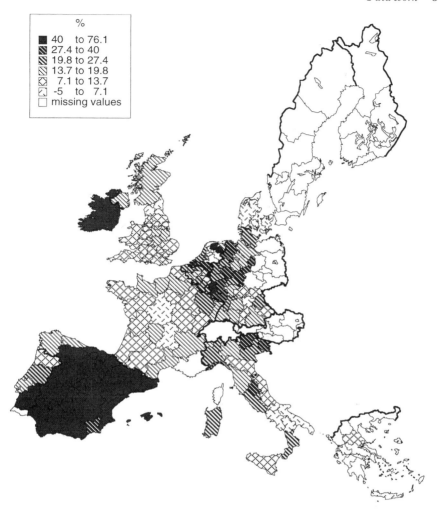

%
- ■ 40 to 76.1
- ▨ 27.4 to 40
- ▨ 19.8 to 27.4
- ▨ 13.7 to 19.8
- ▨ 7.1 to 13.7
- ▨ -5 to 7.1
- □ missing values

Figure 2.2 Change in the female/male activity rate ratio (25–54 years) in the European
Union, 1987–96. *Source*: Eurostat Labour Force Survey.

and seek a professional future. This will perhaps have a progressive impact
on the gender structure of the labour market in this century, although at
present qualifications do not guarantee equal representation in the labour
market. The change for the middle age range reflects the changing structure
of the economy – in particular the widespread decline in traditionally male
jobs and the expansion of employment in service sector activity. However,
the cause of these changes and the gender ascriptions of different kinds of
employment are by no means uniform throughout Europe. In the new member
states (Austria, Finland and Sweden) the developments have been similar
for young women and men, but not for women in the middle age range. In

Finland and Sweden the activity rates have declined by around 10 per cent for both women and men in this age group, while in Austria the developments have been similar to continental Europe (Gonäs 1998; Rubery *et al.* 1998).

Broken down by ages, the regional variations are most pronounced for the women in the middle age range. Young women are found to be economically active to a much higher degree and the pattern is very similar across the different countries. In most regions, women under 24 work nearly as much as men, in many regions even more so than men. The highest activity rates are in eastern and southern Germany, the Netherlands, Austria, UK and Denmark. Young women and men from the Nordic countries do not have specifically high activity rates. Only in southern Italy and in some Greek regions do young women have a significantly lower rate.

For the age group 25–54 a totally different pattern appears. First, the gender differences are very distinct. For women the regional differences follow the national borders and the internal differences within countries are not so apparent compared with men. This pattern suggests that care policies at the national level are the key factor in shaping women's employment patterns, while male patterns are influenced more by the distribution of economic activity. This interpretation is further supported by the fact that the relative position for women and men in different countries is not the same. Taking women in Sweden and Finland as an example, they belong to the group with the highest activity rates, yet men from these countries have activity rate levels similar to regions in western Germany, Italy and southern Spain. Thus it would appear that these Scandinavian countries provide more women-friendly employment conditions.

Figure 2.3 shows the female/male ratio of the active population aged 25 to 54 in 1996, and we can see that the relative activity rate among women is highest in the northern and lowest in the southern countries. On a more geographically disaggregated level southern Italian women have lower activity rates than women in the north of Italy. In Germany, women in the eastern part have a higher rate than women in western Germany. At the same time, women have a higher activity rate in the south, in Baden-Würtenberg and Bayern, than in the northern Niedersaxen, where the rate is low from a mid-European perspective and as low as the rate for the neighbouring women in the Netherlands (see also Perrons 1998a). The picture is similar for part-time workers. The further north, the higher the degree of part-time work (with the exception of Finland, where very few women work part-time).

For the oldest age group yet another pattern appears. Here the gender differences in the regional pattern are not as pronounced as for the other age groups. Scandinavia, Britain, France and Portugal have the highest activity rates compared with central and southern European countries. The activity rates for women aged 55–64 in most Spanish, Italian, Austrian and Belgian regions and in the Netherlands were especially low. Greece and Portugal, where higher rates are found, are the exceptions in the southern countries.

It is important to explain why national legislation and institutional

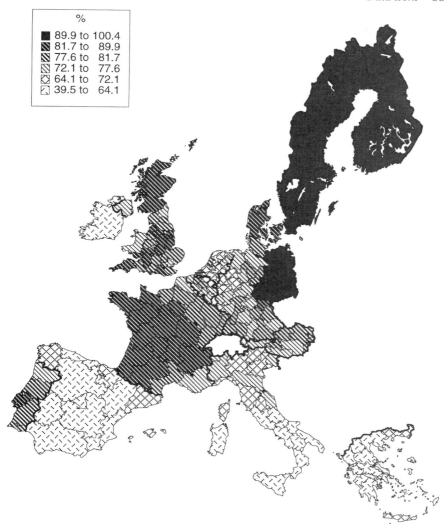

Figure 2.3   Female/male activity rate ratio (25–54 years) in the European Union, 1996.
Source: Eurostat Labour Force Survey.

regulations seem to be more important in influencing women's activity rates
than they are for men, for whom rates seem to be influenced more by the
economic structure. These two lines of inquiry, the market versus the
politically oriented patterns, will be discussed further when analysing gender
structures in later sections of this chapter.

Comparing total activity rate ratios with employment rate ratios for 1996
(Figure 2.4; this is not disaggregated by age), the pattern changes again as
the unemployed are now excluded from the comparisons. The type of welfare
state regime or similarity in national regulations do not seem to play a role.

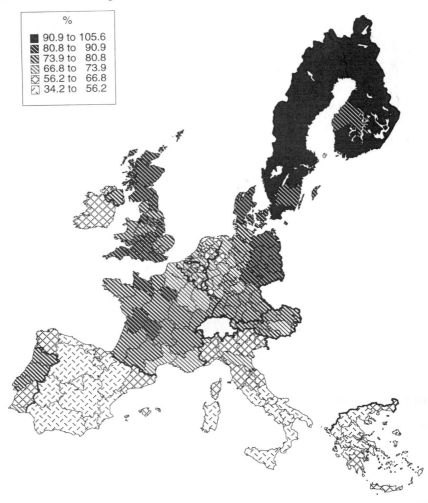

Figure 2.4 Total female/male employment rate ratio in the European Union, 1996.
        Source: Eurostat Labour Force Survey.

This point is illustrated by the cases of Sweden and the UK which stand
together as specific countries where the female employment rate is higher
than the male one. This pattern reflects rising male inactivity in the UK and
the expansion of predominantly part-time jobs for women, in part a
consequence of deregulation policies (see Bruegel and Perrons 1998), rather
than a conversion to a woman-friendly welfare regime. Finland, Austria,
Portugal, Ireland and western Germany form a second cluster. The rest of
the countries – eastern Germany, Denmark, Benelux, France, Italy (especially
the south), Greece and Spain – can be grouped together: here the employment
rate ratio is low and women's employment level is still well below that of
men.

Turning to unemployment levels, as shown in Figure 2.5, the situation becomes very interesting. For women in Sweden, Denmark, the UK, western Germany, Austria and Portugal the unemployment rate in most regions was under 10 per cent in 1996. In the rest of the EU countries the regional unemployment level for women was more than 10 per cent and up to 41 per cent. Only in the UK and Sweden were the female unemployment rates lower than the male ones.

When the female/male unemployment rate ratio is considered it is clear that female over-representation in unemployment has increased during the 1980s and 1990s in Denmark and Spain. Unemployment is most pronounced

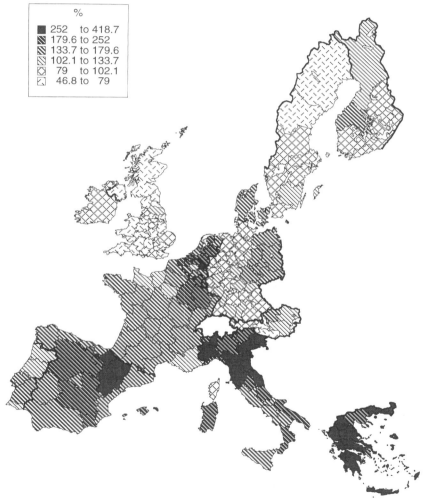

%	
■	252 to 418.7
	179.6 to 252
	133.7 to 179.6
	102.1 to 133.7
	79 to 102.1
	46.8 to 79

Figure 2.5 Female/male unemployment rate ratio in the European Union, 1996.
Source: Eurostat Labour Force Survey.

for young women. Even though – as we have already seen – the labour market participation by the youngest women, under 25 years of age, is almost as high as the male level, the unemployment rates for young women are also very high, especially in the Mediterranean and in France and Denmark. In many regions twice as many young women as men are unemployed.

Long-term unemployment is a more serious problem leading to social exclusion. When a group of people lose their attachment to the labour market for a long period it becomes increasingly difficult for them to return (Forsberg 1998). Most severe is the situation of long-term unemployment in southern Europe, in the former East Germany, and in Belgium and the north of France, where the long-term unemployed constitute up to 20 per cent of the working population. In Italy and the northern part of the Iberian Peninsula, in Northern Ireland and in Belgium this situation is even worse. Here the long-term unemployed form a half or even more of the unemployed. Even in Germany many regions have a high level of long-term unemployment and in southern Germany this tendency has grown in the last ten years.

Weighting the regional level

In Figures 2.6 and 2.7 the regional dimension of gender differences is illustrated by two maps of the weighted female/male activity rate ratio for the age groups 15–24 and 25–54 in 1996. The weighting of the data by the national totals highlights the regional differences within each country (Perrons 1998a). Again, differentiating by age and by gender highlights the differentiated employment relations which are now being formed. For the young age groups the gender differences have a distinct centre–peripheral relation, with the partial exception of women in southern Spain, where young women are much more active than women in the middle age range. Taking the two new member states from the Nordic countries as an example, the Helsinki and Stockholm regions have the highest weighted female/male rate ratios.

For women in the older age groups this pattern is again evident but more varied, with some rural regions also having high female activity rates, for example Galicia in Spain and Thraki (in a similar category to the Athens region) and Kriti in Greece. In these cases the service sector, and in the latter case tourism, may play an important role.

Gender relations in paid work

It is necessary to go beyond a quantitative overview of gender differences in paid work and try to estimate what women and men get out of the efforts they put into the labour market and consider whether they are able to influence their working conditions. To do this it is necessary to analyse gender segregation and the gendered structures of organisations and workplaces. This will be done by using the results of different surveys of gender relations in paid work, though these have been carried out mainly on a national level.

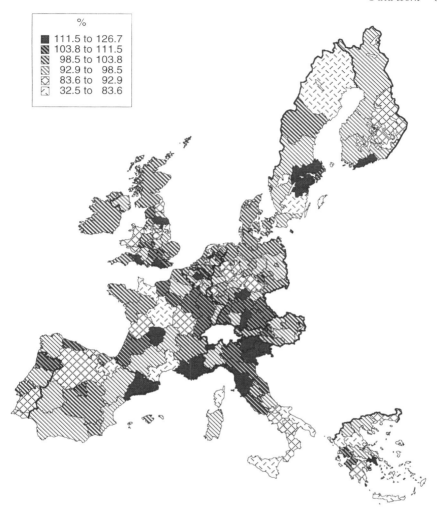

Figure 2.6 Weighted female/male activity rate ratio (15–24 years) in the European Union, 1996. *Source*: Eurostat Labour Force Survey.

In the last decade overall economic restructuring has led to an increase in female and a decrease in male paid employment. The service sector was the only sector to experience job growth in the early 1990s and this is one of the reasons for the comparative increase in female employment. In 1995, 78.9 per cent of women worked in the service sector compared with 75.2 per cent in 1992 (European Commission 1996). However, the service sector is composed of a wide variety of different forms of employment. It includes both highly paid activities, such as many jobs in the financial and business services (10 per cent of total EU employment), and more routine, low paid and irregular jobs, such as those in distribution, hotels and restaurant and personal services,

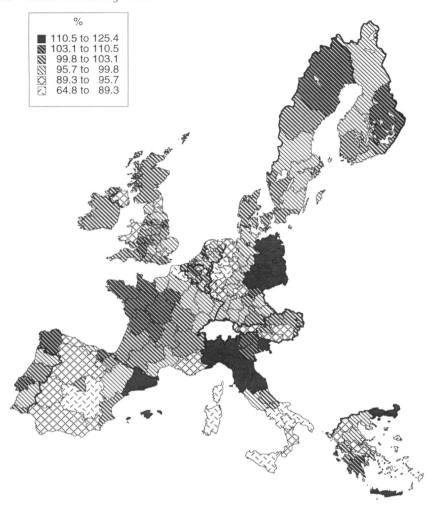

%
■ 110.5 to 125.4
▨ 103.1 to 110.5
▨ 99.8 to 103.1
▨ 95.7 to 99.8
▨ 89.3 to 95.7
▨ 64.8 to 89.3

Figure 2.7 Weighted female/male activity rate ratio (25–54 years) in the European
Union, 1996. *Source*: Eurostat Labour Force Survey.

where 20 per cent of EU employment is found. The public sector, including
public administration, education and health, accounts for 25 per cent of all
EU employment. Furthermore the gender distribution of labour is not even
between these different segments of the service sector, and although there is
some similarity between countries in the horizontal pattern of gender
segregation this is not uniform. In particular, however, women were more
concentrated in the public sector than men (Kauppinen and Kandolin 1998).
This was typically the case in the Nordic countries, where in Sweden 62 per
cent of all women were employed in the public sector, in Finland 57 per cent,
and in Denmark 56 per cent. Luxembourg (51 per cent), Italy (48 per cent)

and the UK (47 per cent) also had a high concentration of women in the public sector.

Gender segregation by economic sector is strong in all EU countries. Figures 2.8 and 2.9 show the regional variations in female and male employment in market services for 1996. The northern and middle parts of Sweden, the south and eastern regions of the UK, all of Belgium and Holland, southern France, southern Spain and almost all capital regions in the different countries had over 85 per cent of women's employment in market services. However, this pattern is composed of different types of service work. The first type is welfare state services, illustrated by the high employment levels

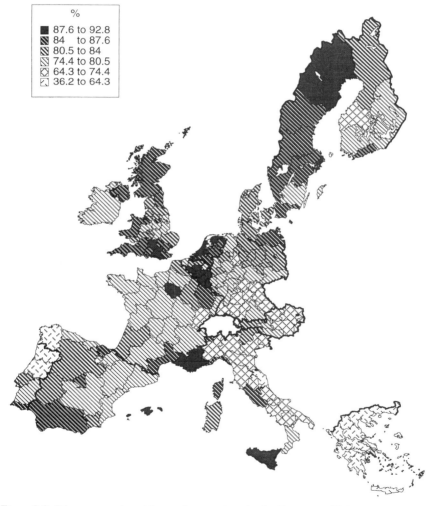

Figure 2.8 Women employed in market services in the European Union, 1996. *Source*: Eurostat Labour Force Survey.

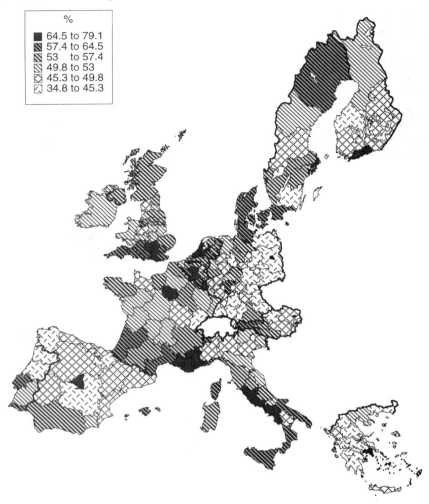

Figure 2.9 Men employed in market services in the European Union, 1996. *Source:* Eurostat Labour Force Survey.

for women in the middle and northern part of Sweden. The second is the tourist industry in the southern parts of Europe and the third is the higher levels of administration, insurance, banking and consulting that are concentrated in the core regions. Male employment in market services was highest in the capital regions, while in the southern coastal regions male employment was highest in tourist industry services. Industrial employment, by contrast, did not have the same concentration in the core regions for either women or men. The traditional manufacturing regions still play an important role in the regional distribution of employment for both genders.

Women formed around one third of the self-employed across the member states. National variations were considerable: whereas the female proportion of the self-employed in Sweden and Ireland was just 22 per cent, it was over 40 per cent in Portugal and Austria. In the UK, 22 per cent of the self-employed women worked in the public sector and in Ireland this figure was 18 per cent. This might be a new trend whereby the public sector uses the services of self-employed women without directly employing them.

The measurement of such occupational segregation is controversial. There are many issues relating to classification, which itself reflects gender segregation by being much more detailed in traditionally male-dominated occupations, the difficulty of harmonisation of categories between countries and the problem of measurement. Many of the countries with high segregation levels include countries with high female employment shares, such as East Germany, the Scandinavian countries, the UK and France. A high segregation level also appears to be combined with high shares of women employed in services. High shares of agricultural employment tend on the other hand to depress segregation as there are few internal categories and therefore women and men are classified as working together (Rubery *et al.* 1996), even though in practice they tend to do different jobs (Stratigaki and Vaiou 1994).

There is consistency in the pattern of segregation throughout the EU. Women are over-represented in occupations such as sales, clerical health and teaching and under-represented among plant and machine operators, the armed forces and managers (Rubery *et al.* 1996). Thus there is a similarity in relation to the gender labelling of work tasks but even so there are some differences. Clerical work, for example, tends to be male dominated in the southern and the Benelux countries and female dominated in the northern countries.

Structural factors explain part of gender segregation at workplaces, but institutional factors related to both internal and external labour markets also set the rules for what can be regarded as female or male work tasks. To this has to be added traditions, values and cultural norms, all of which take part in the process of gendering the labour force. Where horizontal segregation is high then vertical segregation tends to be lower. In other words, where there are gender-divided segments, women and men compete in different markets, and women have greater opportunities in the female-dominated segments. This does not, however, hold for all countries and it is not a very successful strategy for equal opportunity policy in general.

2.3 Explanations: gender regimes, cultures and contracts

The gender contract – a way to understand

As Tim Unwin (1998: 15) reminds us, 'Europe is an immensely varied part of the world'. This statement holds for gendered structures just as much as for economic, social, cultural and political structure. Social and gendered processes and actions have developed in specific places, leading to spatially differentiated gender relations. These differentiated gender relations can be operationalised as 'gender contracts', informal understandings and agreements over the way people carry out their daily lives, including the paid and unpaid work they perform, the type of family they raise and the way they take part in local political decision-making (Hirdman and Åström 1992). These gendered arrangements routinise everyday life. The gender contract guides the perception of what is perceived as proper gender behaviour; that is the gender aspect of social norms. This concept of contract does not reduce the strength of the overall asymmetrical power relation between men and women. The relation in paid and unpaid work is only one of many aspects of the gender contract. It has also been formed by culture, norms and local regimes of power.[3]

In a study of Swedish regions, it became evident that there were regional variations of the national gender contract of the Swedish model (Forsberg 1998). This variation partly correlated with economic structures. Agricultural, mining, metropolitan, university, service societies, all have their specific form of gender contract organising everyday lives. The analysis was structured around slightly transformed concepts of forms and degrees of patriarchy as identified by Sylvia Walby (1994). In the Swedish study, the *form* of patriarchy was translated and operationalised as the rules or the framework under which women and men organise their lives. The *degree* of patriarchy was translated to the (re)actions of individual men and women in their struggle to satisfy social, economic and political needs; that is to what extent patriarchal relations structure the way people cope with different conflicts, such as the family/work dilemma.

Different models

In this section we will try to identify some different archetypes of gender contracts. There has been a vibrant discussion on how to classify different countries and their welfare state arrangements, and many different typologies of welfare state regimes have been formulated and reformulated. These different models are discussed in Chapter 1. But little attention has been given to analysing the changing working and living conditions under which gender relations and gender differences are created and recreated in these discussions. By paying greater attention to the importance of living, and especially working, conditions we try to show that there is no simple correspondence between the welfare state model and the gender contract approach. We try to show the different ways in which welfare provision and the prevailing gender contract enmesh to produce different possibilities for gender relations in the different regions.

One way to discriminate among the European countries on the basis of gender contracts is the public/private dichotomy. Is social infrastructure, as basic social care, carried out privately within the family and other private institutions or is it organised in the realm of public welfare? The two extremes in this case would be the Mediterranean and Scandinavian models.

Let us take the Mediterranean traditional and private welfare system first. This model corresponds to a traditional and segregated gender contract, where women take little part in local politics and in the labour market. However, in terms of the labour market these countries are characterised by a low degree of employment segregation and, in the formal sector at least, comparatively equal earnings. In part this is a statistical artefact as agricultural employment is comparatively high and this sector is not finely differentiated by occupational group and so gives rise to a low segregation index. Furthermore, legislation in relation to equal opportunities is very advanced, especially in Greece (Kyriazis 1998). However, these comparatively favourable conditions do not exist in the comparatively large and unrecorded informal sector where women predominate (Stratigaki and Vaiou 1994; Vaiou 1996). Furthermore, although women do take primary responsibility for managing the household this can be seen as a source of pride and power and not necessarily as a source of oppression. Therefore it is not possible to infer the status of women from the prevailing welfare regime. Rather detailed qualitative work is necessary to explore the actual nature of the gender contract and how it may vary not only regionally but also by social class, in part reflected by labour market status and also ethnicity.

The Scandinavian welfare model, on the other hand, shows another gender contract where women take more part in politics and in the labour market. They do not seem to be as vulnerable as their southern sisters. One important question for equality policy in Sweden has been the sharing of both political and economic power, and family responsibilities, between men and women. One way to achieve this has been to earmark one of the paid months of parental leave to the father. However, employment segregation continues at a high level and women retain overall responsibility for the household (Bellaagh and Gonäs 1998).

Thus presence in the labour market cannot therefore be taken as an indicator of the existence of more progressive gender relations. The nature and form of paid work has to be carefully considered. Similarly the existence of progressive legislation does not necessarily promote more equal gender relations if the way the provision materialises also takes place in a gender-differentiated way.

Culture and traditions

Culture and traditions do not follow national borders, or, more accurately, the political delineation of national territorial interests has seldom taken account of culture and traditions. Consequently phenomena suh as family arrangements will not follow national borders when shown upon a choropleth map. Other patterns related to ethnic and religious divisions also materialise.

Looking at cultural maps of religions, language or political parties, it is striking, if not surprising, how well they correspond with maps of gender contracts, at both the national and regional levels.

An interesting example of culture influences is shown by Elisabeth Bühler (1998) in relation to the situation in Switzerland, where the culture and tradition can be identified by language regions rather than the national border. Gender relations vary significantly between French-speaking, Italian-speaking and German-speaking regions and those relations, or, if you prefer, gender contracts, resemble those in the corresponding regions in neighbouring countries. One explanation is that local and regional public policies are developed in relation to local tradition and not by national state regulations.

Sweden provides another example. Gender contracts at the regional level have been identified on the basis of political, economic, social and demographic indicators. These indicators included women's participation in local government, the employment rate gender ratio, percentage of women in higher managerial work, day care facilities and other welfare services, the migration and fertility rates and size of families, and so on. Using these variables, it is possible to identify a north–south divide, with the most unequal municipalities situated in the south and the more equal in the north. Of course there are also a lot of communes somewhere in between (Forsberg 1998). But there is more than a regional and geographical dimension to this. It is also a question of size and economic structure. The more equal communes are characterised by a greater size, higher level of education and higher percentage of people employed in the service sector. Corresponding to this, the unequal communes are small in scale, based on industry, especially manual work, in small-scale firms, with a low level of education. But at the same time it is important to stress that there are no deterministic relations between geographical or economical factors and gender contracts. For example, not all industrial towns have the same gender contract – it is industrial towns in the same regions that have similar contracts. In other words, it is the combination of geographical (here meaning culture and tradition) and economic structure that constitutes gender relations and the gender contract. This corresponds to a combination of the 'framework' and 'actions'.

The culture you are brought up in gives you your self-identity and a feeling of belonging. But it can on the other hand also be the means of developing alienation from a place and a feeling of exclusion. One way to handle the experience of exclusion – social, economic or political – is to migrate. In the activity and decisions lying behind migration, there are gender-related aspects. Some migrate foremost *to* a place, others migrate *from* a place. In various studies, for example Dahlström's (1996) survey of young women from the north of Norway, the relation between migration and gender relations has been analysed. The result is that the more patriarchal or the more traditional the gender contract, the greater the out-migration of women. The tendency of young women to move from rural areas to cities is a world-wide phenomenon, but on the European scale it is also possible to show that women tend to leave very traditional gender contracts, for instance in Sweden (Forsberg 1998).

Economic transformation and gender relations

As the United Nations points out, for the world as a whole, there is a strong relation between gender inequality and human poverty. This seems to be the case even within Europe. Economic inequality within nations differs significantly throughout Europe. But gender inequality is not necessarily related to specific economic structures or economic wealth. The economic benefit given to men and women respectively is an indication of the gender contract and specifically, given gender segregation, the way society evaluates different activities. Closing the wage gap is of great importance in equality programmes, not least because the possibility of earning enough money to be independent is crucial for the development of an equal gender contract.

The greater the economic transformation, the greater the possibility for change in the gender contract (see Walby 1997). In the path of economic transformations, new forms of opportunities and inequality occur. There have been dramatic changes in the economies of Spain, Portugal and Ireland as well as in the former German Democratic Republic. In the GDR, female employment rates have declined while in the other three countries there have been large increases in GDP and in female employment rates.

However, do these figures give a relevant picture of what has actually happened in these countries? Mireia Baylina and Dolors Garcia-Ramon (1998) present a very different picture of the economic miracle by documenting the conditions of homeworkers working for the prosperous firms of the 'Sunbelt' in southern Spain. Much of the feminisation of employment that has taken place here and elsewhere throughout the EU has been 'flexible', that is part-time, temporary or casual. Although this work provides women with an income, and often a sense of empowerment, it does not really contribute towards providing equal opportunities for women (Perrons 1998b).

Flexible working is advocated by the European Commission as a means of enhancing competitiveness, maintaining employment, and contributing towards economic and social cohesion and towards equal opportunities by enabling people to reconcile work and family life (Perrons 1999). Furthermore, both the cohesion and the equal opportunities policies have been mainstreamed, which means that all policies of the EU have to take into account their effects on cohesion and equal opportunities. Similarly it means that cohesion policies have to take account of the equal opportunity implications (and vice versa).

In this context the European Structural and Cohesion Funds have contributed to the rates of growth in Greece, Spain, Portugal and Ireland. This raises the question as to the degree to which Structural Funds have actually contributed towards equal opportunity policy. The contribution of the overall economic strategy as dictated by the Maastricht criteria has certainly been questioned in this respect (European Commission 1997; Perrons 1999). In the metropolitan regions, by contrast, where the overall gender ratio in employment rates is in general higher, there is another socio-economic change taking place, namely the growth of a new middle class (McDowell 1997). This is a new aspect of feminisation in the central districts, not as poor, social service-dependent women, but as high-flying finance and professional workers and gentrifiers. An interesting conclusion made by Linda McDowell, in her study of this group in London, is that professional women tend to remain single (see also Bruegel 1996), suggesting that the objective of the EU's mainstreaming policy of reconciling work and family life remains very distant. That is, progression in the sphere of work for many women in Britain at least means that the role of motherhood has to be postponed or never realised.

2.4 Afterword

There are many interrelated factors shaping social relations between men and women in the gender contracts. Culture and tradition are two of them, economy and political arrangements are others. There are different gender contracts throughout Europe. Part of the differentiation can be explained by the way the welfare state supports its population. But we can also find variations in these national contracts, formed by cross-national culture and traditions such as ethnic, religious and political factors. Such traditions impose what is morally right and socially acceptable. Economic structure does not seem to determine the gender contract by itself, but where there is an ongoing economic transformation there the form of gender contract is undergoing major change. Evidence of this can be seen today in Portugal, Greece, Ireland and in parts of Spain. Precise employment relations have to be studied in greater detail, however, before the effect of these changes on the gender contract, and whether it can be seen as 'progressive' or not, can be fully assessed. The EU's current mainstreaming statements in relation to equal opportunities policies do address the question of promoting long-lasting changes in the roles of women and men in paid work and in the home, but so far the policy measures are very limited. Perhaps legislation cannot in any case change the way in which people organise their daily lives. Nevertheless, the differences identified in this chapter in relation to paid work suggest that the supra-national, national and sub-national states all play some role in influencing the extent of gender inequality in employment and in establishing frameworks of differentiated opportunities within which people, through their own actions, determine their own specific gender contracts.

Notes

1   The analysis here follows Perrons (1998a,b).

2 The new member countries Austria, Finland and Sweden became part of the EU in 1995. In this section data on the 1990s for these countries have been collected separately as Eurostat does not contain data for them before 1995.

3 The concept of the gender contract does not correspond much with the social contracts of philosophers such as Thomas Hobbes or Rousseau, where people agree on the structure of the contract and where both parties gain from it. On the contrary.

References

Baylina, M. and Garcia-Ramon, D. 1998. Homeworking in rural Spain: a gender approach. *European Urban and Regional Studies*, 5, 55–64.

Bellaagh, K. and Gonäs, L. 1998. National report from Sweden on 'Flexible working and the reconciliation of work and family'. In *Flexible working and the reconciliation of work and family – or a new form of precariousness*. Final report by D. Perrons for DGV Economic and Social Affairs Unit, European Commission. V/768/98 CE-V/22-98-003-EN-C. European Commission, Brussels.

Bruegel, I. 1996. Whose myths anyway? A comment. *British Journal of Sociology*, 47, 175–177.

Bruegel, I. and Perrons, D. 1998. Deregulation and women's employment: the diverse experiences of women in Britain. *Feminist Economics*, 4, 103–125.

Bühler, E. 1998. Economy, state or culture? Explanations for the regional variations in gender inequality in Swiss employment. *European Urban and Regional Studies*, 5, 27–40.

Dahlström, M. 1996. Young women in a male periphery – experiences from the Scandinavian north. *Journal of Rural Studies*, 12, 3, 259–271.

Esping-Andersen, G. 1990. *The Three Worlds of Welfare Capitalism*. Polity Press, London.

European Commission 1996. *Employment in Europe 1996*. Luxembourg.

European Commission 1997. *Employment in Europe 1997*. Luxembourg.

Forsberg, G. 1998. Regional variations in the gender contract: gendered relations in labour markets, local politics and everyday life in Swedish regions. *Innovation*, 2, 161–210.

Gonäs, L. 1998. Has equality gone too far? On changing labour market regimes and new employment patterns in Sweden. *European Urban and Regional Studies*, 5, 41–54.

Gonäs, L. and Spånt, A. 1997. *Trends and prospects for women's employment in the 1990s, the Swedish Report* (submitted to the European Commission Network of Experts on the Situation of Women in the Labour Market). *Arbete och Hälsa*, 1997, 4. National Institute for Working Life, Stockholm.

Hanson, S. and Pratt, G. 1995. *Gender, Work and Space*. Routledge, London.

Hirdman, Y. 1990. *Att Lägga Livet till Rätta: Studier i Svensk Folkhemspolitik*. Carlsson, Stockholm.

Hirdman, Y. and Åström, G. 1992. *Kontrakt i Kris: om Kvinnors Plats i Värlfärdsstaten*. Carlsson, Stockholm.

Jonung, C. and Persson, I. 1993. Women and market work: the misleading tale of participating rates in international comparisons. *Work, Employment and Society*, 7, 2, 259–274.

Kauppinen, K. and Kandolin, I. 1998. *Gender and Working Conditions in the European Union*. European Foundation, Dublin.

Kyriazis, N. 1998. Women's employment and gender relations in Greece: forces of modernization and tradition. *European Urban and Regional Studies*, 5, 65–76.

Lewis, J. 1992. Gender and the development of welfare regimes. *Journal of European Social Policy*, 2, 3, 159–173.

McDowell, L.M. 1997. The new service class: housing, consumption, and lifestyle among London bankers in the 1990s. *Environment and Planning A*, 29, 2061–2078.

Perrons, D. 1998a. Maps of meaning: gender inequality in the regions of Western Europe. *European Urban and Regional Studies*, 5, 13–26.

Perrons, D. 1998b. *Flexible working and the reconciliation of work and family – or a new form of precariousness*. Final report for DGV Economic and Social Affairs Unit, European Commission. V/768/98 CE-V/22-98-003-EN-C. European Commission, Brussels.

Perrons, D. 1999. Deconstructing the Maastricht myth? Economic and social cohesion in Europe: regional and gender dimensions of inequality. In Hudson, R. and Williams, A. (eds) *Divided Europe*, pp. 391–418. Sage, London.

Perrons, D. and Gonäs, L. 1998. Introduction: Perspectives on gender inequality in European employment. *European Urban and Regional Studies*, 5, 5–12.

Pfau-Effinger, B. 1998. Gender cultures and the gender arrangement – a theoretical framework for cross-national gender research. *Innovation*, 11, 2, 147–166.

Rubery, J., Smith, M. and Fagan, C. 1996. *Trends and prospects for women's employment in the 1990s*. Summary report to the European Commission Network of Experts on the Situation of Women in the Labour Market. UMIST, Manchester.

Rubery, J., Smith, M., Fagan, C. and Grimshaw, D. 1998. *Women and European Employment*. Routledge, London.

Sainsbury, D. (ed.) 1994. *Gendering Welfare States*. Sage, London.

Stratigaki, M. and Vaiou, D. 1994. Women's work and informal activities in southern Europe. *Environment and Planning A*, 26, 8, 1221–1235.

Unwin, T. (ed.) 1998. *A European Geography*. Longman, Edinburgh.

Vaiou, D. 1996. Women's work and everyday life in southern Europe in the context of southern European integration. In Garcìa-Ramon, M.D. and Monk, J. (eds) *Women of the European Union: the Politics of Work and Daily Life*, pp. 61–73. Routledge, London.

Walby, S. 1994. Methodological and theoretical issues in the comparative analysis of gender relations in western Europe. *Environment and Planning A*, 27, 1339–1354.

Walby, S. 1997. *Gender Transformations*. Routledge, London.

3 Households and families

Changing living arrangements and gender relations

María José González López and Montserrat Solsona Pairó

3.1 Issues: changing gender relations and living arrangements

This chapter analyses recent changes in family life in Europe. The aim is to identify forms of living arrangements which fundamentally deviate from the main features of the conventional 'housewife marriage' model. This conventional model, as an ideological construction of modern industrial societies, has been strongly contested by feminist scholars since the 1970s and early 1980s for being the main pivot of women's exploitation and economic subordination (see, for instance, Bernard 1973; Hartmann 1976; Barret and MacIntosh 1982; Delphy and Leonard 1992).

The housewife marriage model is supposed to work under the assumption of complementary gender roles whereby women are the main care providers in the household and men the main economic providers. The functionalist approach laid out by social theorists such as Parsons (1949; Parsons and Bales 1955), which has influenced most sociological studies on the family from the 1950s until recently, also attributed to this family model the functions of co-residential partnership, sexuality and reproduction. This traditional family, as a sociological model, was later incorporated into conventional neo-classical economics through the *new household economics* (Becker 1981).

The increase in the society's commitment to egalitarian gender relationships should, therefore, be precisely matched by the decline of housewife marriage. This means that women reject their subordination, including the rigid division of labour between spouses, within hierarchical familial relations. This is why the new role of women becomes the main cause of family change. The rejection of the housewife marriage is reflected either in the formation of alternative living arrangements such as cohabitation, living-apart-together (LAT – defined as an intimate relationship with someone who lives in separate household), one person households, non-family households, single parenthood and so on, or in the postponement of family obligations by simply following an individually centred career. The last option is in fact following in men's footsteps, as a career-oriented life is what most men have always pursued.

Partnerships such as LATs can offer the couple the affective and sexual functions of a relationship without necessarily including the function of procreation, and without obliging them to share a common residence. These partnerships presuppose the economic independence of both partners and, therefore, gender bargaining and mutual commitments are defined in completely new terms. This is not to say that marriage is, by definition, based on hierarchical relations. Married couples can also build their relationship on the principle of gender equality: a dual-career couple may be as democratic as two people living in a LAT. However, in marital unions it is most common that women are economically dependent, given their specialisation in care work. It should also be noted that it is possible to move away from the housewife marriage model as a form within marriage, if an adequate institutional framework is present such as generous public services for working parents. This element of the welfare state will be taken into account in our comparative analysis in sections 3.2 and 3.3.

Recent demographic patterns such as the delay in nuptiality, the decrease in fertility, the increase in non-marital fertility and the increase in cohabitation and divorce are also a clear manifestation of the de-institutionalisation of the 'monolithic family'. Families are no longer the privileged site for reproduction and sexuality. There are other possible living arrangements that are no longer perceived as deviant or stigmatised categories. In fact most policy makers have acknowledged this family change, linked to issues such as an ageing population and declining fertility. In most Western European states they recognise that new trends in family life, lone motherhood for example, require a reformulation of the welfare systems of protection. In this way, states face new challenges for ensuring social protection as societies accelerate the process towards further de-familiarisation and/or individualisation (see European Commission 1994).

In brief, women's role in inducing family change arises out of their attempt to overcome the negative aspects of the traditional housewife marriage. As part of our working hypothesis we expect women to follow a number of individual strategies, which can be summarised as follows:

1   Families are undergoing a profound social de-institutionalisation as more women perceive that they can autonomously make a living without the need to formalise their affective relationship within a marital union. Therefore, women will tend to reject the idea of marriage as the only context for intimate relations and will try out other alternative living arrangements such as the aforementioned LATs, or by living in non-family households (such as living with friends, living alone, and so on).

2   As a result of the de-institutionalisation of family life there is a separation between affective relationships and reproduction. The two elements no longer have to be necessarily taken together as was the case in the monolithic construction of the housewife marriage. Thus, it is hypothesised that women will reject the idea of marriage as the only

context for reproduction. The validation of this hypothesis will mean that there is a clear upward trend in the proportion of women having children in consensual unions or by living motherhood as a lone parent.

While acknowledging the role of men in influencing family life, this chapter will focus on women. Women's roles have changed as a result of their increasing access to education and paid employment as well as their higher awareness of, and motivation to achieve, gender equality. Men's roles, in contrast, have changed less as a result of a concern with gender equality, but more because of their weaker position in the labour force. Nilsson (1994) argues, for instance, that in Sweden the shift in domestic and caring work from women to men is partly compelled by women's absence from the home during working time. This trend, however, is counteracted by the spread of new notions of less committed fatherhood. These notions essentially find their origin in the increasing disruption of the traditional family (Jensen 1998). In any case, neither the traditional dynamic of family formation (the timing of adulthood, marriage and parenthood) nor the monolithic masculine image of the male breadwinner are any longer guaranteed in post-modern industrialised societies.

The signs of this transformation in family life include the increase in new household forms (cohabitation, one parent families, reconstituted families or remarriages, homosexual partnerships, voluntarily childless partners, people living alone or non-family households) and the new terms in which gender relations are defined between partners in these living arrangements. These signs have emerged unevenly between different European states, and between regions within the same state. This is because the spread of these changes depends not only on people's cultural values about family life and gender roles, but also on the structural conditions which enable or constrain particular family forms in the first place. For example, a welfare state that is highly committed to gender equality might provide positive structural conditions (such as comprehensive childcare) for the emergence of dual-career families or lone parenting, which then commonly replace the breadwinner family.

We must also be aware of some of the ambiguities in any comparative study of family change. First of all, the use of the term *change* to describe the transformation of families across Europe can be highly ambiguous. How can we be certain that a newly apparent type of household is really new or, alternatively, if it is new in some places but not in others? For Qvortrup (1989), for instance, *change* in family life has to be interpreted not only according to the starting point and duration of the trend but also with respect to the robustness of the change. When we are examining several European states with substantial historical differences, as in this chapter, then establishing what *change* really entails will be complex.

Similarly, the same type of living arrangement can possess completely different meanings according to the context in which it takes place, even if the arrangements correspond to the same statistical definition. Lone mothers are the classic example. Over the last decades the interpretation of these families has changed from a stigmatised view of a deviant family form towards social recognition as an acceptable alternative form. At the same time, a teenage lone mother living on welfare benefits, and an adult lone mother in a well-paid career job, share the same form but not the same content. They will probably also be given differing social status. Such different meanings that societies attribute to particular living arrangements are, however, not always easy to perceive.

The analysis here is based on secondary data, mainly from the 1990s, drawn from population census data, Eurostat Labour Force Surveys and Fertility and Family Surveys (FFS).[1] The nation state may not necessarily be the best unit in which to analyse family change, as in some cases it may conceal important geographical differences. Data gathered at the regional level would appear to be the best research strategy when states have large socio-economic and cultural differences. This is the case in southern European countries at least. Nonetheless, comparative regional data are rather scarce. We attempt to overcome this shortcoming by introducing regional or local examples when appropriate.

3.2 Patterns: new and old households across European states

The aim of this section is to provide a general description of the prevalent types of living arrangements in Western European states. This description is necessary before we engage in an explanation of family change over time. Here the concept of *household* means one person living alone or a group of people sharing a more or less common pool of resources (a dwelling or the food budget). The concept of *family*, instead, involves members of the extended family related by ties of blood or marriage who do not necessarily live together or share the same pool of resources.

Figure 3.1 provides an overview of the main types of living arrangements. This figure can, however, be misleading. Our task here will partly be to reveal the real meaning behind this typology, which has been drawn from cross-sectional data for 1994. Part of any misinterpretation may result from the fact that this typology is not broken down either by sex or by age of the family members. Furthermore, this is a static picture, which does not say much about family change but focuses purely on *household forms*. The magnitude of the transformation of living arrangements will be further developed in the next section.

Four main household forms are worthy of detailed explanation here: *couples with children, couples without children, lone parents* and *people living alone*. There is a residual category labelled *other households* that includes non-family households and other types not included in the four categories mentioned above such as non-nuclear or extended families. We do not comment further on this category

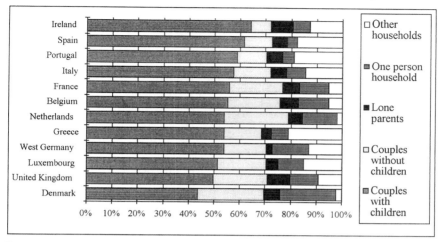

Figure 3.1 Types of living arrangements in the European Union, 1994. *Source:* Eurostat (1996) (Eur-12; see endnote 2). *Note:* Percentages in relation to all family types.

because it is very much like a black-box, where multifarious arrangements can be found such as a household of students living together or a group of adults who have decided to share the same pool of resources for economic reasons.

The first characteristic in this depiction of European living arrangements is the clear weight that the typical nuclear family (married-couple households with and without children) still has in most European states. Indeed, this category includes over 70 per cent of all households (Eurostat 1996, Eur-12).[2] Within the category the high proportion of *couples with children* stands out, comprising 55 per cent of households in the EU in 1994 (Eur-12). Ireland has the highest proportion (64 per cent), closely followed by Spain (62 per cent), Portugal (59 per cent) and Italy (58 per cent). In contrast, Denmark has the lowest proportion, with only 44 per cent of these families. These contrasting groups of countries are the extreme cases within this family type. Is it that southern Europeans like family life more than the Danish do? The answer must be related, on the one hand, to recent national demographic trends and, on the other, to the important role that the family still plays in southern Europe.

In fact this may be partly explained by the way that each country collects demographic statistics on households, since criteria are not always the same everywhere. For example, some countries establish an age limit for children to determine their inclusion as members of a family nucleus (in Denmark, Finland and Sweden, this limit is set at 18), whereas the majority of countries do not have such age limits. This partly explains why Denmark shows so small a proportion of couples with children.

At least three demographic tendencies are important to mention here: emancipation from the parental home, the level of fertility over the last decades and the incidence of divorce. Concerning the age at which children leave the parental home (leaving aside important differences by social group) we find that in Mediterranean countries emancipation occurs at later ages than in northern and central Europe. This clearly favours high rates of families with children in southern Europe. Moreover, in these countries this emancipation generally does not produce a non-family household as it is mostly linked to union formation (eventually with children). This model of family formation explains the high rates of couples with children in the Mediterranean countries. The majority of young people enter partnerships directly via marriage instead of starting with a sort of 'trial period' of cohabitation or living alone as is common in many other European states. Indeed, in the mid-1990s, 87 per cent of Italian and 81 per cent of Spanish women aged between 25 and 29 years entered their first partnership directly through marriage. This figure is dramatically lower in Norway (10 per cent), France (13 per cent) and Finland (17 per cent), while Sweden is the extreme case where only 8 per cent of women entered partnerships directly through a marital union (FFS country reports).

Even though fertility now reaches some of its lowest levels in the world in some southern regions, such as Catalonia in Spain and Liguria in Italy, during the 1970s and the 1980s the number of children per woman was much higher in the Mediterranean countries than in their Western European neighbours. This reinforces the importance of the number of couples with children. Finally, unions are more stable in the south, and divorce laws are more recent, than in other European countries. We thus find fewer lone parent households and more simple-nucleus households constituted by couples with children.

Let us now enlarge on the importance of family relations in the Mediterranean societies. Here there is a kinship family model formed by the strong bonds of solidarity within the extended family of various generations (Jurado and Naldini 1996). This helps explain some other family patterns such as parents' long-term support for adult children or the daily care of under-age children by grandparents. In Spain it is common, for instance, for adult children to live in the parental home without social stigma (Solsona 1998a), whereas elsewhere such action by adult children can be seen as indicating a sort of inadequate, or even suspicious, adulthood. This is not to deny the role of the family in other European states. It is not the case that Scandinavians do not value family life or value it less than elsewhere. It is simply that relationships work differently in Scandinavia partly because they do not need to rely on the extended family. A well-developed welfare state partly undertakes some of the functions that in southern Europe are covered by families. In the case of 'liberal welfare states', such as Great Britain, arrangements may be different again. There, the state takes refuge in the subsidiarity principle whereby it is excused from playing a major role in supporting families. Kinship solidarity plays an important role in facilitating high rates of female employment (see Silva and Smart 1999). For example, a 1980 study of employed women in Britain revealed that the care of pre-school children of those working full-time was provided by the child's father, grandmother or other relatives in 65 per cent of cases, while for those in part-time work this rose to 87 per cent (Clarke and Henwood 1997).

A main difference between working mothers in southern Europe and those in Scandinavia is, therefore, that the latter can stay in the labour force without being forced to drop out owing to the incompatibility of paid and unpaid work. They can rely much more on a universalistic and high-standard welfare system (see Leira 1992). For instance, in Sweden parents of young children (up to the age of 8) can have two hours of the usual working day (unpaid) and up to 60 days of work (at 90 per cent pay) to look after sick children. Additionally, the majority of care for the elderly is provided by the state and they have an extensive system of publicly funded day care centres.

The situation for reconciling paid work and motherhood/fatherhood is rather different in other countries. In Spain, for example, parents can take only the first two days of a child's serious illness at full pay, while in Italy parents can take unpaid leave only until the child reaches three years (European Commission 1996). In Britain there have been no such rights at all until recently. Care for the elderly in southern Europe is mostly informally provided within families and public day care is very insufficient (European Commission 1996). These few examples provide enough elements to distinguish between different roles that families, and mothers, play in societies in the context of welfare state regimes (see Chapter 6 for details of welfare state regimes).

The second type of household which will be described here is that of *couples without children*, embracing 17 per cent of all families in the Eur-12 in 1994 (see Figure 3.1). This group is rather ambiguous as it contains both old couples with adult children who live outside the parental home and young couples without children. The information we have about the age of the couple members does not allow us to draw very definitive conclusions on the relative proportions of these two types, but it does allow us to point out that the number of older couples does not explain country differences. The highest percentages of couples without children are found in Denmark and the Netherlands, followed by the United Kingdom and France where the rate of couples in which both members are less than 65 years old is very high. On the other hand, Jensen (1998, FFS data for adult people aged 25–29 and 35–39) concludes that differences by states in the degree to which people will *finally* end up living in a partnership are very small, and that they tend to disappear with age. She highlights, however, that living with children is the central factor of family change in Europe, rather than living with a partner. She distinguishes between northern countries (Finland, Norway and Sweden), central countries (Belgium, France, West Germany and the Netherlands) and eastern countries (Estonia, East Germany, Hungary, Latvia, Lithuania, Poland and Slovenia). For women aged 25–29 differences between these groups of countries are stark: in the northern group 22 per cent of women were living in childless unions, in the central countries this reached 30 per cent, while in the eastern group it was only 8 per cent. In southern European states such as Spain and Italy, as many as 20.3 and 17.4 per cent, respectively, of women aged 25–29 were living in childless unions (FFS country reports). These figures are close to those in Nordic states.

In her paper Jensen refers to two phenomena included in our initial hypothesis: the separation of sex from parenthood and the separation of parenthood from marriage. She concludes that some paradoxes are taking place in relation to new gender roles as 'women across European regions, and across age groups, tend to live with children to a much higher degree than do men' (Jensen 1998: 98). In sum, the author identifies a trend towards the feminisation of childhood whereby '[a] narrowing in the productive roles of women and men may be coupled with a widening of the reproductive roles if women undertake a larger responsibility for children' (Jensen 1998: 98).

Data on the rate of lone parenthood confirm the aforementioned imbalance between men and women. In the European states (Eur-15) 7.4 per cent of households are headed by lone parents, of which 82 per cent are headed by women. If the data are broken down by age, we find that *lone mothers aged 20–39* account for 6.5 per cent of households as compared with the 0.4 per cent of lone fathers in the same age group (Eurostat 1991). If we compare by countries, the 10.1 per cent of households who are lone parents aged 20–39 in Britain stands out in contrast to the insignificant figure of 2.9 per cent in Spain or 2.4 per cent in Greece (Eurostat 1991). Furthermore, in Spain most lone parents are mature women living with their children as a result of separation, divorce or widowhood, while in Britain around 10 per cent of lone mothers are teenagers (Russell 1994).[3]

The growth of lone parenthood is associated with the recent increase in divorce rates and the growing instability of partnerships in general. The latest data from Eurostat (1998a) shows that for the European Community lone parent families represent 14 per cent of all families with children less than 25 years old (in 1983, this was just 9 per cent). In absolute numbers, this 14 per cent means almost 7 million lone parent families, with an equivalent number of mothers or fathers living alone with dependent children. As far as children are concerned, 10.7 million, or 13 per cent of all dependent children, live in a lone parent household. Eurostat identifies two main routes of entry into lone parenthood: the breakdown of a relationship and the birth of a child outside marriage. Both have increased considerably since the early 1970s and may offer some explanation for the variations between countries. For example, the United Kingdom was the European country with the largest proportion of lone parents in 1996 and also has the highest divorce rate in the European Union, as well as a relatively large number of children born outside marriage.

Duncan and Edwards (1999) found that, although lone motherhood in Britain was rarely a deliberate choice, once they were lone parents most women perceived benefits in escaping from men's dependency and control. Indeed Ermisch and Wright (1991), based on the biographies of 5320 British women in 1980, showed that the richer the lone mothers were in terms of earnings the less likely they were to remarry, and the more likely they were to remain lone parents for a longer time. This result can, however, be counterbalanced by the fact that lone motherhood tends to be highly associated with the feminisation of poverty in most Western European states (Roll 1992; Bradshaw *et al.* 1996). However, the feminisation of poverty associated with lone motherhood is only an expression of the poverty of women living in biparental households.

Scandinavian states are a relative exception to the feminisation of poverty among lone mothers, where most are in paid work and enjoy high levels of social transfer and childcare facilities. In Sweden, for instance, 70 per cent of lone mothers were in paid work and only 2 per cent of these had incomes below half the national average. In contrast, in Britain 60 per cent did not have paid employment and 80 per cent of these were in poverty (Duncan and Edwards 1999). In Spain lone mothers, largely divorcees, have a demographic and socio-professional profile that reflects a selection process contrary to what we would have expected according to the hypothesis of lone parenthood poverty. The absence of a generous welfare state implies that only those women with a good position on the labour market can adequately force divorce (Solsona *et al.* 1998).

Poverty for lone mothers is related not only to the problem of combining employment and motherhood, but also to the father's failure after separation to supply maintenance payments. Around 70 per cent of separated fathers in Britain, and 50 per cent in Germany, failed to contribute to the mother's household expenses after divorce or separation (Meil 1995). Hence, any individual decision to have a child alone, while maintaining an adequate household economy, seems to be an option limited to stable female workers from the middle or upper social classes. It could also be a possibility to those women living in social democratic states where citizenship is based on the principle of universal social rights.

Now we turn to the analysis of households composed of *one person living alone*. Again, it is necessary to know the cause of this arrangement, and whether it originates as a result of an elderly widowhood, or of a young adult person who has decided to form an independent household or of a union disruption. As far as geographical distribution is concerned, the highest proportions of people living alone are found in Denmark (22 per cent), closely followed by Germany (14 per cent), whereas the lowest proportions are found in southern Europe and Ireland where these households account for less than 8 per cent of the total. In southern Europe one person households are especially concentrated in rural villages, where the oldest natives remain, and in inner cities, to which most young people migrate.

Figure 3.1 highlighted broad differences in living arrangements across Europe, but this can be confusing without breakdowns by age and sex of family members. Next we pose a very specific question to move a step further: what type of partnership status did women aged 25–29 have at the time of their first birth? The answer is given in Figure 3.2. Data from the Fertility and Family Survey for selected European states showed that Mediterranean women seemed to prefer motherhood within marriage and very few opted for consensual unions. Sweden is at the other extreme here, where around 60 per cent of women were in consensual unions at the time of the first birth. The most interesting peculiarity, however, is that in Norway, France and Sweden around 10 per cent of women were not in any partnership at all when they had their first child. These are all 'women-friendly states' as far as social policies for working parents are concerned.[4] This specific portrait of women's living arrangements illustrates better the significant differences in living arrangements across Europe. It also poses new questions as to why in some countries motherhood and cohabitation are not compatible, and why some women prefer motherhood within marriage or simply (long term or temporary) lone motherhood. Some answers will be further developed in section 3.3.

Lastly we look at the average size of the households, from which different family systems can be inferred. First of all, the largest families are found in the Mediterranean states, together with Ireland, which in many demographic indicators resembles southern Europe (see, for example, Figure 3.3). These large families are part of the *extended family model* often composed of a multigenerational group of relatives. We ignore the age structure of

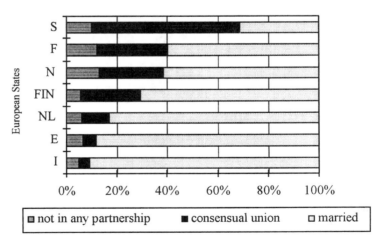

Figure 3.2 Women's partnership status at birth of first child; age group interviewed 25–29*, selected European countries. *Source:* FFS country reports. *Note:* *S, refers to the birth cohort 1964 aged 28 at the time of the interview; N, 1960 aged 28; NL, 1963–68; FIN, 1960–64; E, 1965–70; I, 1966–70. For year of interview see endnote 1 and for country abbreviations see endnote 2.

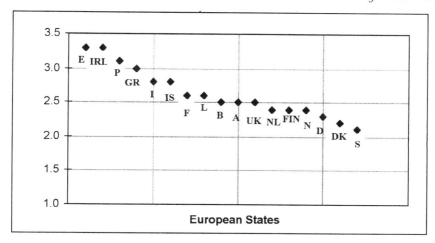

Figure 3.3 Average size of households (number of persons), selected European countries, 1991. *Source*: Eurostat (1997).

households but, given the current low fertility rate in southern Europe (although this was higher than in other European states in the recent past), the large size of families will be due to the presence of adult members. Among mature married couples it is common, for instance, to find one or two grandparents sharing a common pool of resources and enjoying mutual assistance in care work. The large household size in Ireland may, instead, be the result of the large number of children, rather than of adults in extended families.

The concept of the extended family also denotes the existence of a cohesive kinship group in which mutual support and solidarity go beyond the limits of the nuclear family. This system partly reflects the importance of the informal sector of the family (unpaid reproductive work) in the organisation of people's everyday life. The negative side of this whole model lies in the fact that the informal sector mainly rests on women's shoulders and, in this way, it perpetuates their disadvantage in paid employment. This is linked to the fact that southern European states have the highest gender gap in the allocation of unpaid work (see Figure 3.4).

For the Italian case, Saraceno (1998) points to the fact that although domestic work has become more bearable in recent years as a result of new technologies, the gender division of labour remains essentially the same. The higher participation of women in paid work has hardly influenced the degree of men's involvement in family work. Women in general (daughters, mothers, grandmothers and so forth) continue to be more involved than men in daily domestic work. Furthermore, full-time homemaker women who become divorced or separated are more prone to enter paid employment, while the time lone mothers spend on caring and domestic work is far less than for married women.

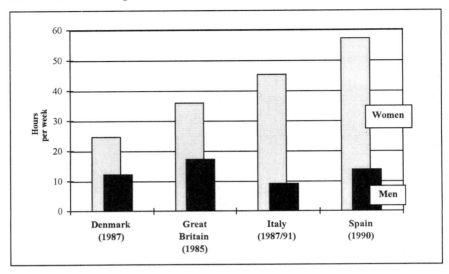

Figure 3.4 Time allocated to household work: women and men aged 25–64, selected European countries. *Source*: Bimbi (1995).

Research evidence suggests that the unequal distribution of unpaid work between women and men is, however, commonplace in all Western European states. Wives, rather than husbands, make the most adaptations in combining paid and unpaid work (see Kaufmann *et al.* 1997). Even in the social democratic states women perform more unpaid work than men. In Denmark, for example, where the unequal gender division of labour has changed most, the care of children aged 0–2 is a joint responsibility in 66 per cent of families and still remains women's sole responsibility in 30 per cent (Knudsen 1997).

If we now turn to the analysis of household composition at the regional level, we see that European patterns are even more complicated. This is because sub-national regions follow their own paths in the transformation of family life. Italy is a good example. In this country fertility decline began much earlier in the industrialised regions of the north, in the early 1970s, and was only later followed by the southern regions. As a consequence, large families are more common in the southern part of Italy where, furthermore, the economic structure largely based on the agrarian sector is completely different (Mingione 1994). In Spain, by contrast, extended families are more commonly found in the northern regions (often the more economically developed regions) where a specific system of property transmission favouring the first child encourages the co-residence of three generations (Solsona and Treviño 1990).

Large families, however, may in the medium term become a rare phenomenon given the striking trend of declining fertility. Currently, the lowest total period fertility rates (sum of age-specific fertility rates) in Europe are to be found in Italy (1.17) and Spain (1.18), followed by Germany (1.25)

(Eurostat 1997a, Eur-15). Indeed, in the fifteen European Union member states as a whole the total fertility rate has declined from 2.59 children per woman in 1960 to just 1.44 in 1997. According to McDonald (1997), present low levels of fertility respond to the clash between current low levels of gender equity in social institutions and women's high aspirations for equality and independence. The contradiction of these two elements then explains women's low fertility levels. This view might therefore also explain why fertility levels are lowest in southern Europe, while they have remained relatively high in the 'women-friendly' Scandinavian countries. Women have gained opportunities in education and employment closer to those enjoyed by men, but without state and employers' recognition of a *gender difference* – that is, without recognition of the inherent fact that women have children and tend to bear the main burden of family responsibilities.

At this stage, we can ask whether there is any patterning in the degree and type of new living arrangements and family systems across European states. The statistical evidence suggests a considerable diversity. In southern Europe the extended kinship solidarity model prevails, while households of people living alone, cohabiting couples or lone mothers are much less significant in statistical terms than in other central or northern states.

This between-country variability in demographic patterns has to be attributed to different cultural patterns as well as to the influence of political and economic structures. 'Latent' wishes to organise family life differently, such as the cases of living alone or having a child as a lone mother, very much depend upon material constraints. At the same time, these constraints will often be related to the nature of the social system of welfare protection (for example the generosity in the provision of public childcare or parental leave). The influence of this on various aspects of women's life is discussed in detail in Chapter 6. However, these structures do not in themselves create family change – there still has to be a cultural shift in values, attitudes and expectations for this to proceed. This is something we will pursue in section 3.3.

Data at the regional level are unfortunately rather limited. The few statistics available suggest that the European map of family life is rather complicated and certainly does not reflect a simplistic north–south European divide. If anything, we subscribe to Boh *et al.*'s (1989) forecast about European families, which Boh describes as 'converging to diversity'. This complexity is additionally illustrated by Kuijsten's (1996) metaphor about family life, which according to the author becomes a sort of history 'à la carte':

> Instead of selecting the standard life course menu, as people used to do especially during the 'Golden Age of Marriage' in the early post-war decades, nowadays each individual composes his or her history à la carte, according to his or her desires and constraints. When choosing their menu people tended, as far as their biography had left them options still open, to select what the decade's chef recommended to them: limiting family

size in the 1960s; premarital cohabitation, divorce and postponement of births in the 1970s; postponement of marriage until a child announces its arrival in the early 1980s; renouncing marriage even after children have been born in the late 1980s and early 1990s. Astonishingly, what was thirty years ago the obligatory entry: formal marriage, has shifted on the quiet to the far less enviable position of an optional dessert.

(Kuijsten 1996: 140–141)

It is certainly true that today there is a large variety of 'menu choices' since individual life courses have become less and less regulated in post-industrial societies. Nonetheless, it is also true that these menus are still very different in different national and regional restaurants. This is precisely the issue that we tackle in the next section: why is it that these geographical differences persist, or are even exacerbated, in Western Europe? Why is it, for example, that Scandinavian women opt more for non-marital unions than southern Europeans? Do these different 'preferences' have anything to do with different gender cultures and family values?

3.3 Explanations: the role of women in inducing family change

In this section two hypotheses which aim to interpret the current transformation of family change over time are explored. Several theoretical approaches have also made the attempt to explain the transformation of the family in Europe, often in terms of the so-called 'family decline'. Post-modernist explanations, for instance, predict the fragmentation of social relationships such as the family centred on the male power. This results not only from women's increased labour force participation, but also from the 'democratization' of relationships. The traditional family model is then replaced by a 'newly integrated family autonomy model' characterised by a low level of female domesticity, a high age of marriage, prolonged female education, more career-oriented individuals and careful mate selection processes (Crouch 1999). It is also argued that there is a process of weakening of the family as an institution. The traditional functions of the family are instead transferred to other private or public institutions such as the state. As Beck puts it:

The individual is indeed removed from traditional commitments and support relationships, but exchanges them for the constraints of existence in the labor market and as a consumer, with the standardizations and controls they contain. The place of *traditional* ties and social forms (social class, nuclear family) is taken by *secondary* agencies and institutions, which stamp the biography of the individual and make that person dependent upon fashions, social policy, economic cycles and markets, contrary to the image of individual control which establishes itself in consciousness.

(Beck 1992: 131)

It is true that the traditional family formation pattern (that is, living first in the parental home and entering marriage for life immediately after) shows clear signs of de-institutionalisation and that the role of families has equally changed in recent years. It is, however, much less clear whether this is the result of individuals' decreasing dependency on family structures. As will be shown, families still play a major role as a safety net and in intergenerational solidarity in many European states, although this is more obvious in southern Europe.

We consider that the transformation of family life only partly results from the enlarged role of public institutions such as the development of the welfare state. Instead, this change is mainly driven by the fact that women cannot put up with the irrationality of the gender division of labour within families any longer. It is primarily the incompatibility between *housewife marriage* and the new social and economic role of women, rather than the replacement effect from private to public institutions as suggested by authors such as Beck, which has triggered most recent changes in family life.

The hypothesis developed in the next section attempts to connect the patterns of family change, as described in section 3.2, to women's new motivation to transform, firstly, the rules of *housewife marriage* and, secondly, their deconstruction of standard life courses to compose their individual biographies *à la carte*. In other words, women now organise the timing of entry and exit to both partnerships and motherhood more as they wish, rather than adapting to some standard model of behaviour.

First hypothesis: rejecting marriage as the only form for relationships

The first hypothesis predicts that the likely disadvantages of gender inequality attached to marital unions will drive many women to reject marriage as the only form of relationship. This statement was implicitly formulated in the marriage theory of Gary Becker (1981). He postulated that the increase in women's attainment of human capital would reduce their interest in or gains from marriage, since the complementary advantages of labour specialisation by partners (where men specialise in market labour and women in domestic work) would no longer hold. Thus, highly educated women with consequent high occupational prospects will simply not be attracted, at least in economic terms, by the project of forming a marital union.

Paradoxically, radical feminist theory has also explicitly formulated the idea of husbands' and wives' differential advantages within traditional marriage. However, such feminists saw women as disadvantaged, rather than engaged in equal exchange, and this was not just a result of husbands' and wives' different economic resources, but also because of inequalities in power and in sexual and emotional relations. As suggested by Delphy and Leonard (1992: 260):

Putting it crudely, what men get from marriage is 57 varieties of unpaid services, whereas the institution of marriage and the family restricts and (ab)uses (married and unmarried) women in all areas of their lives.

Blossfeld (1996) conducted comparative research to test precisely whether Becker's prediction of women's increasing lack of interest in marriage was true. If the hypothesis were accepted, this 'lack of interest' would explain the rise in the age at first marriage which is found in most European states (see Figure 3.5). They concluded that marriage and fertility were *postponed* in most countries, rather than avoided, as women's educational attainment increased. For the cohorts analysed, most women ended up married irrespective of their level of education, therefore it was not a matter of 'lack of interest' associated with the increased opportunity costs of motherhood. Women's different propensities to marry are strongly associated with their level of education in Italy, a little in France and the Netherlands, but the two show no association at all in Swedish and West German women. In turn this suggests the importance of *cultural* rather than purely *economic* changes. Certainly, these trends cannot support a 'rational economic behaviour' in marriage formation as predicted by Becker.

Hence, according to Blossfeld, in countries such as Italy or Spain highly educated women at any age have a lower propensity to marry than the less educated. This pattern is indeed illustrated in Figure 3.6. Around 50 per

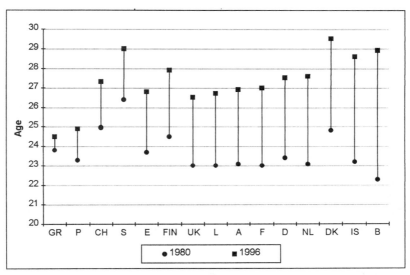

Figure 3.5 Average age of women at first marriage, selected European countries, 1980 and 1996. *Source:* Council of Europe (1997). *Note:* There were no figures for Italy in 1980 and 1996; the nearest data are for 1975 (23.5) and 1994 (26.5). For B, D and IS data refer to 1995; for the UK and E, 1994; and for N, 1993.

cent of women with a primary level of education had married by the age of 22, while for women with a university degree the corresponding age was 26. By the time both groups reached 31 years only 10 per cent of those with primary studies remained single, compared with 30 per cent of those with a university degree. This means that in Spain education is a good indicator of different choices in living arrangements over the life course. However, this association between education and marital behaviour is less clear in northern and central European states (Kiernan 2000).

The main problem with using Becker's theory to examine marital behaviour is that we have to assume a normative concept of rationality. He does not consider varying social norms or ideologies, nor the extent to which the notion of rationality itself is subject to change (see Duncan and Edwards 1999). According to Pfau-Effinger, 'the assumption that there is a homogeneous pattern of actions and orientations for women, with respect to family and waged work, throughout all of Western Europe does not seem very plausible' (1998: 148). Furthermore, from a life course perspective even a lesser educated woman would be interested in paid work if increasing labour force flexibility and job insecurity over the longer term are considered. It is no longer possible to rely on male specialisation in the labour market (Oppenheimer 1994).

Next, we examine women who do not enter marital unions in the first place, but try out the alternative arrangement of LATs (living-apart-together). The FFS survey asked never-partnered people (women and men) aged 20–34 whether they were having an intimate relationship with someone who lived in a separate household. It turned out that 37 per cent of Spanish respondents were in LATs, although only 26 per cent of these (that is, 11 per cent of the

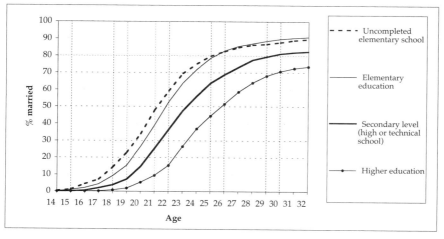

Figure 3.6 Cumulative percentage of married women by educational level: 1955–59 cohort (aged 32–36 in 1991), Spain. *Source*: INE (1991).

total) claimed a LAT was what they really wanted. In Italy 46 per cent answered 'yes', of which 40 per cent claimed this as their favoured option, and in West Germany 32 per cent were in LATs, with as many as 72 per cent claiming to have deliberately chosen a LAT. The issue, then, is not whether they live in LATs; most young people actually have relationships while they stay in the parental home. The important point is whether this is mainly a constrained option, as in Spain, or a choice, as in Germany.

Most studies of young adults stress that in southern Europe they leave the parental home very late, even if their parents' generation followed the convention of entering early into partnerships and forming independent households (Heath and Miret 1996). Bettio and Villa (1998) interpret this new pattern as the *Mediterranean path* to adulthood. This path is particularly interesting from the gender perspective because women, generally more disadvantaged in the labour force than men, can afford to acquire sufficient resources (human capital for instance) to form an autonomous household thanks to their long stay in the parental home. According to these authors, the distinction in southern Europe is that there is a model of *'independence within* rather than *from* the family' (ibid.: 146). That is, emancipation takes place thanks to the parents' transfer of resources which can take the form of affective and economic support, as well as a daily provision via unpaid work (laundry, food preparation, and so on) which is mostly carried out by mothers. Of course, this is also a class-differentiated model of emancipation because low-income families, rather than supporting their children for a long time, may require their help in the household economy as soon as they reach working age.

The fact that young people prolong their stay in the parental home does not mean, however, the perseverance of the parents' control over their children. Young people have tended to negotiate broader areas of individual freedom with their parents, who at the same time are largely permissive with regard to their children's sexual life and autonomy (Mingione 1994; Bettio and Villa 1998). This is illustrated by the fact that, although southern Europeans may leave home very late in comparison to other young Europeans, the median age of first sexual intercourse, which has been declining everywhere, is very similar in all European states (FFS country reports). For instance, the median age at first sexual intercourse in the age group 30–34 was at 20 for the Spanish women, 19.4 for the Italian and 18.5 for the French. There are slight differences but these are by no means as large as the differences in when French and Spanish or Italians leave the parental home (see Figure 3.7).

Not all social classes can afford to support their children leaving the parental home at a late age and, as mentioned above, this pattern involves a certain degree of privilege. A recent study on the Metropolitan Area of Barcelona showed that young people from a working-class background tended to have an earlier emancipation than those with highly skilled parents (Solsona 1998b). The same study revealed that women from working-class

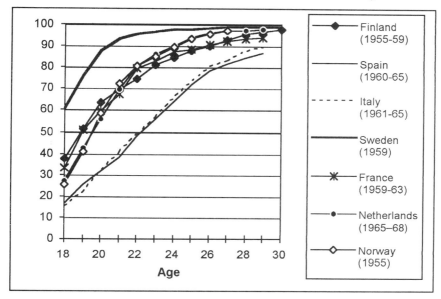

Figure 3.7 Cumulative percentage of women aged 30–34* who have left the parental home by birth cohorts, selected European countries. *Source*: FFS country reports. *Note*: *In Sweden the 1959 birth cohort was aged 33 at the time of the interview, in the Netherlands the 1965–68 birth cohort was aged 33–34, and in Norway the 1955 birth cohort was aged 33. For year of interview see endnote 1.

families tended to leave the parental home even when unemployed – presumably because they joined a working male partner: one out of five emancipated women aged 20–29 reported being a full-time homemaker in the Metropolitan Area of Barcelona in 1995.

In other European states, in the United Kingdom and Sweden for example, entrance into higher education often marks the time at which young people from the middle class leave the parental home. These students usually have residential accommodation provided by the institutions and paid for out of students' income. For working-class non-students in Britain, a good job, after training or an apprenticeship, or a partnership marks emancipation. As Figure 3.7 shows, Swedish women are an extreme case in Europe, leaving the parental home very early (60 per cent had already left at the age of 18), much earlier even than in other Scandinavian states. This may reflect generous welfare state provision for young people in Sweden, or a relative surplus of affordable housing, rather than different cultural values.

If women do eventually decide to enter into a partnership, then are there significant differences in duration of these partnerships across countries? Evidence suggests that this is the case (see Figure 3.8). In general, southern European women seem to stay longer in *legal marriages* than women elsewhere. Spaniards stayed in marital unions for an average of 23.2 years (data from

1985) and Italians for an average of 21.6 years (data from 1988), whereas at the other extreme in Sweden the average was only about 15 years. In Mediterranean Europe cohabitation lasted only for a very short period (0.2 years on average in Spain and 0.4 years in Italy) (De Santis 1992).[5] The Netherlands (2.7 years on average) and France (2.8 years on average) are at a mid-point between southern Europe and the Scandinavian states. In Denmark and Sweden the average duration of cohabitation was 6–7 years in the middle 1980s. Indeed, in these countries women tend to enter partnerships through cohabitation in the first place, which has full legal recognition alongside formal marriage. This partly explains the large proportion of women living in cohabitation. In the age group 25–29 as many as 35 per cent of Danish women and 33 per cent of Swedish women were in cohabitation in 1996 (see Table 3.1). It should be noted, however, that the number of individuals living in cohabitation might vary according to the stage of the life course we look at. In some countries it may be that young people have just begun to live in cohabitation, while divorcees were accustomed to cohabit much earlier, especially where divorce proceedings entail a great deal of legal hassle and time.

A study of cohabiting couples in Sweden showed that cohabitees are often relatively young and their unions generally less stable than married couples (Meisaari-Polsa 1997). This is attributed to the fact that moving apart is always easier for cohabitees without the symbol of marriage, even if the legal situation is similar. Cohabitees by younger partners will also represent a 'trial' partnership. Indeed since the mid- to late 1960s students in the Nordic countries have had access to non-profit flats in which to establish a household. Although non-married unions were relatively few at that time, this did not

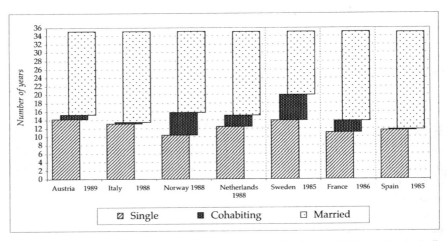

Figure 3.8 Average duration in three conjugal states (single, cohabiting and married) for women (aged 15–49), selected European countries, mid-1980s. *Source*: De Santis (1992).

Table 3.1 Cohabitees according to age group and sex (%), selected European countries, 1996

Country	Women		Men	
	25–29	*30–34*	*25–29*	*30–34*
Greece	1	1	2	–
Portugal	1	1	–	2
Ireland	3	4	6	3
Spain	3	3	2	4
Italy	–	4	–	3
Austria	8	9	10	7
West Germany	9	7	15	11
Luxembourg	10	–	2	4
Belgium	12	7	16	8
Britain	12	7	16	9
Netherlands	16	8	23	13
Finland	27	16	29	14
France	30	19	24	27
Sweden	33	22	39	31
Denmark	35	19	43	23

Source: CEC (1996).

seem to provoke significant cultural resistance. There seems to be little evidence, however, that cohabitation will replace marriage as an institution in the short term in most European countries because cohabiting couples usually marry once they have children (Boh *et al.* 1989). One reason is that there exists the belief that a legalised bond between parents will give a child better chances of support and security than if they grow up in a consensual union (Boh *et al.* 1989), although this belief is less pervasive in Scandinavia and, more recently, in Britain.

De Santis estimated women's median duration for all types of cohabitation (see Figure 3.8), but did not specify the difference in duration according to the type of cohabitation. Kiernan (2000), for instance, provides a more concrete measure that indicates the median duration of cohabitations that had dissolved without converting into marriage (data for both sexes). This provides a rather interesting picture. On the one hand, the median duration of *cohabitations that dissolved* in Spain and Italy is higher (24 and 21 months respectively) than the duration of *pre-marital cohabitation* (16 and 17 months respectively). On the other hand, it is Austria (38 months) and France (34 months), not the Nordic countries, that are in first place with regard to the longest duration of *cohabitations that dissolved*. All this indicates that the label 'cohabiting couples' can mean several things at the same time, and that current statistics hardly reveal this complexity.

Kiernan (2000) also differentiates between social groups who are more prone to cohabit than others. This is for several reasons such as poverty, marriage break-up where divorce was not obtained (post-marital cohabitation), being ideologically opposed to marriage or belonging to the more secular groups in the population. In general, the author also finds that in countries such as Spain or Italy cohabitation is more common amongst the highly educated population, while this relationship does not hold for other countries. Equally interesting, it emerges that cohabitation invariably appears higher among people who experienced parental divorce during childhood, perhaps because they may feel reluctant to make a permanent commitment. Furthermore, the nature of the relationship may vary according to whether they are cohabiting or married. These differences emerged in a recent study in the Metropolitan Area of Barcelona in Spain (Solsona 1998b). Thus, married couples have a higher likelihood of being house owners (an indicator of high expectations of stability) and have a higher fertility rate than cohabiting couples. In contrast, cohabiting couples are more prone to form non-traditional families (women are older or have higher educational attainment than men) and tend to have a more egalitarian distribution of caring work in the household than married couples.

The low popularity of cohabitation in southern Europe could be explained by Sørensen's (1996) hypothesis of a cultural diffusion. She states that in societal contexts where there have not been supportive factors for new living arrangements for young people then the cultural diffusion of non-marital unions as an acceptable institution will take longer to be achieved.

In countries such as Spain childbirth is, in the majority of cases, a reason to formalise a union either by a civil or a religious ceremony. This happens despite there being no real need to be in a legal union for custody or parental rights to the children. Nevertheless, most people tend to perceive that a child will be better off in a marital union. Therefore, cohabitation is only slowly gaining some significance in statistical terms in Spain: 1.9 per cent of the women born in the late 1940s formed a consensual union in their first partnership by the age of 24, while this proportion went up to 9.9 per cent for women born in the late 1960s (FFS data). In contrast, in Britain the legal position of cohabitees with respect to custody, parental rights, inheritance and taxation is more complex than for married couples but, nevertheless, by 1996 some 21 per cent of children were born to cohabiting partners (Barlow and Duncan 1999). Again, this points to the importance of ideological and cultural attitudes rather than legal structures in explaining family change.

Fox-Harding (1996) argues, however, that even in the absence of clear family policies the nature of the welfare state or particular legal regulations can affect the functioning of families. She recognises that particular incentives will not necessarily result in conscious intentions, yet she maintains that the state's 'manipulation of incentives' or 'work on constraining assumptions' affects family life. Fox-Harding's argument can make us think about the reason why people may consider marriage instead of cohabitation. In the case of Spain, for instance, there are a number of legal advantages which make legal marriage the attractive option. Married couples, for instance, have the right to decide whether they wish to be taxed together or separately as well as the right to benefit from the spouse's social security in the case of unemployment or sickness. Cohabitees are completely excluded from these benefits. Moreover, on the death of one of the partners the other cannot inherit the property of his/her companion. This is especially problematic for homosexual couples, who additionally have access neither to marriage nor to adoption.[6] The situation is similar in countries such as Italy since only married couples are recognised in the legislation.

The Netherlands instituted a formal registration of partnerships for both heterosexual and homosexual couples in 1998 giving them the same rights as civil marriages, the only difference being that homosexual couples cannot adopt children. Denmark introduced legal registration of homosexual partnerships in the 1990s. In France a Supreme Court decision in 1989 granted to a large extent the same legal rights to married couples and cohabiting couples in a long-term consensual union without legal marriage. At the time of writing the Jospin French government is introducing legislation to equalise the legal rights of all cohabitees, including same sex couples. In Britain cohabitees continue to have fewer rights than legally married couples, for example the refusal of joint custody for children, despite the growth of this partnership form. Similarly, in Germany unmarried cohabitation is largely ignored by legislation and those parents who remain unmarried do not have the right of joint custody of the children. Additionally, the system of marital tax splitting (incomes are first added and then split into two and taxed separately) favours married couples with only one income. As Federkeil (1997) suggests:

> [M]arrying for reasons of childbirth is rational in the context of German family law so that *we should, on the one hand, expect most people with children to be married, and, on the other hand, expect cohabiting couples to be mostly childless and those with children to be rare*.
>
> (Original emphasis, p. 86)

The question remains, however, as to why a similar legal situation in Britain does not mean that we can make similar assumptions as in Germany. In Britain only 65 per cent of people with children were married in 1996, and around half of cohabitees had children. This may point again to the importance of cultural factors as opposed to legal structures. Nevertheless, in countries such as Britain where divorce is so common as to be almost expected, many women see cohabitation as little different to marriage – it is, after all, 'only a bit of paper' in their eyes (Barlow and Duncan 1999).

Following marriage, the median duration at divorce was estimated in 1995 as 9.7 years (Eurostat 1997a,b). In general, divorce is rising steadily in all European countries. For the Eur-15 the total divorce rate was 30 per cent in 1995; almost one marriage in three was dissolved by divorce (Eurostat 1997a,b). The 1995 total divorce rate (estimated as the age-specific first divorce rates according to the marriage duration) for different countries is given in Table 3.2. Countries are ranked by the incidence of divorce. These figures are complemented with another more illustrative indicator: the proportion of marriages, for different marriage cohorts, which ended up in divorce. (For the correct interpretation of this indicator it should be taken into account that each marriage cohort has had different duration.)

The main outcome is that marriages tend to have a shorter life all over Europe. In the 1960 marriage cohort at least 15 per cent divorced, while this figure was 22 per cent for the 1970 cohort and 27 per cent for the 1980 cohort (see Table 3.2). An interesting finding is that divorce rates are higher among couples who had cohabited before marriage. This might be explained by the fact that these people are more demanding of relationships or have a higher need for self-fulfilment (Lesthaeghe 1995). There are also important national differences, from the very low incidence of divorce in southern Europe to the very high incidence in Denmark, Sweden, England and Wales and Iceland. In the latter states over 40 per cent of unions of the 1980 marriage cohort ended up in divorce (Table 3.2).

The low incidence of divorce in southern Europe tends to be explained by the Roman Catholic tradition there (Boh *et al.* 1989). However, a crucial point is that divorce was legalised only recently in these countries – not until the 1970s in Italy, the 1980s in Spain and only in 1995 in Ireland. In Portugal

Table 3.2 Proportion of marriages ending in divorce by marriage cohorts and total divorce rate in 1995, selected European countries

| | *Marriage cohorts (%)* | | | |
	1960	*1970*	*1980*	*Total divorce rate*
Eur-15 (see note 2)	15	22	27	0.30
Ireland	–	–	–	–
Italy	3	5	7	0.08
Spain	2	5	9	0.12
Greece	–	8	12	0.17
Portugal	5	9	14	0.16
Netherlands	17	25	31	0.37
Austria	18	26	32	0.38
West Germany	18	27	33	0.33
France	16	27	33	0.38
Belgium	–	26	34	0.55
Luxembourg	14	25	36	0.33
Finland	23	31	38	0.49
Norway	20	30	39	0.46
Iceland	21	31	41	0.34
England and Wales	23	34	42	0.45
Denmark	29	40	44	0.41
Sweden	–	38	46	0.52

Source: Eurostat (1997b).

divorce for couples who married in church became possible in 1975. However, a more decisive role seems to be played by other elements such as women's position in the labour force. A recent study in Spain (Solsona *et al*. 2000) pointed at the diffusion hypothesis in the sense that divorce appears to be more selective in countries where the phenomenon is very recent. For example, in societal contexts of low divorce rates education appears to be highly correlated with the level of divorce, similar to the higher cohabitation rates among highly educated women. Thus, the more educated the women or the better their position in the labour market, the higher the likelihood of opting for a divorce and/or cohabitation. However, once divorce becomes normalised this selective effect by education tends to disappear.

Spain and Italy are examples where divorce is a recent phenomenon and, therefore, it is still very selective when compared with countries like Sweden where divorce is a normalised element in a couple's relationship. In a study of divorce in Spain (Solsona *et al*. 2000) economic independence also turned out to have a selective effect. Thus, previous experience of the labour market was positively associated with divorce. The other side of the coin is that as a result of divorce many women will be more inclined to enter the labour force for economic reasons. This supports the idea that job security, or economic independence, is a key factor in understanding women's options to exit relationships.

Remaining high levels of female economic dependency on men are sufficient to limit the options women have to exit from marital unions without falling into poverty. Even if the 'feminisation' of the labour force is increasing everywhere in Europe most women have less well-paid and secure jobs than men. Indeed, higher rates of economic dependency are likely to co-exist with high rates of divorce, with lower labour market participation rates and low divorce rates for women, as in southern Europe and Ireland. Conversely, female employment rates are highest and – crucially – the gender wage gap is lowest in Scandinavia (Walby 1994). Authors such as Hancock (1994) regret the fact that the modern divorce laws of the 1970s and 1980s in Western European countries have been based on 'formal' equality and the presumption of equality in property settlements. In addition, these laws have overlooked substantive inequalities, which stem from a gendered division of labour and a gendered access to resources such as occupational training or education. This has meant that after divorce women on average are materially less well off than their former spouses (Hancock 1994).

We will now take Portugal as a case study of sub-national differences in some of these indicators. We investigate whether consensual unions also have a particular regional pattern (Figure 3.9). Information on childbirth outside marriage, which in the Portuguese case is strongly related to the popularity of cohabitation, has also been included (Figure 3.10). Both maps show the significant distinction between north and south Portugal. The north, together with the islands, has a more traditional pattern of family formation, judging by the low incidence of cohabitation and the low proportion of births outside

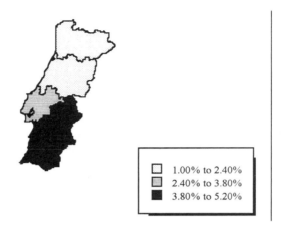

Figure 3.9 Cohabiting women in Portuguese regions, 1991. *Source*: INE (1991). *Note*: The islands of the Azores have 1.1 per cent and Madeira has 1.5 per cent cohabiting women.

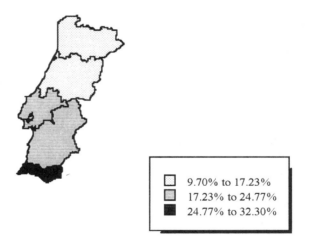

Figure 3.10 Births outside marriage in Portuguese regions, 1991. *Source:* INE Demographic Statistics (1992). *Note*: The islands of the Azores have 10.1 per cent and Madeira has 15.1 per cent births outside marriage.

marriage. This pattern should be understood in the context of agrarian regions of small family holdings which tend to be more attached to traditional cultural values. Quite stunning, however, is the huge number of births outside marriage found in the region of Lisbon and Algarve: they have levels closer to France or Finland (1990 figures). These different patterns might be partly explained by the vast number of migrants from the ex-colonies, the modern character of the industrial and tourist regions of southern Portugal and, last but not least, the high involvement of young adult women in paid employment in these areas – again at rates more like northern than southern Europe.

The Portuguese case is again a good example of the way in which national data can conceal significant regional differences. It also points to the importance of cultural factors as opposed to national-level legislative or welfare structure. These regional differences also point, perhaps, to the possible importance of more emotionally constructed dependencies as well as the purely economic. It is interesting in this respect that 'family-oriented values' as well as economic dependency in other southern European countries such as Spain and Italy have been seen as imposing barriers to the individual-isation of family relations in these countries (Jurado and Naldini 1996).

To conclude, cohabitation has increased among young adult women across all European states and it is becoming more important, even after childbirth, in Scandinavian countries and Britain. This pattern confirms our hypothesis on the rejection of marriage as the only form for relationships. This is not to say, however, that women avoid co-residential partnerships. Some women would rather initially replace marriage by other non-residential intimate relationships such as living-apart-together. Other women would, instead, postpone partnerships to fit their individual projects of occupational career or educational attainment. Both strategies facilitate the formation of more egalitarian relationships, away from the housewife marriage, because these women do not reproduce the same inequalities between partners or spouses in terms of education and occupational experience. These trends have, moreover, shortened the average time women and men spend in marital unions in most Western European states.

Second hypothesis: rejecting marital unions as the only context for reproduction

The second hypothesis predicts that the current process of de-institutional-isation of family life induces a further separation between sexual/affective relationships and reproduction. This process has, nevertheless, created new paradoxes, for example the fact that women carry the major cost of maintaining this separation between relationships and reproduction. One reason is that women, more often than men, have to procure the couple's contraceptive methods, as data on sterilisation and the use of condom show (FFS data). In Finland, for instance, as many as 7 per cent of women aged 30–34 have been sterilised compared with only 0.8 per cent of men of the same age, and in Norway 9 per cent of women aged 33 were sterilised compared with only 5 per cent of men. In Spain the difference is more balanced (7 per cent of women aged 30–34 were sterilised compared with 8 per cent of men), and in the Netherlands rates are even higher for men (10 per cent aged 30–34) than for women (2 per cent). Likewise, women have reported that there is a very low use of condoms among their partners. Thus, for women aged 30–34, only 7 per cent of their partners used them in France, 11 per cent in the Netherlands and Norway (ages 30–33), 17 per cent in Italy, 24 per cent in Finland and 29 per cent in Spain.

The further separation of relationships and reproduction has also encouraged the increase in lone motherhood and motherhood within consensual unions. These living arrangements can also be a way of avoiding abusive patriarchal relationships. The precondition of our hypothesis is that women should be able – if they wish – to organise their own autonomous household without the economic support of a male breadwinner. This would seem, however, to be a difficult condition given the continuing high levels of women's economic dependency on men in many European countries, and the relatively low levels of social transfer available for childrearing.

To test this hypothesis we explore the social meaning of births outside marriage, and lone motherhood, for European states. Iceland, Sweden and Denmark are the countries with the highest levels of births outside marriage. This, as illustrated above, also coincides with high levels of cohabitation. In 1995 as many as 60.9 per cent of children were born outside marriage in Iceland, 53 per cent in Sweden and 46.5 per cent in Denmark (see Table 3.3). These countries were already experiencing an upward trend in the 1960s, while in other states rates increased only in the 1970s.

In countries where cohabitation is not very popular births outside marriage tend to be also low. This is the case in Greece, where just 3 per cent of births take place outside marriage (1995), in Italy (7.7 per cent, 1995) and in Spain (10.8 per cent, 1994) (Council of Europe 1997). In these countries, lone motherhood (women aged 20–39 living with children under 15) did not go beyond 3 per cent in 1991 (European Commission 1994). As mentioned above, in many countries the idea still prevails that children should be brought up in legal unions. A 1994 Spanish survey asked the question 'What would be the main reasons for a cohabiting couple to marry?', to which 55 per cent of respondents replied 'a child', 33 per cent 'religious beliefs', and 29 per cent 'family pressure to formalise the union' (Cruz 1995). In Britain answers to similar surveys are more or less the same. The difference is, however, that more than 20 per cent of children are in fact born to cohabitees (Barlow and Duncan 1999).

Mahon (1997), in her study of Irish mothers, argues that social norms push pregnant women to legitimise their situation in what used to be commonly called *shotgun weddings* or *ex necessitate et post crimen* marriages. Even in Sweden and Denmark many cohabiting couples tend to marry once they have children because they believe that a formal or ritualised bond between parents makes it seem likely that the family will remain complete, and thus provide better support and security for children (Boh *et al.* 1989).

A very recent study based on the Fertility and Family Survey data shows that there is not always a clear relation between cohabitation, childbearing

Table 3.3 Births outside marriage (per 100 births), selected European countries, 1970–97

Countries	1970	1975	1980	1985	Recent years 1990	1994	1995	1996	1997
Greece	1.1	1.3	1.5	1.8	2.2	2.9	3.0	3.0†	3.3‡
Switzerland	3.8	3.7	4.7	5.6	6.1	6.4	6.8	7.3	8.0*
Italy	2.2	2.6	4.3	5.4	6.5	7.4*	7.7	8.3	8.3*
Spain	1.4	2.0	3.9	8.0	9.6	–	11.1	–	–
West Germany	5.5	6.1	7.6	9.4	10.5	12.4	–	17.1	18.0‡
Netherlands	2.1	2.2	4.1	8.3	11.4	14.3	15.5	16.9*	18.6*
Belgium	2.8	3.1	4.1	7.1	11.6	–	–	15.0§	–
Luxembourg	4.0	4.2	6.0	8.7	12.9	12.7	13.1	15.0	16.8
Ireland	2.7	3.7	5.0	8.5	14.6	20.7	22.7	24.8	26.5*
Portugal	7.3	7.2	9.2	12.3	14.7	17.8	18.7	18.7	–
Austria	12.8	13.5	17.8	22.4	23.6	26.8	27.4	28.0	28.8
Finland	5.8	10.1	13.1	16.4	25.2	31.3	33.1	35.4	36.5
United Kingdom	8.0	9.0	11.5	18.9	27.9	32.0	33.6	35.5	36.7*
France	6.8	8.5	11.4	19.6	30.1	36.1	–	38.8*	39.0‡
Norway	6.9	10.3	14.5	25.8	38.6	45.9	47.6	48.3	48.6*
Denmark	11.0	21.8	33.2	43.0	46.4	46.9	46.5	46.3	–
Sweden	18.4	32.4	39.7	46.4	47.0	51.6	53.0	53.9	–
Iceland	29.8	32.9	39.7	48.0	55.2	59.6	60.9	60.1	65.2

Sources: Council of Europe (1997); Eurostat (1998b).
*Provisional data. †Estimated data. ‡National estimates. §Without Transnistria and S. Bender.

in cohabitation and not entering into a union while opting to have a child (Klijzing and Macura 1997). For instance, the percentage of women aged 30–34 living alone at their first birth was very high in East Germany (31 per cent) and very low in Belgium (2 per cent). However, those percentages show no relation with the frequency of cohabitation, and childbearing with cohabitation. In other countries where pre-marital cohabitation is very common, as in the Netherlands, cohabitation does not co-exist with motherhood, as is also the situation in Switzerland.

As well as doing a statistical comparison, in order to evaluate our hypothesis it is extremely interesting to examine the different perceptions that societies have of lone mothers. In Ireland, for instance, a dramatic increase in lone motherhood has recently taken place amongst adolescents and is rather stigmatised. Furthermore, child support for unmarried mothers' allowance is paid on condition that they do not cohabit with the father (Kennedy and McCormack 1997). This law clearly denies their individual right as mothers to receive support from the state. As many as 95 per cent of all births to women aged under 20 were non-marital births (Mahon 1997). A similar pattern of young lone motherhood occurs in the United Kingdom with a similar social perception (Millar 1994).

In none of the cases described above can we state that women are deliberately 'escaping domestic patriarchy', even though many mothers see this as an advantage once they reach this stage (see Duncan and Edwards 1999). On the one hand, we have the example of teenage lone mothers in Britain or Ireland who usually have to rely on relatively low social benefits for their livelihood, as they encounter many obstacles and disincentives to taking up full-time work outside the household while rearing young children. State dependency has been qualified as a simple shift from private patriarchy (that is, women subordinated by structures of male domination within families) to public patriarchy (that is, women subordinated by structures of male domination regulated either by the state or by the gendered labour market; see Walby 1990, 1994). On the other hand, we have the case of middle-aged women across Europe who find themselves becoming lone mothers more by marital breakdown than by any personal choice. Furthermore, these middle-aged women would have less chance than their male partners for remarriage after divorce or separation.

Several reasons may explain the sex biases governing the norms of remarriage in Western European countries. One might be the gendered patterns of courtship whereby men tend to choose younger women (statistically speaking, men marry, in their first union, women two to three years younger on average, and this age gap tends to increase in second unions). Another might be the imbalance in the marriage market whereby men of the baby boom years find more young women available to marry them. Lastly, it might be that lone mothers with co-residential children (82 per cent of lone parent families were headed by women in the Eur-15) are generally seen as being less 'attractive', or are just less able to make social contacts in the workplace or during leisure time.

Welch and Martin (1981) offer another interesting explanation for the sex bias in remarriage. They argue that one could predict the cross-country variation simply by looking at women's relative level of power in domestic contexts, the relative value attached to women's economic contribution, and variation in women's control over property. This would point to the hypothesis that the reduced incidence of female remarriage, compared with that of men from the same age group, is an expression of a society that still incorporates strong patriarchal relationships. Indeed, in countries where second marriages are very common the differences between women and men in the likelihood of remarriage after the first dissolution are very small (Eurostat 1997a,b).

Given the examples above, it seems rather difficult to sustain the argument that female-headed households are very much related to women's emancipation and equality. Marriage still seems the ideal site for reproduction in most of the countries, and the option of being a lone mother is usually a difficult and constrained one. Only in the context of 'women-friendly states' do women have more individual choice in rejecting marriage for reproduction purposes without incurring major economic or personal costs. In these states (Sweden is an example) there is little difference in the meaning of cohabitation and marriage and, therefore, motherhood outside marital unions is widely assumed. These would also be countries that support the independence of women as mothers through the labour market and/or the welfare state, without the need for a male breadwinner (see Chapter 6).

3.4 Afterword

We have interpreted family change as the reformulation of gender relations in new social contexts. Well into the late 1960s most Western European societies tended to protect the figure of the male breadwinner as the supreme economic provider in the household. This was the old institutional context based on the assumption of *the family wage*, which had to sustain the normative model of the *housewife marriage*. This model not only presumed co-residence in the nuclear or extended family and a very rigid gender division of labour, but also had the monopoly of intimate relationships (sexuality) and reproduction as the only site for motherhood/fatherhood.

As societies have modernised the family wage system has tended to disappear in favour of the recognition of women's and men's individual rights as workers and parents. As we initially hypothesised, current principles of gender equality, and more gender egalitarian forms of organising paid and unpaid work, have motivated the formation of *new living arrangements* as an alternative to the housewife marriage. These new arrangements are cohabitation, living-apart-together, motherhood outside marriage or outside a partnership altogether, non-biological motherhood/fatherhood, voluntary childless couples and so on.

Table 3.4 exemplifies two extreme conditions which favour the emergence of old and new living arrangements. It might be the case that none of the states that we have analysed fits entirely within the two ideal type categories here described. These categories essentially correspond to states where *the family wage* persists, which encourage old living arrangements such as the nuclear family based on the housewife marriage, versus states where *individual rights* as wage earners and care givers are fully granted, which facilitates the emergence of new living arrangements. Instead, each country seems to follow their own dynamic of change which results in different forms and combinations of family arrangements (see Solsona 1998a). Indeed, we identify a *great deal of diversity* in family life forms that might be related to different cultural contexts and institutional dis/incentives. However, it proves very difficult to know whether these aspects of family change were mediated more by culture or by institutions or, simply, by the combined effect of both. This is the case when we tried to understand why some women preferred marriage to cohabiting. The example of the Portuguese regional diversity with regard to the proportion of births outside marriage revealed the chief importance of cultural factors, above other explicative variables such as state legislation or social policies, for the understanding of family change.

Much evidence has indicated that the *housewife marriage model* is condemned to almost vanish within future generations. The same cannot be said, however, about the institution of *marriage*. Couples in most Western European states still perceive that with the advent of a child it is better to regulate the relationship in a legal marriage – although this moral imperative is weaker

Table 3.4 Reformulation of gender relationships: new and old living arrangements

Old living arrangements	New living arrangements
'The family wage': male head of household receiving a breadwinner salary and full-time homemaker wife	Recognition of individual rights: both partners or individuals can either be wage earners or care givers
Co-residence in the nuclear family in most Western societies (co-residence in the nuclear or extended family in southern Europe)	Longer or permanent separation of sexuality/intimacy and residence (e.g. living-apart-together)
Specialisation of duties and obligations between spouses (rigid gender division of labour)	Dual-career families (equal share of duties and obligations towards remunerated and unpaid work)
Institutionalisation of reproduction and sexuality within marital unions	Separation between sexuality and reproduction and marriage
Long-term commitment to intimate relationships between spouses and relatives	Commitment while mutual happiness is guaranteed in contingent interests
Cultural and institutional barriers to exit from marital unions	Recognition and de-penalisation of partnership breakdown
Dominant model based on heterosexual partnerships	Visualisation and recognition of homosexual partnerships

in Britain and Scandinavia. Furthermore, after a marital dissolution mothers, more often than fathers, tend to remain in charge of the children. The increase in marital and non-marital dissolution creates new models of fatherhood and motherhood that, at the same time, are associated with complex family arrangements such as second or even third reconstituted families.

Changing gender roles have definitively promoted alternative living arrangements to *housewife marriage*. Some of these new family forms, however, do not necessarily imply more egalitarian relations between women and men, but different ways of arranging family relationships. This creates new paradoxes with regard to gender relations. For instance, there has certainly been a narrowing in gender inequality of *productive* roles, but this has been coupled with a widening in gender inequalities of *reproductive* roles, especially when women undertake greater responsibility for children. Other examples are women's higher burden of caring work after divorce or women's lower likelihood of remarrying compared with men.

The processes of family change here described have several implications for current demographic research. First, complex and divergent paths of family life make traditional demographic indicators, such as women's total fertility rate, inadequate in capturing the degree of change. It is not enough, for instance, to study marriage and fertility only for women. Studies should also focus on men because women's and men's expectations concerning the couple's fertility might be very different. In other words, final fertility should not be formulated as the result only of women's preferences. Furthermore, indicators need to be found for several possible combinations, such as the fertility of women living alone, fertility for cohabiting couples, or for reconstituted families from different biological parents. Second, the study of demographic behaviour should in some cases also focus on *couples* as units of study. Both partners influence each other and negotiate fertility choices and family arrangements with regard to the organisation of paid and caring work. Third, surveys should capture the real significance of emerging families such as *voluntarily childless couples*, and the effect that this arrangement has on gender relationships or on the negotiation processes whereby fertility decisions are taken.

To sum up, the transformation of the role of women in society has affected family life across all of Europe, but the effects have been differently felt in different countries and in different sub-national regions. Thus, in *Nordic* and *central* European states most women will leave the parental home rather early to study (benefiting from more or less generous student grants) or establish themselves in the labour force. They may eventually consider getting married or, most probably, cohabiting. If relationships do not work out, partners would easily split up and live on their own. If necessary, they may claim state support for dependent children.

In *southern* Europe, in the absence of extensive state subsidies or good occupational prospects for young students, most women would rely on their family's solidarity until completing their education or finding a stable job.

Women would eventually consider getting married (with or without pre-marital cohabitation). Many may just marry, instead of cohabiting, to satisfy their family who has, after all, unconditionally supported them. Women may also consider, at the very last minute, having babies (or the baby!) as long as they do not create too much conflict with their occupational career. This, however, will usually occur in the absence of supporting social policies for working parents. Indeed, it is not accidental that southern European women have the lowest fertility rates in the world. In brief, women seem to adapt as far as possible their projects for self-realisation in the labour market, and in relationships, to the cultural, legal and economic conditions which, as other chapters in this book show, vary enormously across European regions and states.

Earlier we emphasised the evident diversity in the dominant family life forms across Europe. We should add to this statement that most emerging living arrangements, such as cohabitation, begin to emerge in a selected group of women: the most educated, certain career women, women from particular generations and so on. This selective factor is crucial in explaining the presence of certain family life forms opposed to housewife marriage, such as having children outside marriage or outside partnerships. These forms initially emerge in the better-off social groups in some countries. In contrast, demographic behaviour which signals that marriage has lost its monopoly of intimate relationships is present everywhere, although it is still restrained to certain social groups (selective effect) in those countries where new living arrangements are still very recent. Hence, cohabitation, divorce and lone motherhood/fatherhood involve a specific type of individual in Italy or Spain, whereas these arrangements would be common to all the population regardless of class, education or age in the Nordic countries and some central European states.

To conclude, the initial hypothesis (rejection of marriage as the only form for relationships) applies to almost all the states analysed here, as the widespread diffusion of arrangements such as cohabitation or living-apart-together indicates. The second hypothesis (rejection of marital unions as the only context for reproduction) would however apply only to those states where gender equality with 'women-friendly' supportive legislation has transformed the private sphere of the family. This would also facilitate experimentation with new living arrangements, for example women making a living without the need for a male partner. Unfortunately, this is still far from a real option for many women in Europe.

Notes

1   The Fertility and Family Survey (FFS) is a long-term sample survey research programme of the Population Activities Unit (PAU) of the United Nations Economic Commission for Europe, which focuses on fertility and family change. This survey conducted two separate questionnaire surveys for women and men aged 20–49 in twenty European and non-European countries between 1988 and

1996 (Denmark, Greece, Ireland, Luxembourg and the UK did not participate in the project). At the time of writing only the following Western European country reports were available: Finland (1989/90), France (1994), Italy (1995/96), the Netherlands (1993), Norway (1988/89), Spain (1994/95) and Sweden (1992/93). Dates within parentheses indicate the year of interview.

2 'Eur-12' refers to the twelve member states of the European Union, and 'Eur-15' includes Austria, Finland and Sweden. Country abbreviations used in this chapter are as follows: A, Austria; B, Belgium; DK, Denmark; FIN, Finland; F, France; D, Germany; GR, Greece; IS, Iceland; IRL, Ireland; I, Italy; L, Luxembourg; NL, Netherlands; N, Norway; P, Portugal; E, Spain; S, Sweden; CH, Switzerland; UK, United Kingdom.

3 Despite low rates of lone parenting in Spain, some studies reveal a higher proportion in urban centres. For instance by 1995, 11 per cent of households with children of 15 years or younger in Barcelona were one parent households (Solsona 1998b), very close to the 1998 European average of 14 per cent of all families with dependent children (Eurostat 1998a).

4 By 'women-friendly states' we refer to those states which enable women 'to have a natural relationship to their children, their work, and public life', and which do 'not force harder choices on women than men' (Hernes 1987: 15). These are commonly seen to be the Scandinavian states.

5 De Santis (1992) classifies Western countries according to how many years, on average, women in the age span 15–49 have been single, cohabiting or married. Data used are cross-sectional and 'intensity' (number of years in each state) is a standardised measure (see De Santis 1992 for methodological details).

6 A new law was passed in the autonomous region of Catalonia (Spain) which introduced a reform in family common law to provide further rights to homosexual and heterosexual cohabiting couples (Generalitat de Catalunya 1998). However, this applies only to employees in the public administration and, in general, is far from being equal to legal protection in marital unions.

References

Barlow, A. and Duncan, S. 1999. *New Labour's communitarism, supporting families and the rationality mistake*. Centre for Research on Family, Kinship and Childcare Working Paper 10. University of Leeds, Leeds.

Barret, M. and MacIntosh, M. 1982. *The Anti-Social Family*. Verso, London.

Beck, U. 1992. *Risk Society: Towards a New Modernity*. Sage, London.

Becker, G. 1981. *A Treatise on the Family*. Harvard University Press, Cambridge.

Bernard, J. 1973. *The Future of Marriage*. Bantam Books, New York.

Bettio, F. and Villa, P. 1998. A Mediterranean perspective on the break-down of the relationships between participation and fertility. *Cambridge Journal of Economics*, 22, 2, 137–171.

Bimbi, F. 1995. *Gender metaphors on paid and unpaid work: time in gender relations*. Paper presented at the conference on 'Gender and the Use of Time'. European University Institute, Florence.

Blossfeld, H.P. (ed.) 1996. *The New Role of Women: Family Formation in Modern Societies*. Westview Press, Oxford.

Boh, K., Bak, M., Clason, C. *et al.* (eds) 1989. *Changing Patterns of European Family Life: a Comparative Analysis of 14 European Countries*. Routledge, London.

Bradshaw, J., Kennedy, S., Kilkey, M. *et al.* 1996. *The Employment of Lone Parents: a Comparison of Policy in 20 Countries*. Family Policy Studies Centre/Joseph Rowntree Foundation, London/York.

CEC 1996. *Eurobarometer: Public Opinion in the European Union*. Commission of the European Communities, Brussels.

Clarke, L. and Henwood, M. 1997. Great Britain: the lone parent as the new norm? In Kaufmann, F., Kuijsten, A., Schulze, H. and Strohmeir, K. (eds). *Family Life and Family Policies in Europe: Structures and Trends in the 1980s*, Vol. I, pp. 155–194. Clarendon Press, Oxford.

Council of Europe 1997. *Recent Demographic Developments in Europe 1997*. Council of Europe Publishing, Belgium.

Crouch, C. 1999. *Social Change in Western Europe*. Oxford University Press, Oxford.

Cruz, P. 1995. *Percepcion de la familia en España*. Opiniones y Actitudes 9. Centro de Investigaciones Sociológicas, Madrid.

Delphy, C. and Leonard, D. 1992. *Familiar Exploitation: a New Analysis of Marriage in Contemporary Western Society*. Polity Press, Oxford.

De Santis, G. 1992. A standardized measure of the years spent in a given conjugal or marital state. *GENUS*, 48, 1–2, 19–46.

Duncan, S. and Edwards, R. 1999. *Lone Mothers, Paid Work and Gendered Moral Rationalities*. Macmillan, London.

Ermisch, J.F. and Wright, R.E. 1991. The duration of lone parenthood in Great Britain. *European Journal of Population*, 7, 2, 129–158.

European Commission 1994. *Social Europe: the European Union and the Family*. Office for Official Publications of the European Communities, Luxembourg.

European Commission 1996. *Social Europe: Developments in National Family Policies in 1994*. Office for Official Publications of the European Communities, Luxembourg.

Eurostat 1991. *Demographic Statistics 1991*. Office for Official Publications of the European Communities, Luxembourg.

Eurostat 1996. *Statistics in Focus. Population and Social Conditions* 5. Office for Official Publications of the European Communities, Luxembourg.

Eurostat 1997a. *Statistics in Focus. Population and Social Conditions* 14. Office for Official Publications of the European Communities, Luxembourg.

Eurostat 1997b. *Demographic Statistics 1997*. Office for Official Publications of the European Communities, Luxembourg.

Eurostat 1997c. *Eurostat Yearbook '97: a Statistical Eye on Europe 1986–1996*. Office for Official Publications of the European Communities, Luxembourg.

Eurostat 1998a. [Lone parents: a growing phenomenon.] *Statistics in Focus. Population and Social Conditions* 12. Office for Official Publications of the European Communities, Luxembourg.

Eurostat 1998b. *Statistics in Focus. Population and Social Conditions* 9. Office for Official Publications of the European Communities, Luxembourg.

Federkeil, G. 1997. The Federal Republic of Germany: polarization of family structure. In Kaufmann, F.X., Kuijsten, A., Schulze, H.J. and Strohmeier, K.P. (eds) *Family Life and Family Policies in Europe: Structures and Trends in the 1980s*, Vol. I, pp. 77–113. Clarendon Press, Oxford.

Fox-Harding, L. 1996. *Family, State and Social Policy*. Macmillan, London.

Generalitat de Catalunya 1998. *Llei 10/1998, de 15 de juliol, d'unions estables de parella*. Collecció "Quaderns de legislació" 16. Generalitat, Catalunya.

Hancock, L. 1994. *Gender and citizenship on the margins: divorce in Western Europe*. Paper presented at the conference on 'Gender and the Use of Time'. European University Institute, Florence.

Hartmann, H. 1976. Capitalism, patriarchy, and job segregation by sex. *Signs*, 1, 3, 137–170.

Heath, S. and Miret, P. 1996. *Living in and out of the parental home in Spain and Great Britain: a comparative approach*. Cambridge Group for the History of Population and Social Structure, Working Paper Series 2.

Hernes, H. 1987. *Welfare State and Women Power*. Norwegian University Press, Oslo.

INE 1991. *Encuesta Sociodemografica 1991*. Nacional de Estadistica, Madrid.

Jensen, A.M. 1998. Partnership and parenthood in contemporary Europe: a review of recent findings. *European Journal of Population*, 14, 89–99.

Jurado, T. and Naldini, M. 1996. Is the south so different? Italian and Spanish families in comparative perspective. *South European Society and Politics*, 3, 42–66.

Kaufmann, F.X., Kuijsten, A., Schulze, H.J. and Strohmeier, K.P. (eds) 1997. *Family Life and Family Policies in Europe: Structures and Trends in the 1980s*, Vol. I. Clarendon Press, Oxford.

Kennedy, F. and McCormack, K. 1997. Ireland: marriage loses popularity. In Kaufmann, F.X., Kuijsten, A., Schulze, H.J. and Strohmeier, K.P. (eds) *Family Life and Family Policies in Europe: Structures and Trends in the 1980s*, Vol. I, pp. 195–224. Clarendon Press, Oxford.

Kiernan, K. 2000. European perspectives on union formation. In Waite, L., Bachrach, C., Hindin, M., Thompson, E. and Thorton, A. (eds) *Ties that Bind: Perspectives on Marriage and Cohabitation*. Aldine de Gruyter, Hawthorne.

Klijzing, E. and Macura, M. 1997. Cohabitation and extramarital childbearing: early FFS evidence. *Conference Proceedings, Beijing IUSSP International Population Conference*, Vol. 2, pp. 885–901.

Knudsen, L.B. 1997. Denmark: the land of the vanishing housewife. In Kaufmann, F.X., Kuijsten, A., Schulze, H.J. and Strohmeier, K.P. (eds) *Family Life and Family Policies in Europe: Structures and Trends in the 1980s*, Vol. I, pp. 12–48. Clarendon Press, Oxford.

Kuijsten, A. 1996. Changing family patterns in Europe: a case of divergence? *European Journal of Population*, 12, 115–143.

Leira, A. 1992. *Welfare States and Working Mothers: the Scandinavian Experience*. Cambridge University Press, Cambridge.

Lesthaeghe, R. 1995. The second demographic transition in western countries: an interpretation. In Mason, K.O. and Jensen, A.M. (eds) *Gender and Family Change in Industrialized Countries*, pp. 17–62. Clarendon Press, Oxford.

McDonald, P. 1997. *Gender equality, social institutions and the future of fertility*. Paper presented at the conference on 'Women and Families'. UNESCO-CICRED, Paris.

Mahon, E. 1997. *Sexuality, reproduction and abortion: an Irish case study*. Paper presented at ESF workshop on 'Gender Inequality in the European Regions: Analysing Gender Culture and Gender Divisions of Power in European Regions'. Trinity College, Dublin.

Meil, G. 1995. La política familiar española durante el franquismo. *Revista Internacional de Sociología*, Tercera Epoca, 11, 47–88.

Meisaari-Polsa, T. 1997. Sweden: a case of solidarity and equality. In Kaufmann, F.X., Kuijsten, A., Schulze, H.J. and Strohmeier, K.P. (eds) *Family Life and Family Policies in Europe: Structures and Trends in the 1980s*, Vol. I, pp. 302–347. Clarendon Press, Oxford.

Millar, J. 1994. State, family and personal responsibility: the changing balance for lone mothers in the United Kingdom. *Feminist Review*, 48, 24–39.

Mingione, E. 1994. *Family structures and family strategies: confronting a changing division of labour in different European contexts*. Paper presented at the conference on 'Gender and the Use of Time'. European University Institute, Florence.

Nilsson, A. 1994. Den nye mannen – finns han redan? In J. Acker *et al.* (eds) *Kvinnors och Mäns Liv och Arbete*, pp. 219–244. SNS Fôrlag, Stockholm.

Oppenheimer, V.K. 1994. Women's rising employment and the future of the family in industrial societies. *Population and Development Review*, 20, 2, 293–342.

Parsons, T. 1949. The social structure of the family. In Huber, J. (ed.) *The Family: its Function and Destiny*. Harper, New York.

Parsons, T. and Bales, R.F. 1955. *Family, Socialization, and Interaction Process*. Free Press, New York.

Pfau-Effinger, B. 1998. Gender cultures and the gender arrangement – a theoretical framework for cross-national gender research. *Innovation*, 11, 2, 147–166.

Qvortrup, J. 1989. Comparative research and its problems. In Boh, K., Bak, M., Clason, C. *et al.* (eds) *Changing Patterns of European Family Life: a Comparative Analysis of 14 European Countries*, pp. 17–51. Routledge, London.

Roll, J. 1992. *Lone Parent Families in the EC*. European Commission, Brussels.

Russell, S.T. 1994. Life course antecedents of premarital conception in Great Britain. *Journal of Marriage and Family*, 56, 2, 480–492.

Saraceno, C. 1998. *Mutamenti della famiglia e politiche sociale in Italia*. Il Mulino, Bologna.

Silva, E. and Smart, C. (eds) 1999. *The New Family?* Sage, London.

Solsona, M. 1998a. The second demographic transition from a gender perspective. *Innovation*, 11, 2, 211–225.

Solsona, M. 1998b. Viure sol, viure amb família. In *Enquesta Metropolitana de Barcelona 1995*, pp. 49–67. Institut d'Estudis Metropolitans, Barcelona.

Solsona, M. and Treviño, R. 1990. *Estructuras familiares en España*. Ministerio de Asuntos Sociales, Instituto de la Mujer, Madrid.

Solsona, M., Simó, C., Houle, R. and Treviño, R. 1998. *Informe analític de les famílies monoparentals a Catalunya*. Institut Català de la Dona, Centre d'Estudis Demogràfics, Barcelona. Unpublished paper.

Solsona, M., Simó, C. and Houle, R. 2000. Separation and divorce in Spain. In González, M.J., Jurado, T. and Naldini, M. (eds) *Gender Inequalities in Southern Europe: Women, Work and Welfare in the 1990s*, pp. 195–222. Frank Kass, London.

Sørensen, A. 1996. Women's education and the cost and benefits of marriage. In Blossfeld, H.P. (ed.) *The New Role of Women: Family Formation in Modern Societies*, pp. 229–243. Westview Press, Oxford.

Walby, S. 1990. *Theorising Patriarchy*. Basil Blackwell, Oxford.

Walby, S. 1994. Methodological and theoretical issues in the comparative analysis of gender relations in western Europe. *Environment and Planning A*, 27, 1339–1354.

Welch, M.R. and Martin, L.L. 1981. Ease of remarriage for females: a cross-cultural test of competing explanations. *International Journal of Sociology of the Family*, 11, 25–37.

4 Reconciling divisions of labour

Eileen P. Drew

4.1 Issues: patriarchy, paid work and the household

According to Sylvia Walby (1990) there are six discrete structures of patriarchy: paid work, household production, the state, male violence, sexuality and culture, in which the 'six structures have causal effects upon each other, both reinforcing and blocking, but are rarely autonomous' (Walby 1990: 20). This chapter explores how patriarchal relations in the household and paid employment continue to interact in a complex manner as exemplifying two sites where women's labour has been appropriated and how gender relations in these arenas have been used to subordinate women. It argues that if women continue to take full responsibility for the reconciliation of paid work and household labour, including housework, childcare and care of adult dependants, then there can be no gender equality either within the home or in the workplace. Women across the EU have made considerable, if uneven, progress in employment and have been willing to adapt their working patterns to other obligations. This chapter shows that to date, with few regional exceptions, men have continued to retain a hegemonic position in all areas of public life, including paid work.

Traditional critiques of women's paid employment patterns have tended to stress the negative effects of women's 'choices' as reinforcing their oppression, through seeking patterns of paid employment outside (and sometimes within) the home which allow them to reconcile their paid and unpaid labour, particularly to care for children and other dependants. Typical of this viewpoint would be Lynne Segal's conclusion that the 'ever increasing part-time, casual, sometimes home-based employment of women has reinforced, rather than reduced, economic inequalities' (1997: 38). In the eyes of many employers/employees, trade unionists and feminist researchers, the problem is sited in women's lack of replication of men's full-time labour market behaviour. Yet, as Ilona Ostner demonstrates, despite working full-time for all their adult lives, women in the former East Germany (GDR) 'did not overcome many fundamental gender divisions. Sometimes these were reinforced. Women were needed, but not on equal terms with men' (1993: 114). For example, state or company childcare in the former GDR 'was a woman's job' (Ostner 1993: 107).

This chapter examines the limited data available on how men and women have adapted their patterns of paid employment to the demands of labour within the household. It posits the view that gender inequality within the European regions can be achieved only through an alteration in men's, as well as women's, relative contributions to paid and unpaid work. Hence the chapter complements Chapters 2 and 3 which, of necessity, examine patriarchal relations within two independent structures (paid employment and the family/household) by showing that paid employment and household must be linked to explain the gendered divisions of labour within and outside the home. In other words, the prevalence of patriarchy in one structure is reinforced by other structures (for example male violence/sexual harassment in employment, state support for working 'mothers' but not 'fathers' and so on; see Walby 1990). Section 4.2 draws comparisons between men's and women's involvement in the labour market, and section 4.3 examines respective contributions to household labour. Since it is the intersection of these dual structures which is of major interest the analysis is based on data for EU member states, subject to availability.

In summary, these data illustrate the range of responses by women to conflicting demands during their life cycle between family and paid work. They demonstrate women's varying degrees of adaptability in response to labour market demands and conditions, for example alternating between full-time employment, 'inactivity', part-time working and homeworking, in patterns which vary across EU member states. In contrast men's labour market responses to the demands of fatherhood and caring are much more consistent across the EU in exhibiting an adherence to full-time continuous working patterns with rising levels of working hours and unsocial work arrangements during years of family formation.

4.2 Patterns: gendered divisions of labour in markets and households

Labour markets

Measuring 'economic activity'

Traditional measures of labour market activity have been based on a 'male' pattern of employment that assumes continuous attachment to the labour market: in employment, unemployment or seeking employment. This means of measuring 'economically active' participants excludes women whose work is not directly remunerated and occurs within the household. Such women, who may be involved in multiple caring activities in addition to 'housework', are deemed 'economically inactive' since they are engaged in 'home duties'. As this chapter shows, the proportion of women assigned to this category varies considerably across member states, despite the fact that the proportion of men so categorised is fairly constant. While the presence of children tends to limit the labour market participation of mothers and other carers, to a greater degree than any other variable, it is clear that economic, cultural and attitudinal factors also operate to encourage/dissuade women from remaining in the labour market. These factors further influence the working time patterns of women workers, which vary widely across the EU, while men's working time patterns show greater consistency in the form of full-time employment.

These activity rates do not include women's and men's contribution to the informal economy which, owing to the fact that they are unreported and unclassified, remain outside the national and EU official statistics. For example, as Sheila Rowbotham and Jane Tate (1998: 112) report: 'Official sources give little information about homeworkers. Their employment is usually unregistered and sometimes illegal. Government surveys which derive their information from official statistics, censuses or from employers' records consequently often omit homeworkers altogether'.

Activity rates

There have been major changes in the activity rates of women and men in the EU over the last few decades. Between 1975 and 1997 male activity rates have fallen in all EU member states with the exception of the Netherlands, Portugal and Denmark, most notably in France (−10.5 per cent), Belgium (−10.3 per cent), Ireland (−9.4 per cent), the UK (−7.3 per cent) and Italy (−6.2 per cent) (Figure 4.1). In contrast, women's activity rates have risen in

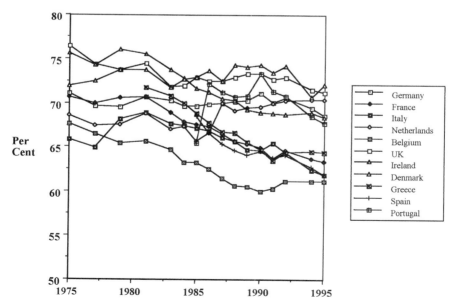

Figure 4.1 Male activity rates, European Union, 1975–97. *Source*: Eurostat Labour Force Surveys, 1975–1997 (Eurostat 1976–98).

all member states, albeit from lower base rates than men's in 1975. Not surprisingly, the countries that had relatively high activity rates for women in 1975 have increased least. These include the UK (+22.6 per cent), France (+20.8 per cent) and Denmark (+31.7 per cent). The rate of increase was highest in the states which, in 1975, had lowest participation: the Netherlands (+133.2 per cent), Ireland (+55.8 per cent) and Italy (+54.7 per cent) (Figure 4.2).

Participation rates are a useful, if crude, measure of the presence/absence of women and men in the labour force. However, they do not differentiate between different patterns of working. As this chapter shows, rising female participation has been accompanied, in some countries, by a rise in part-time employment, particularly for women, and this rise has been most sharply demonstrated in the Netherlands.

Full-time versus part-time employment

The major feature of men's employment throughout the fifteen EU member states (EU 15) is that it occurs as full-time employment. In 1997, 94 per cent of men's jobs were full-time in the EU. It is only in the Netherlands (17.0 per cent) and Denmark (12.1 per cent) that men's part-time employment is a significant proportion of male employment.

The trends in part-time employment for women and men are shown in Figures 4.3 and 4.4. In 1975, part-time employment comprised less than 20

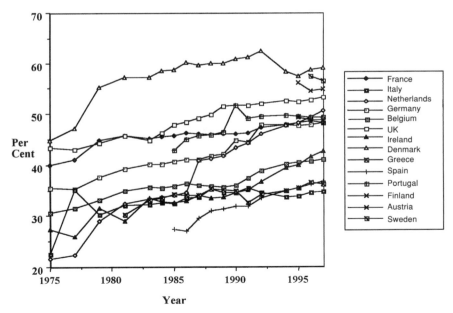

Figure 4.2 Female activity rates, European Union, 1975–97. *Source*: Eurostat Labour Force Surveys, 1975–1997 (Eurostat 1976–98).

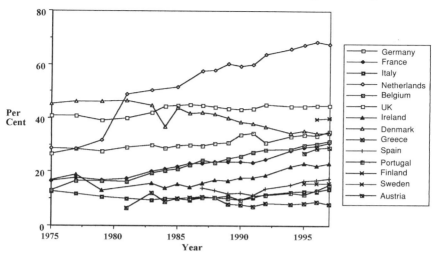

Figure 4.3 Percentage of employed women working part-time, European Union, 1975–97. *Source:* Eurostat Labour Force Surveys 1975–1997 (Eurostat 1976–98).

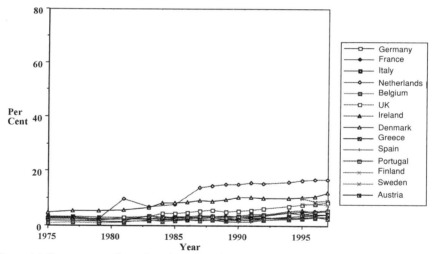

Figure 4.4 Percentage of employed men working part-time, European Union, 1975–97. Source: Eurostat Labour Force Surveys 1975–1997 (Eurostat 1976–98).

per cent of all female jobs in all countries except Denmark (45.2 per cent), the UK (41.0 per cent), the Netherlands (28.8 per cent) and Germany (26.7 per cent). By 1997 the pattern had become more complex, with a decline in female part-time employment in Denmark to 34.4 per cent; a relatively static level of 13.7 per cent in Italy, where the rate had fallen since 1975; a marked increase in part-time female employment in the Netherlands to 67.6 per cent in 1997; and moderate growth in all other member states. Unlike Italy and the Netherlands which represent the extremes, Ireland's increase was from 17.0 per cent to 23.2 per cent, a modest growth compared with Germany (from 16.7 to 35.1 per cent), Belgium (from 13.0 to 31.4 per cent) and France (from 16.7 to 30.9 per cent). In the UK, part-time employment grew more slowly, from 41 per cent to 44.8 per cent between 1975 and 1997. Part-time employment is rising for women in Greece, Spain and Portugal, although at a less rapid rate.

The gendered nature of part-time employment is clear from Figures 4.3 and 4.4, which show the level of female and male part-time employment in 1997. The only exceptions to continuing low levels of male part-time employment are to be found in the Netherlands and Denmark. In the UK 8.7 per cent of men worked part-time. In most member states there has been an increase in part-time working by men, unlike in Italy where it fell slightly from 3.4 per cent of male jobs to 3.3 per cent between 1975 and 1997. Where part-time employment is growing as a proportion of male jobs, the rise has tended to occur during the 1990s, most notably in the Netherlands (since 1987), the UK, Denmark, Ireland and France.

A further, more complex picture emerges if part-time employment among married women is examined. Two decades ago, more than half of married Danish and British women in employment were engaged on a part-time basis. This reflected a well-established pattern of post-war employment of women in these economies in response to labour shortages (Drew 1992). The figure was also high in 1975 for German (32.6 per cent) and Dutch (31.9 per cent) married women. By 1997 it is clear that part-time employment was used as a preferred labour market option in only some member states. In Greece (8.3 per cent), Italy (15 per cent), Portugal (16 per cent) and Spain (18 per cent) the impact of part-time arrangements has been minimal even among married women employed within the formal economy. At the other extreme, part-time working is the normal pattern of work for 81 per cent of employed married women in the Netherlands. It is only in Denmark and Greece that the proportion of married women working part-time has fallen in the years up to 1997.

Reasons for working part-time

Survey data are available, in a somewhat limited form, on the reasons for working part-time. Of the 5 million men working part-time in 1997, 35 per cent of these men 'did not want a full-time job' and 27 per cent 'could not find a full-time job'. Within the EU 15, a further 23 per cent of men were working part-time in order to pursue education or training opportunities; 8 per cent for 'other reasons'; and 5 per cent because of illness/disability (Eurostat 1976–98).

The motivation for working part-time is very different among women in the EU 15. Of the 20 million female part-time workers, 64 per cent 'did not want a full-time job', and these would be considered as working part-time 'voluntarily'. Only 18 per cent of female workers engaged part-time could not get a full-time job. A similar proportion to men were working part-time for 'other reasons' (9 per cent). Women were much less likely than men to be working part-time in order to undertake education or training programmes (6 per cent).

The term 'other reasons' is problematic in some individual countries, where it relates to 'family responsibilities'. However, it is difficult to obtain an accurate and consistent picture across member states when, for example, data for France provide only two responses: 'could not find full-time job' (38.8 per cent of women and 52.9 per cent of men working part-time) and 'did not want full-time job' (61.1 per cent of women and 47.1 per cent of men working part-time). In contrast some countries have placed family care in the category of 'other reasons', which becomes a major explanation for women in part-time employment in Austria (72.4 per cent), Spain (65.8 per cent), Belgium (61.0 per cent), Portugal (50.1 per cent) and Ireland (47.0 per cent). All of these states have relatively low levels of female participation in the labour force. These results are supported by the findings of the European Community Household Panel (ECHP) survey 1994 (Eurostat 1997) which showed that, among the EU 12 (excluding Finland, Austria and Sweden), 55 per cent of women aged 25–59 who worked part-time were doing so because of 'family obligations'. This figure was highest in Germany (76 per cent) and Luxembourg (72 per cent). Another conclusion from the ECHP survey was that 'the decision [by women aged 25–59] to work part-time is often explained by the need to stay at home' (Eurostat 1997: 4).

Family workers

Part-time employment represents one form of adjustment to the dual demands of 'household production' and 'paid work'. Another form of adaptation is through 'family work' which occurs within the market economy (it is not housework) but is undertaken by unpaid family members. The traditional use of female labour has been in agriculture and it is a similarly important component in services. In all sectors, whether in a full-time or part-time capacity, women constitute 69 per cent of unpaid family workers in the EU 15 (Eurostat 1998).

Within the agricultural sector, women represented 69 per cent of full-time family workers and 72 per cent of part-time family workers. In manufacturing, the reliance on family members was much smaller in 1997 compared with the agriculture and service sectors. Women accounted for 55 per cent of unpaid full-time family workers and 83 per cent of part-time industrial workers. The proportion in services was significant, reflecting the emergence of small family-owned service businesses. Women family workers made up 65 per cent of full-time family workers in services and 79 per cent of part-time workers. The largest number of female family workers was in Italy (461,000), followed by Greece (334,000), France (318,000), Spain (239,000) and Germany (260,000). Collectively these five countries account for 55 per cent of all EU 15 female family workers. Whilst this suggests a southern Latin Rim cluster it should be noted that in Portugal the recorded contribution of female family workers is negligible (37,000) and that family workers are important in both France and Germany in agriculture and services.

The imbalance in the utilisation of men's and women's unpaid labour in family enterprises is striking. It points to the predominance of men as business owners, not only in the traditional farm sector but also in emerging service industries in which the labour of female family members is often crucial to business success. However, being engaged in an unpaid and subordinate position, these family members illustrate the gendered nature of family labour.

Other forms of 'atypical' working

TEMPORARY WORKING

Unlike part-time employment and 'economic inactivity', in which there is a consistent divergence in men's and women's levels and forms of 'activity' and 'inactivity', involvement in temporary, shift, weekend and homeworking tend to be similar for women and men within the EU 15. In 1997, temporary working was only marginally more common among men, accounting for 8 million male jobs and 7 million female jobs (Eurostat 1998). Forty-two per cent of the men working in a temporary capacity did so because they 'could not find [a] permanent job', compared with 39 per cent of women. Women were more likely to cite 'did not want permanent job' (10 per cent) than men (6 per cent). Temporary employment is most common in Germany, Spain and France which together accounted for 62 per cent of all temporary workers within the EU 15. In Germany, similar proportions (49 per cent) of female and male temporary workers cited 'contract covering a period of training' as their reason for taking a temporary job, and temporary working is associated with delayed labour market entry while continuing in education/training. This reason was also important for temporary workers in Austria (54 per cent) and Denmark (36 per cent) but was more common there among men than among women (Eurostat 1998).

WEEKEND AND HOMEWORKING

Atypical working can take the form of non-standard full-time hours as well as alternative arrangements of weekly hours as in Saturday/Sunday working and alternative locations such as working from home. Throughout the EU 15 regular or occasional working on Saturdays affected 46.6 million male workers and nearly 28.6 million female workers; regular or occasional working on Sundays affected 26.3 million male workers and 15.4 million female workers in 1997. Similar proportions of women and men usually worked on Saturdays (28 per cent) while more men (25 per cent) than women (18 per cent) sometimes worked on Saturdays. Sunday working was performed by a higher proportion of men (30.2 per cent) than women (24.4 per cent), and it was more common for men to sometimes work on Sunday (18.1 per cent) compared with women (12.7 per cent). Declared homeworking accounted for 6.6 million workers who usually worked from home and a further 11.7 million who sometimes worked from home. It was marginally less important for female workers, with women accounting for 47.5 per cent of those who usually worked from home and 35.5 per cent of those who sometimes worked from home.

As a proportion of total employment, Saturday working as the usual pattern was most common for men in Greece (45.8 per cent), Italy (39.8 per cent) and Spain (36.6 per cent) compared with the average EU 15 level of 28.1 per cent of all male workers usually working on Saturdays. Among women the proportion was similar, with Saturday working most important in Italy (41.7 per cent), Greece (38.6 per cent) and Spain (38.4 per cent) compared with the average EU 15 female rate of 27.8 per cent. This concentration of Saturday working in the Mediterranean countries points to a further structural barrier to the advancement of women in paid employment. Taken alongside the pattern of split day working (with time off in the middle of the day), working on Saturdays would be particularly difficult for primary carers of children and other dependants since Saturday working and extended daytime working would not coincide with school opening hours, or day care arrangements. Hence such working time arrangement would be less than conducive to the many women who are primary care providers in those countries.

The countries in which usually working on Sunday was commonest for men were Finland (20.6 per cent), Ireland (20.1 per cent) and Denmark (18.5 per cent) compared with 12.1 per cent in the EU 15. Among women the proportion usually working on Sunday was highest in Denmark (21.8 per cent), Sweden (18.9 per cent) and Finland (17.3 per cent). This pattern contrasts with the countries which exhibited a high incidence in relation to Saturday working and suggests that Sunday working can be compatible with dual caring within households and may also be an element of part-time working options.

Homeworking, as the usual pattern of working, was highest among men in Finland (12.4 per cent), Denmark (11.2 per cent), Belgium (9.7 per cent), Austria (9.3 per cent) and Ireland (9.0 per cent), while the EU 15 average for men was 4.0 per cent. The levels of male homeworkers were lowest in Spain, Greece, the UK and Portugal. Among women, the highest proportions usually working from home were found in Austria (11.7 per cent), Belgium (10.9 per cent), Denmark (10.5 per cent) and Finland (10.1 per cent) compared with the EU 15 average of 5.0 per cent.

SHIFT WORKING

Shift working was more important for male than female workers in 1997, with men accounting for 63.6 per cent of the 19 million workers who were usually or sometimes engaged in shift work. Evening work, usually or occasionally, was undertaken by 32.5 million men in the EU 15, and only 17.5 million women workers. Night shift working was even more likely to be associated with men, with 16.1 million men working usually or sometimes at night compared with 5.8 million women.

As a proportion of total employment, night shift working was commonest for men in Austria (10.8 per cent), Finland (10.6 per cent), Denmark (9.0 per cent) and Germany (8.7 per cent). It was lowest in Portugal (1.1 per cent) and the Netherlands (2.5 per cent). The overall level of night working was 5.5 per cent for the EU 15. Among women, night working was highest in Finland (7.4 per cent), Denmark (6.6 per cent) and Sweden (5.9 per cent) compared with 3.8 per cent of women who usually worked at night in the EU 15.

CONCLUDING REMARKS

If examined as a whole it is clear that 'atypical' working takes on complex and varied forms, and these tend to be gendered and to exhibit distinct regional variations across the EU 15. Women workers were most heavily involved in part-time working patterns, compared with male workers, and this pattern is least common in the southern EU states. Although, numerically, fewer women were working in a non-permanent capacity, the proportion of temporary workers among women was higher than for men. Some of these may be engaged in temporary work by choice, although among men temporary work was more likely to be due to inability to find permanent jobs than among women. Weekend working was more common and important among male workers. Saturday working was more predominant, for women and men, in the Mediterranean countries: Italy, Greece and Spain. In contrast, Sunday working was highest for women in Scandinavia. The gender difference is even more pronounced among shift workers. Men were much more likely than women to work evening and night shifts, although night shifts were commonest among women workers in Finland, Denmark and Sweden. Homeworking was more evenly distributed among men and women and accounted for a slightly higher proportion of women's jobs.

Overall this analysis of the EU 15 labour markets shows that men and women tend to be situated in different working arrangements. Men are mainly employed in full-time jobs. When they engage in atypical work it is more likely to maximise their take-home pay, by working at times and on shifts which attract a premium, bonus or overtime payments. These conclusions accord with Segal's observations of men's working patterns in the UK:

[W]hereas in Britain two-thirds of married women with children have part-time jobs, the majority of men with young children work extremely long hours in paid employment – an average of 50–55 hours a week, with significant numbers employed for over 60 and 70 hours a week. Where women and men both have full-time jobs, men in general are doing paid work for substantially longer hours ... men work longest hours outside the home when they have dependent children; the reverse is true of women.

(Segal 1997: 37)

These findings are reinforced by a qualitative study of fathering in Italy in which it was noted that 'often fathers spend extremely long hours at work, and, as a consequence, their presence with children is necessarily short during work-days' (Giovannini 1998: 194). A study conducted into childcare in the European Community (Commission of the European Communities 1990: 7) also noted that very few fathers had part-time jobs and that 'overall, fathers work longer hours than mothers, even when comparison is made only for full-time workers: fathers in full-time jobs average 40–49 hours a week compared to 30–39 hours for mothers'. The report showed that fathers' working hours were shortest in France, the Netherlands, Belgium and Denmark and were longest in the UK and Ireland.

If women's atypical working is examined collectively, and part-time and weekend/evening shifts are interwoven, it is more likely that these options will reduce rather than raise their net earnings. Across the EU 15 a pattern emerges in which men's work, whether in full-time typical employment or atypical shift/weekend working, allows them to meet best the 'male bread-winner' (see Drew *et al.* 1998) role. Women's working patterns, in which much of the work occurs outside typical employment, facilitate their reconciliation of work/household commitments and thereby reduce their earnings and career advancement.

'Economically inactive' housewives

The EU Labour Force Surveys do not publish any data on 'housewives' specifically, and indeed these women are, at best, included in the 'inactive' category which is excluded from the labour force for enumeration purposes. According to the Labour Force Survey 1997 the percentage of 'economically inactive' women aged 25–59 ranged from 14.9 per cent in Sweden to 49.2 per cent in Italy (Figure 4.5), compared with an EU 15 average of 33.5 per cent. Levels of female 'inactivity' are highest in the Mediterranean countries (Italy, Greece, Spain) and Ireland. In contrast the lowest rates are in the Nordic countries Sweden and Finland, followed by Denmark, then France, the UK and Portugal. The comparable figure for 'economically inactive' men across the EU 15 was 10.3 per cent.

A European Community Household Panel (ECHP) survey report in 1994 commented that 'cultural factors always play an important role in a woman's decision to stay at home', while acknowledging the importance of economic labour market forces as well as the availability of childcare and part-time work arrangements. The survey also showed that the number and age of

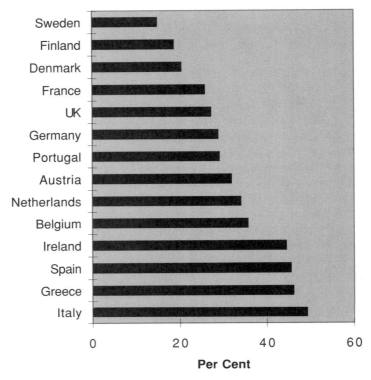

Figure 4.5 Percentage of women aged 25–59 who were 'inactive', European Union, 1997. *Source*: Eurostat Labour Force Survey (Eurostat 1998).

children influenced whether a woman was economically active. Among 25- to 39-year-old women, 52 per cent of those with two or more children and one or more aged less than 5 years were 'economically inactive', compared with 6 per cent of women without any dependent children.

The ECHP study showed that the shift by women from employment into the category 'economically inactive' was rarely associated with marriage in 1994, although 15 and 14 per cent, respectively, of Greek and Spanish women ceased employment for this reason. The EU 12 average was 7 per cent. It was the arrival of children for women (although not for men) that triggered the cessation of employment, for 42 per cent of women aged 25–59 in 1994, and for more than 50 per cent of women in Germany, Luxembourg, the Netherlands and the UK. Among women (aged 25–59 years) not seeking employment, the most common reason cited was 'family obligations (household chores, childcare and/or caring for other people)', which was cited by 84 per cent of these women. Since the proportion of men opting out of employment because of family obligations is so small, there are no comparable data for 'househusbands'.

One significant finding which emerged from the ECHP survey showed that becoming a 'housewife' is strongly correlated with the level of a woman's education. Housewives (aged 25–59) represented 45 per cent of women with a lower secondary education, compared with only 13 per cent of those with tertiary level education. This finding is reinforced by 1997 Labour Force Survey data. Across the EU 15 the average percentage of women aged 25–59 years with tertiary level education who were in employment was 79.9 per cent. Participation was lowest among female graduates in Spain (68.9 per cent) and Italy (75.5 per cent) and highest in Portugal (89.6 per cent), Sweden (87.7 per cent) and Denmark (87.1 per cent). With secondary level attainment, participation drops to an average of 66.3 per cent across the EU 15. This level is exceeded in Sweden (78.5 per cent), Portugal (75.8 per cent) and Denmark (75.5 per cent) (Eurostat 1998).

This examination of mainly labour force survey data demonstrates the employment patterns of women and men during their respective life cycles, and how these diverge. It shows a pattern for men which is predominantly of continuous full-time paid employment (often with extended/shift hours at time of family formation) through to retirement (subject to enforced exit via redundancy or early retirement which is often associated with poor health). In contrast, women tend to be over-represented in discontinuous patterns of employment, with periods of full-time employment alternating with periods of inactivity, part-time, and family or home-based work, particularly during childrearing. While the profile of male employment tends to be fairly consistent across EU member states, this is not true of women's employment patterns. This suggests that the decision to opt for part-time versus full-time, 'inactivity' versus 'activity', and working time arrangements which are better suited to meeting the need to reconcile paid work in the labour market with unpaid work in the household are affected by a range of factors extending beyond economic conditions into social and cultural norms and prevailing attitudes in different countries.

In addition, the state plays a significant role in influencing patriarchal relations and the patterns of women's employment and 'inactivity'. Coinciding with post-war labour shortages, part-time employment was strongly encouraged by the state in the UK and Denmark (Drew 1992). Unlike the UK, Sweden introduced a 'new social gender contract' (Hirdman 1998: 42) in the 1970s to facilitate women's (re)entry into the labour market. This package of reforms related to taxation, childcare provision and parental leave insurance. Despite the gender neutral nature of these reforms, the impact was largely to increase women's participation in the labour market from 53 per cent in 1963 to 86 per cent in 1990 and to contribute to a 'new form of female subordination ... whereby over 1 million women are engaged in part-time employment working in low-paid occupations within the public sector' (Hirdman 1998: 42).

Household division of labour

While labour market presence and absence is carefully monitored by national and EU agencies, it is more difficult to obtain reliable data on the division of labour within the household. The use of Time Budget Surveys is well established in some member states and non-existent in others, such as Ireland. This makes international comparisons difficult to establish and even more difficult to monitor. This section draws upon a limited range of EU data from the European Community Household Panel (ECHP) survey conducted in 1994 for the EU 12 and published by Eurostat, and a Eurobarometer opinion poll on behalf of the Employment, Industrial Relations and Social Affairs department (DGV) of the European Commission in 1996 for the EU 15.

Childcare

The 1994 ECHP survey specifically targeted childcare to establish the relative patterns of involvement by respective parents throughout the EU 12. They concluded that in 'all countries, mothers look after children much more than men', a pattern which is strongest in Greece, Portugal, Luxembourg, Ireland, Italy and Spain. With the exception of Portugal, these are precisely those countries which have lower than the EU average labour force participation rates among women. The gender difference, between respective parents, was least marked in Denmark and the Netherlands, where part-time employment is important and female participation is high by EU standards (Eurostat 1997). The converse expectation, that high female labour force participation is associated with higher involvement by men in household work, including caring, is not borne out by evidence from the former GDR even where full-time employment was the norm for women as well as men (Ostner 1993).

The ECHP survey established that among families where both parents are in employment for a minimum of 30 hours per week and where there are children under 16 years, 77 per cent of women and 50 per cent of men claimed that they looked after them on a daily basis. The time spent minding children was very different for women. Of those who were involved in looking after their children, 32 per cent of men and only 6 per cent of women spent less than 2 hours per day, while 69 per cent of women and 27 per cent of men looked after them for over 4 hours per day. This pattern was observed across all the twelve member states. The differences between the behaviour of mothers and fathers was underlined in relation to the parental care of young children of 5 years and under, with 80 per cent of women looking after their young children at least 4 hours a day as opposed to 32 per cent of men. The survey confirmed that it was in Denmark and the Netherlands that women were able to count most on help from their partners in rearing their children (Eurostat 1997).

Another form of family childcare which, like other family work, is performed for free is provided through 'help from grandparents'. Across the EU, 14 per cent of women and 7 per cent of men aged over 50 years, who were mostly grandparents, looked after children for free. The levels of free childcare by over-50-year-olds were highest in Italy (29 per cent) and Greece (25 per cent), compared with 5 per cent in Denmark. The survey concluded that in all member states, amongst people aged over 50, more women than men look after children. This difference is most noticeable in southern Europe and Ireland where women looking after children devote most time to them. This obviously places an additional moral obligation on older women, who may have only recently finished rearing their own children. It would also reduce their options for return to the formal labour market.

Elder and adult care

As with parental and grandparental care, it was mostly women who cared in an unpaid capacity for family members who are ill or elderly throughout the EU 12. Even selecting from those people in employment for more than 30 hours per week, 9 per cent of women and 5 per cent of men claimed that they devoted part of their time to looking after other people. The predominance of women in this role is more evident in countries such as Italy and Greece. In terms of a daily time commitment of at least 4 hours, the highest levels were found in Portugal, Spain and Ireland.

Arising from the analysis in sections 4.2 and 4.3, there is a major question: when couples have children or family members are faced with the care of an adult dependant (parent, sibling, in-law), why does it fall unequally to female members of the family (mother, sister, sister-in-law, etc.) to feel responsible for that caring role and for the household? Why do women continue, even when they are employed in a full-time capacity, to perform a disproportionate share of housework compared with male partners/members of the household? Why is it women who continue to reconcile the dual (and often multiple) demands of working and family life? And why does the degree of this inequality vary between different European countries and regions?

4.3 Explanations

Explaining unequal gender divisions of labour

This section addresses two key issues: women's continuing responsibility for household work (while men 'help out') and men's unwillingness to adapt their labour market behaviour to the demands of fathering, other caring responsibilities and housework. It provides a brief literature review of some explanatory theories which in some way address the questions posed in section 4.2.

Psychoanalytical theory

In tracing the emotional and relational development of male and female children, psychoanalytical theory has contributed to the debate on mothering, and male and female roles in parenting. Nancy Chodorow (1992: 161) has claimed that 'a child completes the relational triangle for a woman by establishing her maternal place'. She argued that women want and need primary relationships to children, based on their own pre-Oedipal relationship to their mothers and their subsequent mother–daughter relationships as they mature into adulthood.

Chodorow (1992: 167), aware of the lack of clear explanations in psychoanalysis as to why women mother, concluded that having been parented by a same-sex woman, women are more likely than men to seek to be mothers: 'Daughters grow up identifying with their mothers' thereby giving rise to 'a fundamental structure of expectations [that] women naturally take care of children of all ages and the belief that women's "maternal" qualities can and should be extended to the non-mothering work that they do', all of which reinforces and reproduces the ideology of motherhood in which it is women who take responsibility for their children. This suggests a universal and essentialist view of the respective roles of mothers and fathers. It ignores the tantalising questions of what differences, if any, would follow if men substituted for women as 'mothers' or were enabled to act as dual care providers throughout early childrearing years. While addressing the critical role of women in mothering, psychoanalytical theory does not, in any direct way, address the allocation of 'housework' to women, even when this is not necessarily linked to childcare, as in childless households or among post-retirement couples.

Anthropological explanations

Feminist literature has sought explanations for the gendered division of labour in cross-cultural studies. Whilst it would be dangerous to conclude, from these accounts, that gender roles are in some way fixed in time or space, they do point to the importance of culture (another structure of patriarchy) and socialisation in evolving gender segregation and sex typing of male and female labour. Barbara Rogers (1980: 13) concluded that 'there is little physical determinism about which gender performs which role, apart from pregnancy and childbirth'. However, Sherry Ortner (1974) claimed that, regardless of the nature and form of work performed by women across different societies, this work is devalued.

Human capital theory

Gary Becker (1985: 153) sought to explain the lower hourly earnings of married women compared with those of married men 'with the same market human capital'. In full acceptance of functionalist sex-role typing (see next sub-section), Becker noted that childcare 'and other housework are tiring and limit access to jobs requiring travel and odd hours' (Becker 1985: 155).

From this he extrapolated that women, whose energies go into childcare and housework, 'would have less energy available for the market than men would', hence their lower hourly earnings, occupations and investment in human capital. Becker concluded that it was the 'household responsibilities of married women [that] may be the source of much of the difference in earnings and in job segregation between men and women'. Becker further concluded that '[n]ot only casual impressions, but also evidence from time-budgets indicate that the relative contribution of married men to housework in the United States has significantly increased' during the 1970s. While acknowledging the long-term impact of such a trend, leading to a sizeable increase in married women's earnings and a decline in segregation, Becker believed that 'married households would still gain from a division of labor ... no longer linked to sex: husbands would be more specialized to housework and wives to market activities in about half the marriages, and the reverse would occur in the other half' (Becker 1985: 176).

Sylvia Walby (1997) has placed Becker's human capital approach as complementary to the analysis of structural and institutional constraints (such as those examined by Collinson *et al*. 1990; Cockburn 1991; Wajcman 1996). She argued that women 'make choices, but not under conditions of their own making. Women choose the best option that they can see, rationally, though usually with imperfect knowledge, but only within the range of options open to them' (Walby 1997: 25). Exclusion and sex segregation clearly limit women's choices and these are further restricted if women seek only part-time employment within labour markets which attach lower pay and status to such jobs.

Sociological theory

Earlier sociological accounts of men's and women's sex roles can be traced to Talcott Parsons and Robert Bales (1956) in seeking to attribute distinct forms of work allocation within the family. Women were assigned the 'expressive' role in which they would look after the internal family needs of family members, while men's 'instrumental' role meant that they were more oriented to the external world. These gender-assigned roles would, in Parsons' view, maintain stability within the family and society. It could be argued that while women have broken out of their purely 'expressive' role in favour of a wider societal experience, thereby rejecting financial dependence on a male partner, men have tended to adhere to their 'instrumental' role. Further evidence of men's desire to function in the nuclear family comes from the remarriage rate, which is higher among men than among women, reflecting a possibly greater reluctance to remarry, on the part of women, and the higher probability that women will have responsibility for children from a previous relationship (Hoffmann-Nowotny and Fux 1991).

Marxist feminist debates

The contribution of Marxism and Marxist feminist analyses has been the subject of criticism from many sources (including Walby 1990; Delphy and Leonard 1992; Bubeck 1995; Gardiner 1997). Marxism provided a materialist analysis in which to understand different forms of exploitation and in linking household production to capital. This informed the domestic labour debate which emerged in the late 1960s, arguing that housework contributed to the reproduction of labour power and hence benefited capitalism. Writers such as Mariarosa Della Costa and Selma James (1972) claimed that housework was 'work'; that it created both value and surplus value; and that domestic labour contributed to women's oppression.

Another aspiration raised by both Marxists and first-wave feminists related to the 'socialisation of housework' which became an unquestioned goal of socialism, in attaining social ownership and collectivisation of labour. For Jean Gardiner (1997) this approach neglected individual needs to contribute, alongside collective support, to parenting and caring work, thereby alienating working-class women. In socialist countries, for example Germany's former GDR, which had moved closest to the socialisation of some aspects of domestic labour, the effect of high participation of women in wage labour 'had been accompanied by the intensification of other aspects of domestic labour and the perpetuation of traditional gender divisions in the household' (Gardiner 1997: 81; see also Ostner 1993).

Familial exploitation

Walby (1990) assigned the work of Christine Delphy to a 'dual systems' analysis of gender which encompasses Marxist feminism with radical feminism, in assigning the expropriation of women's labour in the home to their husbands. Unlike Marxist feminism in which capital was arguably the benefitee of patriarchal exploitation, for Christine Delphy and Diana Leonard it was individual men. Their analysis claimed that:

> [It is] women [who] do almost all the laundry, ironing and sewing, most of the childcare and care of the sick and elderly, most of the work concerned with helping children's education, and most cooking, washing-up and shopping. Men and children do, however, do odd jobs like taking out the rubbish and some tidying and washing-up.
>
> (Delphy and Leonard 1992)

Evidence from Denmark (Emerek 1998), where a more equitable sharing of household labour might be expected, shows that, despite high female labour force participation, women still have the main responsibility for the time-dependent work in the family such as taking and collecting children to and from the kindergarten, shopping and cooking. Men do the time-independent housework like cutting the grass and washing the car, a pattern very similar to that prevailing in other countries in the Western world. Women, doing the time-dependent work in the family, are more dependent on the time-structuring of everyday life including closing hours in the kindergarten and shopping hours. The more narrow the time-structuring, the fewer the possibilities of planning a life which includes both work and family life with children, and most families with small children need two salaries to survive. This is a dilemma that Danish women try to solve by part-time work while their children are small (Emerek 1998).

Based on the authors' French/British perspective, Delphy and Leonard (1992: 226–227) concluded that 'marriage is precisely a gendered and unequal division of labour, with most wives working more hours a day than their husbands in a subordinate role', even when wives are employed full-time. The authors claimed that when men marry they do half the housework they did as bachelors, whereas women did twice as much, an arrangement in which the wife has overall responsibility and the husband 'helps'. It is argued that the absence of reciprocal supports by men severely limits married women's ability to work overtime, work shifts or travel in their job, and leads to the adoption of working arrangements to meet the demands of family members. They were not optimistic about seeking and adopting solutions to the unequal divisions of labour in the household and paid employment, which are clearly intertwined. Further UK evidence of this is found in the work of Julia Brannen and Peter Moss (1991: 252), who found that women 'changed jobs, cut their hours, postponed seeking promotion, to create more space in their lives for children and domestic work'. Indeed, it seems that men with young children put their own career above their partner's and that for men having a family had the effect of reducing their contribution to household management (Newell 1993).

A study of the contribution by Irish married couples to the allocation of housework concluded that 'wives take on a greater responsibility for day to day household management' (Mitchell 1997: 49) and that this not only reflected apportionment of work but personal agendas 'about the intimacy of marriage and relationships ... this study of Irish couples reveals that housework for wives is *mine, ours*, and *not yours* and for husbands housework is *yours*, and to a lesser extent *ours* but definitely *not mine*' (Mitchell 1997: 50).

Patriarchy at work

Based on recent studies in the United States, Scott Coltrane (1996: 70) noted that the 'time each spouse felt that they had available for doing housework or childcare was dependent on the number of hours employed, the scheduling of those hours, and on the amount of take-home work that their jobs required'. He also noted that it was typically the 'wife' who had more 'free' time since, as in the EU, husbands were more likely to be employed for more hours. Coltrane's sample of American couples mirrored a similar pattern in the

European Union: over half the women were employed part-time: 'These women were much more likely than those working full-time (35+ hours/week) to perform the bulk of the cleaning and cooking'.

Changing masculinities – the role of fatherhood

While inflexible working hours and lack of leave provisions and childcare severely hamper the career prospects of mothers of young children, it is also important to examine the degree to which fathering affects the careers of men. Two studies examined the response and degree of adaptation among fathers: Dino Giovannini (1998) in Italy, representing a strong breadwinner state (see below), and Ulla Björnberg (1998) in Sweden, assigned as a weak breadwinner state. Giovannini's study showed that:

> ...there is no equal sharing whether of childcare or family work. The father is a support, a prop, but does not share. Usually he perceives and admits the inequality of sharing the workload by showing understanding and admiration for what his partner does.
>
> (Giovannini 1998: 198)

Furthermore, fathers in this study were satisfied 'with the present division of roles with regard to family work and think it is not necessary for them to be more involved in domestic work' (Giovannini 1998: 199). From a contrasting Scandinavian welfare state regime, Björnberg (1998) showed that Swedish men and women differed in terms of their motivation to parent a child. Men 'expect that contact with little children will help them to find new insights into themselves and help them to develop aspects of their personality, particularly the emotional side' (Björnberg 1998: 206). In addition she noted that while Swedish men are more child oriented they are 'less motivated to do housework' (Björnberg 1998: 201). As Segal (1997: 58) has noted, 'persuading and enabling men to share childcare and housework entails a struggle on three fronts: personal, ideological and social'.

Explaining spatial differences in inequality: gendered states of welfare

The predominant picture across EU labour markets is one in which it is women who continue to find some accommodation between their paid and unpaid work roles. The explanations reviewed above provide no answer as to why, overall, men have not altered their working patterns. Neither do they explain the different strategies adopted by women across the EU to cope with reconciling work and family life. A major theoretical approach that addresses these is provided by examining the role of the state (a third patriarchal structure) and the assigning of countries to different welfare regimes in terms of their 'woman and family friendliness'.

Building upon the more simplistic dual model by Mary Ruggie (1984) of 'social democratic' and 'liberal' welfare states, Gøsta Esping-Andersen (1990) devised a more complex classification into four types of welfare state regimes. Simon Duncan (1995) has referred to the subsequent analysis using the Esping-Andersen model as 'gendered welfare state models'. This would include the more gender-aware work of Jane Lewis (1993) in her categorisation of 'strong, modified and weak breadwinner' states (as exemplified by Sweden and Denmark as weak regimes, France as a modified state, and the UK, Ireland and the southern European states as representing the strong breadwinner model).

Section 4.2 showed considerable variations in the levels of female participation, part-time employment and the degree to which mothers worked in the home ('economically inactive') versus within the labour market. Part-time employment arrangements, as a reconciliation strategy, were highest for women in the Netherlands, the UK, Sweden and Denmark where they accounted for at least one third of female employment. They were lowest in Greece, Italy Portugal, Finland and Spain (less than 20 per cent of female employment). The level of part-time working among men is more consistent throughout the EU. Only in the Netherlands and Denmark are more than 10 per cent of men employed part-time. There is a strong regional and geographical concentration of low female participation (below 40 per cent) and part-time employment (less than 20 per cent) in Greece, Italy and Spain; this pattern contrasts with high female participation (over 50 per cent) and high levels of part-time working in Denmark and Sweden. However, a distinct north/south convergence does not explain the complex patterns of variation. The Scandinavian pattern is complicated by high female participation and low part-time employment in Finland that bears closest resemblance to female employment in Portugal. Yet in allocating countries to gender systems, Finland falls into the Scandinavian, weak or modified breadwinner, dual role contract while Portugal is classified as Latin Rim and a strong breadwinner state (Duncan 1995). Countries in which there is a moderate level of female activity and part-time employment also straddle different gender welfare state regimes and adherence to strong/modified/weak breadwinner states (UK, Austria, Germany, France).

In relation to household work, the categorisation into gendered welfare states has even less relevance. Lewis's (1993) classification was the first to acknowledge unpaid work, in the form of domestic and family labour that are critical to the re/production of the state. However, even in addressing the mediating role of different welfare state regimes in terms of their support (or lack of support) for women in employment (in the form of childcare, parental leave, equality, flexible working practices and publicly funded eldercare, among other social policy measures), the 'unequal sharing of unpaid work' is not an issue which is being actively addressed in any country, whichever classification they fall into (Lewis 1993: 21). While acknowledging that the Scandinavian countries have gone furthest in valuing women's unpaid work, Lewis concludes: How to value unpaid work at a decent level without perpetuating the idea that it is women's work? And how far and in what ways to claim from men as individuals, whether in the form of financial compensation for women's unpaid work (for example on divorce) or as a demand for men themselves to undertake unpaid labour? (Lewis 1993: 24).

Deborah Mitchell (1998) is also critical of the notion of an 'exemplary' Swedish individualistic model. Drawing upon empirical time-use data she notes:

> It is just as hard in Sweden to get men involved in care and domestic work as it is in Australia. It would seem then that while the individual model does have definite advantages for advancing some aspects of equality in the public sphere, the same is not true for the private sphere.
> (Mitchell 1998: 30)

Janeen Baxter's (1998) comparative work provides further evidence, based on Sweden in comparison with Norway, the United States, Canada and Australia, that there is more consistency than variation in men's contribution to household labour. While in all countries studied men reported doing 25 per cent of the total housework, in Sweden the level was 27.9 per cent. Her pessimistic conclusion was that:

> ...policies aimed at integrating work and family demands ... have little impact on the gender division of labour in the home. One possibility, of course, is that these five countries do not really vary in terms of social and political regimes – even in Sweden, women earn less than men, tend to be concentrated in part-time employment, have a high level of occupational segregation and tend to take up the option of parental leave ... it seems clear that the domestic division of labour is not greatly affected by variations in welfare state design.
> (Baxter 1998: 69)

4.4 Afterword

The redistribution of economic responsibility within paid employment has not been accompanied by a redistribution of domestic and caring responsibilities within the household. Men have been slow to accept parenting and other caring obligations. In theory there are new social arrangements which could provide men with a more varied life such as combining parenthood and caring; a shorter working week; increased opportunities for leisure; and changing work practices to help eliminate segregation within both the employment and household spheres.

However, across the EU fifteen member states women's integration into the labour market is still hampered by their caring obligations and individual family circumstances. Predictably, women who face caring obligations have sought ways of 'reconciling work and family life' through flexible working practices and, where available, formal childcare (Drew *et al*. 1998). In some countries, particularly in Sweden, Denmark, the UK and more recently the Netherlands, the strategy for many 'working mothers' has been to opt for part-time employment, especially when their children are young. In other countries, for example France and Finland, there has been a longer tradition of women, including mothers, holding full-time employment, facilitated by state childcare provision and allowances, particularly for children who attend school. However, this attachment to full-time paid employment does not necessarily ensure that men adopt an equal share of household labour.

Across the EU, it is mainly women who seek to balance work and family life, through part-time and other forms of 'atypical' work. This creates a vicious circle in which, for example, part-time working and job-sharing is perceived as a female option (Humphreys *et al*. 1999), signalling that the woman lacks commitment to the job, and has limited career aspirations, and hence the practice is an unattractive option for men who might otherwise seek to spend more time with their partner and family.

Francis Höpflinger (1991) has observed that 'while the development towards greater equality is a slow process, there are some indications that role sharing will become more widespread in the future. Younger Swedish couples are markedly more egalitarian than older ones, even when education and family life-cycle were controlled for' (Höpflinger 1991: 310). It will be important to observe whether this tendency (1) is a long-term trend, (2) extends to all forms of caring and (3) is being adopted in other European states. A less optimistic picture is painted by Leonore Davidoff:

> Despite some public shifts in attitudes, it is still women who are seen today as basically responsible for servicing members of the family, protecting them from the pollution of dirt, waste products and untidiness, for transforming the raw into the cooked; and for transforming 'little savages' into civilised adults. In the vast majority of cases it is women (particularly mothers, but also the women responsible for the elderly and chronic sick) who peel the potatoes, wash, sort and put away the socks, mop up the vomit, change the nappies and the sheets. These activities are still performed for love (and support).
>
> (Davidoff 1991: 91)

Two alternative scenarios are outlined by Nancy Folbre (1994). In the first, women have the same rights as men, but class and race inequalities remain. In the second, men have the same responsibilities as women, across class and race lines. In the first scenario, women's full-time labour force participation rates reach those of men. Former 'women's work', such as teaching and childcare, is performed by men and women from disadvantaged groups who would work for a minimal wage to provide institutional and home-based care of children, the sick and elderly. In Folbre's second scenario men would substantially increase their hours of unpaid work, devoting more time to home, children and community. Their formal labour force participation rate would decline to levels more typical of women's today. Forms of work that women once specialised in, such as childcare and teaching, would be re-valued (Folbre 1994). Only the second scenario assigns responsibility for family and household-based work equally to men and women. Folbre recognises that the latter scenario would be more difficult to achieve 'because it would require more sustained collective effort and co-ordination' (Folbre 1994: 103).

References

Baxter, J. 1998. Moving towards equality? Questions of change and equality in household work patterns. In Gatens, M. and Mackinnon, A. (eds) *Gender and Institutions: Welfare, Work and Citizenship*, pp. 55–72. Cambridge University Press, Cambridge.

Becker, G. 1985. Human capital, effort, and the sexual division of labor. *Journal of Labour Economics*, 3, S33–S58.

Björnberg, U. 1998. Family orientation among men: a process of change in Sweden. In Drew, E., Emerek, R. and Mahon, E. (eds) *Women, Work and the Family in Europe*, pp. 200–207. Routledge, London.

Brannen, J. and Moss, P. 1991. *Managing Mothers: Dual Earner Households after Maternity Leave*. Unwin Hyman, London.

Bubeck, D.E. 1995. *Care, Gender, and Justice*. Clarendon Press, Oxford.

Chodorow, N. 1992. The psychodynamics of the family. In Crowley, H. and Himmelweit, S. (eds) *Knowing Women: Feminism and Knowledge*, pp. 153–169. Polity Press, Oxford.

Cockburn, C. 1991. *In the Way of Women: Men's Resistance to Sex Equality in Organisations*. Macmillan, Basingstoke.

Collinson, D.L., Knights, D. and Collinson, M. 1990. *Managing to Discriminate*. Routledge, London.

Coltrane, S. 1996. *Family Man: Fatherhood, Housework, and Gender Equity*. Oxford University Press, New York.

Commission of the European Communities 1990. *Childcare in the European Community 1985–90*. Women of Europe Supplement, No. 31. Commission of the European Communities, Brussels.

Council of Europe 1991. *Seminar on present demographic trends and lifestyles*. Council of Europe, Strasbourg.

Davidoff, L. 1991. The rationalisation of housework. In Leonard, D. and Allen, S. (eds) *Sexual Divisions Revisited*, pp. 59–94. Macmillan, Basingstoke.

Della Costa, M. and James, S. 1972. *The Power of Women and the Subversion of the Community*. Falling Wall Press, Bristol.

Delphy, C. and Leonard, L. 1992. *Familiar Exploitation*. Polity Press, Oxford.

Drew, E. 1992. The part-time option? Women and part-time work in the European Community. *Women's Studies International Forum*, 15, 5/6, 1–8.

Drew, E., Emerek, R. and Mahon, E. (eds) 1998. *Women, Work and the Family in Europe*. Routledge, London.

Duncan, S. 1995. Theorizing European gender systems. *Journal of European Social Policy*, 4, 263–284.

Emerek, R. 1998. A/typical working time: examples from Denmark. In Drew, E., Emerek, R. and Mahon, E. (eds) *Women, Work and the Family in Europe*, pp. 131–139. Routledge, London.

Esping-Andersen, G. 1990. *The Three Worlds of Welfare Capitalism*. Polity Press, Oxford.

Eurostat 1976–98. *Labour Force Surveys 1975–1997*. Eurostat, Luxembourg.

Eurostat 1997. *European Community Household Panel*. Eurostat, Luxembourg.

Folbre, N. 1994. *Who Pays for the Kids? Gender and the Structures of Constraint*. Routledge, London.

Gardiner, J. 1997. *Gender, Care and Economics*. Macmillan, Basingstoke.

Giovannini, D. 1998. Are fathers changing? Comparing some different images on sharing of childcare and domestic work. In Drew, E., Emerek, R. and Mahon, E. (eds) *Women, Work and the Family in Europe*, pp. 191–199. Routledge, London.

Hirdman, Y. 1998. State policy and gender contracts: the Swedish experience. In Drew, E., Emerek, R. and Mahon, E. (eds) *Women, Work and the Family in Europe*, pp. 36–46. Routledge, London.

Hoffmann-Nowotny, H.J. and Fux, B. 1991. *Present Demographic Trends in Europe*. See Council of Europe 1991.

Höpflinger, F. 1991. *The Future of Household and Family Structures in Europe*. See Council of Europe 1991, pp. 291–338.

Humphreys, P., Drew, E. and Murphy, C. 1999. *Gender Equality in the Civil Service*. Institute of Public Administration, Dublin.

Lewis, J. 1993. Introduction: Women, work, family and social policies in Europe. In Lewis, J. (ed.) *Women and Social Policies in Europe*, pp. 1–24. Edward Elgar, Aldershot.

Mitchell, D. 1998. Life-course and labour market transitions: alternatives to the breadwinner welfare state. In Gatens, M. and Mackinnon, A. (eds) *Gender and Institutions: Welfare, Work and Citizenship*, pp. 19–37. Cambridge University Press, Cambridge.

Mitchell, E. 1997. *Yours, mine or ours? The contribution of married couples to the allocation of housework*. Unpublished MPhil dissertation in Women's Studies, Trinity College Dublin.

Newell, S. 1993. The superwoman syndrome: gender differences in attitudes towards equal opportunities at work and towards domestic responsibilities at home. *Work, Employment and Society*, 7, 2, 275–289.

Ortner, S. 1974. Is female to male as nature is to culture? In Rosaldo, M. and Lamphere, L. (eds) *Women, Culture and Society*. University Press, Stanford.

Ostner, I. 1993. Slow motion: women, work and the family in Germany. In Lewis, J. (ed.) *Women and Social Policies in Europe*, pp. 92–115. Edward Elgar, Aldershot.

Parsons, T. and Bales, R. 1956. *Family Socialization and Interaction Process*. Routledge & Kegan Paul, London.

Rogers, B. 1980. *The Domestication of Women*. Tavistock, London.

Rowbotham, S. and Tate, J. 1998. Homeworking; new aproaches to an old problem. In Drew, E., Emerek, R. and Mahon, E. (eds) *Women, Work and the Family in Europe*, pp. 112–123. Routledge, London.

Ruggie, M. 1984. *The State and Working Women*. Princeton University Press, New Jersey.

Segal, L. 1997. *Slow Motion: Changing Masculinities Changing Men*. Virago, London.

Wajcman, J. 1996. Women and managers: careers and equal opportunities. In Crompton, R., Gallie, D. and Purcell, K. (eds) *Changing Forms of Employment: Organisation Skills and Gender*, pp. 259–277. Routledge, London.

Walby, S. 1990. *Theorising Patriarchy*. Basil Blackwell, Oxford.

Walby, S. 1997. *Gender Transformations*. Routledge, London.

Part II

Gender divisions of power – citizenship, rights and control

5 Gender and European welfare states

Context, structure and agency

Henrik Bang, Per H. Jensen
and Birgit Pfau-Effinger

5.1 Issues: the need to contextualise welfare state policies

The way in which the welfare state affects the position of women is a highly contested issue, as the perception of causes and effects varies with the theoretical viewpoint from where observations and interpretations take place. For example, theories of patriarchy (Walby 1990, 1994) argue that the welfare state is an instrument used by men for the oppression of women, while the empowerment hypothesis (Hernes 1987; Siim 1994a), on the other hand, argues that welfare state institutions may pave the way for the improvement of women's lot as workers, mothers and citizens. Such controversies as to how the welfare state is conferred with meaning have intensified in recent years, not least as a result of the paradigmatic shift from 'modernity' to 'post-modernity', and from 'feminism' to 'post-feminism' (Brooks 1997).

'Modernist' feminism is marked by essentialism anchored in an egalitarian rhetoric. As such, modernist feminists seem to have found the truth of women's nature, since they have developed normative and universalistic assumptions about 'what is good for women'. Starting from such a unified gender identity, modernist feminists then argue how a welfare state ought to be constructed in order to meet women's needs and aspirations. For instance, the welfare state should guarantee women's right to be 'commodified' (Orloff 1993) or, alternatively, the welfare state should provide the possibility for women to form and maintain an autonomous household (Lister 1995).

From an anti-essentialist perspective, institutions and individuals cannot be analysed independently of the historical and social conditions that constitute them in their specificity for a given society and a given moment in time (Bourdieu *et al.* 1991). Given this, welfare state institutions have no virtual existence of their own. Rather, the properties of individuals and institutions arise from the broader cultural system to which they belong. This means that social relations, culture and contextualisation must be given primacy in the analysis of the welfare state – and especially in a comparative perspective.

Anti-essentialism entails a move from abstract ideas of gender equality to a debate about gender equality in relative terms. For example, the promotion of part-time work might benefit women in one cultural context, while being disadvantageous to women in another cultural setting. As such, conclusions as to what is beneficial for women can differ across countries because of cultural differences, just as women can lean towards different cultural models of gender equality.

Even though essentialism and anti-essentialism are two distinct approaches, we have witnessed some attempts to integrate the two divergent perspectives. In a recent article, Birte Siim (1999) argues for normativity and contextuality simultaneously. On the one hand, from a normative standpoint Siim tends to universalize conceptions about what is good for women, arguing that specific types of welfare state institutions are in accordance with women's identities and aspirations. An example is that of good quality childcare institutions. On the other hand, Siim insists that contextualising the framework of citizenship is crucial for analysing the driving forces behind the development of women's social and political rights.

We consider it logically impossible to combine a contextual approach with a general normative one. Furthermore, we will argue, much confusion in the debate occurs as a result of the essentialist understanding of anti-essentialism as 'relativistic' or 'nihilistic'. Anti-essentialism has its own contingent methodological and theoretical foundations. Therefore, the first aim of this chapter is to give answers to the following questions: What does it mean to include an anti-essentialist perspective on culture in analyses of the relationship between women and the welfare state in a comparative perspective? What does it mean to speak of contingency with regard to the framework of citizenship? In answering these questions the main empirical focus of this chapter is the different social constructions of motherhood in Britain, Denmark, Finland, Germany, Italy, the Netherlands and Sweden. Such a country comparison will highlight the need for contextualisation in the face of well-known variations in welfare state regimes (Esping-Andersen 1990).

Furthermore, anti-essentialism raises new challenges as to how to come to grips with the dynamics of social change. From the point of essentialism social change is generated either by a 'self-unfolding' social structure or by the deliberate decisions of a rational actor. Anti-essentialism, in contrast, invites us to reconsider the relevance of this modern understanding of order as opposed to disorder, and of structures as opposed to actors. The contextualisation of gender relations first of all seems to require a new notion of the political which allows for contingency and which does not take the hierarchical type of authority to be the only possible type. Therefore, the second aim of this chapter is more programmatic in discussing and identifying the transforming capacities of society.

5.2 Patterns: variations in the gender policies of welfare states and problems of interpretation

Since World War II we have witnessed an overall increase in female labour force participation. The feminisation of the labour force in Europe is, however, marked by huge national and local variations. These variations become even more striking if we consider the labour force participation among mothers with children under 11 years of age. As we see from Table 5.1, the participation rate among mothers for our case study countries varies from 49 per cent in Italy to 84 per cent in Denmark. As the labour force participation of mothers is normally lower compared with all women in the age group 25–54, it seems as though motherhood in general discourages women from participating in the labour market. This discouragement effect, however, differs markedly across Europe. As Table 5.1 shows, motherhood leads to a dramatic drop in female labour force participation in Germany, the Netherlands and Britain, while the Danish experience seems to indicate that motherhood actually encourages labour force participation (see also Chapter 9). Similarly, there seems to be no clear-cut pattern in the relationship between full-time and part-time employment. As Table 5.1 shows, the Netherlands and Italy exhibit similar participation rates for mothers of young children, but diametrically opposed situations for shares of part-time and full-time work.

The distribution between part-time and full-time for working mothers may be dependent on demand or supply-side factors. From a demand-side perspective Anne Marie Berg (1989: 229) has argued that 'part-time work in itself is the ideal manifestation of the female population as a "reserve army of labour" '. But what are the meanings and consequences of such statements? Does it mean that women serve as a reserve army to a larger extent in the Netherlands and Britain than in Finland and Italy, where only a very small proportion of mothers are working part-time? Conversely, from a supply-side perspective it has been argued that part-time jobs may bridge the juxtaposition between family and work and as such contribute to the integration of women into society as a whole (Nätti 1993). According to this line of argument, jobs have been constructed as part-time jobs in order to meet women's needs, and hence women in the Netherlands and Britain would be better integrated into the labour market than those in Finland and Italy. Thus, part-time work may be infused with negative or positive meanings depending on whether we look at the phenomenon from a demand- or a supply-side perspective (see also Chapter 2).

When we are doing comparative research another question is whether part-time work, as a social phenomenon, is actually comparable cross-nationally. In Britain, for instance, women's part-time jobs are largely located in the private service sector; often this is unskilled work, where usually the degree of unionisation is low, wages are low, employment is unstable, employment protection is weak, hours are low, and so on. In the Scandinavian countries, in contrast, part-time work is largely located in the public service sector, the work is skilled work as social programmes are the primary fields of public employment, the degree of unionisation is high, wages are relatively high, employment is stable, hours are not far below full-time, and so on. Furthermore, in the Scandinavian countries part-timers can fully participate in the social security and benefits system as individual workers. [The fact

Table 5.1 Women's labour force participation: case study countries, 1993

	Labour force participation: women aged 25–54	Labour force participation: women with children aged 0–10	Per cent mothers working part-time	Per cent mothers working full-time	Per cent mothers unemployed
Denmark	82.1	84	25	49	10
Sweden	86.2	82	40	35	7
Finland	85.1	77	8	57	12
Germany	72.1	59		37	
East		88	14	55	19
West		50	28	18	4
Italy	53.7	49	6	6	6
Netherlands	65.7	51	41	18	5
Britain	74.0	59	35	18	6

Source: European Commission Network on Childcare (1996).

that part-time workers have access to unemployment benefits may contribute to the explanation of the relatively high unemployment rates among women in the Nordic countries (see Table 5.1), as there is an incentive for part-timers to be registered and stay in the labour market as unemployed.] Thus, as the substance of part-time work differs markedly across Europe, we can state that part-time work is not part-time work, is not part-time work.

In the social science literature the integration of women into paid employment is treated mainly as a supply-side phenomenon. However, within mainstream literature it is possible to make a distinction between two major approaches. First, the economic literature argues that the relative wages of women are crucial for the decision of mothers to enter the labour market, inasmuch as the higher the relative wages of women the higher the utility of entering paid employment (see, for example, Gustafsson and Jacobsson 1985; Mincer 1985; Blau and Ferber 1986; Becker 1993). As such, the decision of mothers to participate in the labour market is seen to be based on calculative reasoning. The relative wages of women may also be structured by the welfare state in the form of equal pay and equal treatment legislation, on the one hand, and the welfare state as employer, on the other. Second, childcare and parental leave institutions enter into most discussions of women and the welfare state, in that there is a substantial literature on how these institutions allow women's autonomy and independence by facilitating female labour force participation (see, for example, Kamerman and Kahn 1981; Leira 1992; Pringle 1998). That is, childcare and parental leave policies are considered to be central indicators for the measurement of the commitment of the welfare state to integrate women into the workforce. From these two major perspectives the key elements in a definition of citizenship of mothers has been outlined (Table 5.2).

Tables like this are commonly used in comparing different types of welfare regimes (Jensen 1996; Pfau-Effinger 1998a). Most often such tables are based on an underlying assumption about causal dynamics and linear model thinking. Thus, on the one hand, we may argue from Table 5.2 that cross-national differences in the pace, degree and form of women's labour force participation are an outcome of institutional differences. From such a perspective, the behaviour of women may be interpreted as an automatic or mechanistic response to the opportunity structures of the welfare states; that is, the behaviour of women is more or less programmed or determined by the state. On the other hand, we may argue that women's labour force participation is a deliberate response to the utility of a given behaviour. Thus, women's informed and premeditated decision to participate in the labour market is based on instrumental rationality.

We find such interpretations understandable, but also highly problematic. A first reading of Table 5.2 may indeed support linear model thinking as differences between welfare states seem to 'fit' with variations in the labour force participation of mothers. A second and more careful reading, however, reveals that there are no simple interrelationships between these key elements

Table 5.2 The labour force participation of mothers, ratio of female to male earnings, publicly funded services for children, and maternity/paternity leave arrangements: case study countries, around 1990

	Labour force participation of mothers with children aged 0–10	Women's wages relative to men's (1996)	Publicly funded day care for children aged 0–3: per cent covered	Publicly funded day care for children aged 3–6: per cent covered	Duration of maternity leave (weeks)	Parental leave Mothers	Parental leave Fathers
Denmark	84	0.85	48	82	14	Yes	Yes
Sweden	82	0.90	33	72	72	Yes	Yes
Finland	77	0.77	21	53	9.5–12.5	Yes	Yes
Germany	59				14	Yes	Yes
East	n/a	n/a	50	100	n/a		
West	n/a	0.73	2	78	n/a		
Italy	49	0.85	6	91	12	Yes	No
Netherlands	51	0.79	8	71	10–12	Yes	No
Britain	59	0.68	2	60	29	No	No

Sources: OECD (1988, 1996); Eurostat (1991); European Commission Network on Childcare (1996); Millar and Warman (1996).
n/a, not available.

of citizenship. For instance, from Table 5.2 it is very difficult to explain the low level of participation in the labour market among mothers in Italy. First, as we see from Table 5.2, the ratio of female to male earnings is very high in Italy and equals, for example, the Danish situation. Thus, from an economic perspective, participation in the labour market has a high degree of utility. However, mothers in Italy do not enter the formal labour market to the same degree as in Scandinavia. Second, as Table 5.2 reveals, the combined effect of (1) day care institutions for children between 3 and 6 and (2) maternity leave arrangements is relatively high and equals, for instance, the situation in Denmark. That is, welfare institutions in Denmark and Italy allow mothers to participate in the labour market to a similar extent, but mothers in Italy still exhibit far lower participation rates than in Denmark.

Such inconsistencies are often labelled 'misfits'. 'Misfits' are, however, only rarely mentioned in mainstream literature on gender and the welfare state and, if they are, they are mentioned parenthetically. For instance, Millar and Warman (1996: 21) write that 'the fit is perhaps not so close here' without addressing what are the consequences of such misfits, and how can we account for the misfits?

Misfits often occur because similar institutions, or institutions with similar names, have different meanings and different steering effects in different social and cultural contexts. For instance, high female wages may be interpreted as an egalitarian measure stimulating the entry of women into paid employment. High female wages, however, may also be interpreted as a measure making it uneconomic for employers to take on women workers. Historically, this has been the case in Italy, where female wages reached 83 per cent of male wages as early as 1945–46 (Lorini 1975). Or, conversely, institutions which from the 'outside' look very different may actually have the same nature or structure. For instance, historically Sweden has had high-quality maternity leave schemes in terms of coverage, duration and entitlements while, alternatively, Denmark has had a high degree of coverage by high-quality day care institutions (see Table 5.2). Nonetheless, maternity leave and day care institutions may be functional alternatives to the same problem, that is to organise conditions allowing entry of mothers into the labour market. As such, different institutions with different names may actually have the same meaning and harbour the same goals.

Similarly, it is not sufficient to observe whether welfare schemes are present or absent in one country or another, because properties of welfare institutions differ markedly cross-nationally. This is the case, for instance, for day care institutions (Moss 1990). First, day care may be constructed in order to improve the socialisation, life quality and welfare of children vulnerable to neglect or abuse. Second, day care may be constructed to bridge the needs of mothers in combining childrearing with paid employment. Third, day care may be considered as an institution of relief in order to improve the welfare and functioning of the family. All these motives may be present in the day care institutions in a given society. However, one motive often predominates.

In Britain, for instance, public day care has up to now been effectively limited to 'problem children'. Services provided in the Nordic countries are much influenced by the intention of enabling women to combine motherhood with paid employment, which, among other things, is reflected in the opening hours of the day care institutions. In Italy social and educational motives predominate. This is also the case in West Germany. Here, public day care is seen as part of the educational system and as a means to socialise children in groups at a time when families are getting smaller and having siblings is less common (Kaufmann 1995). Only recently has the political aim to give mothers the possibility of combining parenthood and employment (at least by working part-time) been added in Germany, although this is still limited to pre-school children aged from 3 to 6 years. A right for children to participate in public or publicly financed childcare was introduced in 1996 and includes the possibility for full-time care, even though many childcare institutions are still limited to part-time care. This is not simply a question of public provision of childcare but also one of the demands of parents who often do not want their children to spend the whole day in a childcare institution. Although former East Germany is now integrated into the same welfare state, local government there normally provides both full-time childcare for pre-school children and after school care as well, and this better matches the demands of women who are traditionally more oriented towards continuous full-time employment (Pfau-Effinger 2000). Thus, in Germany, even within the same welfare state context, different cultural and institutional traditions, and different demands from citizens, have contributed to a differing public provision.

A focus on the presence or absence of one scheme or another also tends to neglect the quality of such schemes in terms of level, coverage and staff. In Germany, for instance, we find rather generous maternity arrangements in which women receive benefits for 14 weeks at 100 per cent of previous earnings. Such generous benefits do not, however, necessarily overcome the problems of juggling family and employment. In Germany, the generous maternity arrangements are counteracted by the low level of coverage of services for children. That is, the generous maternity arrangements in Germany do not function as a 'bridge' back to employment. Instead they function within an overall framework of public policies directed at promoting traditional family norms, and encouraging women to take on a 'homemaker' role for at least three years. Therefore, the maternity arrangements in Germany are a flexible *exit* mechanism from the labour market, quite different to the *entry* intentions of maternity leave arrangements in the Nordic countries.

We can see that parental leave arrangements are designed to achieve different aims in different parts of Europe. It makes a difference, for instance, whether the parental leave arrangements are designed to complement a female 'homemaker' model, as in Germany, or are constructed with the aims of supporting equality among husband and wife in the caring and upbringing of children, as in Scandinavia. If the latter is the case, parental leave will be paid and will normally be supplemented with a paternity leave scheme (see Table 5.2). On the other side of the coin, Britain has only very recently introduced a parental leave scheme and it remains unpaid. That Britain is a latecomer to parental leave, and that the leave is unpaid, mirrors a specific cultural and historical legacy according to which society is committed to values such as individualism and privacy, which in turn favour a traditional gender division of labour. Parental leave in Germany can be seen as something in between. It was designed in the middle of the 1980s with the intention of keeping mothers of children under 3 years old out of the labour market, and this fits into the cultural ideals of private childhood and a homemaker role for mothers with small children. It is paid, but means tested, so that the care-giver is dependent on a (usually male) breadwinner. It also mirrors in part the orientation towards waged work in the younger generation. Thus parental leave in Germany builds a bridge back to employment by including a right for parents to return to the former employer for up to three years. This is ambivalent, however, since the law did not include a right for parents to work part-time at the previous employer – which is the type of employment which mothers of young children prefer for it fits with the new cultural orientations. This is one reason why childbirth in Germany still ends, in many cases, with a long period of unemployment for women (Pfau-Effinger and Geissler 1992; Holst 2000).

So far, it seems as though welfare state institutions have no virtual existence of their own, as the properties of similar institutions vary cross-nationally. We assume that the properties of institutions arise from the broader cultural system in which the institutions are located. Therefore, to analyse, classify and explain differences in welfare states with respect to gender policies, it is necessary to consider the existence of different cultural and institutional traditions. This is because cultural ideas penetrate the functioning of welfare state institutions.

5.3 Explanations: welfare state policies in the context of gender arrangements

In this section we wish to present an explanatory framework as to how culture and social actors may be included in the analysis of welfare states. This will then allow us to understand the properties of welfare state institutions and their dynamics of change. In the first section we present a conceptual framework as to how welfare state policies and culture interrelate, and in the second section we discuss more generally how to avoid essentialism in gender analyses.

The interrelations of welfare state policies with cultural and institutional frameworks and with social agency

What does it mean to include 'culture' in analysis or to 'contextualise' the framework of social citizenship? We suggest the theoretical framework of 'gender arrangement' as described by Pfau-Effinger (1996, 1998a, 1999a) as a way of doing this. This theory conceptualises the interplay of welfare state policies with culture, institutions, social structures and social actors, and considers the dynamic of change which may develop within these mutual interrelations. This is a further development of the 'gender system' and 'gender contract' approach of Yvonne Hirdman (1988, 1990; see Pfau-Effinger 1994, 1998a).[1]

According to the idea of a gender arrangement, a gender cultural system can be identified which includes values and ideals about gender relations, such as the gender division of labour, power relations and dependencies, motherhood and fatherhood. The gender cultural system is the result of conflicts, negotiation processes and compromises of social actors with differing power at an earlier stage of historical development. It has a strong impact upon the gender discourses and practices of each new generation of actors. The gender cultural system also forms a main reference point for social action and policy formulation at the level of the welfare state, where it is implemented as norms and expectations about what is normal, and in other institutions like the labour market and the family, as well as by collective actors and individuals themselves. However, under certain circumstances individuals or groups of social actors develop new ideas, or adopt ideas from different contexts, and may try to negotiate a new dominant gender arrangement. Change at the level of gender culture can thereby contribute to change in welfare state policies. The outcome is influenced by the power relations between these actors, for instance between the feminist movement as a new social movement on the one hand and conservative political parties on the other. The cultural foundations of welfare state policies are thus mutually interrelated with the dominant cultural ideals about family and gender relations in the population, and these also form a cultural reference point for other institutions such as the labour market and the family (Pfau-Effinger 2000).

Crucially, however, the way welfare state policies refer to those gender cultural models which are dominant in the population can vary. The interrelations may be more harmonious or, alternatively, they can to a certain degree be characterised by asynchronies and discrepancies. For example, the relationship between welfare state policies and gender culture was relatively harmonious in the Netherlands in the 1950s and 1960s, when welfare state policies exclusively promoted the housewife model of the male breadwinner family to which the broad majority of women and men were oriented (Ishwaran 1959; Heiligers 1992). In the 1970s, however, contradictions and asynchronies developed, for the cultural orientations of women were changing whereas welfare state policies still promoted the housewife model (Heiligers 1992; Bussemaker and van Kersbergen 1994; Knijn 1994a,b).

We do not support an ideational approach here, however, where the explanation of welfare state policies is restricted to the influence of cultural values and ideals alone. Welfare state policies are also the result of differing interests of social groups – and some social groups have more power than others. Welfare state policies can therefore contribute substantially to the development of social inequality, including gender inequality. In this view, gender culture, institutions, gender structures and social actors are mutually interrelated within the gender arrangement, and the concept therefore forms an appropriate framework for cross-national analyses of differing welfare state policies and their dynamics of change (see Chapter 10).

This theoretical framework can also be used to analyse the degree to which welfare state policies can contribute to the empowerment of women and the promotion of gender equality. We would argue that welfare states promote the aim of gender equality best if they refer to dominant ideals and orientations towards gender equality among women. The Netherlands represents a good example of the importance of the analysis of the interrelations between welfare state policies and the cultural ideals of women. Part-time work by women (and also by men) has been substantially promoted by the state, in a relatively protected form and of similar quality to full-time jobs (Plantenga 1996). One could draw the simple conclusion that this promotion of part-time work for women was a more traditional gender policy, based on the exclusion of women from full-time employment. However, this would be a misleading interpretation. An analysis of change in cultural orientations in the attitudes and behaviour of women (and men) towards waged work helps to understand and interpret this development more adequately. In the Netherlands, a new and more egalitarian gender cultural model, based on part-time work by mothers and fathers, has developed at the level of cultural orientations by the majority of adults, mainly by women but also by a considerable proportion of men (see Haller and Höllinger 1994; Pfau-Effinger, 1998a). The promotion of part-time work by the state can be seen here as an element of an equalising gender policy, and is also supported by the feminist movement as a contribution to greater gender equality. In social practice this model had been realised only to a rather limited degree by the millennium. Even though the rate of men working part-time was the highest in Europe by 1998 (67 per cent; OECD 1998: 192), it is still mainly women who work part-time, and this means that they are dependent on the income of their male breadwinner as long as they are partnered. To empower women adequately with respect to the dominant cultural model of gender equality, a stronger promotion of part-time work for men would be needed. Moreover, some kind of substitute for the loss of full-time income would also be necessary, in order to free part-time workers from dependency on a full-time breadwinner. There is, however, strong pressure for change towards more equal family and employment patterns. Moreover, post-divorce social protection for carers is relatively high. A universal retirement scheme with a minimum retirement pension which is above the subsistence level also minimises the risk of poverty for workers who previously combined employment and care by working part-time (Bussemaker and van Kersbergen 1994; Knijn 1994b; Plantenga 1996). This is different for instance to Germany, where no minimum pensions exist (Veil 1996; Ginn and Arber 1998).

In other words, the promotion of part-time work in this particular context of time and space was an important step towards greater gender equality (Plantenga 1996; Pfau-Effinger 1998b). In contrast, in Finland a cultural model of full-time employment for all adults and comprehensive public childcare is dominant (Haavio-Mannila 1985; Anttonen 1997). Here, the traditional gender cultural model of both partners contributing to agricultural work was transformed, during the transition to an industrial and service society, into a dual breadwinner/state carer model. The tradition of full participation of all women in employment was maintained during this process, but adapted to the new situation of work outside the home by a strong expansion of the public social service sector and of comprehensive public childcare provision. The cultural tradition of the housewife family, and the idea of private, individualised childhood in the family, was never dominant in Finnish history. Therefore part-time work by mothers does not have any cultural basis, and does not match the employment orientations of women. Instead, women in Finland are usually oriented to continuous full-time employment (Pfau-Effinger 1994, 1998a, 1999). The social practice of women fits to this orientation and the share of women working part-time has since the beginning of the 1970s always been about 10 per cent (OECD 1996: 192; OECD 1998: 192). In this societal context, any promotion of part-time work by the state would not contribute to the empowerment of women.

Cross-national differences in the gender policies of welfare states can therefore be substantially explained by differences in the gender cultural foundations to which welfare state policies refer, and by the interests of those social groups which are influential in the reconstruction of old compromises, or in the struggle for new compromises. It should be noted that the gender policies of welfare states overlap in a specific way with those policies of welfare states which refer more closely to the differing class interests of capital and labour, the varying outcome of which has been conceptualised by Esping-Andersen (1990) as 'welfare regimes'. The respective combination of gender cultures with class-based welfare regimes contributes substantially to cross-national differences of social policy between societies with similar gender cultures (Pfau-Effinger 2000). Simon Duncan and Ros Edwards (1999) have introduced a framework using such a combination, which they call the 'genderfare' model for the classification of social policy. This is based on the assumption that policy variations reflect variations in both the capital–labour contract and the gender contract (or gender culture), and that these are mutually interrelated. According to this model, welfare states vary according to the specific way both kinds of contracts are shaped and interrelate.

The classification of gender cultural models

To analyse gender policies of welfare states in their cultural context, we need a classification of gender cultural models. Pfau-Effinger (1998a, 1999) suggests a classification based on the following criteria:

1   Cultural ideals about the gender division of labour, the main spheres of work for women and men, the social valuation of these spheres, and the way dependencies between women and men are constructed.
2   The cultural construction of the relationship between generations, that is the construction of childhood, motherhood and fatherhood.

Using this classification model it is possible to distinguish between at least six gender cultural models in Western Europe, which include more traditional and new cultural models. The different models can be characterised as follows (Pfau-Effinger 1998a, 1999):

(1) THE FAMILY ECONOMIC GENDER MODEL

This model is based on the cooperation of women and men in their own family business (farm or craft business), in which both genders contribute substantially to the survival of the family economy. Children are treated as members of the family economic unit, that is as workers, as soon as they are physically able to contribute. There may exist a strong sexual division of labour within the family economy, which varies according to context of time and space. This model was previously widespread in the agrarian regions of Europe, particularly where the agrarian structure was based on small family farms (Honnegger and Heintz 1981).

(2) THE MALE BREADWINNER/FEMALE HOME CARER MODEL

This model conforms to the idea of the basic differentiation of society into public and private spheres. Women and men are seen to be complementarily competent for one of these spheres: men are regarded as breadwinners, earning the income for the family with waged work in the public sphere, whereas women are primarily regarded as being responsible for the work in the private household, including childcare. This is also based on a social construction of childhood, according to which children need special care to be supported comprehensively as individuals. This model was dominant at the cultural level in many Western European countries after the transition to industrial society, for example in Germany since the turn of the nineteenth century, and has lasted much longer in other countries such as Ireland. It also forms the cultural basis for model (3):

(3) THE MALE BREADWINNER/FEMALE PART-TIME CARER MODEL

This is a modernised version of the male breadwinner model. The idea is that women and men are to an equal degree integrated into waged work as long as there are no dependent children in the household. During the phase of active motherhood, however, the combination of part-time waged work and caring is seen as appropriate for mothers. This model is dominant at the cultural level in West Germany and Great Britain, for instance.

(4) THE DUAL BREADWINNER/STATE CARER MODEL

This model conforms to the idea of the 'completed labour market society' (Beck 1994), with full-time integration of both sexes into the employment system. Women and men in marriage are seen as individuals, who are both breadwinners earning income for their own livelihood and that of their children. Like the male breadwinner/female carer model, childhood is constructed as a phase of life with its own worth, in which the individual child needs much care and support. But in contrast, caring for children is not primarily seen as the task of the family, but to a considerable extent the task of the welfare state, which is also seen as more competent for fulfilling this task than private households. The dominant gender cultural model in Scandinavian countries, particularly in Finland, approaches this model. Whereas the Scandinavian version of this model is in principle based on the idea of gender equality, a Russian version of this cultural model is more connected to the idea of male superiority, as can also be said for the dominant model in former East Germany (Nickel 1995). In France this model seems to be combined with pervasive ideas of women's femininity and motherhood.

(5) THE DUAL BREADWINNER/DUAL CARER MODEL

This model reflects the notion of a symmetrical and equitable integration of both genders into society. In contrast to the preceding model, childrearing is to a large extent a responsibility of the family. The basic idea is that the family economy consists of an equal distribution of domestic labour – in particular childminding – and waged labour between a female and a male head of household. This is possible only because the labour market is organised in such a manner that structurally allows parents to fulfil a 'dual responsibility'. Such a model requires that domestic labour be financed on the basis of a family wage or on the basis of a state transfer system. This model has gained dominance at the cultural level in the Netherlands.

(6) THE DUAL EARNER/MARKETISED FEMALE CARER MODEL

This model is based on the idea of full integration of women and men into full-time waged work. The family is seen as responsible for organising and paying for marketised childcare, by using commercial childcare facilities or by employing childminders in the household. This is a new model which has gained increased importance in countries such as Britain and the USA, but is not yet dominant at the cultural level (Crompton 1998; Yeandle 1999).

There also exist mixes between these models, as in Sweden, where a dual breadwinner/dual carer model is combined with elements of private care for children, and mothers in the phase of active motherhood tend to work part-time (although mostly with long hours not much below the level of full-time employment). In some countries different gender cultural models are dominant at the same time, as in Germany where in former West Germany the male breadwinner/female part-time carer model is dominant, while in former East Germany the dual breadwinner/dual carer model is the central model. A co-existence of two dominant models can also occur when the gender arrangement is in transformation from one dominant family model to another, as in the Netherlands, where at the cultural level the dual breadwinner/dual carer model is dominant, whereas in practice most couples still live in correspondence with the male breadwinner/female part-time carer model (Pfau-Effinger 2000).

It should be remembered that even though there is a mutual interrelation between the economic structure and gender cultural models there is no deterministic impact of the former on the latter. Thus in Holland of the seventeenth century, which was an agrarian society (with elements of a commercial society), instead of the family economic model (which was the cultural basis for the family in many agrarian societies) the housewife model of the family was apparently dominant at the cultural level of the whole society (Schama 1988; Pfau-Effinger 2000).

Cross-national differences in welfare state policies, as indicated in Table 5.1, can to a considerable part be explained by the gender cultural model(s) to which welfare state policies in each country refer. This is not a simple interrelation, however. It should be noted that social policies are constituted by complex interrelations between different kinds of institutions and policies, as outlined above, including the way in which they interrelate with welfare state outcomes of the capital–labour relation (see the 'genderfare' approach of Duncan and Edwards 1999). In times of social, institutional and cultural change these interrelations may be characterised by asynchronies, and traditional and more egalitarian policies may be combined in discrepant or even contradictory ways.

The interrelations between welfare state policies and social practices of individuals are also very complex. The social action of individuals is not a simple outcome and is not determined by state policies, although this is often assumed when data on behaviour (such as the labour force participation rates of women) are used as an indicator for welfare state policies. Such an assumption does not take into account the fact that the social behaviour of individuals is a process which takes place in a very complex field of influences, where cultural ideals and values also play an important role. Thus Duncan and Edwards (1997, 1999) have criticised the assumption of 'rational economic man' on which analyses of the impact of welfare state policies on behaviour are often based. According to their argument, individuals do not simply act according to principles of 'economic rationality' but also with respect to principles of 'moral rationality'. In turn these principles are related to cultural ideals and values. Similarly Pfau-Effinger (1998a, 2000) found that cross-national differences in the development of female labour force participation rates and part-time working in Finland, the Netherlands and West Germany could not be explained by simply referring to welfare state policies, but rather by the complex interplay of culture, institutions, structures and social actors.

As long as the respective gender arrangement is coherent, the labour force participation rate of women may to a large degree conform with the aims of welfare state policies. This is because in such cases welfare state policies and behaviour refer to the same set of cultural values and ideals on gender relations, as for example in West Germany and the Netherlands in the 1950s and 1960s. Things can be different, however, in times of social and cultural change in the respective gender arrangement. Women may act according to new cultural orientations in spite of welfare state policies which are traditionally oriented, and sanction their new behaviour negatively, so that this even seems to be 'irrational'.[2] For example, in the Netherlands and West Germany in the 1970s many women became culturally more oriented towards waged work and increasingly participated in the labour force, whereas welfare state policies were still conservative and promoted the housewife model of the family. Change may therefore take place at the level of culture and in the behaviour of individuals, while welfare state policies still promote more traditional gender cultural models – particularly in those cases in which the power relations still favour traditional (usually male) elites (Pfau-Effinger 2000).[3]

To conclude, cross-national variations in the gender policies of welfare states can be more adequately understood if these policies are analysed with respect to the ways in which they are embedded in the social context. This includes the complex interrelations of culture, institutions, social structures and social agency.

5.4 Afterword: from essentialism to anti-essentialism in gender analysis

The chapter so far has shown that gender theory must reconsider the relevance of the state–civil society opposition for understanding and explaining changes and continuities in gender relations (Bang and Sørensen 1999). It is far from evident that either the state, or civil society, is the natural starting point for assessing how new gender identities and activities affect, and are affected by, political institutions. The legitimate domination of the state may indeed be employed to set people free in certain contexts. Yet this freedom is acquired at the expense of political self- and co-governance by social actors (Bang *et al.* 1997). Furthermore, integrative norms and other forms of social capital may be the 'glue' that holds a society together. However, they are simultaneously the site of orthodoxies in the social which prevent the pluralisation of gender differences, and the balancing of uneven gender relations.

As Foucault was one of the first to stress, 'power isn't localised in the State apparatus and … nothing in society will be changed if the mechanisms of power that function outside, below and alongside the State apparatuses, on a much more minute and everyday level, are not also changed' (Foucault 1980: 60). Norms and administrative power do walk hand in hand in the social.

However, this does not necessarily imply that role and identity building must always be enwrapped in a circle of power and counter-power, as Foucault suggests. Power could function on the basis of the reciprocal acceptance of difference rather than as a relationship of superordination and subordination. Hence, power might be employed to do away with relations of class, race and sex, and other kinds of uneven relations, which subvert difference (Bang and Dyrberg 2000).

We see a possibility of using a notion of political solidarity, understood as the reciprocal acceptance of difference, to merge Bourdieu's theory of culture and the new institutionalism in political analysis as an alternative logic of exclusion and inclusion (March and Olsen 1989, 1995; Bourdieu 1990; Swartz 1997). This may help to demonstrate that although political authority has traditionally been interpreted as resembling the legitimate domination of the state, it could be extended into the social as a condition for establishing relations of self- and co-governance within the various fields of power–knowledge constituting a society. If political authority is understood as conditioning access to solving common problems, it becomes evident that the ideal of gender equality is dependent on the transformative capacity of authority, that is, on power (Giddens 1979, 1992). What is of importance here is the fact that analyses of the inclusion or exclusion of the ideals and discursive practices of gender equality do not obey the logics of the rational calculation of utilities and the internalisation of a common good. They rely more on specifications of the power conditions that enable or hinder the articulation of personal and collective differences. Hence, new concepts and ideals are needed that do not trace gender equality to some comprehensive doctrine of 'order', 'rationality', 'normative integration', or 'class struggle' but simply to the mutual acceptance and recognition of difference (Butler and Scott 1992).

The social contextualisation of gender relations and the introduction of a cultural framework for different societies, as understood in sections 5.2 and 5.3, thus require a new notion of political authority as a guarantor of difference, contingency and change. Political authority is effective only when people accept it and consider themselves bound by it (Easton 1953). However, its acceptance need not be univocal; nor does its social bonding require a comprehensive normative agreement. It is a type of power–knowledge that allows for continuous disagreement and struggle, as a continuous presence in the social, which may appear in multiple, irreducible forms (Bang 1998).

The multiplicity of relatively autonomous forms made available by authority indicates why the governance and integration of gender differences should not be narrowed down to a matter of combining 'strong steering' and 'thick solidarity'. However, this is often what happens in gender analysis. There still is a tendency to envelop gender problems in the more or less hidden agenda of the opposition between *the state* as the playground of the dynamic, the rational and the powerful, and *civil society* as the social embodiment of the stable, the understanding and the good (Keane 1991;

Cohen and Arato 1994; Hirst 1994; Etzioni 1995; Held 1996). Perhaps what is really wrong is the hidden presupposition of much gender analysis that just as women must grow hair on their breasts, if they are to gain influence over the big games that rational men play within the sphere of the state, so men must be soft and harmony-seeking when partaking in the solving of the small issues of everyday life in civil society. This is, of course, just another version of essentialism. Rather, we find it more appropriate to speak of gender within a framework of continuous battles and disputes over the distribution of valued things (Bourdieu and Passeron 1997). In such a framework, gender inequality is not merely a matter of sealing the life-world off from power, or alternatively of meeting 'the system' with counter-power and counter-rationality. It is much more a matter of exclusion – of particular meanings, of certain identities, of special discourses, of specific resources. Exclusions and so on are not the sign of 'distorted communication' or 'social anomalies'. They are on the contrary a constitutive part of the social, making inclusion possible. Exclusion manifests lack, or the privileging, of certain modes of self- and co-governance in the social, which may both enable and constrain and lead to freedom as well as to domination.

Hence, we approach gender problems as a matter of political inclusion and exclusion rather than as a problem of decommodification, depaternalisation or empowerment. We adopt an anti-essentialist stance towards all comprehensive gender doctrines, whether of a biological, functionalist, evolutionist, statist, or 'society centrist' nature. However, we do not deny the relevance of analytical theory. We merely hold that there are only *contingent foundations* and that any theoretical foundation has a political aspect which makes it crucial to ask what it is that a theory authorises by its foundation and, as a consequence, what it excludes. The continuous presence of the political in the social necessarily implies that gender relations could always have been shaped otherwise – even if their conditioning by culture and structure often make them peculiarly resistant towards change (De Certeau 1997; Swartz 1997; Gunnell 1998). We believe that this contingent foundationalism requires at least three methodological breaks with modern gender analysis:

1   *The first break* is with the tendency to oppose order and disorder, space and time, or the static and the dynamic.
2   *The second break* is with the actor-structure dichotomy and its many echoing oppositions such as those between rational man and irrational society, preference calculations and integrative norms, self-interest and the common good.
3   *The third break* is with the dichotomisation of power and knowledge, and thereby of authority and democracy.

We will briefly deal with these in turn.

Social capital – beyond the dichotomisation of order and disorder

The state–civil society opposition lays out many snares for gender analysis. One of the most basic is the tendency to empty the social of all political tensions and conflict. By perceiving unity, homogeneity and consensus as the constituting elements of civil society, the focus is removed from its constitutive political aspects: the handling of differences, diversity and dispute in everyday life (Connolly 1991, 1995; Mouffe 1992, 1993).

Robert D. Putnam, whose notion of social capital has been widely acclaimed, puts this well. 'Political participation,' he writes, 'refers to our relations with political institutions. Social capital refers to our relations with one another' (Putnam 1995: 665). Gender relations and social interactions are here simply defined as non-political. They become political only when they are politicised as claims upon the state which 'affect the prospects for effective, responsive government' (Putnam 1993: 16). The political has in this conception nothing to do with the social 'as such' which is why we must distinguish 'social trust – trust in other people – and political trust – trust in political authorities' (Putnam 1995: 665). There is nothing political outside the sphere of governmental power and the formal institutions of the state.

For Putnam, gender interactions appear as non-political and as important solely for the building of social capital. To the extent that one can speak of political capital, it is something that derives from the support for appropriate political authority by active citizens and social movements. A virtuous social order, the argument is, requires that the state is effective and responsive to the needs for equilibrating relations in the social. Hierarchy, political coercion and other forms of asymmetries in political domination are acceptable as long as they guarantee progress and enjoy legitimacy, and as long as the building of social capital is made independent from them. Only by keeping the political out of the social will 'virtuous circles result in social equilibrium with high levels of cooperation, trust, reciprocity, civic engagement, and collective well-being. These traits define the civic community' (Putnam 1993: 177). If the political is allowed to intrude on the social, social capital will erode. For 'the *un*civic community is also self-reinforcing. Defection, distrust, shirking, exploitation, isolation, disorder, and stagnation intensify one another in a suffocating miasma of vicious circles' (ibid.).

In Putnam's frame of reference, democratic political authority functions as an instrument of rational choice and as a medium for social order preventing such vicious circles from occurring. Like Talcott Parsons, Putnam tends to take it for granted that the functional problem for political authority is the 'minimizing of disruptive behavior and the motivation to it' (Parsons 1951: 30). This presumption leads both authors to put primary stress on the legitimation of authority as a binding or appropriate norm, deriving from the autonomy of the social. However, authority is not linked to the problem of social or normative order but to the problem of how to distribute values for a certain field or domain. It is a type of communicative relationship between a sender (A) and a receiver (B). It occurs (1) when B receives an explicit message from A; (2) when B then accepts A's message as the basis of decision and action; and (3) when B's grounds for doing so are the practical recognition that messages received in this way must or ought to be obeyed without evaluating the merits of the proposed conduct in the light of one's own comprehensive doctrines or normative judgments (Easton 1955: 28–29). Hence, the opposite of authority is not disorder but communication breakdowns, meaninglessness, and patternlessness.

It is important for gender analysis to recognise that if the terms 'order' and 'stability' are to have any sensible meaning they must represent a condition in which the rate of disorder and change of authority relations is slow enough to create no special communicative problems due to such disorder and change. There will always be some disorder and change. Hence, the basic problem of authority is not whether it is stable, harmonious or consensual but what is excluded and included by it. Authority does not and cannot guarantee the separation of order from disorder and thereby the discovery or the imagination of a protected locus where the 'Ideal of Enlightenment' prevails. But it does communicate that in principle and in the imagination, at least, things could always have been done otherwise.

The Third Way – beyond the actor–structure dichotomy

The actor–structure dichotomy is often called into being 'in the light of a rationalized life-world in which system imperatives *clash with* independent communication structures' (Habermas 1989: 391). This methodological clash is supposed to derive from the study of the opposed ideologies of liberalism and socialism, both of which tend to insulate the individual from the community as an actor–structure duality. The liberals tend to see the social as an essentially private association where interests are calculated and pursued by individuals independently of, and prior to, the concerns of the social community. The state here appears as a public instrument of aggregating individual interests and of protecting their free realisation in the private sphere. The socialists, in contrast, tend to conceive of the social as much more strongly communal in content, insisting that social bonds are prior to individual interests, manifesting the 'real' interests of classes in the capitalist economy. In this view, the state appears as a class agency for integrating the social in terms of an ideology of the common good, hindering the objective interests of workers from taking effect within the social community.

Jürgen Habermas, Gøsta Esping-Andersen and Birte Siim alike tend to conceive of their models as a 'third way' between liberalism and socialism, the practical embodiment of which is the (Nordic) welfare state. Most famously, Anthony Giddens has put this together in terms of a political programme, which in some respects has furnished an ideology for the centre-left in its response to liberalism, particularly in Britain (Giddens 1979). The developed welfare state, their joint argument seems to be, sets us all free as a public agent of emancipation, linking together concerns for individual autonomy in the marketplace with the requirements for social solidarity in the civic culture. Thus the problem of order is made into a methodological problem of actors versus structures. The discussion of gender is situated within the *'difference between steering problems and problems of mutual understanding ...* between systemic disequilibria and lifeworld pathologies, between disturbances of material reproduction and deficiencies in the symbolic reproduction of the lifeworld' (Habermas 1987: 363). The instrumental rationality of actors is claimed to be necessary to release both men and women from the fixities of tradition, safeguard their human rights, and enlarge their economic opportunities. However, it has to be constrained by 'the abstraction of universal lifeworld structures from the particular configurations of totalities of forms of life that arise only as plural' (Habermas 1987: 344). The communicative logic of the life-world is the medium for integrating gender differences with the common good, bringing about a peaceful socialisation of the capitalist economy, reducing anarchic competition and economic waste, and protecting 'the weak', in particular women, against the 'excesses' of industrialist capitalism (see Esping-Andersen 1990).

The problem shared by such 'third way' social democratic perspectives is that it makes little sense to speak of either a political individual or a political community in these models because political community is considered opposed to the individual and because this community is identified with either the state or the family. Furthermore, the state appears as deriving from something outside the political, namely from the clash between private and social interests in society. This apolitical stance, indicative of most modern actor–structure methodologies, seems to derive from an exclusion of the political from the domain of the theoretical. It blocks any understanding of the political as an aspect of the social, composed of a set of regularised practices in the duality of structures (Easton 1953; Giddens 1979; Bourdieu 1990).

We believe new methodologies of gender are needed to put theory and epistemology in their proper relationship. We must accept that 'any form of unity, articulation, and hierarchization that may exist between the various regions and levels [of society] will be the result of a contingent and pragmatic construction, and not an essential connection that can be recognized' (Laclau 1990: 186; Connolly 1991). The social sciences, like all other metapractices, stand in a distinctive discursive space established by society as a set of regularised practices. We see outlines of such an alternative methodology in both sociological and political research. In sociology, it is most prominent, perhaps, in Bourdieu's cultural theory of action which asks, as we did earlier in this chapter, 'How do regular patterns of conduct occur over time without being the product either of some abstract external structure or of subjective intentions?' (Swartz 1997: 95). The argument is that both individual dispositions and social structures are shaped in conventional fields of social interaction and that it is therefore the discursive construction of the social as 'habitus' and 'field' which reveals how the social can exist both inside and outside of individuals, both in their minds and in 'things' (ibid.). Individual subjectivity and societal objectivity, in such a conception, appear as properties of their mutual interpenetrations in practice. In this understanding the argument that social structures have subjective consequences is not incompatible with saying that the social world is constructed by individual actors.

We experience the same movement from individual preferences and social structures to regularised practices in the new institutionalism political research. The new institutionalists 'begin with the belief that political and administrative phenomena can not be adequately described, explained or predicted without considering the *structuring* quality and the independent effects of institutions (the meso-level)' (Olsen 1992: 7). This belief reflects an 'empirically based prejudice, an assertion that what we observe in the world is inconsistent with the ways in which contemporary theories ask us to think, that the organization of political life makes a difference' (ibid.: 1). On such a practical conception 'political democracy depends not only on economic and social conditions but also on the design of political institutions' (March and Olsen 1989: 17). The latter shows the articulation of conventional practices within a given field as 'collections of standard operating procedures and structures that define and defend values, norms, interests, identities, and beliefs' (ibid.).

We would suggest that the theory of culture and the new institutionalism are combined together in a new approach to politics and policy, which identifies the political not with government or the state but rather with *practices of governance*. We understand the political as fields or networks of relatively autonomous practices or institutions for authoritatively allocating values. This indicates how disputes and struggles over value differences can cross all established boundaries between public and private, national and international, and state and civil society. Such disputes and struggles constitute subjects through exclusions establishing a domain of de-authorised subjects erased from view (Butler and Scott 1992: 13). As such they also guarantee that these excluded and de-authorised subjects in their practices are the embodiments of political potentials for continuous rearticulations of authority relations.

When one gives up the old metapractices of defining the individual and the political in terms of the private and the state, it becomes possible to put forward the argument that the personal and the public – far from being antithetical to each other – are, in fact, articulated with each other politically. To sum up, the debate on gender through notions of emancipation, social capital, the caring state and the like simply models the political after the modern opposition between 'rational man' and 'normative society'. This opposition will most likely create more problems than solutions when studying how gender equality can be created, sustained and expanded. It does not only prevent us from discussing the difference between a commonality which is oriented towards the good and the attainment of mutual interests (social solidarity) and one which is oriented towards rights and the solving of common concerns (political solidarity). It also directs our attention away from critically reflecting upon the tendencies in the modern state to make experts rather than 'ordinary' citizens the meta-principle of democracy and of the authoritative allocation of society's valued things. In contrast, our notion of democratically regularised practices as grounded in the mutual acceptance and recognition of difference allows for analyses of democratic political communities which are 'weak' enough to make room for the powers of both elites and lay-actors, and 'thin' enough to provide space for their various conceptions of the good (Rawls 1995, 1997).

Beyond the dichotomy of power and freedom

The idea of equality of the sexes seems intrinsically related to the outline of a political democratic practice in which 'I would accept and recognize that you make a real and significant difference, if you could accept that I do so as well' (Bang and Dyrberg 2000). Such interpersonal relations, meanings and symbols in the social are more directly based on experiences with, and images of, self- and co-governance than on exchange relations or shared mutual obligations (Strong 1994). They establish political rather than social 'habits of the heart' which spring less from trust in authorities than from trust in the capacities of lay-actors for political decision and action. The importance of such political 'capital accumulation' for democracy simply disappears from sight within the framework of modern social science. This neglect of authoritative mechanisms of inclusion and exclusion hangs together with a failure to appreciate the problem of order in (or from) disorder and the play of political individuality and commonality in the social, as discussed above.

It seems important to employ the idea of the political as the making and implementing of difference, and hence to bring authority back in as the twin pair of power–knowledge in the social. The political, in this conception, is a condition of *both* hierarchy *and* self- and co-governance. We see remarkable convergences between the theory of culture and the new institutionalism with regard to these issues. Factually, they both encourage examinations of how hierarchy and domination can persist and reproduce from one generation to the next without powerful resistance and conscious acknowledgement on the part of lay-actors. Normatively, they lead us to ask how lay-actors can be related to authorities and other experts in ways that allow for self- and co-governance in both directions. Bourdieu's sociology reveals the social world as one of conflict and struggle over valued resources and definitions that are hierarchically ordered. This notion of the social as a web of interweaving fields of struggle over various kinds of valued resources should be of considerable interest to the new institutionalists. For they are brought up within a tradition according to which 'political science is reaching towards an understanding of the very things that men consider most vital: *their differences over ... the authoritative allocation of values*' (Easton 1953: 50, italics added). This tradition, where politics appears as the 'interweaving of power and the authoritative allocation of values' (ibid.: 133), seems very much in line with a sociological tradition which 'does not oppose one value judgment to another but takes account of the fact that the reference to a value hierarchy is objectively inscribed in practices and in particular inscribed in the struggle over this hierarchy itself and is expressed in the antagonistic value judgments' (Bourdieu in Swartz 1997: 25).

The kind of power–knowledge intrinsic to the operation of political authority in the social thus indicates that gender should be studied as regularised practices that have reflection over, and involvement in, politics and policy as their content. Authority should be regarded as a communicated message, which applies to getting things expressed and *done* in practice. It is a means of settling disputes and struggles over the distribution of values. Authority thus indicates that whereas the acceptance and recognition of political difference are intrinsic to the balancing of uneven gender relations stability and consensus are not. The prospects for gender equality are far more dependent upon unceasing dispute, pluralisation and change than upon reaching normative agreement and consensus. Gender relations are neither logically nor practically connected with the problem of social order; they do not concern the employment of state power as either an instrument of preference aggregation or a medium of normative integration; and they do not reveal the consequences that administrative domination may have for economic effectiveness and social support. They principally concern the ability to carve out spaces of self- and co-governance in the various contexts of everyday life. This ability to convert ideas and resources into political identities is exercised in and through the institutions or regularised practices that are the issue of political life, no matter whether they operate 'below', 'above' or 'within' the state. It manifests a socio-political ontology of potentials enabling persons and groups to construct meaningful accounts of what they themselves and others are doing and to employ these for the exclusion of what are regarded unacceptable alternatives, identities or meanings.

Acknowledgement

Many thanks to Simon Duncan for valuable comments on an earlier draft.

Notes

1 In Hirdman's approach, in contrast to that taken here, culture and social order are not conceptualised as relatively autonomous and the concept is based more on the assumption of coherence. Gender inequality is seen always as a structural basis of the 'gender system', whereas here we leave space for equalisation processes. The term 'arrangement' is also preferred here to that of 'contract': the idea of a societal contract was developed in theoretical thinking and is based

on the assumption of free and equal citizens entering the social arena; the 'arrangement' approach is a more open sociological and analytical concept which leaves more space for the analysis of social and gender inequality.

2 For criticism of the idea about economic rationality in the labour market behaviour of women see Duncan and Edwards (1999). Women also may use the political and institutional framework of the welfare state in new ways which deviate from the original aims of these policies.

3 This does not mean, however, that the dividing line between traditional and more equal orientations to the question of gender equality is identical with the split between women and men, for there are different social groups with differing interests and orientations among both sexes. See also Mósesdóttir (1995).

References

Anttonen, A. 1997. The welfare state and social citizenship. In Kauppinen, K. and Gordon, T. (eds) *Unresolved Dilemmas: Women, Work and the Family in the United States, Europe and the former Soviet Union*, pp. 9–32. Ashgate, Aldershot.

Bang, H.P. 1998. David Easton's postmodern images. *Political Theory*, 26, 3, 281–316.

Bang, H.P. and Dyrberg, T.B. 2000. Governance, self-representation and the democratic imagination. In Saward, M. (ed.) *Democratic Innovations*. Routledge, London.

Bang, H.P. and Sørensen, E. 1999. The Everyday Maker: a new challenge to democratic governance. *Administrative Theory and Praxis*, 21, 3, 325–342.

Bang, H.P., Dyrberg, T.B. and Hansen, A.D. 1997. Elite eller folkestyre – demokrati fra oven eller neden. *Journal Grus*, 51, 5–31.

Beck, U. 1994. *Reflexive Modernisation*. Polity Press, Cambridge.

Becker, G.S. 1993. Nobel Lecture: The economic way of looking at behaviour. *Political Economy*, 101, 3, 385–409.

Berg, A.M. 1989. Part-time employment – a response to economic crisis? In Rosenberg, S. (ed.) *The State and the Labor Market*, pp. 221–231. Plenum Press, New York.

Blau, F.D. and Ferber, M.A. 1986. *The Economics of Women, Men, and Work*. Prentice-Hall, New Jersey.

Bourdieu, P. 1990. *The Logic of Practice*. Polity Press, Cambridge.

Bourdieu, P. and Passeron, J.-C. 1997. *Reproduction in Education, Society and Culture*. Sage, London.

Bourdieu, P. *et al*. 1991. *The Craft of Sociology – Epistemological Preliminaries*. Walter de Gruyter, Berlin.

Brooks, A. 1997. *Postfeminisms – Feminism, Cultural Theory and Cultural Forms*. Routledge, London and New York.

Bussemaker, J. and van Kersbergen, K. 1994. Gender and welfare states: some theoretical reflections. In Sainsbury, D. (ed.) *Gendering Welfare States*, pp. 8–25. Sage, London.

Butler, J. 1990. *Gender Trouble*. Routledge, New York.

Butler, J. and Scott, J.W. (eds) 1992. *Feminists Theorise the Political*. Routledge, New York.

Cohen, J.L. and Arato, A. 1994. *Civil Society and Political Theory*. MIT Press, Cambridge.

Connell, R. 1987. *Gender and Power: Society, the Person and Sexual Politics*. Polity Press, Cambridge.

Connolly, W.E. 1991. *Identity/Difference*. Cornell University Press, Ithaca.

Connolly, W.E. 1995. *The Ethos of Pluralization*. University of Minnesota Press, Minneapolis.

Crompton, R. 1998. Explaining women's employment patterns: "orientations to work" revisited. *British Journal of Sociology*, 49, 118–136.

De Certeau, M. 1997. *The Capture of Speech and other Political Writings*. University of Minnesota Press, Minneapolis.

Duncan, S.S. and Edwards, R. 1997. Lone mothers and paid work: rational economic man or gendered moral rationalities? *Feminist Economics*, 3, 2, 29–61.

Duncan, S.S. and Edwards, R. 1999. *Lone Mothers, Paid Work and Gendered Moral Rationalities*. Macmillan, London.

Easton, D. 1953. *The Political System*. University of Chicago Press, Chicago.

Easton, D. 1955. A theoretical approach to authority. *Office of Naval Research*, Report 17, 1–59.

Esping-Andersen, G. 1990. *The Three Worlds of Welfare Capitalism*. Polity Press, Cambridge.

Etzioni, A. (ed.) 1995. *New Communitarian Thinking*. University of Virginia Press, Virginia.

European Commission Network on Childcare 1996. *A Review of Services for Young Children in the European Union, 1990–1995*. Brussels.

Eurostat 1991. *Earnings – Industry and Services*. Luxembourg.

Foucault, M. 1980. *Power/Knowledge: Selected Interviews and other Writings 1972–1977*. Pantheon Books, New York.

Giddens, A. 1979. *Central Problems in Social Theory*. Macmillan, London.

Giddens, A. 1992. *The Transformation of Intimacy*. Stanford University Press, Stanford.

Ginn, J. and Arber, S. 1998. How does part-time work lead to low pension income? In O'Reilly, J. and Fagan, C. (eds) *Part-time Prospects*, pp. 156–174. Routledge, London.

Gunnell, J.D. 1998. *The Orders of Discourse, Philosophy, Social Science, and Politics*. Rowman & Littlefield Publishers, Inc., Lanham.

Gustafsson, S. and Jacobsson, R. 1985. Trends in female labour force participation in Sweden. *Journal of Labour Economics*, 3, 256–274.

Haavio-Mannila, E. 1985. The state, the family and the position of women in the Nordic countries and Poland. In Risto, A. *et al.* (eds) *Small States in Comparative Perspective*. Oslo.

Habermas, J. 1987. *The Philosophical Discourse of Modernity*. Polity Press, Cambridge.

Habermas, J. 1989. *The Theory of Communicative Action*, Vol. 2. Polity Press, Cambridge.

Haller, M. and Höllinger, F. 1994. Female employment and the change of gender roles: the confluctual relationship between participation and attitudes in international comparison. *International Sociology (Journal of the International Sociological Association)*, 9, 87–112.

Heiligers, P. 1992. *Gender and changing perspectives of labour and care*. Paper presented at the First European Conference of Sociology, August 1992.

Held, D. 1996. *Models of Democracy*, 2nd edn. Polity Press, Cambridge.

Hernes, H.M. 1987. *Welfare State and Women Power: Essays in State Feminism*. Norwegian University Press, Oslo.

Hirdman, Y. 1988. Genussystemet – reflexioner kring kvinnors socialaunderordning. *Kvinnovetenskaplig Tidskrift*, 3, 49–63.

Hirdman, Y. 1990. Genussystemet. In Statens Offentliga Utredningar, *Demokrati och Makt i Sverige*. SOU, Stockholm.

Hirst, P. 1994. *Associative Democracy: New Forms of Economic and Social Governance*. Polity Press, Cambridge.

Holst, E. 2000. Die Stille Reserve am Arbeitsmarkt. Grösse – Zusammen – Setzung – Vethalten. Sigma, Berlin.

Honnegger, C. and Heintz, B. (eds) 1981. *Listen der Ohnmacht: Zur Sozialgeschichte weiblicher Widerstandsformen*. Suhrkamp, Frankfurt am Main.

Ishwaran, K. 1959. *Family Life in The Netherlands*. The Hague.

Jensen, Per H. 1996. *Komparative Velfaerdssystemer: Kvinders reproduktionsstrategier mellem familien, velfaerdsstaten og arbejdsmarkedet*. Nyt fra Samfundsvidenskaberne, Copenhagen.

Kamerman, S.B. and Kahn, A.J. 1981. *Child Care, Family Benefits, and Working Parents*. Columbia University Press, New York.

Kaufmann, F.X. 1995. *Zukunft der Familie im Vereinten Deutschland*. Schriftenreihe des Bundeskanzleramtes, Vol. 16. Beck, München.

Keane, J. 1991. Democracy and the Idea of the Left. In McLellan, D. and Sayers, S. (eds) *Socialism and Democracy*, pp. 6–17. Macmillan, Basingstoke.

Knijn, T. 1994a. Social dilemmas in images of motherhood in the Netherlands. *European Journal of Women's Studies*, 1, 183–206.

Knijn, T. 1994b. Fish without bikes: revision of the Dutch welfare state and its consequences for the (in)dependence of single mothers. *Social Politics*, 2, 83–105.

Laclau, E. 1990. *New Reflection on the Revolution of our Time*. Verso, London.

Leira, A. 1992. *Welfare States and Working Mothers*. Cambridge University Press, Cambridge.

Lister, R. 1995. Dilemmas in engendering citizenship. *Economy and Society*, 24, 1–40.

Lorini, M. 1975. *Trent'anni di lotte delle lavoratrici italiane*. Editrice Sindacale Italiana, Proposte No. 33, Roma.

March, J.G. and Olsen, J.P. 1989. *Rediscovering Institutions*. Free Press, New York.

March, J.G. and Olsen, J.P. 1995. *Democratic Governance*. Free Press, New York.

Millar, J. and Warman, A. 1996. *Family Obligations in Europe*. Family Policy Studies Centre 7, London.

Mincer, J. 1985. Intercountry comparisons of labor force trends and of related developments. *Journal of Labor Economics*, 3, 3, 1–32.

Mósesdóttir, L. 1995. The state and the egalitarian, ecclesiastical and liberal regimes of gender relations. *British Journal of Sociology*, 46, 4, 623–642.

Moss, P. 1990. *Børnepasning i de Europæiske Fællesskaber 1985–1990*. Kommissionen for de europæiske fællesskaber.

Mouffe, C. (ed.) 1992. *Dimensions of Radical Democracy*. Verso, London.

Mouffe, C. 1993. *The Return of the Political*. Verso, London.

Nätti, J. 1993. Temporary employment in the Nordic countries: a "trap" or a "bridge"? *Work, Employment and Society*, 7, 3, 451–464.

Nickel, H. 1995. Frauen im Umbruch der Gesellschaft: Die zweifache Transformation in Deutschland und ihre ambivalenten Folgen. *Aus Politik und Zeitgeschichte: Beilage zur Wochenzeitung das Parlament*, B 36–37/95, 1, September, 23–33.

OECD 1988, 1996, 1998. *Employment Outlook*. OECD, Paris.

Olsen, J.P. 1992. Analyzing institutional dynamics. *LOS-senter Notat*, No. 14, 1–38.

Orloff, A.S. 1993. Gender and the social rights of citizenship. *American Sociological Review*, 58, 303–328.

Parsons, T. 1951. *The Social System*. Free Press, New York.

Pfau-Effinger, B. 1994. The gender contract and part-time paid work by women – a comparative perspective. *Environment and Planning A*, 26, 8, 1355–1376.

142   *Gender divisions of power*

Pfau-Effinger, B. 1996. Analyse internationaler Differenzen in der Erwerbsbeteiligung von Frauen – theoretischer Rahmen und empirische Ergebnisse. *Kölner Zeitschrift für Soziologie und Sozialpsychologie*, 48, 3, 462–492.

Pfau-Effinger, B. 1998a. Gender cultures and the gender arrangement – a theoretical framework for cross-national gender research. *Innovation*, 11, 2, 147–166.

Pfau-Effinger, B. 1998b. Culture or structure as explanations for differences in part-time work in Germany, Finland and the Netherlands? In Fagan, C. and O'Reilly, J. (eds) *Part-time Perspectives*, pp. 177–198. Routledge, London.

Pfau-Effinger, B. 1999. Defizite der Theoriebildung zu den Grenzen wohlfahrtsstaatlicher Geschlechterpolitik. In Hradil, S. (ed.) *Verhandlungen des 29. Kongresses der Deutschen Gesellschaft für Soziologie, des 16. Österreichischen Kongresses für Soziologie und des 11. Schweizerischen Kongresses für Soziologie "Grenzenlose Gesellschaft?"* in Freiburg, Bd. 1, pp. 203–218. Centaurus, Plenumsveranstaltungen, Freiburg.

Pfau-Effinger, B. 2000. *Kultur und Frauenerwerbstätigkeit im europäischen Vergleich*. Leske und Budrich, Opladen.

Pfau-Effinger, B. and Geissler, B. 1992. Institutioneller und soziokultureller Kontext der Entscheidung verheirateter Frauen für Teilzeitarbeit – Ein Beitrag zur Soziologie des Erwerbsverhaltens. *Mitteilungen aus der Arbeitsmarkt- und Berufsforschung*, 25, 3, 358–370.

Plantenga, J. 1996. For women only? The rise of part-time work in the Netherlands. *Social Politics*, 4, 3, 57–71.

Pringle, K. 1998. *Children and Social Welfare in Europe*. Open University Press, Buckingham.

Putnam, R. 1993. *Making Democracy Work*. Princeton University Press, New Jersey.

Putnam, R. 1995. Tuning in, tuning out: the strange disappearance of social capital in America. *Political Science and Politics*, 28, 4, 664–683.

Rawls, J. 1995. Reply to Habermas. *Journal of Philosophy*, 42, 3, 132–180.

Rawls, J. 1997. The idea of public reason revisited. *University of Chicago Law Review*, 64, 3, 765–807.

Schama, S. 1988. *The Embarrassment of Riches. An Interpretation of Dutch Culture in the Golden Age*. University of California Press, Berkeley, CA.

Siim, B. 1994a. Engendering democracy – the interplay between citizenship and political participation. *Social Politics*, 1, 3, 286–306.

Siim, B. 1994b. Køn, medborgerskab og politisk kultur. In Andersen, J. and Torpe, L. (eds) *Demokrati og politisk kultur*, pp. 125–159. Systime, Herning.

Siim, B. 1999. Towards a gender sensitive framework for citizenship. In Bussemaker, J. (ed.) *Citizenship and Transition of European Welfare States*, pp. 85–100. Routledge, London.

Strong, T.B. 1994. *Jean-Jacques Rousseau: the Politics of the Ordinary*. Sage, London.

Swartz, D. 1997. *Culture and Power*. University of Chicago Press, Chicago.

Veil, M. 1996. Zwischen Wunsch und Wirklichkeit: Frauen im Sozialstaat. Ein Ländervergleich zwischen Frankreich, Schweden und Deutschland. *Aus Politik und Zeitgeschichte: Beilage zur Wochenzeitung das Parlament*, 29–38.

Walby, S. 1990. *Theorizing Patriarchy*. Blackwell, Oxford.

Walby, S. 1994. Is citizenship gendered? *Sociology*, 28, 2, 379–395.

Yeandle, S. 1999. Gender contracts, welfare systems and "non-standard working": diversity and change in Denmark, France, Germany, Italy and the U.K. In Felstead, A. and Jewson, N. (eds) *Global Trends in Flexible Labour*, pp. 95–118. Macmillan, Basingstoke.

6 Gender, migration and social inequalities

The dilemmas of European citizenship

Marina Calloni and Helma Lutz

6.1 Issues: gender, contracts and citizenship

The main interest of this book is to reconsider the interaction between economy, society and culture from a gender perspective and to both describe and explain differences in how this occurs in the European Union. The aim of our chapter is to refocus this interest and to shed light on it from a different angle. By taking into account the position of migrant individuals and groups we want to indicate the persistence and the increase of new forms of social inequality and gender discrimination in the European Union.

In particular, in the present section we will reframe the social, political and ideological theory of the 'gender contract' and the structure of national constitutions, by including the perspective of 'foreigners', that is non-citizens, and migrant women among them in particular. In the second section we will consider the influence of migration on the constitution of the European Union. For European unification has transformed previous definitions of migration, and of who have to be considered migrants. (Hence the 'old migration' refers to that before 1989, when the EEC became the EU; see section 6.2.) In fact, since 1989 migrants in the EU have been considered only as those individuals who are not citizens of a European member state. (The 'new migration' is thus after 1989; see section 6.2.) Migration, however, cannot be considered to be culturally and economically homogeneous. For this reason, in section 6.3, we will discuss the phenomenon of the 'feminisation' of migration. This is of fundamental importance for understanding the structure of gender roles in a trans-cultural way and the emergence of new forms of social inequalities within each European nation state. The case of domestic workers, who are mostly employed by indigenous women, will be taken as an example. Finally, taking as background the new situation of migrants in Europe, and the increase in new kinds of discrimination (including that between women), in section 6.4 we will try to indicate some perspectives which can help us to conceptualise European citizenship in a new way. This should not be based any longer on the principle of the *ius sanguinis* (literally the 'right of the blood'), but should be understood as a negotiable and flexible political and cultural construct, open to 'new workers and citizens'.

We will introduce our argument by questioning the theory of 'gender contract'. In recent years some social scientists have developed the concept of the gender contract as a theory, practice and perspective, in order to reformulate the traditional comparative approach to welfare state regimes (Esping-Andersen 1990) and to illuminate prospects for their reform in Europe. Furthermore, many female scholars (for example Orloff 1993, 1997) stress that these traditional theories have been 'gender blind'. Thus, 'gender contract' theorists (Hirdman 1988) suggest that (1) 'virtually all areas of life are divided into male and female categories', and (2) the distinction between these two categories is a hierarchical one, where 'the male is the norm and the female is ascribed lower value' (as noted in Duncan 1995: 271).

Yet, although we agree with the critique of the limits of the previous welfare state models implicitly based on the figure of the 'male breadwinner', we think also that the gender contract approach is insufficient for adequately understanding a multicultural society. The problem with this approach is that it excludes the central questions of 'race', 'ethnicity' (Williams 1995) and 'culture' (Archer 1996; Pfau-Effinger 1998). Therefore, it cannot give adequate answers to the questions of why these issues are simultaneous with 'economy', 'gender' and 'society' (Kovalainen 1999), and how they contribute to perpetuate traditional forms of social exclusion, as well as to generate new forms of social inequality. Consequently, culture has not only to be considered in a cross-national way (comparing the different European countries, their welfare regimes and forms of gender relations), but also to be analysed in its multiplicity (as with the co-presence of 'foreigner communities'). Social inequalities can thus arise from both the maintenance of local discriminatory traditions and from the increase in new patterns of life based on disadvantage.

Starting from this point, we want to argue that some issues (like race and ethnicity) have been underestimated in the debate on gender contracts and the reform of the welfare state. Rather, we want to examine the issue of citizenship in the European Union, and the idea of mobility of 'human capital' (as codified in the Maastricht Treaty), in connection to questions about migrant populations, gender and socio-political inequalities. Gender inequalities in Europe cannot in fact be considered in a monolithically and culturally homogeneous way, and referred only to 'native populations'. Cultural differences and gender inequalities have thus to be approached from a dynamic viewpoint, considering also people who are 'politically' excluded, but moving from one country to another, that is migrants.

However, migration – as labour importing and labour exporting at the global and regional level – also has to be reconceptualised. It has to be understood as a consequence of the new processes of modern rationalisation, such as technological and financial innovations which are deeply changing the previous forms of production, human relationships and political institutions. This epochal transformation induces a necessity to reframe the earlier analyses of social, cultural and political differences, which were based on the class distinctions produced by industrial society.

In modern terms migration has always been defined in relation to citizenship, belonging and borders (Williams 1995; Bader 1997; Lister 1997). Furthermore, the idea of 'contract' has been a key category and metaphor for understanding modernity and its forms of political legitimation. Namely, contract is not only a relevant concept in the legal sphere and economic system, but in the political domain as well. Since early modernity this has informed theories of citizenship – from Hobbes to Rousseau – and nowadays also influences the conceptualisation of a theory of distributive justice (Rawls 1971). Contract theory has also been used as the basis for the critique of marriage as a sexual contract, where the construct is a metaphor for modern capitalist and liberal citizenship based on the idea of an abstract individual (Pateman 1988). However, in the debate over gender and welfare state regimes, the concept of 'gender contract' has also been used as a construct able to indicate a specific socio-political compromise and negotiation, which takes place between women and men in social democratic societies (Hirdman 1988). This has been particularly developed by Nordic scholars, in the context of 'women-friendly' welfare states with official gender equality – but where gender inequality remains. This has then been used as an explanatory and classificatory concept in analysing the position of women in welfare states (see Pfau-Effinger 1998).

Therefore, if we look carefully at the different interpretations of gender contract mentioned above, we have to admit that they start from opposite assumptions regarding contract and human relations. The first 'legal–political' interpretation starts from the assumption of a universalistic concept of contract, considered as a product of mutual agreement based on 'equality' and freedom of involved parties and individuals. Against this neutral liberal definition of human beings and formal equality among them, the second 'socio-cultural' interpretation deconstructs the ideology of contract, indicating the roles of power and the structure of the patriarchal order, on which gender relations and domination are based. The third conceptualisation, that developed by Nordic scholars, comes from particular socio-political experiences, contextualised and institutionalised in specific European countries, which refer to a joint and collectively possible negotiation between women and men both at work and in the household. Yet all these different theoretical and social ideas of contract (related to persons and goods) do not face the specific type of socio-political inequality we are dealing with, that is migration and in particular the specific issue of women coming from different cultural traditions.

At the same time, the egalitarian assumption and the ideological framework of the concept of contract can now be found in the definition, and in the legal regulation, of migration in Europe. Namely, we can observe in many constitutions and laws the coexistence both of the 'symmetrical tradition', which normatively expresses the moral dimension of mutual respect among human beings and the acceptance of 'moral disagreement' (Gutmann and Thompson 1996), and the 'asymmetrical factor', which refers to the real mistreatment of human beings, who are not yet considered 'citizens'. The gender issue related to migrant women combines these two different aspects.

In the case of migration, contract is agreed under unequal conditions between dissimilar parties and individuals, who have at their disposal an unequal distribution of socio-political rights and resources. Furthermore, in the case of migration there is a third factor: the dynamic of 'inclusion/ exclusion'. Although foreigners are not recognised as interested citizens of a specific constitutional contract, their presence is assumed, admitted and considered by democratic national pacts. In fact, every foreigner has to be protected under human rights and he/she is usually a citizen of another nation state which has the duty and the right to act on his/her behalf. Because of the interconnection, but also the disparity, between human and political rights, each government has the duty to implement laws for the regulation of migration as a social/ economic phenomenon, but at the same time it has to face questions related to the political and constitutional status of foreigners in general and individual migrants in particular. In such a way, the condition of 'strangers', who live and work in a specific place, can be thus compared to the situation of women since they obtained the right to vote. They certainly have civic, economic and social rights, but not the political status of full citizens.

Yet migration is also a complex issue in Europe, because it is treated under two different political and economic perspectives: from the viewpoint of each nation state and from the standpoint of the European Union. These two perspectives are often divergent, because of different constitutional traditions, political compositions of national governments and the weakness of the European Parliament (EP) as a legislative assembly. Indeed, the political institution which decides European policies and subscribes to treaties is not the EP but the Council of Ministers, composed of national Prime Ministers. Migration is thus considered in an ambivalent way as a result of the constitution of European citizenship.

The divergence between the different national governments in Europe is concerned with both economy and politics, and the control of the new power centres. The process of pursuing the establishment of a new entity is led by those nation states which assume that the name of a continent – like the case of the United States of America – indicates an economic and political union as well as cultural commonalities. However, de facto Europe is not yet a given entity, but its political, social and cultural definition is in the process of constitution. There are now numerous activities initiated by EU bodies which strive to construct common denominators. One example is the definition of European citizenship, formulated in Article 7 of the Maastricht Treaty (1992). This definition has had 'internal' as well as 'external' consequences. The right of all Europeans to partake in local elections of the country of their residence has not only permitted a stronger cohesion between European citizens, but also accentuated their difference from the 'others', that is the non-European (Sayad 1991). The constitution of a European citizenship is thus ambivalent, because it includes those who are in possession of membership status of a national state, while excluding those who are defined as outsiders. This dialectic indicates a new step in the traditional notion of citizenship, based on the assumption of a reciprocal and free contract between institutions and individuals.

An ambivalent dialectic related to the constitution of a common 'European identity' and the exclusion of the 'others' can also be observed in the present 'politics of borders'. These treaties on boundaries indicate that new cultural and political dynamics are at stake. A look at the Schengen Treaty[1] elucidates how on the one hand it permits the opening up of frontiers between the EU member states on the basis of the liberal principle of the free movement of people and goods. On the other hand, it has constituted new borders inside the states and between human beings with regard to foreigners. Now boundaries are no longer equivalent to state borders, but are constructed inside states as well as delimitating Europe as a whole.

For example, in Germany public spaces such as undergrounds, airports and harbours were recently declared 'dangerous places'. Here the police are entitled to search and arrest every suspicious person (declaration of the Interior Minister, quoted in Das Argument 1998). All European citizens can potentially be dangerous border crossers, but in reality only those who are 'suspicious looking', often foreigners, are exposed to this procedure. The former inside becomes the new outside. Meanwhile all European airports now have 'extra-territorial zones' where refugees are kept and from where they can be deported to another place, without 'entering' the country and thus being able to claim rights of political asylum.

The Schengen Treaty also engenders a new development in the concept of a 'political contract', which by territorial inclusion creates freedom of movement and a new social space, but at the same time provokes new exclusive boundaries. However, this treaty has specific features. It was concluded by the Council of Prime Ministers in Brussels and was only later presented to national parliaments for ratification. Furthermore, the treaty also differs from previous forms of international relations because it is not a 'contract' stipulated between foreign nation states, but is connected through a common European project. This situation also indicates that various new international strategies are implemented in the case of migration and the definition of migrants.

Taking as a background the political and cultural transformations which are occurring at the European level, and the critique of the traditional idea of citizenship as merely based on a symmetrical contract among individuals, we also want to argue that a theory of gender contract based on the Nordic model of the welfare state perpetuates the limits of previous approaches. This is because it does not take 'cultural variables' enough into account and neglects the issue of who starts with disadvantage and without equal opportunities. In fact, it is based on the individualistic assumption of free personhood, where men and women negotiate their rights, duties and strategies, including the use of time (for themselves, for caring and for work). Yet in the case of migration this approach is inappropriate for two reasons in particular. First, the conditions for symmetrical negotiations (that is joint rights and equal starting points for all the interested individuals) do not apply, and second there is a different understanding of the individual in relation to space, loyalties, family, networks, ethnic belonging and cultural collectivities.

Reconsidering Western gender contract theory in relation to the issue of migration and cultural differences in Europe also requires a re-analysis of the sources and the nature of social inequality. In fact, gender inequality can be considered as coming from the interaction between different cultures, supported by both local and foreigner individuals and communities. A more complex and interlinked comparative analysis can thus point out the structure of gender relations and the consistency of social inequalities at three different levels: (1) in a specific territory, that is region or nation state, (2) comparatively in different countries, and (3) in the European Union. However, considering social inequalities, criticising injustices and promoting social policies for a common welfare also require the development of a normative viewpoint, which allows social criticism and pragmatic intervention. This refers to the basic moral and political assumptions of citizenship, such as equal respect, recognition and participation (Fraser 1999), which have to be at the basis of a theory of a distributive social justice (a fair distribution of resources among human beings).

The question of gender, migration and citizenship in Europe has therefore to be discussed on five different but interconnected levels: (1) the moral level: respect for human beings; (2) the political level: the impact of the state and the meaning of citizenship; (3) the social level: human capital and its composition; (4) the economic level: the work system and its organisation; and (5) the cultural level: the coexistence of traditional and post-traditional ways of life, starting from the family and the presence of minorities. Our society is a composite and multistratified complex of individuals, communities, systems and networks, where the possibility of entering the public sphere and the labour market is interlinked with differentiated forms of discrimination and segregation, often related to the '(gender) difference' (Benhabib *et al.* 1996). But traditional forms of unequal opportunities or harassment now become related not only to native but also, in particular, to migrant women.

We are conscious that citizenship has always been and remains a matter of 'frontiers' and 'rights'. Yet our interest is not only to understand why (internal and external) boundaries can be a matter of exclusion and a cause of new forms of social inequalities (different status and salary among workers, new segregation in the domestic work sector, employment without social assistance, unequal opportunities for youth and so on). We also want to understand if migration in Europe can be regulated in a new way, so that it will become possible to avoid discrimination among human beings as well as among genders. Yet if we want to support this argument, it is necessary to explain the features and patterns of migration in Europe and the change in its meaning (such as the 'old' and 'new' migrations) and its composition over time. In particular, we have to stress the changing profile of migration including the phenomenon of feminisation. We have also to emphasise that since World War II the European countries have had different reactions and legislation regarding migration as a result of their different constitutional traditions, national backgrounds and geographical position. And this now causes many difficulties for the creation of a common law and policy on migration in the European Union.

6.2 Patterns: migration in post-war Europe

The old migration and its aftermath

Before 1989, 'Europe' referred to those countries included in the 'European Economic Community' (EEC) along with the other liberal democracies of Western Europe. Later, with the signing in 1992 of the Maastricht Treaty by the member states, the EEC was changed into a political union and renamed the 'European Union' (EU). Furthermore, the fall of the Soviet bloc together with the end of the Cold War have brought into focus questions like 'what is Europe' and what are its boundaries (Balibar 1990; Brah 1996).

Since then, a search for alternative organising principles able to unify Europe has been under way and this has often focused on the elusive concept of 'European civilisation'. De facto, since the decolonisation process started after World Wars I and II, the redefinition of 'what Europe is' has been an ongoing project. The 'old Europe' referred to a discourse about its superiority and domination over the South and was constructed through the process of colonisation, the settlement of Europeans in other parts of the globe, the formation of empires and the struggles against indigenous populations (Balibar 1990). In contrast, the 'New Europe' seems to be a rather defensive discourse of striving to construct a 'pure Europe' as a symbolic continent, cleansed of foreign and 'uncivilised' elements. In the search for intrinsic features of 'Europe', discourses of culture, politics and space have become closely intermeshed with discourses on nationalism, racism and 'home' versus 'foreigners' and 'otherness' (Lutz *et al*. 1995; Räthzel 1995; Brah 1996; Yuval-Davis 1997).

Migration movements have been and still are at the heart of these cultural and political developments. Indeed, contrasting with the popular image of a sedentary Europe, historians have proved that Europeans have moved both inside and outside Europe over the last 500 years at least (Moch 1992; Lucassen and Lucassen 1996). Even though migration is by no means a new phenomenon in Europe, nevertheless it has entered, and at times dominated, political debates and action after World War II in a particular way. However, it has been considered in various terms and at different times in different

European countries. For this reason, we want – although briefly – to map out some of the most significant developments, using Germany, the Netherlands and the United Kingdom as prime examples.

To begin with, not every movement was automatically perceived as 'migration', at least not in the sense attached to this terminology today. In Britain post-war migration has had a major impact on society, although it has not been perceived in these terms. After this period, according to Robert Miles (1993: 129), notions of 'race' and 'race relations' were widely employed within sociology for considering migration and its consequences. These concepts were used for indicating that post-war migration to Britain came from the Caribbean, the Indian subcontinent and other 'New Commonwealth' countries. Miles rejects this approach as a seriously flawed portrayal of history. He has proved in fact that as early as 1946 there was an active recruitment policy organised by the British Labour government in the displaced persons camps, which encouraged European migrants (including many women) to come and resolve the major labour shortage in industries, considered as essential for the economic recovery of Great Britain (Kay and Miles 1992).

Between 1947 and 1950, British workers were joined by ex-prisoners of war and short contract workers from Italy and Germany, exiles and refugees from Poland and other East European countries as well as widows from Germany and Austria (Kay and Miles 1992: 59–64). The significant shortage of nurses in the public health sector was mainly solved through recruitment from abroad. In 1946, 2000 Latvian, Lithuanian and Estonian women from displaced persons camps went to work in English sanatoria as part of the so-called 'North Sea and the Balt Cygnet recruitment programme' (Holmes 1988: 213). In spite of initial employment restrictions, the arrival of these migrants was widely welcomed as their potential for assimilation was viewed as an asset. In sharp contrast, at around the same time, the arrival of British subjects from the Caribbean, mainly from Jamaica, was discussed in a quite different way: as 'coloured people' they were perceived as a problem and as non-assimilable. From that time on the British government discussed and appointed measures to prevent Black migrants from immigration to the British mainland. In fact all these measures, among which the Commonwealth Immigrants Acts of 1962 and 1968 and the British Nationality Act of 1981 are most important, can be seen as a means of institutionalising racist migration control and thereby racialising the New Commonwealth (Kay and Miles 1992; Miles 1993; Harris 1995). Through and by these measures the British state has recreated its national borders as well as reconstructed the British post-colonial nation.

In post-war migration a clear split between colonial and non-colonial European states can be noticed. Former colonial states used their human resources from former colonies to fill the gaps in the labour market. Critical researches, however, also show that the British state tried as long as possible to prevent Black citizens from the colonies from migrating to the United Kingdom and, when this became difficult, it gradually changed the citizenship status in a direction which served this purpose. Thus the citizens of the British Empire no longer became part of one Commonwealth, but were differentiated into citizens belonging to the Old Commonwealth (the British settler societies of Australia, New Zealand and Canada) and the New Commonwealth (the British colonies in Africa, the Caribbean and Asia). While the former category has to meet few requirements to get access to the UK, the latter has been gradually subjected to more and more restrictions. (For an analysis focused on how women were targeted by immigration control, see Bhabha and Shutter 1994 and Lutz 1997).

In the Netherlands the development of migration was similar, albeit with differences regarding target groups and resources. The Dutch post-war migration history is characterised by two different migration profiles, which in part succeeded each other and in part overlapped: the first is a kind of migration coming from the former colonies, the second concerns the 'guest worker' recruitment from the Mediterranean countries. After the declaration of independence, transforming in 1949 the former colony of 'Dutch Indies' into the state of Indonesia, 'repatriates' were 'moving back' to the 'motherland' until the early 1960s, amounting to some 300,000 people (Cottar and Willems 1984; Schuster 1999). Not all of them, however, were equally welcome.

The Dutch government constructed in fact two different categories of the 'Indische Nederlanders', the 'Western oriented' and the 'Eastern oriented', based on 'racialisation', which was already part of the colonial discourse in the Dutch Indies. While there were minor problems with the acceptance of the former category (White or mixed Dutch, so-called Eurasians), the latter was perceived to be unassimilable, so that ministers and state officials did everything they could in order to prevent them from moving to 'Holland'. As this differentiation could not be easily transferred into juridical categories, the 'Eastern oriented' Indische Nederlanders could not be excluded on the basis of the equal treatment of all Dutch citizens. Furthermore, the Dutch government felt responsible for the integration of the newcomers and promoted their integration through support systems (in housing and the labour market) as well as through radio speeches, on the basis of the Dutch self-understanding of being a tolerant nation (for an elaborate analysis see Schuster 1999). This attitude, however, changed significantly when, in the 1960s, immigration of Black people from Surinam and the Dutch Antilles in the Caribbean became an issue.

The Dutch government preferred the recruitment of South European and Mediterranean workers (from Italy in the 1950s, then from Spain, Greece, Portugal, Turkey, Yugoslavia and Morocco in the 1960s) as 'guest workers' rather than admitting the 'human resources' from the 'West Indian' Caribbean colonies. The declaration of independence by Surinam in 1975 was preceded and followed by large-scale emigration from the country to the Netherlands. The Dutch state reacted by limiting the period of free movement between the former 'parts of the Empire' to five years. After that period visa requirements were installed. In the 1990s the number of immigrants from the former colony of Surinam has almost reached the number from the former 'Dutch Indies'. There is, however, a significant difference between the way these two immigrant groups have been dealt with: while the latter has never been considered as an ethnic minority and is now seen as the 'model minority', fully integrated into Dutch society, the former is instead the main target group (followed by Turkish and Moroccan immigrants) of state minority policies, established in 1983.

Comparing the Dutch and the British state regarding the post-war history of immigration control, John Schuster (1999: 313) emphasises various similarities:

> The governments' reactions to the arrival of the former colonial subjects are expressions of confusion over the indeterminacy of these migrants. As long as potential migrants were still in their countries of origin, they could easily be represented as fellow countrymen. They became strangers as soon as they bridged the geographical gap between their native countries and Great Britain or the Netherlands and transgressed the boundaries of the nation states. Their indeterminacy originated in the failure of the classifying function of language, since they defied the purity of the opposition between citizen and foreigner.

As in the Netherlands and the United Kingdom, the de-colonisation process as a result of the collapse of old empires led to significant changes of state borders and consequently to a re-definition of national identities in Europe as well as in the former colonies. France is the other leading example. As every empire had created its own colonial system of hierarchical 'belonging', the question of who had to be admitted to the 'motherland' became a question for all state bureaucracies of the involved nations. It was in this context that the term 'repatriate' emerged. It is a category which implied selection criteria, based on perceived differences between those who – despite their long-term absence – 'belonged' to the patria and therefore were assumed to be capable of assimilation, and those who did not belong because of real or imagined cultural and ethnic differences (Lutz 1997).

A look at the migration development in post-war Germany makes this observation even clearer. West Germany admitted 12 million people between 1949 and 1961 on the basis of the conviction that these were 'ethnic' Germans – of whom 9 million (called *Aussiedler*) were predominantly expelled from East European countries and 3 million (called *Übersiedler*) were refugees from the former GDR – who originally 'belonged' to Germany by *ius sanguinis*. This assumes that nationality and culture is inherited from the parents. The *ius sanguinis* principle, which is at the heart of the current citizenship debate in Germany (see Lutz 1999), is contrasted by the *ius soli* principle supported by the French republican tradition according to which migrants have the right to citizenship after a certain period of sojourn in a nation state and in which migrants' children are considered nationals if they are born in that country. While Germany and Austria adhere to the *ius sanguinis* rule and France – though reluctantly – operates the *ius soli*, most of the other West and North European countries combine the two principles in various ways. Britain is an exception as it handles these questions differently according to the 'racial' differentiations between the Old and New Commonwealth countries, as established by the Nationality Acts (which themselves can be seen as a sort of *ius sanguinis*).

The migration process of the ethnic Germans was seen as re-settlement, an act of repatriation to the 'fatherland' of their ancestors, from which some of them had been absent for more than 300 years. The most significant difference between this post-war immigration flow and the simultaneous 'guest workers' immigration – involving the recruitment of workers from Italy in the 1950s and from Spain, Turkey, Yugoslavia, Greece and Portugal in the 1960s – was the fact that ethnic Germans were granted citizenship from the very day of their entry, while this possibility was and still is denied to the majority of the labour migrants and their children. As in the Netherlands, the 'ethnics' were welcomed by the state through radio speeches making an appeal to the 'indigenous' population to treat these migrants as fellow countrymen. Between 1961 and 1988, another 1.5 million ethnic Germans (now called *Spät-Aussiedler*) arrived in the FRG and since then the number of those coming from Russia, Romania, Poland and other parts of Eastern Europe amounts to approximately 250,000 persons per year (Morokvasic 1993; Rudolph and Hübner 1993; Münz 1996; Rudolph 1996).

In this context, it is also important to stress the change in terminology and the transformation of the perception of 'migrants' in those European countries which recruited migrant labourers from the Mediterranean regions (West Germany, the Netherlands, Belgium, Luxembourg, Sweden, Denmark, Austria).[2] These people were called 'guest workers', in order to avoid the contaminated term of 'foreign workers' and also because their sojourn was considered to be of a limited duration. From the 1980s onwards terminology changed gradually into 'migrants' and, since the expansion of the EU and the gradual amelioration and acceptance of membership rights, Italians, Spaniards, Portuguese and Greeks have now become 'Europeans'. The Maastricht Treaty has in fact recognised European citizenship (Article 7), which includes the right of free settlement and access to work for all European citizens as well as the right to participate in local elections.

While the legal and social status of Southern European immigrants has been improved through their nations' integration into the EU (ex-Yugoslavs and Turks being excluded from this category), non-EU immigrants and the former colonial citizens are exposed to increasing exclusion. As a counter to the 'European national', the 'Third Country National' has emerged as an antagonistic category.

Concluding this section, it should be mentioned that the 'old migration' is closely linked, and significantly contributed, to the recovery of the European economies during the early post-war period as well as to the modernisation and prosperity of the Western and Northern European countries, many of which were thereby enabled to develop their welfare state system. Old migration can thus be characterised by three movements: (1) the influx of former colonial subjects to the 'motherland'; (2) the influx of 'ethnic' repatriates to the so-called fatherland; and (3) the recruitment of primarily but not exclusively young and healthy male workers from the Mediterranean countries, followed by their spouses and children.

While the gender balance for the first two movements was often equal from the beginning, or was even dominated by females in the case of certain groups coming from the Caribbean islands, the third category was originally male dominated.[3] However, considerable numbers of women were recruited by some industries (such as the electronics, textiles and food processing industries), in particular in West Germany, where in cities like Berlin 40 per cent of the Turkish workforce in 1973 was female. As well as thousands of single female workers, who left their homes in order to work abroad, many of those who came as spouses also joined the labour market as low-status labour. There are, however, hardly any studies of these female workers from Mediterranean countries, who pioneered migration movements. Perhaps this lack of research and consideration has unintentionally contributed to the stereotype of migration being a male project rather than a family project, or indeed one in which women can be active social agents and agents of control. A 'different' consideration of female migration in the 'new Europe' is thus necessary.

The 'new migration' and the constitution of a 'new Europe'

A 'new Europe' has been emerging in the 1990s as an answer to the global economy and the political reorganisation of the world. There is evidence that, since 1989 and the opening of the borders between East and West, Europe has faced a 'new migration' (Koser and Lutz 1998) which is in some ways the legacy of the old one.

The settlement and stabilisation of immigrant populations originating in post-colonial migration and the old guest worker system is in fact perpetuated through ongoing family reunification and marriage migration. According to the latest SOPEMI report (OECD 1998) immigration to the OECD countries, including the EU, is still predominantly linked to family reunion. This is largely due to the establishment of restrictive entry regulations since the 1970s, preventing any migrant settlement except for family reasons (a right which has been recognised by the last international conference on 'Population and Development' held in Il Cairo in 1994; United Nations 1995). In addition, several West European countries have implemented a new guest worker system. For example, Germany has issued tens of thousands of temporary work permits to Poles, Hungarians and Czechs since 1990, with clear restrictions on rights and duration. In order to avoid the violation of the official 'recruitment stop' released in 1973, the 'recruitment-stop-special regulation' (the so-called *Anwerbestoppausnahmegenehmigung*) insists on strict compliance with rotation-regulation including the rejection of family reunification rights (Rudolph 1996).

There are also aspects which significantly distinguish the new migration from the former. The first is in terms of numbers. Fassmann and Münz (1994) suggest that between 1989 and 1994 four million people migrated into the EU, while, at the same time, the outbreak of war in the former Yugoslavia triggered the flight of an estimated five million refugees (UN-ECE 1995). The extent of this migration is said to outnumber any other migration in Europe since the end of the World War II (Fassmann and Münz 1994; King 1994; Münz 1996). Other features which distinguish the 'new' migration from earlier movements include changing migrant profiles, shifting geographies, new policy responses and changing migration strategies (Koser and Lutz 1998). Owing to lack of space, we will describe these aspects only briefly, and will focus on one which is most relevant in the context of this chapter, namely 'feminisation'.

By 'changing migrant profiles' commentators refer to the increase in the range of migrant 'types', amongst which the most significant are highly skilled workers (from East to West and vice versa), clandestine migrants and asylum seekers (Champion 1994; Rudolph and Hillmann 1998). Shifting geographies are characterised by new developments in which countries of emigration become countries of immigration (as for example Southern Europe), while they can also be both at the same time (Russia and other East European countries) though to a different extent (Wallace *et al.* 1996; Codagnone 1998; Pilkington 1998). New policy responses are increasingly important on political agendas. These responses carry signs of a moral panic in many European societies, where undocumented migrants and asylum seekers are represented as abusing the welfare state, committing crimes and threatening the employment of established citizens (Cornelius *et al.* 1994). Changing migration strategies, partly as a result of the aggressiveness of policy responses, are also seen to be undermining the effect of new restrictions (Koser 1998; Staring 1998).

The feminisation of migration is, finally, receiving more attention and is increasingly visible. Researchers have (1) rejected the assumption that women's migration motivations can be reduced automatically to family reunification, even if they use this mode of entry, and (2) expanded the investigation of migration data to undocumented migrants (Morokvasic 1993; Kofman 1996; Phizacklea 1998). However, even though it acknowledges that the labour market participation rates of foreign women have increased over the last fifteen years, the SOPEMI report (OECD 1998) on the trends of international migration still presents only a single table on this development (see Table 6.1). This can presumably only be explained by the long-lasting gender bias in migration research.

Second, there is an increasing movement of female migrants into the

Table 6.1 Participation and unemployment rates in selected OECD countries by sex, place of birth and nationality, 1995

	Women (%)				Men (%)			
	Born in the country	Born overseas	Foreigners	Nationals	Born in the country	Born overseas	Foreigners	Nationals
Participation rates								
Australia	67.6	58.0	–	–	86.8	82.5	–	–
Austria	63.1	62.5	64.5	62.9	81.4	84.8	86.1	81.3
Belgium	53.2	42.0	38.1	53.2	72.8	71.2	68.9	73.1
Canada	70.9	71.0	–	–	86.5	89.2	–	–
Denmark	74.2	56.4	48.3	74.2	86.8	80.0	78.7	86.7
France	62.2	54.6	46.8	61.8	75.5	79.2	76.3	75.2
Germany	–	–	50.8	62.8	–	–	79.3	80.4
Italy	42.9	51.1	49.8	42.9	73.5	88.6	84.7	73.5
Luxembourg	40.6	51.8	51.2	40.7	72.7	83.2	80.3	74.1
Netherlands	59.7	48.1	39.8	59.4	81.9	70.4	64.1	81.7
Portugal	61.4	47.0	35.1	61.4	80.7	66.4	64.3	80.5
Spain	45.2	52.2	48.6	45.3	74.8	80.4	85.1	74.9
Sweden	80.3	64.0	60.2	80.0	84.6	73.3	69.7	84.5
UK	67.7	58.3	56.1	67.4	85.3	80.0	76.5	85.2
Unemployment rates								
Australia	7.7	10.0	–	–	8.5	9.8	–	–
Austria	4.6	7.4	7.8	4.6	3.6	6.5	6.2	3.7
Belgium	11.2	23.8	31.5	11.0	6.3	16.9	19.8	6.0
Canada	10.0	10.7	–	–	10.2	9.7	–	–
Denmark	8.4	16.7	24.4	8.4	5.3	13.2	16.2	5.4
France	13.5	19.0	14.8	13.6	9.1	16.5	20.2	9.2
Germany	–	–	22.6	9.2	–	–	15.1	6.1
Italy	16.2	27.3	24.3	16.2	9.2	–	23.1	9.2
Luxembourg	7.7	19.8	7.7	8.2	4.8	19.4	6.5	5.3
Netherlands	7.5	19.8	27.0	6.3	4.8	19.4	6.5	5.3
Portugal	7.5	18.5	15.6	7.0	7.7	24.1	20.7	8.1
Spain	30.3	30.1	27.0	30.1	17.9	24.8	23.5	18.0
Sweden	6.5	18.5	15.6	7.0	7.7	24.8	23.5	8.1
UK	6.6	10.9	11.7	6.7	9.8	14.0	16.4	9.8

Source: OECD (1998). – = no data.

(informal) economy of the highly industrialised nation states in Europe. Because of a steadily growing demand for female labour in certain sectors both in and outside the formal economy, such as the service industries, domestic work, the entertainment industries and prostitution (AGISRA 1990; Weinert 1991; Council of Europe 1993; Phizacklea 1998), the presence of female migrants in Europe is growing. Recruiting or trafficking in women from either developing countries or Eastern Europe satisfies the quest for female workers. Before we go into further details of recent studies conducted on female domestic work and prostitution, we wish briefly to present some data on the current state of female immigration in the EU.

Figures on the total number of immigrant women in Europe vary significantly. A Eurostat Report (1993–98) suggests that 14.1 million 'non-nationals' were identified in the statistics of the EU member states as resident on 1 January 1991 (undocumented residents were excluded); of these 6.4 million were females, accounting for 4 per cent of the total female population of the EU. One third of these female 'non-nationals' were citizens of another EU member state. All figures, however, have to be read with caution, because they are based on varying national definitions and registration practice. In addition reliable numbers of undocumented migrants – because of their temporary and clandestine nature – are not available, even though the importance of this phenomenon is in general recognised. Thus, Table 6.1 records only the legally registered participation rates of foreign women in selected EU member states.

For the interpretation of the table it is important to remember that national figures refer to different modes of registration and national definition which in addition have been changing over time. For example, while French statistics, owing to the *ius soli* principle, include all citizens born in France, the German statistics, following the *ius sanguinis* definition, categorise all non-German citizens and their offspring – no matter how long they stayed in the country or whether they were born in the country or not – as *Ausländer* (foreigners). Contrary to the case in the Netherlands, there is no registration of birthplace in Germany. In the Netherlands this registration is seen as an indicator for 'ethnic descent' and policy making on behalf of 'ethnic minorities' is based on these figures.[4]

Another problem concerning the presentation of figures is the fact that so far the majority of the available statistics do not break numbers down into males and females. Although European policy makers are partly aware of the limitations of their registration systems, for example the lack of useful data on the so-called 'unregistered' or 'illegal' immigrants, there is little space for doubts in this debate: migration is a highly ideological subject and so are the ways of dealing with it. While the SOPEMI report (OECD 1998), for example, acknowledges and indeed highly regards the ongoing in-migration into Europe as a means of compensation for population decrease and the ageing of the indigenous population, this phenomenon is at the same time seen as a threat to the population balance and social cohesion by many politicians throughout the EU. No single EU member state has declared itself a 'country of immigration' although there are tremendous national differences and disparities in dealing with migrants and migration. Against this background it becomes obvious that talking about migrant women today means talking about an extraordinarily heterogeneous group, encompassing significant differences in educational, social, cultural and ethnic backgrounds.[5]

These differences are, however, only of little importance for the labour demand-oriented policies of European nation states. It did not matter in the 'old migration' that many of the primarily recruited 'guest workers' in the 1960s were skilled workers or even university students in their home countries, as they were often set to work in areas of uneducated, unhealthy, dangerous and low-status labour.

Throughout migration studies it is almost seen as a 'law of nature' that pioneering migrants have to start from the lowest point of the social ladder and that only through generation change can social mobility be achieved. The fact that through this policy 'brain-drain' is engendered, which also leads to brain-waste, is an important element of the new migration. The unequal terms of trade in the global economy in which some countries put their human resources at the disposal of others, and where the remaining part of the population partly lives on remittances from abroad (as in the Philippines or Malaysia), seems to become the order of the day. We will illustrate this situation in the next section, where we will focus on a specific group among female migrants: the domestic workers.

6.3 Explanations: feminised migration – the case of female domestic workers

Through the analysis of the working and living conditions of female migrants, we will try to illuminate the interconnection between international trends, national changes, local aspects and the private sphere. The asymmetrical interaction between the Western and Southern European women as employers on the one hand, and the female workers coming from Eastern European, African, South American or East Asian countries on the other, also forces us to admit that the conventional gender perspective on inequality has to be revised and shifted to consider the inequalities which have been created *within* gender.

The case of 'Nanny Gate'[6] has brought to public attention a phenomenon which is often 'invisible' but is widespread in Europe too: indigenous European women who enter the (qualified) labour market and hire immigrant women to be domestic workers or live-in maids. They do so in many regions and situations, especially in countries such as Italy, Spain and Greece, where childcare and elder care facilities are lacking, and where the majority of husbands and fathers are still reluctant to share in 'care work'. 'Solving' this problem by employing women (in some cases men) or au-pairs as caretakers has become common. Most countries in Europe have introduced measures to regularise this labour flow through quota systems. In some countries, such as France, where the payment for domestic workers is tax deductible, nearly a million families are registered as employers of domestic workers. There is also evidence, however, of large numbers of undocumented domestic workers (Anderson and Phizacklea 1997; Phizacklea 1998). However, in those areas of Europe where state provision of both children and elder care is widespread and men participate more in care work (as in Scandinavia) the use of migrant domestic workers may be much less common.

It is very difficult to estimate the number of domestic female workers in Europe as the nature of this work is often clandestine or semi-legal, and welfare contributions are paid by only some of the employers. This situation is due to different factors: (1) the one year limitation on work permits which most European countries have installed as part of the immigration defence policy; (2) the relatively high expenses of a legally employed worker; and (3) the fact that current regulations tie a domestic worker to the very employer who originally hired her.

In their report on the situation of migrant domestic workers in Europe, Bridget Anderson and Annie Phizacklea (1997) came to the conclusion that, although there are no sound data on this question, the sector is to be characterised as growing. They deduce as follows:

> In January 1997 Mintel Survey shows that overall Britain will spend 4 billion pounds on domestic work in private households, four times as much as ten years ago. In France the employers' federation now claims 900,000 members. In Germany estimates of the number of employers in 1996 range between 700,000 and 1 million. Domestic workers in Italy accounted for nearly one third of the work permits issued in 1995, while in Spain it is the largest single area of female employment. Despite the lack of public and governmental interest in domestic work in Greece, it has been found to be, both in this study and others, the largest employer of migrant female labour in Athens.
>
> (Anderson and Phizacklea 1997: 1)

In addition, the authors have found that:

> ...a hierarchy of labour operates with domestic workers earning different wages depending partly on their countries of origin, and partly on their skin colour. In general migrants from sub-Saharan Africa and Sri Lanka tend to earn less than others, as do some migrants from Eastern Europe (Albanians in Greece and Ukrainians in Germany).
>
> (ibid.)

Domestic workers operate in a situation where they are highly dependent on the good will of their employers. Living and working conditions are dependent on their legal status, with undocumented workers, naturally, in the most precarious situation. Workers' problems include the demand to be 'on call' for twenty-four hours a day (particularly true for live-in domestics), sexual harassment, violence and psychological abuse (often reported by female employees), the enforcement of additional work for employers' friends and relations, and the demand to undertake all domestic chores, whether or not this is care for the elderly, for children or for animals (Anderson and Phizacklea 1997: 2–3). Very often the children of these domestic workers have been left in the care of other family members in the country of origin, and do not accompany their mothers in migration. Maltreated or sexually abused workers are forced to find a new employer at the expense of their legal employment permit. The highly personalised relationship between the worker and the employer is the source of many conflicts.

In Italy, Spain and Greece, and to some extent Great Britain and the Netherlands, the Philippines provide the main group of live-in maids (the Philippine self organisation talks of a total of approximately 500,000 Philippinas) (Lutz 2000). While Italy and Spain often recruit from the territories of their former colonies (Campani 1993) or from Catholic countries and missions (in both Africa and Asia, but also in Poland; Andall 1998), countries like Germany and Austria profit greatly from the proximity of Eastern Europe, with Polish, Hungarian, Czech and Slovakian women functioning as the available reservoir of domestic workers, many of whom commute (Morokvasic 1991, 1993; Rerrich 1996).

Annie Phizacklea stresses that this development de-masks the myth of the new 'spousal egalitarianism':

> The hiring of a full-time domestic worker means that patriarchal household and work structures can go unquestioned, women pursuing a career and a family need not 'rock the boat' and any guilt over exploitation is assuaged by the knowledge that a less fortunate woman is being provided with work. Thus racialised and class privileges are preserved as well as patriarchal structures and privileges.
>
> (Phizacklea 1998: 34)

Among the many issues for feminist consideration arising from this case are the following:

1   As a consequence of changing labour market profiles and changing family structures, the debate on the meaning of 'public' and 'private' has to take into consideration differences within gender: the very place that means 'home' for the female employer means work, social isolation and strangeness to the worker. Yet it is work which guarantees salaries on which the workers' families are dependent. Seen from this perspective, the public–private divide is as much an ethnic and class phenomenon as it is gendered.

2   Ageing has become a major concern, which is shared not only by

demographers but also by policy makers all over Europe. Feminists are interested in this issue because it turns out that older women are more likely to be living alone: in 1996 only 18 per cent were cared for by spouses, compared with 53 per cent of men who were cared for by their wives ('European Union Report' quoted in Anderson and Phizacklea 1997: 5–6). Elderly women are more likely to be in need of (professional) care than older men. This gap between need and supply of care is often solved by the employment of domestic workers. Ageing and care are thus in more than one sense a gendered issue.

3   The new middle-class life style leads to more domestic work: for example some clothes using natural fibres need to be washed by hand using ecological products, and this requires as much work as formerly (Gregson and Lowe 1994).

4   Many domestic workers who have higher education, and who have even attended university, work in Western European households (as is often the case with East European women). While these women help their Western employers to pursue a career, their own education is devalued and wasted (Friese 1996).

In the light of these issues, in the next section we will reconsider gender contract theory and the issue of the 'feminisation' of migration in relation to the present debate on citizenship in Europe and cosmopolitan democracy (Held *et al.* 1999).

6.4 Afterword: multiculturalism, globalisation and cosmopolitanism: towards a negotiated citizenship

In section 6.1 we stressed the theoretical limits of the gender contract approach in considering the issue of migration. In sections 6.2 and 6.3 we examined the case study of migrant women, and by so doing demonstrated both the socio-political limits of gender contract theory and the traditional concept of citizenship. We argued that the gender contract approach cannot be simply applied to migrants in general and female migrants in particular. Following on from these considerations, in this last section we will link theoretical arguments and empirical situations in considering the future of European citizenship as a negotiated and dynamic process among people having different cultures and nationalities.

We have employed female migration as a case study in order to show how the link between gender difference (as women) and cultural difference (as foreigners) can lead to new forms of social inequality and political exclusion. Yet the phenomenon of migration (referring here to non-EU citizens) shows two different spatial dimensions of inequality. The first is 'dynamic' and relates to globalisation and the mobility of foreign workers and refugees into different countries. The second is 'static' and refers to the local context of the daily life of foreign citizens who work and live permanently within the borders of a nation state. In both cases non-EU migrants have less power and fewer rights[7] than the native inhabitants because they do not have political rights, that is the right to vote and to be represented. However, 'inequality' refers not only to the lack of political rights, but also to a cultural marginalisation. In the case of migrant women, the two dimensions of political exclusion and cultural diversity, combined with gender difference, can both cause social injustice and perpetuate traditional forms of subjection.

Taking into account all these factors, we have to admit that female migration is a very multifaceted phenomenon, even though it has been 'socially discovered' only recently. Indeed, until the end of the 1980s the involvement of women in international migration was not really considered as publicly relevant by either social researchers or international organisations. There was little gender perspective in the analysis of social issues, and little consideration of the existence of female migrant workers (Apitzsch 1996; Lutz and Huth-Hildebrandt 1998), and in general a lack of knowledge about them. Consequently there was a deficiency in social policies and political intervention. For example, until the 1990s statistics and classification systems on migration were not structured by sex (United Nations 1994). However, starting from the world conference held in Nairobi in 1995, female migration has become a central issue for the advancement of women.[8]

By the millennium, the situation of migrant women has become more nuanced and diversified, although the major problems of equal conditions of opportunities and work for female migrants have not been resolved. Yet the picture of migrant women given by the Nairobi resolution and by some EU directives in the 1980s and early 1990s does not reflect the condition of all female migrants. Indeed, the totalistic image of migrants as uneducated and poor women from developing countries does not correspond to reality.

After the fall of communist regimes in Eastern Europe, the explosion of ethnic conflict and the deportation of populations, a 'forced migration' (Zugic 1999) obliged many women (mostly from Poland, the former Soviet Union and Yugoslavia) to move to EU countries. Many of them have higher degrees, professional skills and university careers (Ercomer 1999; Soros Foundation 1999). Even though they have had initially to accept less qualified jobs, nevertheless many of them decided to start again by attending vocational training courses, obtaining new university qualifications and finding employment in professional work. Yet a majority do not want to remain in the EU forever, but rather want to go back to their native countries and participate in the national reconstruction (UNHCR 1999).

Migrant women can thus be discriminated against or underestimated (in relation to their professional qualifications and skills), but they cannot be reduced to 'passive' subjects. They are indeed active both in their communities, in their 'new' civil societies, and at work. Moreover, migrant women often use the networks of extended families, who migrated to different parts of the world, or continue to live in their own countries, for developing the exchange of products, materials, and so on. This constitution of new forms of entrepreneurship and cooperation thus shows the interdependence of agency and creativity. In some cases these companies are formed by different groups and generations of female migrants coming from different countries and with different experiences and education.

Cooperation is often based on collaboration between the 'old' political migrants (most of whom were escapees from dictatorships in the 1970s), the 'new' refugees (who left their countries because of ethnic cleansing and civil war) and the economic migrants (who decided to come to EU countries to escape poverty, even hunger, or simply to improve their quality of life).[9] But in many cases the 'community of origin' to which the migrant women refer is symbolically 'recreated' (for example in the use of 'traditional' costumes) in relation to the commercial interests of the host society and to the new biographical experiences of the migrant women themselves (Calloni 1999).

New socio-economic factors, such as the weakening of previous forms of the welfare state and the crisis of industrial production in Europe, have thus complicated the issue of migration. Yet each nation state reacts differently to the economic crisis and to the new migration, depending on its history and constitutional background. This means that the EU does not yet have a common way to approach socio-political issues. How can the EU overcome the limits of the nation state, finding common strategies? Can the European Union be successful in this aim, when financial globalisation overcomes the borders of the nation state and the geo-political position of some countries makes their borders more 'problematic' than in the past? (as for example in the case of Italy, where hundreds of migrants, refugees and deportees arrive daily through the Mediterranean coasts from Eastern Europe, Africa and Asia). How could European citizenship be constituted given this change in frontiers, borders and boundaries?

To answer this question we have to stress that European citizenship cannot be based on the idea of an assumed homogeneous political community having common origins. Europe cannot be considered either a 'homogeneous neo-nation state' or a country threatened by the invasion of foreigners considered as 'enemies', criminal or deviant (Palidda 1996; Dal Lago 1999). These stereotypes have to be deconstructed (Zincone 1998). The traditional approach to citizenship as based on a common origin has to be challenged because of the interlinked perspective between the 'indigenous populations' and the 'foreigners'.

Indeed the traditional idea of citizenship refers to the constitution of the modern nation state and is based on the recognition of a set of equal rights for individuals having the same national belonging. Citizenship was grounded on the principle of the '*ius sanguinis*' (blood) and/or '*ius soli*' (territory). The 'others' were 'excluded', although they had civil rights as human beings and socio-economic rights as workers. Citizenship (Marshall 1964; Barbalet 1989) was thus related to the struggle of different human groups, who fought first for the recognition of their political rights and later for the achievement of their socio-economic rights in the construction of the welfare state. In the case of migrants, social inclusion (the right to benefits and insurance) is combined with political exclusion (the impossibility of having the right to a representative citizenship). Therefore, civil society is not identical in number and composition to the political community and its representation in parliament. Moreover, the 'last generation of rights' – the cultural rights – differs from the previous tradition of political, economic and social rights. This concerns the protection of specific traditions against forced assimilation and defends the rights of minorities on the basis of the principle of self-determination.

Migration has therefore to be set within the interconnection between four different generations of rights: civic, political, socio-economic and cultural. Yet all these kinds of rights are linked by the normative assumption that people (both as individuals and as members of communities) are born free and equal in dignity and liberty. Migrants are thus acknowledged and in some cases 'protected' both as individuals under human rights (Soysal 1994) and as a member of foreigner communities and ethnic minorities who have to be culturally respected. However, we think that these different theoretical traditions and historical dimensions are not incompatible. Indeed, they could form a basis for a new idea of 'social, political and cultural contract' as long as interested parties and subjects (natives as well as foreigners) understand their political and cultural belonging as flexible, multiple and continuously in change. It means that citizenship has not to be understood as an immutable and ontologically fixed characteristic. Therefore EU citizenship has not to be referred to a strictly defined political status, but has to concern stratified 'circles of belonging' and the acceptance of 'multiple cultural/political identities'. This will also imply the transformation of 'national identities' because many of the EU countries do not yet recognise themselves as 'multicultural' countries. Gender contract will also be reframed within a new dimension of citizenship, where the interests of the new society do not clash with the traditions of the native countries and gender relations could be fairer. The political idea of 'borders, boundaries and contracts' will be replaced by a concept of citizenship as a continuous and mobile process of negotiation and struggle for claims of validity in reinforcing democratic societies. Within this framework the perspective of a 'cosmopolitan citizen' could be conceptualised. As David Held and colleagues put it, he/she is:

> ...a person capable of mediating between national traditions, communities of fate and alternative forms of life. Citizenship in a democratic polity of the future, it is argued, is likely to involve a mediating role: a role which encompasses dialogue with the traditions and discourses of others with the aim of exchanging the horizons of one's own framework of meaning, and increasing the scope of mutual understanding.
>
> (Held *et al.* 1999: 449)

A 'differentiated universalism' (Lister 1997: 29), which implies the application of human rights, the 'recognition' of diversity and the struggle against discrimination of excluded or marginalised groups and individuals, is aimed at reinforcing human agency and autonomy starting with the outsiders. The development of human capabilities (Nussbaum and Sen 1993; Nussbaum and Glover 1995) and the perspective of social justice (Commission on Social Justice 1994) have to start at the basis of a new politics of participation, representation and presence (Phillips 1996). Justice not only means fair distribution of resources, benefits and opportunities, but also implies the possibility of avoiding humiliation (Margalit 1996).

The modern nation state is coming to an end and the welfare state is in crisis. The European Union must not repeat the limits of the previous cultural–political form of the nation state. Citizenship is not an ontological characteristic based on blood. It is a dynamic form of belonging and a negotiating relationship (Stasilius and Bakan Abigail 1997) among human beings having rights, duties, and different cultures. Taking into account all these aspects, citizenship could be reconceptualised as a differentiated and multidimensional contract, which can be permanent for foreign individuals who live stably in a territory and temporary for people who commute between the EU and their own countries of origin. After all, this solution is experienced by many migrant women, who continue to maintain their families and children in their countries of origin, even though they work temporarily in the EU.

We are conscious that the tension between politics (national boundaries) and morality (cosmopolitan perspective) still remains. Yet a legitimate democracy has to find a fair balance between insiders and outsiders (Phillips 1999). Democracy implies always the perspective of inclusive rights (Bobbio 1996), who is different or excluded, as the case of gender and migration has underlined. We need new and common roles for increasing forms of trans-border cooperation. The European Union can play a fundamental role in renewing democracy and in the struggle against social inequalities and gender discrimination. National identity can only refer to multicultural and multinational societies and the existence of differentiated political communities, which overlap and are permanently in change. The presence of the 'others', the development of self-regulating associations at both the local and global level, and the increasing importance of international public spheres oblige us to look in the direction of a 'cosmopolitan and negotiated citizenship'.

Notes

1   The Schengen Treaty was first signed in 1985 by France, Germany and the Benelux countries. It aims to initiate common visa policies throughout the Schengen territory and control entry and movement of non-EU citizens, including asylum seekers, through a common electronic database system. In addition to the five original states, the treaty has been signed by Spain, Italy, Greece and Austria but it has not yet been implemented in all of these countries.

2 France also recruited from Italy, Spain, Portugal and the North African Maghreb countries, but the terminology used was slightly different.

3 'Asian' immigration to Britain, from India and Pakistan, was also originally heavily dominated by younger males.

4 The policy for ethnic minorities focuses mainly on four groups: colonial immigrants from the Caribbean (but not from the former Dutch Indies), labour migrants from the Mediterranean region, people living in caravans (among them gypsies), and refugees.

5 For a detailed analysis of the commonalities in the access regulations for immigrant women in the EU see Lutz 1997.

6 'Nanny Gate', in spring 1994, was the first public and political scandal of Bill Clinton's presidency and government. Clinton had appointed Zoe Baird as attorney general, but she had to turn the appointment down when investigations proved that Baird had employed an undocumented Peruvian couple as domestic workers without paying their income and social security taxation.

7 This is even though several conventions on 'equality of opportunity and treatment' have been signed since the 1970s, for example the 'European Convention on Social Security' (1972) and the 'ILO Migrant Workers Convention' (1975). The last convention aims at ensuring that all persons resident in the territory of a contracting state – including nationals of other contracting parties, refugees, and stateless persons – enjoy equality of treatment with nationals as regards the benefits available to them under social security schemes.

8 'The decade has witnessed the increasing involvement of women in all forms of migration, including rural–rural, rural–urban, and international movements of a temporary, seasonal or permanent nature. In addition to their lack of adequate education, skills, and resources, migrant women may also face severe adjustment problems due to differences of religion, language, nationality, and socialisation as well as separation from their original families. ... It should be given special attention by the Governments of host countries, particularly with respect to protection and maintenance of family unity, employment opportunities, and equal pay, equal conditions of work, health care, benefits to be provided in accordance with the existing social security rights in the host country, and racial and other forms of discrimination' (quoted in United Nations 1994: 300–301).

9 See for instance the experience of the 'Cooperativa Proficua' (at the 'Lega Italiana per i Diritti e la Liberazione dei Popoli') in Milan.

References

AGISRA 1990. *Frauenhandel und Prostitution – eine Bestandaufnahme*. Beck, München.

Andall, J. 1998. Catholic and state constructions of domestic workers: the case of Cape Verdean women in Rome in the 1970s. In Koser, K. and Lutz, H. (eds) *The New Migration in Europe: Social Constructions and Social Realities*, pp. 124–142. Macmillan, London.

Anderson, B. and Phizacklea, A. (eds) 1997. *Migrant Domestic Workers: a European Perspective*. Report for the Equal Opportunity Unit, DGV. Commission of the European Communities, Brussels.

Apitzsch, U. 1996. Frauen in der Migration. In Helfrich, H. and Gügel, J. (eds) *Frauenleben im Wohlfahrtsstaat: Zur Situation weiblicher Existenzbedingungen*, pp. 66–91. Daedalus, Münster.

Archer, M.S. 1996. *Culture and Agency: the Place of Culture in Social Theory*. Cambridge University Press, Cambridge.

Bader, V. (ed.) 1997. *Citizenship and Exclusion*. Macmillan, Basingstoke.

Balibar, E. 1990. The nation: form, history and ideology. *Feminist Review*, 13, 3, 329–361.

Barbalet, J.M. 1989. *Citizenship*. University of Minnesota, Minneapolis.

Benhabib, S. (ed.) 1996. *Democracy and Difference: Contesting the Boundaries of the Political*. Princeton University Press, Princeton.

Benhabib, S., Butler, J., Cornell, D. and Fraser, N. (eds) 1996. *Feminist Contentions: a Philosophical Exchange*. Routledge, New York.

Bhabha, J. and Shutter, S. 1994. *Women's Movement: Women under Immigration, Nationality and Refugee Law*. Trentham Books, Stoke-on-Trent.

Bobbio, N. 1996. *Left and Right: the Significance of a Political Distinction*. Polity Press, Cambridge.

Brah, A. 1996. *Cartographies of Diaspora: Contesting Identities*. Routledge, New York.

Calloni, M. 1999. Das Öffentliche und das Private: Migration/Geschlecht/Biographie und 'Beschäftigungspolitik'. In Calloni, M., Dausien, B. and Friese, M. (eds) *Migration, Biographie, Geschlecht*. Universität Bremen Verlag, Bremen.

Campani, G. 1993. Immigration and racism in Southern Europe: the Italian case. *Ethnic and Racial Studies*, 16, 3, 507–535.

Champion, A.G. 1994. International migration and demographic change in the developed world. *Urban Studies*, 31, 4–5, 653–677.

Codagnone, C. 1998. The new migration in Russia in the 1990s. In Koser, K. and Lutz, H. (eds) *The New Migration in Europe: Social Constructions and Social Realities*, pp. 39–59. Macmillan, London.

Commission on Social Justice (ed.) 1994. *Social Justice: Strategies for National Renewal*. Vintage, London.

Cornelius, W.A., Martin, P. and Hollifield, L. (eds) 1994. *Controlling Immigration: a Global Perspective*. Stanford University Press, Stanford.

Cottar, A. and Willems, W. 1984. *Indische Nederlanders: Een Onderzoek naar Beeldvorming*. Moesson, Den Haag.

Council of Europe 1993. *The Council of Europe's Work on Violence against Women*. Council of Europe, Strasbourg.

Dal Lago, A. 1999. *Non-persone: L'esclusione dei Migranti in una Società Globale*. Feltrinelli, Milano.

Das Argument 1998. Special issue on 'Grenzen', 40 (1–2).

Duncan, S. 1995. Theorizing European gender systems. *Journal of European Social Policy*, 5, 4, 263–284.

Ercomer 1999. *Highly Skilled Intellectual Immigrants of some Eastern European Countries in Western Countries: a Project*. http://www.ercomer.org/research/zz.html

Esping-Andersen, G. 1990. *Three Worlds of Welfare Capitalism*. Polity Press, Cambridge.

Eurostat 1993–98. *Population and Social Conditions: Female Population by Citizenship in the European Community*. European Community, Luxembourg.

Fassmann, H. and Münz, R. 1994. *European Migration in the late Twentieth Century*. Edward Elgar, Aldershot.

Fraser, N. 1999. *Social justice in the age of identity politics: redistribution, recognition, and participation*. Unpublished paper.

Friese, M. 1996. Arbeit im Privathaushalt: die Rückseite der Individualisierung. In Scholz, H. (ed.) *Aufbrüche, Brüche, Ausbrüche in Ost und West. Nation – Kultur – Geschlechternverhältnisse*. Berlin.

Gregson, N. and Lowe, M. 1994. *Servicing the Middle Classes: Class, Gender and Waged Domestic Labour in Contemporary Britain*. Routledge, London.

168   *Gender divisions of power*

Gutmann, A. and Thompson, D. 1996. *Democracy and Disagreement*. Harvard University Press, Cambridge.

Harris, C. 1995. *Post war immigration, the state and the reproduction of racism in Britain*. Paper presented at the Conference on Migration, University of Nijmegen, 14–17 December.

Held, D., McGrew, A., Goldblatt, D. and Perraton, J. 1999. *Global Transformations: Politics, Economics and Culture*. Polity Press, Cambridge.

Hirdman, Y. 1988. Genussystemet – reflexioner kring kvinnors socialaunderordning. *Kvinnovetenskapligt Tidskrift*, 3, 49–63.

Holmes, C. 1988. *John Bull's Island: Immigration and British Society, 1871–1971*. Macmillan, London.

Kay, D. and Miles, R. 1992. *Refugees or Migrant Workers? European Volunteer Workers in Britain 1945–1951*. Routledge, London.

King, M. 1994. Policing refugees and asylum seekers in "Greater Europe": towards a reconceptualisation of control. In Anderson, M. and den Boer, M. (eds) *Policing across National Boundaries*, pp. 69–84. Pinter, London.

Kofman, E. 1996. *Female "birds of passage" a decade later: immigration, gender and class in Europe*. Unpublished paper presented at the Conference on Gender and Global Restructuring, San Diego, CA.

Koser, K. 1998. Out of the frying pan and into the fire: a case study of illegality amongst asylum seekers. In Koser, K. and Lutz, H. (eds) *The New Migration in Europe: Social Constructions and Social Realities*, pp. 185–198. Macmillan, London.

Koser, K. and Lutz, H. (eds) 1998. *The New Migration in Europe: Social Constructions and Social Realities*. Macmillan, London.

Kovalainen, A. 1999. The welfare state, gender system and public sector employment in Finland. In Christiansen, J., Koistinen, P. and Kovalainen, A. (eds) *Working Europe: Reshaping European Employment Systems*, pp. 65–96. Ashgate, Avebury.

Lister, R. 1997. Citizenship: towards a feminist synthesis. *Feminist Review*, 57, 28–48.

Lucasson, J. and Lucasson, L. 1996. Migrations, migration history, old paradigms and new perspectives. In Lucasson, J. and Lucasson, L. (eds) *Migrations, Migration History, Old Paradigms and New Perspectives*, pp. 1–29. Lang, Bern.

Lutz, H. 1997. The limits of European-ness: immigrant women in Fortress Europe. *Feminist Review*, 57, 93–111.

Lutz, H. 1999. Von Grenzen, Pässen und Rechten: Europäische Szenarien. In *L'Homme. Zeitschrift für feministische Geschichtswissenschaft*. Schwerpunkt 'Staatsbürgerschaft', 1, 63–78.

Lutz, H. 2000. *Geschlect, Ethnizität, Professim. Die neue Dienstmädchenfrage im Zeitalter der Globalisierung*. IKS Querformat, Münster.

Lutz, H. and Huth-Hildebrandt, C. 1998. Geschlecht im Migrationsdiskurs. *Das Argument*, 40, 1–2, 159–173.

Lutz, H., Phoenix, A. and Yuval-Davis, N. (eds) 1995. *Crossfires: Nationalism, Racism and Gender in Europe*. Pluto, London.

Margalit, A. 1996. *The Decent Society*. Harvard University Press, Cambridge.

Marshall, T.H. 1964. *Class, Citizenship and Social Development*. Greenwood, Westport.

Miles, R. 1993. *Racism after "Race Relations"*. Routledge, London.

Moch, L. 1992. *Moving Europeans. Migration in Western Europe since 1650*. Indiana University Press, Bloomington.

Morokvasic, M. 1991. Fortress Europe and migrant women. *Feminist Review*, 39, 4, 69–84.

Morokvasic, M. 1993. "In and out" of the labour market: immigrant women in Europe. *New Community*, 19, 3, 459–484.

Münz, R. 1996. A continent of migration: European mass migration in the twentieth century. *New Community*, 19, 3, 287–300.

Nussbaum, M. and Glover, J. (eds) 1995. *Women, Culture, and Development: a Study of Human Capabilities*. Clarendon Press, Oxford.

Nussbaum, M. and Sen, A. (eds) 1993. *The Quality of Life*. Clarendon Press, Oxford.

OECD 1998. *SOPEMI: Trends in International Migration: Continuous Supporting System on Migration*. Annual Report 1998. OECD, Geneva.

Orloff, S.A. 1993. Gender and the social rights of citizenship: the comparative analysis of gender relations and welfare states. *American Sociological Review*, 58, 322–323.

Orloff, S.A. (ed.) 1997. A discussion of gender and welfare regimes. *Social Politics*, 4, 2, 157–160.

Palidda, S. (ed.) 1996. *Délit d'immigration: La construction sociale de la déviance et de la criminalité parmi le immigrés en Europe*. EUR 17472 FR/EN. European Community, Brussels.

Pateman, C. 1988. *The Sexual Contract*. Cambridge University Press, Cambridge.

Pfau-Effinger, B. 1998. Gender cultures and the gender arrangement – a theoretical framework for cross-national gender research. *Innovation*, 11, 2, 147–166.

Phillips, A. 1996. *The Politics of Presence*. Clarendon Press, Oxford.

Phillips, A. 1999. *Which Equalities Matter?* Polity Press, Cambridge.

Phizacklea, A. 1998. Migration and globalisation: a feminist perspective. In Koser, K. and Lutz, H. (eds) *The New Migration in Europe: Social Constructions and Social Realities*, pp. 21–38. Macmillan, London.

Pilkington, H. 1998. Going home? The implications of forced migration for national identity formation in post-Soviet Russia. In Koser, K. and Lutz, H. (eds) *The New Migration in Europe: Social Constructions and Social Realities*, pp. 85–108. Macmillan, London.

Räthzel, N. 1995. Nationalism and gender in West Europe: the German case. In Lutz, H., Phoenix, A. and Yuval-Davis, N. (eds) *Crossfires: Nationalism, Racism and Gender in Europe*, pp. 161–189. Pluto, London.

Rawls, J. 1971. *A Theory of Justice*. Harvard University Press, Cambridge.

Rerrich, M. 1996. Modernizing the patriarchal family in West Germany. *European Journal for Women's Studies*, 3, 27–37.

Rudolph, H. 1996. The new Gastarbeiter system in Germany. *New Community*, 22, 2, 287–300.

Rudolph, H. and Hillmann, F. 1998. The invisible hand needs visible heads: managers, experts and professionals from western countries in Poland. In Koser, K. and Lutz, H. (eds) *The New Migration in Europe: Social Constructions and Social Realities*, pp. 60–84. Macmillan, London.

Rudolph, H. and Hübner, S. 1993. Repatriates – guest workers – immigrants: legacies and challenges for German politics. In Rudolph, H. and Morokvasic, M. (eds) *Bridging States and Markets: International Migration in the Early 1990s*, pp. 265–290. Edition Sigma, Berlin.

Sayad, A. 1991. *L'immigration ou les Paradoxes de L'altérité*. De Boeck-Wesmael, Brussels.

Schuster, J. 1999. *Poortwachters over Immigranten. Het debat over immigratie in het naoorlogse Groot-Britannie en Nederland*. Het Spinhuis, Amsterdam.

Soros Foundation 1999. *Forced Migration Monitor*. http://www.soros.org/fmp2/html/fm_monitor_99toc.html

Soysal, Y.N. 1994. *The Limits of Citizenship: Migrants and Postnational Membership in Europe*. Chicago University Press, Chicago.

Staring, R. 1998. "Scenes from a fake marriage". Notes on the flip-side of embeddedness. In Koser, K. and Lutz, H. (eds) *The New Migration in Europe: Social Constructions and Social Realities*, pp. 224–241. Macmillan, London.

Stasilius, D. and Bakan Abigail, B. 1997. Negotiating citizenship: the case of foreign domestic workers in Canada. *Feminist Review*, 57 (Special issue on 'Citizenship: Pushing the Boundaries'), 112–139.

UN-ECE 1995. Population trends and population-related issues. In *Countries in Transition: the Need of International Assistance*. UN, Population Activities Unit, Geneva.

UNHCR 1999. *UNHCR Report on Resettlement Activities*. http//:www.unhcr.ch/resettle/97report.htm

United Nations 1994. *The Migration of Women: Methodological Issues in the Measurement and Analysis of Internal and International Migration*. United Nations, New York.

United Nations 1995. *Report of the International Conference on Population and Development, Cairo, 5–13 September 1994*. United Nations, New York.

Wallace, C., Chmouliar, O. and Sidorenko, E. 1996. The eastern frontier of western Europe: mobility in the buffer zone. *New Community*, 19, 3, 259–286.

Weinert, P. 1991. *Foreign Female Domestic Workers: Help Wanted!* International Labour Organisation, Geneva.

Williams, F. 1995. Race/ethnicity, gender, and class in welfare states: a framework for comparative analysis. *Social Politics*, 2, 127–159.

Yuval-Davis, N. 1997. *Gender and Nation*. Sage, London.

Zincone, G. 1998. Multiculturalism from above: Italian variations on a European theme. In Bauböck, R. and Rundell, J. (eds) *Blurred Boundaries: Migration, Ethnicity, Citizenship*, pp. 1–43. Ashgate, Aldershot.

Zugic, J. 1999. *Education, Refugees and Migration: the Barriers to Resettlement in former Yugoslavia*. Proposal for Research, Institute of Education, London.

7   Male violence and control

Constructing a comparative European perspective

Carol Hagemann-White

7.1 Issues

Defining a comparative project

Male violence, intertwined with men's control over women, seems endemic in European societies. The effort to raise awareness of this disturbing fact has stood in the way of considering possible spatial variations and the conditions to which these might be attributed. This chapter will look at how and why male violence might differ between countries, regions or subcultural spaces, examine the available European data, and discuss how possible differences might be interpreted.

As yet, no cross-national comparative research on men's violence towards women exists in Europe or elsewhere; furthermore, studies within countries rarely differentiate by region. Nonetheless, introductory overviews commonly cite information from other countries without mention of methods or sources, or refer to numbers without specifying the location (or even the continent) in which they were generated, in support of a statement on the universal nature of the problem. Thus, the increased visibility of men's violence to women has not led to identifying concrete patterns, but rather to diffusing them. Yet, as will be shown, there is a growing basis of careful, representative studies in European countries from which a comparative project could be built, and there are good reasons to presume that regional differences do exist.

Seeking to trace a spatial dimension in the gender inequality structure manifested as male violence and control is uniquely challenging. There is no prior tradition of research to which this undertaking can refer. Unlike other, long documented dimensions of gender inequality, violence towards women was neither recognised as a social problem nor studied empirically until it emerged as a feminist issue of public concern in the 1970s. The success of feminist activism in creating hotlines, shelters and counselling agencies for women made male violence and control visible as a structural element in gender relations. In response, many countries have acted to change legal definitions, procedures and police responses; these reforms have an impact on the reporting and recording of violence. As a result, it is extraordinarily difficult to identify spatial patterns in the underlying phenomena, since the data available in any given state, region or community at any point in time are a product of what might be called the 'visibility triangle' of interacting forces (see Figure 7.1).

More profoundly, any attempt to describe patterns in the potential and actual deployment of violence empirically must come to terms with the protean and subjective nature of violence itself. There is no clear-cut set of actions which define violence. It can exist on a structural, an organisational and an interpersonal level; it is perhaps best described as a strategy that can make use of an almost infinite variety of means of expressing dominance and/or enforcing subordination. As Jalna Hanmer (1996a: 9) notes, 'interlocking behaviours of control and domination can be physical, sexual, emotional and economic'; their impact on women, through which a particular act becomes a violation, is very much dependent on relationship context, personal history and social situation. Thus, findings of incidence or prevalence vary with methodology as well as with women's perception of the possible consequences (negative or positive) of naming violence.

There is no other area of gender inequality of which the reality and oppressiveness is so brutally obvious, while at the same time social facts, patterns and data remain so elusive. Quantitative data on violence are constituted by the theories used to define them and by the social processes that lead to naming events as such. Thus, the 'facts' cannot be presented without delineating how they emerge. In an approximation towards the common approach in this book, it was decided to restrict the discussion to *interpersonal* violence with a clear *gender* dimension, and to focus primarily on 'men's violences towards *known* women' – a useful concept introduced by Jeff Hearn (1996). Interpersonal violence is more accessible to quantitative study than organisational or structural violence. The acts, behaviours and systems of abuse on the part of men who know women personally (whether in a close relationship or by acquaintance) bring dominance and subordination home

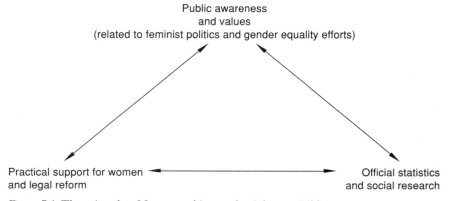

Figure 7.1 The triangle of forces making male violence visible.

to women in a very different way from victimisation – although this is devastating as well – by stranger violence, violation in war, or commercial exploitation.

Theories of violence and links to spatiality

European discussions within research as well as in the policy field largely agree on a gender perspective; that is, they interpret violence against women as symptomatic of a gendered and unequal society in which men dominate or control women. Within this general consensus, several schools of thought can be distinguished. A brief typology of relevant theories can suggest where to look when searching for spatial variations in male violence.

First are theories that aim to explain the commonality of male violence in a wide range of societies by deriving it from some basic cause. Two main subtypes can be distinguished according to preference for a biological or a social departure point. Biosocial and evolutionary explanations take a high level of male violence and aggression (between men and towards women), in conjunction with sexual jealousy and need for control, to be biological or adaptive in origin and thus a given from which civilising strategies must proceed (see Archer 1994; Daly and Wilson 1994). Generalised theories of patriarchy also see a wide range of violent behaviour (rape and battering, but also war and environmental destruction) as integral to men's global oppression of women, and emphasise similar phenomena in widely differing societies (see Dobash and Dobash 1979; Heise 1994). These approaches, although they engage in heated controversy, share a common premise that all societies everywhere show high levels of male violence. They highlight converging data from widely different times and places to prove their respective theoretical points, and thus do not recognise a spatial dimension in violence against women.

Second, theories of individual and family dynamics aim to explain why particular men become rapists, batterers or sexual abusers of girls and/or of boys while others do not. These theories vary greatly in the scope of violent behaviour in their purview, in the distinctions which they draw between violent and non-violent men as well as in their theoretical orientation (see Minssen and Müller 1998). They could be inserted into theories of differing societal structures, welfare states or gender regimes, although it is difficult to define the connection between individual biographies and social conditions. At present, when they enter into social theory, they are usually both over-simplified and over-generalised. For example, Lothar Boehnisch and Rainer Winter (1993) see abuse of women in relationships and sexual violence as completely distinct; in their view, men become batterers due to psychological deprivation in childhood and to social disintegration that confuses them about male norms, while they explain sexual violence as a result of men having suffered sexual abuse in early years. Jørgen Lorentzen and Per Are Løkke (1999) conclude from their experience of therapy with batterers that the absent father, or the father experienced as remote or aggressive, socialises men towards 'hypermasculinity' and violence. In both writings, a possible differentiating factor is generalised to all violent men, and then to men at large. Paul Gilbert (1994) presents a complex biopsychosocial model including psychological, socio-economic and evolutionary explanations that seems more promising for investigating variation, but his focal point remains the individual. He does, however, suggest a number of social group characteristics that may influence the likelihood of using violence as a strategy, including cultural values and scripts for successful males, religion, family patterns of aggression and control, peer group relationship styles and degrees of social and economic inequality. All of these vary spatially and regionally.

Third, sociostructural explanations derive violence against women from gender inequality, sometimes also from class inequality. They hypothesise that men's violence towards women, particularly towards women known to them personally, will be greater where women's economic and social dependence is stronger (Gillioz *et al.* 1997), and, conversely, that progress towards gender equality in the economic or political sphere will reduce violence against women (Gislason 1997). Within the same framework, it is often thought that loss of power, for example when men suffer unemployment or traditional family roles break down, may generate violent attempts to re-establish dominance (see Boehnisch and Winter 1993; Wetzels *et al.* 1995). Thus, the social power explanation can work both ways: one can predict a higher level of male violence under conditions of social disadvantage that weaken men's position as breadwinners, or a lower level of violence when the status of women improves and male power is diminished. Neither claim has been linked explicitly to spatial differences in Europe except in very general terms, and to do so would require a complex theory of resources and negotiations in interpersonal relationships.

Fourth, theories of differential vulnerability hypothesise that damaging past experiences and present circumstances (prior victimisation, social exclusion by ethnicity, handicap, poverty, marginalisation) will increase the probability of becoming a victim (see Gillioz *et al.* 1997; Wetzels 1997; Heiskanen and Piispa 1998). Feminist research has been sceptical of considering such links out of concern for reviving traditions of victim-blaming (see Mullender 1996), while simultaneously emphasising the need to explore differences among women (Hester *et al.* 1996). A resolution of this ambivalence would require an understanding of *situated* vulnerability that is not restricted to the psychological history of the individual. A closer look at social class could suggest how the use of interpersonal violence might be related to gender culture. For example, it could be hypothesised that a gender culture that values a male breadwinner and a mother at home with children (see Pfau-Effinger 1998) also makes well-educated women with real labour market options vulnerable to specifically middle-class types of violence and control, as described for Austria by Cheryl Benard and her colleagues (1991). Alternatively, a link could be made between differential vulnerability and welfare state variations. It seems evident that levels of state benefits and the extent of their eligibility would be directly relevant to women's economic power to protect themselves from, or to leave, abusive relationships.

Finally, cultural theories describe connections between concepts of masculinity and the ability or inclination to use physical force in relationships, or coercion to achieve sexual access (see Lundgren 1995; Hearn 1998). Many authors are inclined to generalise about 'men' or 'masculinity' (Godenzi 1989; Seidler 1991; Jukes 1999), while others try to distinguish and contextualise different masculinities (Connell 1995; Hearn 1996). Like theories of patriarchy, cultural explanations link men's violence to women (both domestic and sexual) with other forms of masculine violence (such as violence to male homosexuals, or ritualised violence in sports). They have the potential to locate specific cultures of masculinity in social and geographical space (see Kandiyoti 1994), but also struggle with the dangers of stereotyping inherent in culturalism. It would seem useful to link a cultural approach to violence and masculinities with theories of differential vulnerability of women, but this has yet to be attempted.

Surveying the range of explanatory theories, two dilemmas emerge:

- the *explanandum* shifts with the theory used to explain it; for example, some theories claim to explain sexual and sexualised violence, others focus on physical injury, others on instrumental aggression;
- the *skandalon* – that men are violent to the very women with whom they have close ties – lends every statement about spatial or social differences the connotation of a moral value judgement on the country, region or subculture said to have more or less violence.

These dilemmas need to be admitted, examined and confronted if research is to move beyond the repetition of the obvious, that all European societies see a great deal of men's violence to known women, and that this violence functions to intimidate and control. Truly useful information about spatial variation or differing patterns will not be possible until some cross-regional and trans-national standards for data collection have been developed that can secure a minimum of comparability.

Visibility: identifying and documenting the problem

The literature on male violence to women has been dominated by publications from the USA and to a lesser degree from Canada and Australia. This chapter is based on empirical material from European countries; the restriction is a first step towards distinguishing what might be regional specificity. Empirical studies from Austria, Denmark, England and Wales, Germany (East and West), Ireland, Iceland, Finland, France, the Netherlands, Norway, Portugal, Scotland, Sweden and Switzerland were accessible; additionally, reports of the Group of Specialists (Council of Europe) and of the Regional Office of the World Health Organisation (WHO) on violence against women yielded some data. North American work is cited on methodological issues.

Much existing research has developed out of documenting women's accounts when seeking help, leaving a violent man or attempting to protect their children from sexual abuse (see Benard and Schlaffer 1978 on Austria; Dobash and Dobash 1979 on Scotland; Hagemann-White *et al*. 1981 and Teubner *et al*. 1983 on West Germany; Hanmer and Saunders 1984 on England; van Stolk and Wouters 1987 on the Netherlands; Hanetseder 1992 on Switzerland). Subsequently, there has been some empirical and theoretical study of the behaviour and motives of violent men, most based on samples available through agencies of social control; the fact that such research is still very scarce in Europe is directly related to the low level of intervention in most countries (but see Godenzi 1989 for Switzerland; Sørensen 1990 for Greenland; Nini *et al*. 1995 for Germany; Hearn 1996 and Jukes 1999 for England).

Owing to patterns of under-reporting and under-recording wherever violence has been a normal aspect of gender relations, police and court statistics are largely useless for comparative analysis, either trans-nationally or over time within countries. Both reporting and recording depend on police procedures, available redress, judicial rules of handling complaints, and the general social climate. Even where (more recently) reporting acts of gender-based violence is encouraged, standard procedure in recording crimes against the person excludes information on the relationship between (alleged) perpetrator and victim, so that stranger violence cannot be disaggregated statistically from men's violence to known women (European Women's Lobby 1999).

The political context of research in this field has been both a strength and a weakness (Hagemann-White 1998). Women's experience of violence reached public awareness in the context of concern about its specific forms and sites: rape, battering, sexual abuse of girls (and boys), marital rape, sexual harassment at work and in public places, objectifying pornography, and sex tourism. Each of these has appeared as a separate and specific 'issue'; data estimating prevalence have been put forward, qualitative studies have described how women become victims, cope and resist.

More recently, research has shown that different forms and sites of violence are interrelated. Data converge to suggest that both physical and sexual abuse of children frequently occur where mothers are battered (see Hester *et al*. 1998). There is empirical evidence that having suffered abuse in childhood increases the probability of re-victimisation, although this has only been confirmed for women who were both sexually and physically abused as children in the home (Wetzels 1997). Liz Kelly (1988) has suggested that re-victimisation may often be due to the later husband's knowledge of the woman's history. She has also shown how stranger violence and threats (such as stalking) can make women more dependent on male partners and thus more vulnerable to domestic violence. Battering cannot be separated from sexual violence: many – probably most – women beaten by their husbands are also raped or forced into unwanted sexual practices (see Hagemann-White *et al.* 1981; Elman and Eduards 1991; Lundgren 1995) as well as experiencing economic deprivation, emotional abuse and deliberate humiliation (see Benard *et al.* 1991). Kelly (1988) introduced the concept of a 'continuum of violence' to describe both the wide range of women's encounters with threat and violence as well as their interlocking impact. Thus, both our empirical and our theoretical knowledge call for an integrated approach which focuses on how gender, power and violence are related.

Methodological quandaries: defining and measuring violence

Cultural values and theories of injurious violence enter, often implicitly, into research methodology. For example, many feminist authors postulate that, as a result of the power structures of gender relations, any physical blow or threat to a woman from a man should be qualified as violence, while this may not apply when women slap or kick men (Dobash *et al.* 1992; for empirical justification see Schwartz 1987). In fact, the consistent research finding of a gender disparity in reporting women's aggression – men are less likely to report having been hit by women than those same women report hitting a man – tends to confirm that men see slaps or punches by women as harmless. Women, on the other hand, may overestimate the potential damage of blows from a man (see Stets and Straus 1990). Emphasising the structural significance of gender has been grounds for focusing exclusively on women as victims and men as agents; it is then easier to include a wide range of physical, psychological, economic and social means of hurting, restricting or gaining compliance.

In contrast, an influential school of family violence follows what might be called the 'domino theory' of hitting. According to this view, physical aggression is always more problematical than verbal, because once hitting is accepted, it can and very likely will escalate into abuse (Straus and Gelles 1990). Authors of this school require that empirical studies define single acts as (to a greater or lesser degree) intrinsically violent and examine gender differences in both actions and resulting degree of injury independently. Many studies using this methodology focus on the 'upper half' of the listing, dividing this, again, into 'less severe' and 'more severe' forms of violence. Implicitly, any form of physical contact is seen as more dangerous than any form of verbal or indirect aggression, restriction or deployment of power.

Both theoretical approaches tend to downplay or disregard the cultural meanings of actions, and to avoid grappling with the more complex issue of what – short of demonstrable physical injury immediately caused by a single act, such as breaking a bone – constitutes a violation of another person's integrity. Although apparently very concrete, they are actually very much abstracted from the process of violence in relationships (Lundgren 1995) and thus are not useful for identifying connections between gender and violence with respect to men's control of women.

Critiques of this abstraction from process, context and patriarchal control have lent credence to definitions based on the subjective experience of being violated or referring to the abuse of an existing structural power imbalance (see Hagemann-White 1992). In the research, women have described a broad range of threatening, restricting, humiliating and terrifying actions by men that imply the possibility of bodily harm and sexual violation, but may not actually include carrying these out. Thus, as Jalna Hanmer (1996a: 8) has written: 'The most general expression of women's definition of violence in relation to individual men is being unable to avoid becoming involved in situations and, once involved, being unable to control the process and outcome'. This perspective leads away from counting isolated acts or incidents, but is difficult to translate into definitions for quantitative study. The question remains how violence should be measured, and under what research conditions respondents are likely to give accurate information about it.

In all countries, many women do not report assaults to statutory agencies. Much violence is trivialised and made to seem 'normal'; both sexual and domestic violence are strongly associated with secrecy, shame and isolation; women may have good reason to fear retribution and further violence if they speak out; they may have no practical access to official bodies, or no faith that they will be believed or treated with respect. Not only do official statistics depend on a 'climate of confidence' (Group of Specialists 1997: 19), but research does so as well. All of the reasons which inhibit reporting to official bodies also weaken surveys trying to estimate the extent of the problem. 'Under-reporting' emerges in research as women's reluctance to name the violence of a present partner or to describe the pain of past violence, and in the failure of many studies to empower them to do so. For women currently in a violent relationship it is often not safe to speak to an interviewer – they disappear in the category of 'refusals' (Gillioz *et al.* 1997). 'Under-recording' is typical for much survey research when the range of events defined as 'violence' is too narrow or too technical to include much of what women experience. As will be seen below, the greatest variation in prevalence data is not cross-national or regional, but between detailed questionnaires or in-depth studies on the one hand and short-form surveys on the other. Thus, research methods must be re-examined continually in the light of what we know about the dynamics of violence in relationships.

By necessity, large-scale survey research uses standardised catalogues of single acts which could be considered violent, often placed in a sequence interpreted as signifying severity. To avoid suggestive questioning, terms such as violence, rape or abuse are avoided and concrete, everyday language is used: hit, kick, bite, throw objects. This raises two major methodological problems:

1   Catalogues reiterate the dominant thinking which segments violence within relationships into unrelated 'incidents', and mirror both the classic approach of agencies of social control and the way in which men

themselves describe their violence to known women. The concept of the incident is a reduction that constructs violence as an exception to the fabric of everyday life (Hearn 1998). Yet the controlling dimension of violence arises precisely through its 'normalisation' (Lundgren 1994).

2   Most everyday acts in a family, home or relationship fall in a middle range whose impact is not evident from the verbal category under which they are usually subsumed. Unequivocal acts of injury such as stabbing with a knife are infrequent; the characterisation as a violent act usually requires some evaluation of context. Thus kicking is a very different action as part of a sibling wrestling match from when applied to someone who has just been knocked to the ground.

Surveys in the general population often find roughly equal numbers of women and men reporting physical acts within the family or household which could be violent, most of which are various types of 'hitting'. Within gender neutral victimisation surveys only a small proportion of the population reports physical aggression or violence by the current partner. On the other hand, qualitative and quantitative studies, especially (but not solely) those linked to shelters, have documented physical and sexual violence far beyond slapping and shoving, often requiring medical care. Against such a backdrop even the smallest threat or slap can create terror.

It may be difficult to access this kind of experience of violence with the methods of survey research, either because battered women are prevented from responding, or because women who have not yet left a threatening situation may not name what is happening to an outsider, or possibly even to themselves. Murray Straus, whose insistence that violence by women is a serious social problem in the US has remained controversial (see Gelles and Loseke 1993), has suggested that survey research and shelter-based studies are not in agreement because they reach different populations. For the US he contrasts the frequency and severity of attacks sustained by women in two studies carried out in shelters – who averaged 65–68 assaults in the previous year – with the results of the 1985 US National Family Violence Survey, where women who had been hit by their husbands sustained an average of six attacks. Straus (1991) concludes that severe wife abuse is so infrequent that even in a large representative sample there are too few cases for statistical analysis. From existing knowledge of the dynamics of isolation and control in wife-battering, this seems an arbitrary assumption. More apposite is his warning that the 'clinical fallacy' – drawing conclusions about the general population from the group of those seeking help – must be seen in balance with the 'representative sample fallacy' – assuming that what does not appear in survey research does not exist.

More recent studies suggest that survey research can capture a larger proportion of more severe violence when attention is given to gender and to sensitive communication. Higher levels of reporting seem to result when surveys specifically address women and distinguish violence by men in relationships from other violence. A Finnish comparison between telephone survey and postal questionnaire results found that the mail survey – with the very high response rate of 70.3 per cent – identified more violence by present or ex-partners than the telephone survey, while the telephone survey located a larger proportion of experiences of violence by strangers (Heiskanen and Piispa 1998). A 1992 criminological survey in Germany combined the traditional standardised interview with a drop-off questionnaire specifically targeting violence by a member of the family or household; the prevalence rate for rape and sexual assault doubled when the results of the written, sealed questionnaire were combined with the reported prevalence in the interview. Also, more severe violence was reported in response to an open screening question than when women responded to a checklist (Wetzels *et al*. 1995). It is possible that women's willingness to report men's violence within relationships is increasing, yet remains highly sensitive to methodology.

Mapping male violence and control

Given the lack of comparable prevalence data, estimated patterns in male violence against women are often political exercises in raising awareness. More pertinent to the concerns of this book, the number of events of violence occurring, even assuming that the data were available, cannot be regarded as an indicator of the level of patriarchal control existing in a region. Men may employ violence to reassert control or in reaction to a sense of losing the power and respect that they 'ought' to have, while at the same time the practice of violence is in itself a form of exerting power. Thus, not only can social power breakdown in gender relations work both ways, violence can also substitute for other forms of power or compensate for losses consequent to social change. Unlike many resources, violence against women is readily available to the vast majority of men, so the appropriate research question may be not why (some) men use it, but 'why not?'; that is, what are the conditions under which men reject or do not even consider this option (Godenzi 1993; Sørensen 1998).

Furthermore, the efficacy of male violence towards women as a structure of (patriarchal) control is largely based on its relative 'invisibility'. This is a multifaceted phenomenon, comprising the exclusion of such violence from the public sphere, the collusion of agencies of the state in normalising it, the various factors leading women to accept blame for the violence exerted against them, constructs of masculinity, femininity and heterosexuality which confound violation with intimacy, and other elements. Certainly, in the past, low levels of reporting have correlated with high levels of acceptance of violence in everyday life. The first step towards challenging male violence as a power structure consists in making it visible. Thus, a rise in the number of rapes and rape attempts reported to the police could signal a decreasing acceptance of sexual violation and possibly even a real decrease in the number of rapes occurring. It is not possible to draw any conclusion about changes in the prevalence of male violence over time from police statistics or from representative surveys, since public awareness and political challenges to the normality of violence are the context within which such data are collected.

Another approach to the spatial dimension of gender is suggested when we consider the implications of challenges to male violence. Their focal point is undermining the power of men's violence to exert control, on the premise that only a woman without resources to counter, or protect herself from, a threat can be controlled by it. Violent men implicitly rely on the socialisation of women to non-violence as well as on the evident readiness of society to punish violent women much more severely than men (Oberlies 1995).

The power of male violence at the interpersonal level is connected to structures that allow it to function as a means of control. Such functioning is disrupted, for example, by shifts in court decisions on women who have killed a violent husband, or after changes in criminal law, when acts formerly outside the purview of intervention become punishable offences. Certainly reports on court-mandated programmes for batterers in the US and Canada suggest that their effectiveness is partly attributable to men experiencing being controlled, humiliated and punished by statutory agencies. For a comparative analysis of the gender dimension of welfare state regimes, it would thus be useful to document changes in state policy and intervention on violence against women. Examples would be legal reforms that improve a woman's option to pursue a complaint of rape (eliminating the 'marital exception', expanding the rape definition, limiting the admissibility of humiliating questions on past sexual activity) or give her better police and court protection from battering. In some cases, official statistics have been restructured to document the extent to which women actually use the protection of the state.

A plausible research design to map indicators for a stronger or weaker structure of male violence and control would be a combination of the following:

- prevalence/incidence surveys with follow-up over time;
- information on changing legal and procedural access to redress, with accompanying statistics;
- data on available resources (shelters, hotlines, intervention centres) for women's 'resisting and coping' (Kelly 1988), accompanied by data on their utilisation.

To date, the combination of all three kinds of data is not available for any country or region.

7.2 Patterns

Prevalence surveys

Until very recently, there has been little effort to co-ordinate quantitative studies on the incidence and prevalence of violence so as to arrive at comparative data. Existing representative studies not only differ in their methodological approach and in the questions asked. They also differ in their research topic (ranging from violence against women to criminal victimisation in general), in the age range and sex of respondents, in the types of violence included, in the locations (in the family or household, by partner, in private, public or workplace), and in the time frame.

Few such studies have published their questionnaires or tables, or made their data available for further analysis. Thus, the results are accessible only in the numbers (often percentages) calculated by the authors for the questions they pursue, which (predictably) differ. Even with allowance for margins of error due to different approaches, there is no way to make the data comparable cross-nationally, nor to break them down regionally. At the same time, data do now exist in a number of countries, and – taken with due caution – the differences are suggestive; yet it is still imperative in each case to place them in their methodological context. Table 7.1 summarising data on adult women's experience of physical violence in the home was possible only through considerable simplification, ignoring variation in the definition of violence, the precise age range in the survey and the time span to which the questions referred. Thus, this overview must be understood as heuristic.

Taken as a first approximation, the Table 7.1 shows lifetime prevalence figures for the adult female population ranging from 8.6 per cent (Ireland) to 30 per cent (Finland). Physical violence by the current partner appears in a range from 1 per cent (Denmark) to 15 per cent (Finland). Where women were asked about recent experience of physical violence in the home (within the past year), the spread of figures was from 3.8 per cent in Portugal (Lourenço et al. 1997: 68) to 10.2 per cent in Germany (Wetzels et al. 1995: 158). It should be noted, however, that some percentages refer to the adult female population as a whole (Denmark, Iceland, Finland, Portugal), thus including many women who no longer have a partner, while others refer to women aged 18–60 (Germany, the Netherlands). Some studies (Finland, Ireland), after giving an overall figure, focus their analysis on percentages of those women who have ever lived in an intimate relationship with a man, and others (Switzerland) include only women currently living in a couple relationship or recently separated. The spread of figures thus reflects not only variation in methods and a possible impact of growing public awareness, but also differing choices on the presentation of figures.

A better sense of the state of our knowledge can emerge when studies are grouped according to similar methodology. Classic crime victimisation surveys are based on the entire adult population, and they use standardised lists of (potentially criminal) acts, specified in a few words or phrases; three of the studies in Table 7.1 followed this procedure. Women and men are asked if they have ever been subjected to these acts, and, if so, by whom. Such studies often use the misleadingly named 'Conflict Tactics Scale' (CTS; Straus and Gelles 1990), because it is well standardised. Not in fact a scale, it is used without reference to previous 'conflict' or to whether the acts in question are 'tactics' (see Römkens 1997). The CTS lists items in a sequence of increasing physical violence, beginning with a general category of hitting. These may be condensed for short surveys.

Table 7.1 Overview of representative prevalence data on physical violence by partner or member of household in European countries

Authors	Year of survey	Sample size	Country	Per cent of adult female population aged c.18–60
Extended questionnaires or in-depth studies				
Römkens	1986	1016	Netherlands	26.3% ever
Wetzels *et al.*	1992	>1600	Germany	18.9% (West) past five years 18.4% (East) past five years
Gillioz *et al.*	1994	1500	Switzerland	6% in past year* 12.6% ever
Lourenco *et al.*	1995	1000	Portugal	6.7% past year 16.6% ever
Women's Aid	1995	679	Ireland	8.6% (10.3%) ever†
Heiskanen and Piispa	1997	4955	Finland	15% (22%) present partner† 30% ever
Multiple data sources				
Schröttle	1989/90		East Germany	15–20%
Short-form surveys				
Christiansen and Koch-Nielsen	1991	1000	Denmark	1% present partner‡ 13% former partner
Government	1995	1500	Iceland	6% present partner‡ 14% former partner

*Women currently living with a partner; combined prevalence for physical and sexual violence ever by husband/partner was 20.7%.
†The figure in parentheses gives percentage for all women who had such a relationship.
‡Percentages for 'general' and 'severe' violence were added, although there was certainly overlap; the figures could be lower if overlap could be eliminated.

The 1991 telephone survey in Denmark, replicated in Iceland in 1996, asked respondents whether they had ever, since the age of 15, experienced one of four categories of actions, beginning with being 'pushed, shaken or mildly slapped' (Christiansen and Koch-Nielsen 1992; Gislason 1997). The agent of violence was classified as present partner, previous partner or 'other'. In both studies, women were much more likely to report violence at the hands of their former partner than by the current one. Although men had encountered substantially more violence than had women, they had considerably less experience of violence by a past or present partner, and were much less likely than women to be subjected to more severe types of violence more than once. Overall, the levels of violence reported in Iceland were higher than those in Denmark.

A crime survey approach with a differentiated checklist based on the CTS was also taken in the 1992 German study; however, several measures were used to increase reporting, and the results are based on a complex data set. Like the short-form surveys in Denmark and Iceland, the German analysis divided violent acts by prior definition into mild violence (slapping and hitting) or severe violence (hitting with an object, kicking, and beyond); unlike the other two, this study specifically referred to a domestic context, and asked about experiences in the previous five years or within the last year. This had the advantage of prompting more vivid recall of even minor incidents, but the data do not reflect lifetime prevalence. Respondents were not asked to specify which member of the household or family was involved; for example, the younger age group may have referred to siblings or parents.

The German study offers a rare example of regional analysis (Wetzels *et al.* 1995). The data were gathered one year after unification. For women aged 16–59 the overall prevalence of domestic violence scarcely varied (18.9 per cent in Western and 18.4 per cent in Eastern Länder), but more severe violence did differ, affecting 6 per cent of women in the West and only 4 per cent in the East. A further indicator of regional differences was the impact of unemployment. Where the head of household was unemployed, 24 per cent of respondents in the West had experienced domestic violence, as opposed to 17.2 per cent of those with an employed breadwinner. No significant difference was evident in the East, although unemployment was dramatically higher there. East Germans were accustomed to a different 'gender contract' than in the West, rejecting the housewife ideal (see Zentrum für interdisziplinäre Frauenforschung 1995; Institut für Praxisorientierte Sozialforschung 1997). Unemployment was a new, collective experience with external causes, and not interpreted as a failure of the man as breadwinner. Regional differences in economic conditions thus need to be seen in the context of cultural meanings.

All crime survey studies face a dilemma with respect to what they should include. The vague general category of hitting covers acts of low impact which many people would not consider violent, as well as blows causing pain, fear and injury; it can refer to a rare quarrel or to repeated battering. To avoid exaggerating the extent of the problem, hitting is usually categorised as mild or general, and analysis is focused on 'severe' violence. This highlights gender differences, but underestimates prevalence. The implicit division into acts that are 'not so bad' and those that are 'real violence' derives from criminal law, where the abstract probability of injury in a fight has shaped distinctions on assault in most legal systems. As the Irish study found, women may not make this distinction in the domestic context: 97 per cent of the women assessed a man's use of actual physical violence of any type, including hitting, as 'extremely bad' (Kelleher *et al.* 1995: 12).

The predominant approach in more recent surveys is to seek information from women only, presenting items appropriate to typical experiences of women. Most include psychological and sexual violence as well as physical assault, and they try to distinguish hurtful and threatening acts from those that women regard as not serious. The surveys in the Netherlands, Ireland,

Switzerland and Portugal were explicitly aimed at violence against women. The earliest representative survey in Europe was carried out in the Netherlands in 1986 by Renée Römkens (1992, 1997). Using in-depth personal interviews, she found that 20.8 per cent of women aged 20–60 had suffered unilateral physical violence in a heterosexual relationship; a further 5.4 per cent described mutual, mild violence. Römkens derived her measure of severity of violence empirically, considering frequency, resulting injury and women's sense of their degree of control. In her sample 11.1 per cent described repeated violence, and for over half of these women it had recurred monthly, weekly or even daily, with increasingly severe injuries.

Subsequent studies have each created their lists of items independently (only Gillioz refers to Römkens' work), some using, but expanding on, the CTS. For example, the Portuguese questionnaire also asks about 'socio-cultural discrimination', distinguishing acts at the workplace, the home and in public places. The telephone survey in Switzerland added items for the use of pressure and force to obtain sexual compliance. The Irish study included threats of physical violence as a distinct category. Low-threshold approaches differed: in Portugal, questions on physical violence begin with 'pulling hair', in Ireland with 'pushing, shoving'.

All three studies arrive at lower overall prevalence figures than in Römkens' in-depth interviews, but they describe a greater variety and extent of violence than the crime survey studies. Offered specific categories for psychological violence by husbands, 40.3 per cent of Swiss women said that they had experienced this at some time (Gillioz *et al*. 1997), as did 28.6 per cent of Portuguese women (Lourenço *et al*. 1997) and 12.5 per cent of Irish women (Kelleher *et al*. 1995). The differences may be related to prompting of recall: the Portuguese items delineate a pattern of obsessive isolation and control, the Irish items emphasise verbal abuse.

Studies focusing on violence against women also seem to elicit more information on injurious violence. In percentages of women who are or have been living with a male partner, the Swiss study finds 12.6 per cent, the Irish study 10.3 per cent reporting physical violence in the past. Most of this seems to resemble 'severe' violence in the crime surveys (around 5 per cent of women in Germany, Denmark and Iceland), since in the Irish group seven out of ten women say that it resulted in actual physical injury.

Most recently, there has been a trend to replicate or adapt the survey instrument developed by Statistics Canada (Johnson 1996), and to follow that model in presenting the survey as a study of women's safety. A representative postal survey by Statistics Finland (Heiskanen and Piispa 1998) arrived at quite high prevalence figures. Two fifths of all Finnish women had experienced 'physical or sexual violence or threats' after their 15th birthday. Violence by the *current* partner was reported by 15 per cent of all women, comprising 22 per cent of those married or cohabiting. Of women who had had at least one prior relationship with a man, fully one half (50 per cent) had experienced violence (this corresponds to slightly less than 14 per cent of the total sample). The violence did not terminate upon separation, and in some cases it even began at that point.

This study highlights the value of relating reports on experienced violence to the subgroup to which they refer; the figures on violence by a past partner come out dramatically higher when taken (correctly) as a percentage of those women who have had a prior relationship. Similar surveys are currently under way in Sweden and France (personal communications from Eva Lundgren and Maryse Jaspard).

Across different surveys, it seems clear that there is much overlap among types of violence, and, in particular, that domestic violence has sexual aspects. In the Swiss survey 11.6 per cent of the women said that a partner had used force to make them submit to sexual relations (Gillioz *et al.* 1997), while Römkens found that, of battered women, 23 per cent were also raped or physically forced to have sex (Römkens 1992). In the German survey of women aged 16 and older, 5.7 per cent had been victimised sexually within the home and most of these rapes were by husbands or cohabiting men. Battering during pregnancy could be a related phenomenon: in Ireland, one third of the women subjected to physical violence had been beaten during pregnancy (Kelleher *et al.* 1995); in the Finnish survey, this was the case for 15 per cent (Heiskanen and Piispa 1998).

Patterns of interpersonal violence in everyday life

A regional approach needs more than total numbers based on checklists, however these may be improved. Meaningful data should give some picture of how and where violence arises and is made use of in the lives of women and men. Who is affected, what strategies of control are employed towards whom, by whom? How does physical violence connect to other forms of dominance and subordination?

The statistical analysis of the Finnish data profiles the vulnerability of specific groups: younger women (aged 18–24), women who are cohabiting rather than being married, and single mothers with children under the age of 7 are twice as likely to have suffered violence from a current partner within the past twelve months (Heiskanen and Piispa 1998). These groups were also most often victimised in prior relationships. A substantial number of women have been subject to violence for many years: 35.6 per cent of those whose current partner had ever been violent say that this first occurred more than ten years ago, and although for two fifths (41 per cent) of these women the violence has ceased over a quarter had been beaten within the past twelve months.

In the Swiss study an 'index of dominance' was constructed including men's decision-making power, control of daily life and demeaning criticism of the wife. This proved the best predictor of violence, also correlating with low levels of communication within the couple and of social interaction outside the home. There was *no* confirmation of the hypothesis that economic or social inequality is related to violence. The woman's actual economic contribution to the family income, her relative level of professional training (labour market potential), and the man's participation in housework had no influence on the presence or absence of violence (Gillioz *et al.* 1997). The Finnish survey also looked at men's use of power and control. The most widespread form of control is the 'demand to know where she goes, with whom, and when she will return'; 39.9 per cent of the men violent within the last year, but also 15.2 per cent of the men of whom no violence is reported, place this restriction on women. Other forms of control used by violent men – but rarely by non-violent men – are name-calling, trying to humiliate, jealousy, and attempting to prevent the woman from seeing her relatives. This confirms the pattern described by Jeff Hearn (1998) that men who use violence also use a number of other strategies of control.

There seems little doubt that, in all European countries and regions, violence against women persists and functions as an anchor of male dominance. At the same time, when prevalence data are sought from both women and men, it appears that men also encounter much interpersonal violence, often more than women; the German data indicate that this is also frequent within the family or household, especially for younger men (aged 16–20), who may come to blows with siblings, parents or other household members. It is difficult to tease out the gender dimension from data collected with differing methods, but theoretical considerations suggest that men's violence to women cannot be discussed in isolation.

The rather schematic information from Denmark and Iceland indicates that nearly all of the very considerable violence that men encounter (around 36 per cent and 45 per cent respectively) occurs not with partners, but with 'others'. In fact, when asked what leads to violence, men attributed it primarily to alcohol, drugs and fights on the street. By comparison, men in West Germany aged 18–60 reported – for a reference period of the previous five years – considerably lower (21 per cent) prevalence of experiences of violence in general, but much higher (18.7 per cent) within the household or family sphere. It is possible that patterns of everyday life may habituate men to giving and receiving blows to a greater or lesser degree, or in a more private or public context.

Peter Wetzels (1997) found that three quarters of the German adult population reported having been physically punished by their parents in childhood; 38.8 per cent had experienced this more than just rarely, 10.6 per cent had been physically abused (defined as blows with a fist or worse) at least occasionally. The proportion of men having grown up with corporal punishment was significantly higher than that of women, and they had been hit more frequently. This could mean that hitting those who are smaller and weaker has been experienced as a normal occurrence in the home, and reflects a value system in which boys are expected to tolerate being struck more than girls. Such norms could foster casual hitting of partners in anger, but may not always mean that physical aggression is used to injure, dominate or control. It is also not clear whether a high level of general male violence, as documented in the data from Iceland, corresponds to a high frequency of battering of wives, although both are apparently higher than in Denmark, and Bo Wagner Sørensen (1998) suggests such a connection for Greenland.

With all caution, it can be hypothesised that local cultures which 'casualise' hitting will influence the *forms* of violence chosen when a strategy of domination is employed. Qualitative studies of 'middle-class battering' point to such a connection. Middle- and upper-class men may use purely physical violence less frequently, but have specific forms of financial cruelty, social sadism (degrading and ridiculing their wives in public) and social destruction at their disposal (Benard *et al.* 1991). Other cultural backgrounds may heighten the probability that men who use violence to control women may be more likely to do so in a highly sexualised way.

Overall, large numbers of men encounter physical violence outside a partnership. Being hit, kicked or attacked appears to be a 'normal' occurrence in the life of a man, but one that is typically situative in nature. Living with a partner is not a site of danger. Women may experience less overt physical violence than men, although Wetzels and his colleagues (1995) emphasise that this is true only if rape is discounted. In their data, women, especially younger women, had suffered a significantly higher proportion of severely violent crime (including rape) by comparison with men. Non-sexual violence seems to be more frequent among men, but women are more likely to experience repeated violence, and they are much more likely to suffer both physical and sexual violence within marriage or cohabitation.

Challenges to male violence and control

Violence as a medium of men controlling women has been a political issue in all European countries. In recent decades, the major challenges to the unobtrusive functioning of violence and control in everyday life have been legal reform, social services and political self-help for women's self-determination and safety; public awareness-raising and education; and lobbying for the legitimacy of alternative forms of living.

Legal reform in all countries has tended to move towards introducing similar changes: improving women's rights within marriage; facilitating non-punitive divorce for women; redefining abuse within marriage as a criminal offence and developing more effective procedural rules; expanding the range of acts punishable as rape; recasting the complainant in cases of sexual violence as a bona fide victim rather than as a suspect; and eliminating the marital exemption from rape law. Yet comparison of the legal situation remains difficult. Rape and sexual assault may be categorised as offences against public morality (Italy, the Netherlands, Norway), against sexual self-determination (Germany), against the human person (France), against sexual liberty (Greece, Spain), against the sexual dignity of women (Switzerland) or as a sexual offence (UK); and there is no unified feminist view on which categorisation best addresses the problem. The UK and Ireland have replaced the use of force or coercion with the criterion of the woman's consent. However, as Sue Lees has shown, this is understood to mean requiring proof that the defendant knew that the woman did not consent (Lees 1996). Lees also shows that official policy on prosecution can coexist with actual refusal to prosecute: while the number of women reporting rape and attempted rape to the police trebled from 1985 to 1993, the rate of attrition – that is, the proportion of cases not prosecuted – rose even more sharply. In many cases, reported rapes are – despite guidelines to the contrary – not recorded as crimes when the police think a conviction unlikely (Gregory and Lees 1999). As Christine Delphy (1996) has shown for France, Spain and the Netherlands, legal reforms expressing greater respect for women's right to give or withhold consent may not signify any greater real challenge to men's violence, since actual practices can remain unchanged. Legal reforms are thus not a reliable indicator for societal limits to men's sexual violence.

Services and increased options for women have included shelters and other services for battered women; counselling and/or free legal advice in case of rape or sexual violence; improved medical procedures and special training for female police officers to respond appropriately to rape and domestic violence victims and collect evidence effectively; crisis intervention centres and hotlines and women's advocacy services for victims of any kind of violence; further education and awareness-raising across all areas of social, legal and medical services; training women for assertiveness and self-defence, and awareness-raising campaigns.

Despite superficial similarities (hotlines, shelters) there are distinct patterns in the development of intervention strategies which suggest differences in how the state is positioned towards this gender power structure. Data to describe patterns are hard to come by: shelters and hotlines have been reluctant to publish statistics of their utilisation, and it is difficult even to map their existence and capacity (but see Egger *et al.* 1995). Yet it is suggestive that new approaches towards addressing domestic violence have differed, emphasising criminal law in Sweden, civil law in Austria and multi-agency community co-operation in the UK and Germany. They are embedded in the history of interaction between that state and the feminist challenges to male violence and control.

Germany presents an example of feminist 'autonomy' gaining substantial public recognition, while remaining distrustful of the state. The first German shelter in West Berlin was funded in 1976 as a model project on a scale probably unique in Europe (sixteen employees, 70–90 beds, day care for children). It was in the hands of an independent association and presented a strong feminist profile based on women's solidarity and self-help (all female staff, residents' self-organisation, staff as a resource), the need for safe women's space in a patriarchal society (address secret, shelter open twenty-four hours to any woman who feels threatened) as well as a programmatic intent to work politically against violence against women. In the following years, shelters were opened throughout Germany, numbering over 400 by 1999, all receiving some public funds. They are only loosely united with little formal structure. In the late 1980s, the need for broader community intervention at the local level came into focus, generating controversy among feminist projects concerned that multi-agency networks could endanger their existence or compromise their principles. Co-operation with the police – seen as a profoundly patriarchal institution – has been viewed with particular scepticism. Nonetheless, feminist shelters are increasingly involved in community initiatives with support from federal, state and municipal governments.

The Austrian shelter movement shared essentially identical feminist principles with that in Germany, but grew more slowly. The first publicly funded feminist project on violence was the shelter in Vienna, opened in 1978. The spread of shelters to the rest of the country was gradual but continuous (Egger *et al.* 1995); relative to the population, Austria today has about half as many shelters as Germany. Despite a lower level of public funding and a lower growth rate, the independent feminist shelters formed a formal umbrella organisation and developed working partnerships with key state agencies. Through their central organisation they took on responsibility for training police on violence against women and were directly involved in drafting a new law, passed in 1997, focused on civil protection orders.

In Sweden, feminist initiatives created the first women's crisis centres in 1979. Although their number increased more rapidly than in Austria, they are less well established; many operate as crisis lines without housing. In 1984 they chose to create a formal umbrella organisation that receives government funds for its work. Swedish shelters differ from those in Germany and Austria in their limited official opening hours. They rely heavily on volunteers, and insist that it is not the task of feminist projects to provide alternative social services or housing. Requests that shelters, in return for public funding, be accessible on evenings and weekends or provide a telephone emergency service – considered constitutive of the feminist shelter idea in Germany and Austria – may in Sweden be interpreted as attempts to exploit women's political work and to delegate a core responsibility of the welfare state (see Eduards 1997).

Efforts to address violence against women on a more structural level in Sweden have turned to criminal law as the instrument of choice. As with the prohibition of physical punishment of children twenty years earlier, the law is understood to articulate a consensus and generate social pressure against reprehensible behaviour. The innovative law of 1998 defining 'gross violation of a woman's integrity' was intended to sanction repeated violence of men towards women within close relationships. However, implementation has encountered substantial obstacles. The shelter movement has been less involved in this process and seems to have low expectations of its practical relevance for women. The criminal law approach in Sweden can be interpreted not as opting for actual prosecution and punishment, but rather as expressing a normative public statement.

These three cases share characteristics missing in many other European countries, in having both strong shelter movements as well as innovative state measures to counteract domestic violence. Yet the differences between them make it clear that the dynamics of challenging men's violence cannot be the same when the relationships between feminist movements and the state differ.

Summary

At present, data on the prevalence, nature and extent of male violence to women do not provide a clear picture. Regional differences are probable, but to discuss them is to indulge in speculation. There are suggestive hints that the use of violence as a strategy of control relates to other patterns of violence in everyday life, such as punishment and abuse of children or violence among men. However, we know little about these either. It seems clear that violence controlling women is a specific phenomenon, even after comparison with men's experience of violence.

With the patterns of violence so indistinct, a plausible approach to comparative analysis is to look for patterns in breaking the link between violence and control, since on the level of social theory, as well as of politics, it is not violence itself so much as its purposes and effects that are of interest. An overall move towards legal reform, strengthening women's rights, can be traced throughout Europe, but comparisons of progress are extremely difficult and would require a detailed, case-by-case study. A fruitful alternative is the comparison of overall strategies of intervention, whose components and their interaction do seem to differ and point to a gender cultural context as well as to different understandings of the role of the welfare state. Contrasting case studies may thus help locate a spatial dimension in how individual male violence functions, or is impeded from functioning, as a structure of patriarchy.

7.3 Explanations

Does progress towards economic and political equality reduce violence against women?

There is a widespread belief that, since men's violence to known women is a matter of power, policies which aim to reduce men's relative power over women will also reduce the prevalence of men's violence. This is at least over-simplified. Direct shifts in the balance of power *within* a relationship clearly do not prevent violence. Studies of the dynamics of wife-battering point out that one of the two great 'danger points' for a woman living with a potentially or overtly violent man is the moment when she acts to assert her independence. Women are more likely to be murdered by their spouses/former cohabitees when they separate or seek divorce than in any other situation.

This suggests an initially higher incidence of male violence when the control function of intimidation and threats begins to break down. Only over the longer term, when gender relations have become restructured in the direction of valuing equality, can the incidence and prevalence of violence be expected to decrease. Until then, acts of violence are symptomatic *both* of a high level of men's direct personal domination of the women personally known to them, *and* of any decrease in the success of such domination strategies.

Social change, when seen solely in terms of economic power, is also ambivalent. Scepticism over the role of economic equality in reducing violence is suggested by two cases for which we have prevalence estimates, Finland and East Germany. One could argue for similarities in their gender arrangements: the lack of a 'bourgeois' cultural period; in Finland a transition from an agrarian culture, in the GDR from a proletarian culture (which was similarly egalitarian), to industrialised regimes which defined women as productive workers and individualised them. Both developed a normative culture of gender equality, and indeed one which ignored gender; in both, gender-separatist women's projects and movements could not easily take root. For Finland, representative data are now available (see section 7.2). In East Germany, no such research was carried out, yet, as Monika Schröttle has shown in a thorough search of sources and indicators, ideological and political constraints on public discussion of interpersonal violence coexisted with violence against women within the home (Schröttle 1999). Considerable gender equality in employment and a proclaimed 'gender contract' granting women economic independence from men did not prevent sexual and domestic violence. For example, in a 1990 representative regional study, 15 per cent of East German women reported physical violence by their current partner, and court data from the 1980s suggest that men's violence was a factor in at least one quarter of divorces (ibid.). Ideological constraints, together with factors such as the heightened value attached to the family as a retreat from pressures of the state, may have made it even more difficult for women to challenge private patriarchal domination underpinned by violence.

An egalitarian gender culture, where women's economic dependence on men is relatively low, may actually inhibit revealing male violence in the home, since couple relationships are presumed to be consensual. Furthermore, Finland and the GDR appear to have little culture of negotiating conflict verbally. The prevalence estimates for sexualised violence in these two countries are among the highest available. With all caution, one might at least conclude that economic independence, participation in production and egalitarian social norms do not, by themselves, reduce male violence as a means of control.

These overtly gender neutral societies doubtless retained a substrate of gender inequality integrated into the organisation of economic, political and private life. Progress towards gender equality in the fullest sense of the term – interpreted to mean 'equal visibility, empowerment and participation of both sexes in all spheres of public and private life' (Council of Europe 1998)

– would, by definition, involve not only the elimination of gender-based systems of abuse and violence, but also work to deconstruct the entitlement claims to masculine domination which seem to drive efforts towards controlling women within relationships. At present, this is a vision rather than a hypothesis for empirical research.

Do 'masculine' cultures maintain a higher level of male violence than 'feminine' cultures?

Cross-cultural social psychology has often described entire cultures as being more or less violent, frequently based on ethnological data from many parts of the world (see Felson and Tedeschi 1993). However, there is no plausible literature on more or less violent cultures within Europe that takes interpersonal behaviour as the point of reference.

Geert Hofstede (1998) has developed an empirically founded concept of masculinity and femininity as a dimension of national cultures. He defines culture as a 'collective programming of the mind', and his cross-national study aims to capture dominant value systems. The dimension of masculinity versus femininity (tough versus tender) was derived by factor analysis from the responses to a values questionnaire on work-related goals, and thus has, as yet, no component concerning personal relationships in the private sphere. The original data come from a survey of employees in national subsidiaries of the IBM corporation; a replication by Michael Hoppe drew on alumni of the Salzburg Seminar, a high-level international study centre in Austria.

In this theory, masculinity 'stands for a society in which men are supposed to be assertive, tough, and focused on material success; women are supposed to be more modest, tender, and concerned with the quality of life. The opposite pole, femininity, stands for a society in which both men and women are supposed to be modest, tender, and concerned with the quality of life' (Hofstede 1998: 6–7). The difference between 'masculine' and 'feminine' cultures mirrors the presence or absence of a certain masculine stereotype as a positive value. At first glance, it also seems to represent a difference in whether the sexes are expected to be different or alike. However, Hofstede finds that, in terms of actual self-perception, women and men tend to describe themselves more similarly in the masculine cultures, both laying claim to the more highly valued 'masculine' characteristics, whereas in feminine cultures gender stereotypes differentiate more strongly between women and men.

Between the original study and the large-scale replication by Hoppe there were interesting shifts in the ranking of some countries such as Germany and France. The most consistent finding is the existence of a cluster of countries characterised as feminine, comprising the Scandinavian countries and the Netherlands. These cultures also share a preference for a low power distance within society. It seems a possibility that in cultures of this group the inclination or decision to use male violence to control women might be less widespread or less well tolerated, although there are no prevalence data supporting this.

The values on masculinity yield a much less clear picture, and the interaction between gender and power distance values may play into this. Austria and Germany show a marked normative disinclination towards power distance, while France, Greece and Italy, also rated as masculine, value power distance and authority in a positive way; Spain and Portugal emerge as feminine cultures that affirm power distance. It seems likely that the masculinity factor also conflates a gender dimension of culture with traditionalism and the persistence of gender division of labour in the home; these may in fact be different dimensions.

There is at present no basis for estimating whether masculinity of the culture as a whole promotes male dominance in the home or male sexual aggression, although this seems plausible from the literature on the masculinity socialisation of violent men. In Hofstede's collection of papers, only one (Van de Vliert 1998) mentions violence at all, and this uses a measure of political violence, while referring to an evolutionary explanation (drawing on parental investment theory) for greater male sexual jealousy in warm climates. This is one of many examples of explaining one type of data with a theory derived from an entirely different type, a confusion all too frequent in discussions of male violence. Perhaps the best conclusion to be drawn from the available material is that more culture-specific measures of masculinity need to be developed (see Best and Williams 1998) before conclusions on national or regional differences are drawn.

What might explain differences in women's vulnerability to male violence and control?

Differential vulnerability could be described and explained on three levels:

1   The differing risk of encountering violence; a discussion of women's vulnerability should also take account of women's emotional and social resources to resist and cope with violations.
2   The degree to which women can be subjected to a continuous pattern of abusive behaviour, such as sexual harassment, pressure to participate in unwanted sexual acts, or battering.
3   The degree to which society enables a woman to challenge the domination of a specific man, and empowers her to lead an assertive life independent of belonging to a heterosexual couple.

These levels do not necessarily correlate.

The *first level* will depend on the *social psychology* of gendered relationships and communities. Poverty, drug addiction or deteriorating social networks are obvious vulnerability factors, but there may be cultural spatial dimensions as well. The connections between battering of wives and child abuse described in Germany and in the UK suggest that women there may be more likely to encounter (or expect) being struck by their husbands. Deniz Kandiyoti (1994) suggests that Mediterranean sex segregated societies have not only defined the public sphere as masculine and the domestic as feminine, but forced boys to make a transition from intense interaction with women in childhood to separation, possibly laying a foundation for sexual violence to maintain the division. When agrarian societies make a rapid transition to industrial life, or in migration to urban regions, women may lose the wider social networks that both constrict and protect them, while men can have a heightened tendency to cast the idealised pure woman as a nostalgic symbol for what has been lost, and to punish women for activity outside the home.

The *second level* of vulnerability could depend on the way in which *gender cultures* define what are a woman's duties and a man's right, but also on the material realities underpinning such cultures. Cultural expectations that women should welcome men's sexual advances as a compliment (while avoiding actual promiscuity with skill or by attaching themselves to a protecting male) make it extremely difficult for them even to put a name to sexualised aggression; as Delphy suggests, this may be true of Southern European gender cultures. Cultural and religious norms that a wife and mother should try to keep the marriage going at whatever cost to herself 'for the sake of the children' will allow little alternative but to put up with a husband's abuse, whether physical, psychological or sexual. In the early years of shelters in the UK, the Netherlands and Germany, women often reported having been refused help with equivalents of the phrase 'you have made your bed', or 'it is the woman who makes the marriage work'. This has changed; van Stolk and Wouters (1987) describe the shift in Dutch women's interpretation of husband's violence as 'from misfortune to injustice'. Where traditional gender norms taught women that having a violent husband was just bad luck that had to be borne, in the new normative framework they can feel deprived of an essential social right, and thus they feel justified in turning to the community for support and redress.

It must be noted, however, that structural vulnerability of all kinds makes women more likely to become victims of long-term abuse, which in turn debilitates their self-confidence and erodes their access to social networks and other resources. Women in migration whose legal right to remain in the country depends on maintaining their marriage, as has been the case in most European countries, have little choice but to submit to domestic violence. Women in a weak labour market position, but also highly educated women whose careers depend on proving themselves successful in a given position, such as doctoral candidates at university, may also see no possible recourse and thus accept sexual harassment over long periods.

On a *third level*, vulnerability defines whether a woman can resist what she feels to be a violation of her well-being and integrity or prevent its repetition. To a significant degree this depends on whether she is – economically and socially – at liberty to reject any particular heterosexual relationship without regard to whether or not a new partner is available. It is here that the gender dimension of the *welfare state* becomes most relevant. Theoretically, equal participation in employment offers women independence from any given man. In actual fact, however, employment is not a protective factor unless women both have earnings equal to those of men and are relieved of the additional expense (material and immaterial) of caring for children, older family members or others in need of home-based care. This is not the case in any European country at present. An analysis of regional variation in women's vulnerability to men's violence and control must, therefore, examine the *combination* of access to employment income and welfare state transfer payments, particularly those available to lone mothers or to women carrying responsibility for care work in the family. Employment alone places most women, during the years in which they have caring responsibilities, in a situation where they may pay a high price for rejecting a male partner. State welfare benefits alone imply for many of these women a life close to poverty.

The analysis of the combinations of benefits and employment is a complex task. Sainsbury (1996) has attempted it for three European countries and the USA, and finds that in the multiple and multilayered systems of welfare states and the complexities of entitlement to benefits the net effects are often paradoxical. It seems probable, however, that benefits based on the principles of citizenship and of the care principle, when combined with the practical possibility of employment for mothers, as is the case in Sweden, offer (at present) the best material foundation for a woman, enabling her to resist and – if she so chooses – leave a man who tries to dominate and control her. Perhaps these advantageous conditions for women's relative economic autonomy, despite gender-based family responsibilities, also make shelters or services for victims seem less urgent and less central to challenging violence against women.

Mothers and wives: why is violence addressed differently in different countries?

Although the early feminist discourse on male violence and control of women was international, the sequence of issues that were presented to a broader public, the priority of demands for action and their relative success have differed from country to country and regionally as well. It seems plausible to assume that such differences relate to gender cultures, but possibly also to differing realities in the presence and use of violence with varying gender arrangements.

In France, as Jalna Hanmer points out, 'the first issue to be taken up, as in the United States, was rape. In Britain and the Netherlands the initial focus was on home-based violence from husbands, cohabitees and boyfriends. The family was conceptualised as a major site of women's oppression...' (Hanmer 1996b: 133). Christine Delphy discusses the French case in terms of lagging behind: 'In matters of social policy and feminist activism, Europe is clearly

cut at least into two halves: feminist projects are far fewer in Southern Europe
– Italy, Greece, Spain and France' (Delphy 1996: 149).[1] Her own choice of
cases centres on sexual violence and abortion: she points out that there has
never been even one rape crisis centre in France (ibid.). Following a
recommendation of the European Commission in 1991, France was the first
country to legislate against sexual harassment, thus underlining the high
profile of sexual violence; but the law has proven of little practical relevance.
In defining the problem as 'abuse of authority to obtain sexual favours', the
law implies that only certain means are sanctioned, while seeking sexual
access belongs to the 'natural' interaction of men with women: 'In France,
gendered behaviour is sexualised, passed as sex, and sex is good' (ibid.: 153).
Feminist activism against men's violence has focused on this very
sexualisation, at the cost of being seen as a threat to normal sexuality and to
the cultural self-image of the French; it has been largely unable to engage
the state in efforts towards change.

In the Northern European countries there seems to be a stronger tradition
of locating the gender relationship in the context of the family, seeing women
as mothers perhaps even more than as part of a heterosexual couple. The
historical roots cannot be discussed here, but it might be noted that the French
Revolution aimed at eliminating intermediaries between the individual and
the state, while the northern countries relied strongly on the family as an
intermediary in preserving and policing the social order. Mary Ann Glendon
(1989: 289) comments that the French approach in family law 'is distinguished
by a relatively greater solicitude for the status of legal marriage', whereas
the parent–child relationship was radically privatised in the Civil Code of
1804 (unrestricted paternal power) and not reformed until 1970, when a
notion of parental duties was introduced (ibid.). Germany and the Nordic
countries have a longer tradition of regulating parental rights and
responsibilities and setting explicit norms of parenting (ranging from the
Prussian General Code of 1794, which regulated issues such as the duration
of breast feeding, over which the father had authority, to the Swedish
prohibition of physical punishment in 1979). Although family law in all these
countries has shifted its focus to individuals, the differences in legal tradition
may indicate differences in the interest of the *polis* in the gender relationship:
has the woman been perceived – for the purposes of social policy – primarily
as part of a couple, while children are property of the man, or has she been
seen primarily as a mother, who (until recently), while deserving protection,
needed to be subjected to benevolent male control?

It seems plausible that a tradition of locating women in the family and
valuing them primarily as mothers, rather than as wives or lovers, contributed
to making battering in the home a particularly scandalous issue. In these
countries, feminist outrage could be framed as a challenge to the family as
such, describing it as a site of violence and domination. In the early days of
the movement, this fed into the struggle for liberation and supported
separatist tendencies. Wife-battering as an issue was thus ideally suited to

mobilise women and to translate abstract political goals into concrete projects. At the same time, precisely because these states had claimed to value, protect and support mothers, they found it relatively easy to offer funding to services, saving marriages being less important than promoting healthy families and competent mothers. Thus, Germany, Austria and the Netherlands, which share an orientation towards the mother as the primary carer and guarantee of child welfare, remain committed to maintaining a network of shelters where battered women can seek refuge and receive counselling and support.

Some Scandinavian countries have moved from mother-centred welfare state policies (up to the 1950s) to state-supplied childcare and increasingly energetic measures to engage fathers in the actual care of children. As a result, equality policy comes into direct collision with measures supporting mothers who try to leave violent men. As a case in point, in 1998 Sweden introduced, on the one hand, an energetic law package addressing domestic violence, and at the same time a law encouraging the courts to grant joint custody after divorce even against the expressed will of one of the parents. The new law created the offence of 'sabotage of child contact' as a legal reason for withdrawing custody. This could mean that a mother who does not actively support child contact with a violent husband can lose her right even to joint custody.

The patterns of activism and policy (and their interrelationships) are not simple. In Sweden, feminists found it very difficult to place sexual violence on the public agenda. It was a government commission which, in 1976, gave the first impetus to public debate on violence against women, as a consequence of its recommendation that – in the spirit of modern sexual liberation – rape should be considered a 'minor crime', the penalties on sexual assault be reduced and penalties on incest be abolished altogether. But although women reacted with a rare display of public outrage, activist initiatives – addressing women's oppression broadly – were not able to maintain a visible profile on sexual violence, but gradually became accepted as projects for battered women, evidently a less controversial goal. Sweden's first rape clinic, established in Stockholm in 1977, closed after five years, and the therapists who had worked there published a report with the expressed aim of promoting 'understanding rape from the rapist's perspective' (Elman 1996: 71–76).

In the early 1990s, feminist efforts to bring sexual violence into public debate were renewed, and much work was put into educating professionals and the public to an awareness that this was a real and serious problem. The impact of this work resulted in the establishment of a National Centre for Raped and Battered Women in 1993, funded by the Swedish government (Posse and Heimer 1999). The centre now provides emergency and medical services on a twenty-four-hour basis as well as further education for the health care community, social services and the justice system.

The tenor of current government reports is that the prevalence of rape is a challenge that has been met. As in France, the self-image of the country as a place where heterosexual relationships are relaxed and pleasurable seems to stand in the way of pursuing either public debate or policy response to sexual violence. But in Sweden, concern for the welfare of children finally pushed the state into a more active role of intervention.

State patriarchy or women's autonomy? Comparing intervention strategies in Sweden, Austria and Germany

Across the various theoretical classifications of welfare state and gender regimes, Sweden, and Austria with Germany, are commonly considered illustrative of contrasting categories. Austria and Germany have been classified as conservative compared with Sweden's social democratic welfare state regime, as strong breadwinner states compared with Sweden's weak, as private patriarchy as opposed to Sweden's public form, or as 'housewife contract' states to Sweden's 'equality contract' (for a summary see Duncan 1998). Germany, although in many respects close to Austria, may be seen to have some commonalities with Sweden in its corporatist tradition, and is characterised by both an east–west and a north–south divide (Sackmann 1998). Yet these three countries also stand out in Europe with respect to their current active and innovative strategies of the state towards violence against wives. This raises the question of how gender regimes may affect state involvement in a struggle to reduce male violence and control.

In all three countries, the concept of the welfare state has been expanded to include:

- the responsibility to protect women who suffer violence, especially violence from known men;
- the redefinition of violence against women as a public, not a private, concern, and its prevention and elimination as a task of the *polis*;
- the normative expectation that interpersonal (gendered) violence as a means of control be effectively de-legitimised under threat of sanctions.

It is suggested that the different ways of challenging violence also reflect different definitions of the woman as victim, the gender relationship and the relationship between the state and civil society.

In all three countries, although rape and sexual violence were mobilising themes of great impact in the early feminist movement, it was the problem of men's battering their wives and partners that defined the relationship of the movement to the state, because it was here that state involvement in protecting or supporting victims was successfully claimed. In both *Germany* and *Austria*, shelters define themselves as places of refuge in crisis situations; they see it as essential to be able to take in women and children at any time of the day or night (Egger *et al.* 1995). Women often arrive at a shelter with nothing but what they are wearing, are taken in regardless of ability to pay, and are offered the opportunity to consider their alternatives in peace. In theory women should be allowed to stay in a shelter as long as they need to;

in practice scarce resources have led to time limits between six months and one year. The staff provide individual counselling, and protective and supportive accompaniment when the women go home to collect their possessions, to the police, or to various agencies. Great importance is attached to 'group work', which refers both to egalitarian team structure in the staff and weekly meetings of the residents. These characteristics of shelters are directly linked to theoretical foundations of political struggle (comprising three pillars of empowerment of women, working against male violence, and working to change the unequal power of men and women in society) and feminist social work.

Founding shelters in *Germany* involved a strategic alliance between the feminist groups or non-profit associations and the state, resulting in rapid public visibility of the problem of domestic violence. In this alliance, the state was defined as patriarchal and its agencies as unable or unwilling to support women: its role was to supply funding to the groups that laid claim to competence. Community co-operation projects encounter scepticism from shelters because of the mere participation of state agencies; they proceed on principles of voluntary participation and consensus, protecting the interests of the 'weak' projects against the 'strong' established agencies.

The *Austrian* shelters, while retaining the theory of the state as a vehicle of patriarchy, have built a different kind of alliance, leading to their direct involvement in police reform and legislative innovation. The distinguishing feature of the new Austrian approach was the decision to use civil rather than criminal law: the focus is not upon sanctions for men, but upon protecting women. The most striking element of this new law is the introduction of a 'go-order' directly issued by the police when they are called to a situation involving domestic violence. At the scene of an assault, the individual posing a threat can be expelled from the home and its immediate vicinity for seven days, without regard to the relationship to the victim or to ownership of the house. During this time, the woman can apply for an extension of the ban on the male batterer returning to the domestic area. The law also provided for establishing and certifying 'intervention centres' that receive the name of the woman from the police and seek contact with her to offer support.

Based, as it was, on almost a decade of co-operation and training with the police, the law had an immediate impact. Within the first year after its introduction, nearly 2000 men were evicted from their homes and barred from returning, and close to 600 women requested court injunctions giving them further protection. Amazingly, the ban on returning seems to be obeyed in the great majority of cases, although the procedure is not effective with extremely violent men (Logar 1998). Possibly a conservative gender culture and/or an authoritarian mentality among batterers inclines them to submit to police orders. It seems clear that the Austrian shelter movement is strongly identified with the new approach, while at the same time – some observers see this as a paradox – pursuing a policy of permanent institutionalisation of shelters based on a standard number of beds per 10,000 population. The overall strategy might be characterised as securing a maximum of benevolent protection for women in a variety of situations.

The *Swedish* shelter concept constructs the situation of the battered woman differently from that in Austrian or German feminist shelters. The woman is assumed to be employed, to have functioning social networks from which she can receive short-term temporary assistance, and to have both the wish and the ability to plan the changes involved in leaving a violent man. Women in acute crisis situations who must respond without planning are construed as the exception. Implicitly, it is assumed that the presence of third parties operates as social control, so that friends and relatives will not be endangered by taking a battered woman in. The police and the health care system are seen as the responsibility of the state, and the shelter's role is to insist that the state agencies do their job. Women, in turn, must be encouraged to claim their rights.

It seems probable that some groups of women are served particularly well and others badly by each approach. Immigrant women (or other marginalised groups) in Sweden may be excluded by a shelter system that presumes integration into social networks, a decent job with privacy to make phone calls and resources for planning. On the other hand, there are probably women in Austria who resent the police taking action without their consent, who would rather be given useful advice on safety planning than be told to leave everything and just come to the shelter to be protected and guided, while living at close quarters with complete strangers. Some German women doubtless wish to avoid uprooting their children, leaving their possessions to the violent man to sell or destroy, and living in crowded shelters, and may find the long and slow negotiations between agencies and projects do too little to address their acute needs. Every kind of social service, whether feminist or not, finds confirmation of its approach in a self-selected clientele. Nonetheless, the predominance of such contrasting approaches, each firmly convinced that theirs are feminist politics, suggests that gender culture and gender arrangements may create a different background for challenging violence.

Summary: interacting explanations and perceptions

From the discussion it will have become evident that describing patterns and explaining them are extremely difficult to separate, especially given the absence of even moderately well defined 'facts' for comparison. The interaction between explanations and perceptions noted at the end of section 7.1 is thus not so much a product of inadequacies in existing theories, but results from the complexity of the problem and the way it is rooted in the sphere of private life.

Different types of theory are more or less relevant depending on whether we are trying to explain why and how (certain groups of) men employ strategies of violence, or why and how (certain groups of) women are vulnerable or remain subjected to repeated violation, or which limits on men's violence are considered legitimate or pressing in some countries sooner than in others, or how the roles of the state and of feminist activism vary in their challenges to male violence and control. Not only that, but even the grouping of welfare states, gender relations and gendered culture seem to aggregate in different configurations according to the aspect of male violence and control under examination.

7.4 Afterword: heterosexuality, violence and culture

In the long run, analysis of regional variation in male violence and control will not be able to avoid the issue of sexuality. This is a question which can only be raised, but not answered, here; it would require investigating regional differences in the understandings and practices of sexuality and how they are embedded in socio-cultural patterns. It is perhaps not coincidental that there is as little comparative research on sexuality (see Hofstede 1998) as there is on male violence.

The links between masculinity, violence and heterosexuality have been shown to be pervasive: men encounter them in their socialisation into sport culture (especially football, rugby and ice hockey), into the military and during their sexual socialisation through peers, media and pornography. Religion may convey the same message (see Lundgren 1994). On the other hand, even on the most general level of 'Western culture', masculinity is not unitary. As R.W. Connell (1995) has emphasised, violence is part of the process that divides different masculinities from each other. It is difficult to locate research in European countries differentiating between men who batter or rape and men who do not. But Lundgren as well as R. Emerson and Russell Dobash have described the process character of becoming a violent (and violently gender-stereotyped) husband from relatively slight beginnings. Hearn (1998) also suggests that the interaction of violence and heterosexuality has a process character: not only does violence become sexualised, but heterosexuality becomes suffused with violence. This would suggest that there are mechanisms at work which could respond to intervention or social control.

Understanding how culture prefigures sexualised male violence while shaping gendered subjectivity is useful for locating what might be called the point of departure for such mechanisms. It is striking that – despite a significant growth of moral consensus against violence – the institutions of social control and the agents of social sanctioning have difficulty drawing a line between normal heterosexual intimacy and violence against women. Repeatedly, physical violence and murder are partially excused when a woman is said to have injured a man's (sexual) honour, insulted his potency or his expectation of gender-based respect. Most legal codes define rape by the additional, non-sexual violence employed to make the actual rape possible. The sexual violation itself – which is painful, harmful and humiliating – thus appears legally and morally indistinguishable from consensual heterosexual intercourse.

Scripts of sexuality can, of course, be a bridge towards mutuality or pleasure. At the same time, scripts are normative and abstract; they shape and limit the possible expressions of desire. Surely the probability of rape will be higher in a culture that teaches men that successful sex depends on them alone. Convicted rapists, as Diane Scully (1990) has shown, draw upon this model in their own accounts to legitimate their actions as 'not rape'. We know little about how sexuality and violence interact with the temporal and spatial variation of gender regimes and power structures.

The present survey of evidence and theories to describe or explain spatial variation within Europe was an exercise in distilling at least moderately precise information out of a wealth of generalisations and emotions, and involved a patient search for published data in nine languages, with the help of colleagues in translating the less accessible information. Building a European research network has been indispensable to laying the groundwork, even to describe what patterns might exist. Yet the past decade has also seen considerable progress both in the political and in the scientific approaches to the problem; awareness of the issues and of the need for accurate knowledge and appropriate action has grown in many countries and in the European community as a whole. Comparative study of male violence and control is a complex but sorely needed task, since it addresses a dimension of patriarchal social relations that is independent of other structures of social, economic and political inequality, even as it interacts with them. Understanding and changing gender inequality in society cannot progress without giving attention to male violence and control and developing differentiated strategies to overcome it.

Acknowledgements

I thank Ingolfur Gislason for providing me with data from Iceland and Denmark and Mona Eliasson, Amy Elman, R.W. Connell, Renate Klein, Celia Valiente and Sylvia Walby for comments on earlier versions of this chapter. Thanks also to the Swedish Tercentenary Foundation and the Sociology Department of Uppsala University for supporting the research.

Note

1 This is overgeneralised; there are substantial differences among the Mediterranean countries. In 1997 there were 129 shelters for battered women in Spain (Instituto de la Mujer 1997: 117).

References

Archer, J. (ed.) 1994. *Male Violence*. Routledge, London.
Benard, C. and Schlaffer, E. 1978. *Die ganz gewöhnliche Gewalt in der Ehe: Texte zu einer Soziologie von Macht und Liebe*. Rowohlt, Reinbek.

204   *Gender divisions of power*

Benard, C., Schlaffer, E., Mühlbach, B. and Sapik, G. 1991. *Gewalt in der Familie: Teil I: Gewalt gegen Frauen*. Bundesministerium für Umwelt, Jugend und Familie, Wien.

Best, D.L. and Williams, J.E. 1998. Masculinity and femininity in the self and ideal self: descriptions of university students in 14 countries. In Hofstede, G. (ed.) *Masculinity and Femininity: the Taboo Dimension of National Cultures*, pp. 106–116. Sage, Thousand Oaks.

Boehnisch, L. and Winter, R. 1993. *Männliche Sozialisation: Bewältigungsprobleme männlicher Geschlechtsidentität im Lebenslauf.* Juventa, München.

Christiansen, E. and Koch-Nielsen, I. 1992. *Vold ude og hjemme.* Socialforsknings-instituttet, Copenhagen.

Connell, R.W. 1995. *Masculinities.* Polity Press, Cambridge.

Council of Europe 1998. *Gender Mainstreaming: Conceptual Framework, Methodology and Presentation of Good Practice.* Final report of Activities of the Group of Specialists on Mainstreaming (EG-S-MS). Council of Europe, Strasbourg.

Daly, M. and Wilson, M. 1994. Evolutionary psychology of male violence. In Archer, J. (ed.) *Male Violence*, pp. 253–288. Routledge, London.

Delphy, C. 1996. The European Union and the future of feminism. In Elman, R.A. (ed.) *Sexual Politics and the European Union: the New Feminist Challenge*, pp. 147–158. Berghahn Books, Providence, RI.

Dobash, R.E. and Dobash, R.P. 1979. *Violence Against Wives.* Free Press, New York.

Dobash, R.P., Dobash, R.E., Wilson, M. and Daly, M. 1992. The myth of sexual symmetry in marital violence. *Social Problems*, 39, 71–91.

Duncan, S. 1998. The spatiality of gender – and the papers in this issue. *Innovation*, 11, 2, 119–128.

Eduards, M. 1997. The women's shelter movement. In Gustavson, G., Eduards, M. and Rönnblom, M. (eds) *Towards a New Democratic Order? Women's Organizing in Sweden in the 1990's*, pp. 120–168. Publica, Stockholm.

Egger, R., Fröschl, E., Lercher, L., Logar, R. and Sieder, H. 1995. *Gewalt gegen Frauen in der Familie.* Verlag für Gesellschaftskritik, Wien.

Elman, R.A. 1996. *Sexual Subordination and State Intervention: Comparing Sweden and the United States.* Berghahn Books, Providence, RI.

Elman, R.A. and Eduards, M. 1991. Unprotected by the Swedish welfare state: a survey of battered women and the assistance they received. *Women's Studies International Forum*, 14, 3, 413–421.

European Women's Lobby (EWL) 1999. *Study: Unveiling the Hidden Data on Domestic Violence in the EU.* Report presented to the German presidency/European Commission Conference on Domestic Violence, Cologne, 28–30 March 1999.

Felson, R.B. and Tedeschi, J.T. 1993. A social interactionist approach to violence: cross-cultural applications. *Violence and Victims*, 8, 3, 295–310.

Gelles, R.J. and Loseke, D.R. (eds) 1993. *Current Controversies on Family Violence.* Sage, London.

Gilbert, P. 1994. Male violence: toward an integration. In Archer, J. (ed.) *Male Violence*, pp. 352–389. Routledge, London.

Gillioz, L., de Puy, J. and Ducret, V. 1997. *Domination et violence envers la femme dans le couple.* Editions Payot, Lausanne.

Gislason, I.A. 1997. *Violence against women in Iceland.* Unpublished manuscript presented at the Dublin workshop of the GIER network, July 1997.

Glendon, M.A. 1989. *The Transformation of Family Law: State, Law and Family in the United States and Western Europe.* University of Chicago Press, Chicago.

Godenzi, A. 1989. *Bieder, brutal: Frauen und Männer sprechen über sexuelle Gewalt.* Unionsverlag, Zürich.

Godenzi, A. 1993. *Gewalt im sozialen Nahraum.* Helbing and Lichtenhahn, Basel.

Gregory, J. and Lees, S. 1999. *Policing Sexual Assault.* Routledge, London.

Group of Specialists for Combating Violence Against Women (EG-S-VL) 1997. *Final Report of Activities of the EG-S-VL including a Plan of Action for Combating Violence against Women.* Council of Europe, Strasbourg.

Hagemann-White, C. 1992. *Strategien gegen Gewalt im Geschlechterverhältnis.* Centaurus, Pfaffenweiler.

Hagemann-White, C. 1998. Violence without end? Some reflections on achievements, contradictions, and perspectives of the feminist movement in Germany. In Klein, R.C.A. (ed.) *Multidisciplinary Perspectives on Family Violence*, pp. 176–191. Routledge, London.

Hagemann-White, C., Kavemann, B., Kootz, J., Weinmann, U., Wildt, C.C., Burgard, R. and Scheu, U. 1981. *Hilfen für mißhandelte Frauen.* Kohlhammer, Stuttgart.

Hanetseder, C. 1992. *Frauenhaus: Sprungbrett zur Freiheit? Eine Analyse der Erwartungen und Erfahrungen von Benutzerinnen: Beitrag zur Evaluation eines feministischen Projekts.* Haupt, Bern.

Hanmer, J. 1996a. Women and violence: commonalities and diversities. In Fawcett, B., Featherstone, B., Hearn, J. and Toft, C. (eds) *Violence and Gender Relations: Theories and Interventions*, pp. 7–21. Sage, London.

Hanmer, J. 1996b. The common market of violence. In Elman, R.A. (ed.) *Sexual Politics and the European Union: the New Feminist Challenge*, pp. 131–146. Berghahn Books, Providence, RI.

Hanmer, J. and Saunders, S. 1984. *Well-founded Fear: a Community Study of Violence to Women.* Hutchinson, London.

Hearn, J. 1996. Men's violence to known women: historical, everyday and theoretical constructions by men. In Fawcett, B., Featherstone, B., Hearn, J. and Toft, C. (eds) *Violence and Gender Relations: Theories and Interventions*, pp. 22–37. Sage, London.

Hearn, J. 1998. *The Violences of Men: how Men talk about and how Agencies respond to Men's Violence to Women.* Sage, London.

Heise, L.L. 1994. Gender-based abuse: the global epidemic. In Dan, A.J. (ed.) *Reframing Women's Health: Multidisciplinary Research and Practice*, pp. 233–250. Sage, London.

Heiskanen, M. and Piispa, M. 1998. *Faith, Hope, Battering: a Survey of Men's Violence against Women in Finland.* Statistics Finland, Helsinki.

Hester, M., Kelly, L. and Radford, J. 1996. *Women, Violence and Male Power: Feminist Activism, Research and Practice.* Open University, Buckingham.

Hester, M., Pearson, C. and Harwin, N. 1998. *Making an Impact: Children and Domestic Violence.* Barnardo's, Barkingside

Hofstede, G. (ed.) 1998. *Masculinity and Femininity: the Taboo Dimension of National Cultures.* Sage, Thousand Oaks.

Institut für Praxisorientierte Sozialforschung (IPOS), Mannheim 1997. *Gleichberechtigung von Frauen und Männern – Wirklichkeit und Einstellungen in der Bevölkerung 1994.* Kohlhammer, Stuttgart.

Instituto de la Mujer 1997. *Las mujeres en cifras 1997.* Instituto de la Mujer, Madrid.

Johnson, H. 1996. *Dangerous Domains: Violence against Women in Canada.* Nelson Canada, Scarborough.

Jukes, A.E. 1999. *Men who Batter Women.* Routledge, London.

Kandiyoti, D. 1994. The paradoxes of masculinity: some thoughts on segregated societies. In Cornwall, A. and Lindisfarne, N. (eds) *Dislocating Masculinity, Comparative Ethnographies*, pp. 197–213. Routledge, London.

Kelleher and associates with Monica O'Connor 1995. *Making the Links: Towards an Integrated Strategy for the Elimination of Violence against Women in Intimate Relationships with Men*. Women's Aid, Dublin.

Kelly, L. 1988. *Surviving Sexual Violence*. University of Minnesota, Minneapolis.

Lees, S. 1996. Unreasonable doubt: the outcomes of rape trials. In Hester, M., Kelly, L. and Radford, J. (eds) *Women, Violence and Male Power: Feminist Activism, Research and Practice*, pp. 99–115. Open University, Buckingham.

Logar, R. 1998. *The new intervention projects in Austria*. Paper presented at the third interdisciplinary meeting of the European Network on Conflict, Gender and Violence, Stockholm, 23–26 August 1998.

Lorentzen, L. and Løkke, P.A. 1999. Men's violence against women: the need to take responsibility. *IASOM Newsletter* 6, 2 (June 1999, Special issue on 'Men and Violence'), 30–35.

Lourenço, N., Lisboa, M. and Pais, E. 1997. *Violência contra as mulheres*. Cedernos Condicão Feminina No. 48. Comissão para a igualdade e para os direitos das mulheres, Lisboa.

Lundgren, E. 1994. "I am endowed with all the power in heaven and on earth": when men become men through "Christian" abuse. *Studia Theologica*, 48, 33–47.

Lundgren, E. 1995. *Feminist Theory and Violent Empiricism*. Avebury, London.

Minssen, A. and Müller, U. 1998. *„Psycho- und Soziogenese von männlicher Gewaltbereitschaft gegenüber Frauen" – Eine Literaturauswertung*. Ministerium für die Gleichstellung von Frau und Mann NRW, Düsseldorf.

Mullender, A. 1996. *Rethinking Domestic Violence: the Social Work and Probation Response*. Routledge, London.

Nini, M., Bentheim, A., Firle, M., Nolte, I. and Schneble, A. 1995. *Abbau von Beziehungsgewalt als Konfliktlösungsmuster – Abschlussbericht – 1994*. Kohlhammer, Stuttgart.

Oberlies, D. 1995. *Tötungsdelikte zwischen Männern und Frauen*. Centaurus, Pfaffenweiler.

Pfau-Effinger, B. 1998. Gender cultures and the gender arrangement – a theoretical framework for cross-national gender research. *Innovation*, 11, 2, 147–166.

Posse, B. and Heimer, G. 1999. The multiple traumas of sexual violence: educating staff working in the medical services. *Women's Studies Quarterly*, 1–2, 133–139.

Römkens, R. 1992. *Gewoon geweld?* Swets & Zeitlinger, Amsterdam.

Römkens, R. 1997. Prevalence of wife abuse in the Netherlands: combining quantitative and qualitative methods in survey research. *Journal of Interpersonal Violence*, 12, 99–125.

Sackmann, R. 1998. European gender roles: public discourses and regional practices. *Innovation*, 11, 2, 167–190.

Sainsbury, D. 1996. *Gender Inequality and Welfare States*. Cambridge University Press, Cambridge.

Schröttle, M. 1999. *Politik und Gewalt im Geschlechterverhältnis*. Kleine, Bielefeld.

Schwartz, M.D. 1987. Gender and injury in spousal assault. *Sociological Focus*, 20, 61–75.

Scully, D. 1990. *Understanding Sexual Violence: a Study of Convicted Rapists*. Unwin Hyman, London.

Seidler, V.J. 1991. *Recreating Sexual Politics: Men, Feminism and Politics*. Routledge, London.

Sørensen, B.W. 1990. Folk models of wife-beating in Nuuk, Greenland. *Folk*, 32, 93–115.

Sørensen, B.W. 1998. Explanations for wife beating in Greenland. In Klein, R.C.A. (ed.) *Multidisciplinary Perspectives on Family Violence*, pp. 153–175. Routledge, London.

Stets, J.E. and Straus, M.A. 1990. Gender differences in reporting marital violence and its medical and psychological consequences. In Straus, M.A. and Gelles, R.J. (eds) *Physical Violence in American Families: Risk Factors and Adaptation to Violence in 8,145 Families*, pp. 151–165. Transaction, New Brunswick.

van Stolk, B. and Wouters, C. 1987. *Frauen im Zwiespalt. Beziehungsprobleme im Wohlfahrtsstaat. Eine Modellstudie*. Suhrkamp, Frankfurt am Main.

Straus, M.A. 1991. New theory and old canards about family violence research. *Social Problems*, 38, 2, 180–197.

Straus, M.A. and Gelles, R.J. (eds) 1990. *Physical Violence in American Families: Risk Factors and Adaptation to Violence in 8,145 Families*. Transaction, New Brunswick.

Teubner, U., Becker, I. and Steinhage, R. 1983. *Untersuchung "Vergewaltigung als soziales Problem – Notruf und Beratung für vergewaltigte Frauen"*. Kohlhammer, Stuttgart.

Van de Vliert, E. 1998. Gender role gaps, competitiveness, and temperature. In Hofstede, G. (ed.) *Masculinity and Femininity: the Taboo Dimension of National Cultures*, pp. 117–129. Sage, Thousand Oaks.

Wetzels, P. 1997. *Gewalterfahrungen in der Kindheit: Sexueller Mißbrauch, körperliche Mißhandlung und deren langfristige Konsequenzen*. Nomos, Baden-Baden.

Wetzels, P., Greve, W., Mecklenburg, E., Bilsky, W. and Pfeiffer, C. 1995. *Kriminalität im Leben alter Menschen: Eine altersvergleichende Untersuchung von Opfererfahrungen, persönlichem Sicherheitsgefühl und Kriminalitätsfurcht*. Kohlhammer, Stuttgart.

Zentrum für interdisziplinäre Frauenforschung an der Humboldt-Universität Berlin (ZiF) (eds) 1995. *Unter Hammer und Zirkel: Frauenbiographien vor dem Hintergrund ostdeutscher Sozialisationserfahrungen*. Centaurus, Pfaffenweiler.

Part III

Gendered understandings – cultures and values

8 Challenging and negotiating the myths

Gender divisions in the situation comedy

Liza Tsaliki

8.1 Issues: differentiated gender cultures and the sitcom

This chapter discusses the relationship between values and practices in Western European gender roles and their representation in contemporary situation comedy, and examines how gender inequality is experienced in different cultural contexts. It does this by looking closely into the different ways in which situation comedies represent stereotypical and alternative myths of femininity and masculinity, from the point of view of female participation in paid work, the domestic division of labour, and the institutions of marriage and family using four case type countries, Britain, Sweden, Greece and Spain.

The argument is that, although gender inequality is an over-arching characteristic in human history, women in different societies and in different social and historical circumstances experience subordination and imbalance of power differently, showing considerable divergence in their relations to men (Duncan 1995). Therefore, if we are to develop a critical understanding of gender inequality, rather than a gender-blind account of it, we need to theorise difference and understand 'where gender inequalities come from, ... how they are produced, maintained and changed'. Towards this goal we have to examine 'how structures [of gender inequality] can vary, what the various outcomes are and how they are differentially caused' (ibid.: 264).

The theoretical framework of gender inequality is well discussed amongst theorists of social policy, and can be broadly conceptualised within three theoretical perspectives. The first, signposted as 'gendered welfare modelling', revolves around the ground-breaking work of Gøsta Esping-Andersen, *The Three Worlds of Welfare Capitalism* (1990). Esping-Andersen offers a taxonomy of state welfare regimes premised on the extent to which different welfare states erode the commodity status of labour within capitalism. The fact that welfare regimes are gendered, having different implications for men and women, has escaped Esping-Andersen, and constituted one of the major criticisms of his work. In reaction to this weakness, various alternative taxonomies have been formulated, as with Jane Lewis's differentiation between strong, modified, and weak 'breadwinner' state regimes (Lewis 1992).

However, a more gender-aware categorisation is what Duncan has called 'differentiated patriarchy', based on Sylvia Walby's theorising of patriarchy as embodying difference in the levels and types of gender inequality. Following this model, a revised map of gender inequality within Western Europe has been devised taking into account geographical differences in patriarchal culture by looking into the *form* of patriarchy (how women's subordination is maintained) and the *degree* of patriarchy (to what extent are women exploited). Finally, another categorisation of gender systems across Europe originates from Scandinavian ideas of 'gender contracts', that is those mechanisms, entrenched within society, which encode gender roles – what men and women are, what they think and expect, and what they do (Duncan 1995, 1998). A conceptual framework which accommodates the models of both differentiated patriarchy and gender contracts seems to offer a better and more critical understanding of regimes of gender inequality across Western Europe by 'describing variations [as well as] …building up an explanatory account of how social structures differentially operate' (Duncan 1998: 121). This is the conceptual and methodological framework which will be used in this chapter in order to analyse differences in the ways in which gender disparities are represented in situation comedies in Europe.

More specifically, this chapter will take a close look at television comedy in Britain, Sweden, Greece and Spain. A comparative, cross-national analysis was deemed essential as no researcher's experience of gender inequality can be taken to have universal applicability. On the contrary, social processes of gender inequality do not take place in a spatial–cultural vacuum. They are formed in specific places, within specific cultural contexts, where they are in dynamic interaction with pre-existing social norms (Duncan 1998; Pfau-Effinger 1998). The reason why these particular countries were chosen is because, from a social policy perspective, they are seen to represent type models of welfare state regimes (the Esping-Andersen model), of differentiated patriarchy, and of gender contracts. Thus Britain is an example of a liberal welfare state with a homemaker gender contract, Sweden is representative of the social democratic welfare state regime, with an equality or at least 'dual role' gender contract, while Greece and Spain belong in a 'southern Mediterranean' model with more 'traditional' gender contracts (ibid.; see also Crompton 1998; Sackmann 1998). The issue then becomes to what extent televisual representations of gender relations within various comedy programmes in different national contexts resonate with the above classification.

At a different level, the choice of the four countries also depicts quite differentiated broadcasting systems. Despite national variations in the way different broadcasting systems have developed and operate, they all more or less fit into a model of European public service broadcasting, as opposed to an American market-oriented one (Blumler 1992, chapter 2). Furthermore, in all four broadcasting systems, politics has played a defining role over the years, often impinging on broadcasting freedom in the shape of differentiated patterns of public regulation and state intervention. This primacy of politics, however, is gradually giving way to the primacy of markets as public service broadcasting across Europe experiences the backlash of increased commercialisation and internationalisation (Humphreys 1996). This is even more evident if we take a closer look at the level of changes brought into European broadcasting, where in the 1990s 'dual' systems (that is systems where a public sector coexists with a private commercial one) replaced previously existing 'pure' public monopolies (that is systems funded solely by the licence fee) which existed up to the 1980s. Sweden is such an example. 'Mixed revenue' systems (that is public monopolies funded by licence fee as well as advertising) have also been replaced by dual systems in the 1990s. Greece and Spain belong to this category. Britain has belonged to the 'dual' systems category for a considerable time (Brants and Siune 1992: 104).

The question to address now is why the sitcom? What is it within the situation comedy that makes it a useful tool for the description and examination of mechanisms of gender inequality in different spatial, cultural and broadcasting contexts? A prime reason is that the situation comedy has become particularly associated with the popular articulation of femininity and masculinity, and with family and gender relations both in domestic situations and in the workplace. Its domesticated humour and broad-based appeal have made it one of television's preferred modes for addressing the 'nation's families' (Spigel 1992: 154). The situation comedy also has salient features as a genre: it has a half-hour format, it is based on humour, and is capable of constant reproduction – the weekly problem will be resolved in a way that a new problem will replace it in the following episode. On the other hand, narrative development never occurs at the expense of the rhythms of the half-hour slot, nor does it lead to such a disclosure of knowledge that would jeopardise the need for the series to return the following week. This relatively uniform structure makes national comparison easier, therefore. The narrative development in the situation comedy also follows a structure whereby the state of initial equilibrium is disrupted before things can return to a new state of equilibrium (Todorov cited in Neale 1980: 20). The thematic typology of sitcoms revolves around themes that can accommodate continuous repetition, which inevitably leads to the use of stereotypical myths of representation (Eaton 1985). It is these stereotypical myths which promote a key to the analysis of gender culture in different countries.

Television comedy could not function without stereotyping, for jokes need an object, a victim easily and immediately recognisable to its audience, and comic characters need to be 'a representative embodiment of a set of ideas or a manifestation of a cliché' (Medhurst and Tuck 1982: 43). Television comedy has also to be socially relevant, and to this goal it references the social world through widely accepted notions of what is typical; in this way, it represents 'what [is] recognized as true to life' (Lovell 1986: 159). The construction of the 'typical' will draw on 'what everyone knows', folk wisdom and proverbialism, and on common sense truisms. In this respect, 'typical' comedies are rarely seen to challenge traditional patterns of behaviour and expectations. The sitcom thus works towards the normalisation of heterosexual love, marriage and family (and for this reason it has often been accused of being conventional and conservative). Disruption can come either from conflict within the family or from intrusions from the 'outside', but in general any threats to the domestic sexual hierarchy tend to be rejected, side-stepped or forgotten by the next episode. The genre, then, invests in the 'bourgeois' traditional family and the gender division of roles within it as a model of stability and 'normality' (Neale and Krutnik 1990). The sitcom is also marked by an interplay between dominant norms (heterosexual love leading to marriage and children; a structured sexual division of labour) and marginality (reversal of gender roles; disconnection of marriage and family) as it depicts the social transformations which have become resonant in the wider culture. Concurrently, the sitcom seeks the middle ground audience, without alienating the more liberally minded, 'quality' demographic categories (Feuer 1992). However, and this is a key point for this chapter, *what* family situation is seen as 'normal' and 'abnormal', and *how* it is represented in the sitcom varies between countries.

The sitcom evolved from pre-existing forms of entertainment, through which it is seen to *naturalise* the family unit. Representations of the family in the situation comedy can be traced back to the 'parlour theatricals' of Victorian times, to the various sketches of domestic life printed in the American mass-circulation newspapers during the 1870s and the comic strips which replaced them from the late 1890s. Later on, in the early 1930s, the radio sitcom was developed by merging vaudeville and theatrical realism before the format made the final transfer to television between the late 1940s and early 1950s, thus providing a middle ground for reaching the family audience (Neale and Krutnik 1990; Spigel 1992).

The sitcom format initially flourished within an American and British framework. However, following the proliferation of broadcasting across Europe, it became transplanted in different national contexts where it was differentially appropriated, thereby producing distinct national variants. There is scant evidence in academic literature about the historical development of television comedy in any other national context apart from the United States (and Britain to a certain degree). Such an account needs to be set within the confines of the material available, in itself a methodological limitation. Having said that, even by following the steps of US situation comedy towards generic adulthood, television comedy constitutes a powerful tool in the representation of gender roles and cultures within particular societies as it is closely related to ongoing social change.

During the mid-1950s to the early 1960s, the situation comedy in the United States was the primary device in naturalising family life, and the allocation of gender roles within it, by making it appear as the only possible living arrangement. Women had to be persuaded to return to their homes after their war-time draft and undertake their family role, and the family sitcom of the 1950s made a significant contribution to the social reconstitution of women (Silverstone 1994). The family comedy of the mid-1950s brought female comics into the limelight, though in a way that would not upset middle class codes of femininity: comediennes were depicted as loving daughters or charming housewives, whose femininity, though, was not erotically charged. The family sitcom also domesticated men, making them appear as predominantly family types; following the increasing presence of women in the public sphere, men were becoming more involved in family life. This form of 'masculine domesticity' allowed men to become involved in anything from housework and childrearing to interior decorating and family amusements, and to offer more 'compassionate' marriages (Spigel 1992: 20).

However, as the historical conditions of contemporary Western societies started to change, the nuclear family gave way to new social formations. Rising divorce rates, increasing female participation in paid employment, the disconnection of family from marriage are among the changes that inflect contemporary notions of family life and demonstrate the destabilisation of gender dynamics in the home (see Chapter 2). In the 1970s and 1980s the women's movement began to have a steady, subversive impact on long-established assumptions and stereotypes about the sexual division of labour at home and in the workplace, and about family life in general. As the feminist critique of patriarchy became part of the public discourse, it legitimised 'women's issues' as a 'relevant' topic in television programming and led towards a 'prime-time feminism' (Taylor 1989). Gradually, the sitcom moved towards the depiction of social dissidence and family disorder by breaking away from traditional representations of the family, and thus questioning the inevitability of the nuclear family. This historical transition happened at a different pace, and in different ways, in different national situations. In the next section, I will examine the particular experiences of Britain, Sweden, Greece and Spain.

8.2 Patterns: the sitcom and gender representations

The previous section put the notion of gender disparities into context by stressing difference in the way women's power imbalance with men can be experienced, and presented a number of theoretical models of gender regimes across Europe drawing on existing literature in social policy. It also introduced a conceptual framework for the comparative analysis of television comedy in Britain, Sweden, Greece and Spain. This section will now focus on the textual analysis of specific situation comedies in terms of three indicators: (1) female employment participation; (2) the division of domestic labour; and (3) marriage and family. In this way, the section will illustrate the depiction of dominant, and marginal, gendered myths and patterns of behaviour within different spatial and cultural contexts in Western Europe.

Barthes (1973) has argued that a myth is a story through which a culture explains or understands some aspect of reality or nature. In fact, for him myths are class based: their meanings are constructed by the socially dominant and accepted by the subordinate since they have been 'naturalised'. Primitive myths are about life and death, men and gods, good and evil, while contemporary myths are about masculinity and femininity, about the family, about success. Myths work to naturalise history, which suggests that they are actually the product of a social class that has achieved dominance, and operate by trying to present the meanings they carry as 'natural', not as historical or social as they are in reality. In this way, they mystify or obscure their origins and thus their political or social dimension. Women, for example, are 'naturally' more nurturing than men, therefore their natural place is at home with their husband and children, whereas men are the 'natural' breadwinners with a natural place in paid work and the public sphere. By presenting these meanings as natural, myth disguises their social and historical origin, while at the same time it gives them a universal appeal and makes them look unchangeable and fair. As a result, the meaning of femininity has been constructed in terms of nurturing, domesticity, sensitivity, and the need to care. In contrast, masculinity has been translated into strength, assertiveness, independence and the ability to operate in the public sphere (Fiske 1990). However, the changing role of women in contemporary society and the changing structure of the family has meant that the dominant position of these myths, and their status as natural, is challenged. New gender myths have therefore been introduced in order to accommodate the career woman, the 'sensitive' man, and the single parent. The sitcom offers particularly potent, current examples of these new gender myths.

Attitudes towards female employment

The presence of women in paid work is prevalent in sitcoms in all four case type countries. However, this prevalence is felt to varying degrees and with different potential for creating gender conflict, depending on the particular spatial and cultural context presented by each country.

Contemporary British comedy has a number of women professionals to show, ranging from the strong-willed and down-to-earth Dorothy in *Men Behaving Badly* to the fashion-addict and hopeless Eddie in *Absolutely Fabulous*. Dorothy works as a nurse, a profession that resonates the 'traditional' feminine traits of empathy, nurturing and caring. Despite that, Dorothy does not represent the stereotypical loving female, as she always has the last word in the relationship with boyfriend Gary. Dorothy is fully aware of Gary's shenanigans, usually performed with his 'mate' Tony, but is also fully equipped to bring Gary back into 'order'. Gary and Tony, the personification of lager-drinking, working-class lads, 'philosophise' about sex and women, but any exhibition of 'bravado' attitudes quickly falls into shambles as soon as Dorothy's down-to-earth persona and razor-sharp comments enter the room.

Eddie (short for Edwina), one of the main characters in *Ab Fab*, is in contrast found in a much more middle-class setting, a working mother running her own media business who lives with her daughter Saffron in a very fashion-aware house. This is a typical setting for 1960s hippy parents. Permanent fixtures of the household are also Eddie's mother and Eddie's alter ego, Patsy (or 'Pats' as Eddie likes to call her). However, Eddie is not just any working mother as she turns expected gendered norms and myths against themselves.

Femininity has long been cherished for its caring qualities, as women are seen to have a 'natural' talent for nurturing others. However, towards the end of the millennium, in Britain, the 'new traditionalism' of family values allows more fluidity in the conception of motherhood; mothers are now permitted to be unruly, carry filofaxes and have a sexual appetite as well (McDonald 1995). The situation comedy in Britain, and *Ab Fab* in particular, accommodates this trend as it is about breaking boundaries and going against type. Eddie is far from the stereotype of the 'ideal mum'. She challenges the dominant myth of the caring and sharing mother and introduces unruliness, excess and immaturity. In a prime example of norm-breaking, Eddie is the one who needs to wise up and be taken care of, while Saffron fulfils the demand for maternal advice. There is a generational conflict between Eddie and Saffron that represents the tension between the liberalism of the 1960s, and the rationalism and individualism of the 1990s. Contrary to the modern myth of the capable and efficient career woman who successfully juggles between family, motherhood and professionalism, the only thing Eddie is good at is being unruly, excessive and politically incorrect, and indulging in booze, sex, and dope with soulmate 'Pats'.

In the case of Sweden, female characters are portrayed in a strongly positive light. Women in television comedy have wits, understanding, tolerance, and the best lines; they are smart, flexible and sophisticated. They have successfully made the transition to the post-modern society – unlike men who still cling to the modern society – and thrive in both the domestic and the public spheres. Women have control over their personal lives, and are more in tune with the interests and worries of young teenagers than are their male partners. Men, on the other hand, are the butt of the jokes. They appear as hopelessly out-of-touch and old-fashioned, relics of the forgone era of Swedish social democracy, and slow to catch up with contemporary social transformations. They represent the old welfare state system, which was based on a policy of negotiations between the labour unions and the state, on strong industrial production and a huge public sector. Most male characters are employees in the public sector and see themselves as social democrats, thereby embodying the 'Swedish model' itself. They are also sensitive and emotional, but they end up being over-stressed and preoccupied with family life, and their children in particular.

Women professionals are active members in plot development, at least within a middle-class family context. They successfully combine profession-alism with motherhood, and are allowed the lead. In what is a case of role reversal, the wife in the *Svensson Family* is ascribed 'male' features: she is the main breadwinner, having a high-profile job which requires long hours in the office, frequent trips, and working at home. She is also very sophisticated and outspoken with a tendency towards sharp comments. In fact, she could easily be 'the man' in the sitcom. This does not mean that she is robbed of her 'femininity' either: she is taking good care of herself, being very desirable and elegant in her middle age, and of her children too, being more in tune with the whims and anxieties of pre-puberty and adolescence than her husband. This is a case of 'Mother knows best' rather than *Father knows best* – a very popular American sitcom screened in the mid-1950s about a suburban American family.

Shifting now to a Mediterranean context, in Greece the situation comedy illustrates the transition from tradition to modernity, which is a characteristic feature of Greek society and culture (Tsaliki 1995). Television comedy in Greece represents the coexistence of traditional and alternative family structures, and allows the inversion of stereotypical gender roles and myths. It also marks the continuation of a cinematic tradition, which was in itself rooted in variety theatre. The growth of the Greek cinema industry, from the 1950s onwards, lured comedy writers into writing film scripts. As Elefteriotis (1995) notes, the popular film industry in Greece in the 1960s and 1970s principally revolved around the problems and pleasures of life within the network of family and friends. In a similar way, the Greek television comedy from its earlier days until today has not strayed significantly from this strand (Tsaliki 1995).

There are many powerful women in Greek situation comedy. Representing women as powerful is not uncommon, since strong female characters have had a regular presence even within the earlier theatrical and cinematic comedies. Along the dimension of machismo, there exists in Greece the popular stereotype of the overpowering, domineering female, the strong matriarch in the capacity of wife, mother, sister, in-law. This is an element of popular culture that the situation comedy capitalises on. There is, for example, Katerina and Maria in *The Top Floor*. They are both in full-time employment, married, middle-aged, and they are both 'fat texts' (Rowe 1995) with a sharp tongue. There is also Athina in *The Mess*, who inverts dominant myths of masculinity and femininity. She is engaged and about to get married to Spyros. She comes from a wealthy, upper-class family and happens to be the President of the Board of Directors, while Spyros is one of her employees – high ranked, but still subordinate. This constitutes a prime example of role reversal, as the heroine occupies a 'traditional' male job (President of the Board) and marries one of her executives. Usually it is the other way round, with the male protagonist ending up marrying his secretary. In this way, the programme marks a transgression towards a modern world where women occupy the dominant posts in a man's world. Another example of gender inversion is Anna, the high-flying, power executive in *Making the same mistake twice*.... Anna is the elegant managing director of a television station called *Media Channel*. Both her husband Petros and her lover Yiannis work in the same television station and are subordinate to her. Anna also turns stereotypical gender roles against themselves, being on top and in control in both the professional and the private realm.

The situation comedy in Spain is a genre that is informed by a constant feedback with its social reality, depicting the complexity of a culture where tradition and modernity, freedom and restraint coexist. The sitcom constructs a complex notion of femininity where women are assertive, intelligent, experienced and independent, while also allowing for more traditional versions of womanhood. Not only do we have strong female participation in paid employment, but we also see many mothers with professional careers and a private life as well. Most of these women are set in a positive light, being financially independent, confident and strong, and appear to have experience in personal relationships. Some are more ambitious than men, but this is not necessarily a negative attribute; instead, these female protagonists show that today's women run complicated and demanding lives where the personal and the professional may conflate. Men, on the other hand, are portrayed as confused and bewildered by the presence of these strong women, their machismo being simultaneously a handicap and under threat. Myths of masculinity in transition are constructed whereby a more progressive type of Spanish man is offered, one which, after having gone through a process of 'social learning', is more informed, sophisticated and not afraid to get in touch with his 'feminist' side.

In most cases, it is middle-class women who are more likely to combine successfully the public and the private. For example, in *Medico de Familia* (*Family doctor*), Nacho's second wife is an ambitious radio journalist who is in close touch with her large family. In *A las 11 en casa* (*At home at eleven*) we are met with an ex-wife, who is economically independent, self-confident and in control of her relationships, and with a current wife – in this case, a career academic, also in control of her private life. Similarly, in *Querido Maestro* (*Dear teacher*) Mario, a thirty-something teacher in a rural school, is emotionally involved with the Director of School, a divorced mother of one and Mario's first love from his youth. These examples show that Spanish women can have professional aspirations without losing their sensitivity and need for romance. If there is a feminist way to cruise through life, then this is it; instead of taking onboard 'masculine' features of assertion and aggressiveness, and sacrifice personal life in search of professional achievement, in Spanish sitcoms women offer an alternative that combines both worlds.

The domestic division of labour

The representation of gender roles in the domestic sphere plays with traditional and stereotypical role allocation between the sexes, while also allowing for 'casting against type'. In Britain the extent to which household chores are shared between partners is a corollary of gendered class attitudes. It is Dorothy who takes responsibility for domestic duties in *Men Behaving Badly*, certainly not out of choice but out of necessity: boyfriend Gary and his 'mate' Tony have a low level of resistance against increasing piles of beer cans and pizza boxes. Furthermore, both men take it for granted that the house is a 'girl's concern'. *Ab Fab*'s Eddie, on the other hand, never does any housework. 'Chores' is just not a word in Eddie's vocabulary, and household duties are 'done' by some kind of divine intervention (in the form of her daughter Saffron). This is a result of Eddie's inability to do anything right apart from going out, getting hopelessly drunk and making a spectacle of herself. Consideration of housework is a very 'bourgeois' habit, beyond Eddie's world and, simply, not an option.

The division of domestic labour also seems to be a matter of class in Swedish comedy. From a working-class point of view, women are portrayed in a more stereotypical way. Myths of femininity are hereby constructed along the lines of patriarchal culture. Women reside in the private sphere, caring for the welfare of their husbands and of the household in general. In *Rena rama Rolf* (*Simply Rolf*), a programme making fun of industrial, working-class Gothenburg with its big car-manufacturing and ship-building industries, we meet middle-aged tram-driver Rolf and his housewife Bettan. Rolf is the epitome of working-class manliness, thrusting an Elvis-inspired hairdo, and taking great pride in his profession. He represents the male chauvinist *par excellence* who expects everything from his wife, and sees himself as the exclusive breadwinner in the household. Bettan, on the other hand, personifies the stereotype of the obliging, tolerant and caring housewife, who sees it fit that she stays at home and takes care of the housework.

In Greece, gender segregation of domestic roles within the situation comedy illustrates the transitional state of contemporary Greek culture, wherein modernising gender myths coexist with more traditional and stereotypical ones. In that respect, Greek television comedy appears fully aware of the mixed patterns of relations and gender roles that exist within Greek domesticity. Thus, when the mother-in-law in *The Top Floor* drops by to see the newly wed couple, she is astonished to find her son wearing an apron, ready to do the washing-up. She mutters that he is not in 'good hands' since her daughter-in-law is not a good *nikokyra* (housewife), and that a 'man's place is not in the sink'. The unspoken rivalry between the wife and the mother-in-law, who is inclined to believe that her son does not have what he deserves, is easily recognisable within Greek culture. She personifies the mentality of the older generation wherein daily chores were allocated according to gender and each partner knew their place. At the same time, though, the programme depicts modernising attitudes and changing perceptions about gender roles amongst the new generations.

Even so, this does not mean that there is no conflict amongst the younger generation either. When Spyros, a yuppified ex-lefty in the series *The Unacceptables*, invites his boss for dinner he has very clear ideas about what (house)wife Dimitra must prepare. She, however, has a mind of her own, and a very independent one indeed, and decides against Spyros's 'directions'. By the end of the evening, not only has Dimitra utterly 'captivated' their guest, but receives his praise for her impeccable cooking and housekeeping techniques, and her choice of food and music, much to Spyros's dismay. In this sense, even in the case when the man is the main breadwinner while the wife commits herself in the domestic sphere, there is plenty of room for role reversal and female emancipation. Dimitra manages to reduce Spyros's superior status as the cultured, professional male, thus evoking a positive understanding of female domesticity. The ability of Greek women to occupy a high-status position by staying at home has already been stressed by Kyriazis (1995) who has noted the overt significance of women in Greece in their capacity as mothers and housewives, a point I will come back to later in this chapter. As a result, then, Dimitra initiates a reversal of gender subordination, and comes across as the modern representative of *nikokyra*: self-confident, outspoken and assertive.

Spain forms another example of a culture in transition, where the play between tradition and modernity is at work, with class being a determining variable. Domestic duties are as much a matter of gender as they are of class: both in *Medico de Familia* and in *A las 11 en casa* housework is undertaken by the female domestic aid, leaving the 'mistress' of the house to get on with her career and family in both programmes. In *Manos a la obra* action revolves around two working-class men who do 'chapuzas' for a living (they mend things in the home). They both share a stereotypical mentality regarding participation in domestic duties, expecting women to inhabit the domestic sphere in the capacity of housewives. On the other hand, *Querido Maestro*'s Mario offers a more progressive type of masculinity as he takes an active role in the division of domestic labour. It appears that the more conformist mentality to the dominant institutional patterns, and the more conventional representations of men and women, are 'reserved' for the working class within the Spanish sitcom, while the middle class is portrayed as more enlightened.

Marriage and family life

Unsurprisingly, although the sitcom as a genre revolves around family structures and issues of domesticity, there are divergent attitudes towards marriage and family across the four countries. In Britain, the sitcom deconstructs nuptiality to a greater or lesser degree, following increasing divorce and cohabitation rates in real life. Dorothy starts by living on her own while going out with Gary; later on, however, she moves in with him and Tony. With Dorothy being thirty-something, discussions about marriage and children abound, giving Gary tormenting nightmares. At some point in the sitcom, not being able to cope with Gary's and Tony's laddish behaviour and daily routine, Dorothy delivers an ultimatum before finally moving out. Dorothy's dream of getting married and starting a family, even with someone like Gary, is no different from any other working-class girl's. Eddie, on the other hand, stands for a different world – and a different class status for that matter. Eddie is past marriage, her ex-husband having finally found true

happiness in a relationship with a younger black man. She is also past
motherhood, as she is still 'traumatised' by pregnancy and childbirth, an
experience she, 'fortunately darling', did not have to live twice. In a way,
Eddie has reinvented marriage through her relationship with 'Pats'. For both
of these women, their friendship is priceless and better than any man (one-
night stands aside).

In Sweden, marriage and family do not always go together, as the household
in *Papas flicka* (*Dad's daughter*) shows. Father Frank is a divorcee teacher who
epitomises the 'nineties-man', the enlightened 'new man' who exhibits the
feminine traits of caring and nurturing. In that respect, the younger
generations of Swedish men, like Frank, represent another facet of
masculinity, one which is not afraid to show its sensitive, romantic and
emotional self. These men have taken 'masculine domesticity' (Spigel 1992:
20) to another dimension: they compensate for the absence of the mother by
becoming 'motherly' themselves and experiencing the worries and
contradictions of single parenthood. Having said that, it is not that marriage
is now defunct within Swedish society and comedy. Allan in *Svennson, Svennson*
is a caring father, taking active interest in his 2.4 family.

From a Greek point of view, contemporary situation comedy often disrupts
traditional and conformist notions of family and domesticity, while nuptiality
is still retaining its conceptual currency. *Making the same mistake twice...* is a
text which breaks established middle-class, patriarchal values of family and
sexuality. The series, which was widely accepted by the public as well as the
critics, breaks conventional bourgeois domestic structures by introducing an
extreme erotic consensus into everyday family life. In this way, marriage and
adultery merge into a new type of relationship as the sitcom recognises
abundant female sexuality, and defies middle-class behavioural conformities.
Middle-class familialism is, thus, undermined from the inside, and the
stereotypical patriarchal culture is seriously challenged – especially if we
consider that, in the last series of the programme, Anna is expecting a baby
outside wedlock without knowing who the actual father is. From this
perspective, the Greek sitcom offers an alternative version of traditional
family structures, and of myths of femininity and masculinity.

However, it is the interplay between tradition and modernity that
characterises Greece, a clinging to the past within the concurrent influence
of modernity that remains a staple feature in the situation comedy. In *The
Unacceptables*, the social expectations following the convention of middle-class
nuptiality and respectability apply even to Yiannis, the gay character in the
series. This conforms with traditional and stereotypical norms according to
which men are expected to be straight and get married to a 'nice girl' (*kopella*).
Nevertheless, as social mores gradually become more tolerant towards
homosexuality, 'deviant' behaviour is openly discussed and less marginalised,
and Yiannis is allowed to lead his own life in the end.

Spanish television comedies present us with a wide variety of family
structures, which have departed from the stereotypical bourgeois nuclear

family of 2.4 children. There are extended families of the 'meccano' type (offspring from previous relationships along with children from the present one), and families where close relatives share the domestic bliss; there are also dysfunctional families and 'surrogate' families, as well as traditional versions of domestic life. In this, Spain forms another example of a culture in transition. Take for instance the three friends who share a flat after their divorces in *Todos los hombres son iguales* (*All men are the same*), thus forming a 'surrogate' family. They are middle-aged, educated and spend time with their children (who, however, live with their mothers), each one of them representing a different type of Spanish man, ranging from the stereotypical macho type to the more sensitive. In a similar way, Mario, the school teacher in *Querido Maestro*, shows that a man in the 1990s can still be a man even if he endorses 'feminine' characteristics such as sensitivity and commitment to a notion of romantic monogamy. Mario cohabits with his first love who is now a divorced mother. Divorced mothers and fathers also feature in *Medico de Familia* and *A las 11 en casa*, an indication that trouble has begun in marital paradise and that Spanish sitcom has been quick to pick this up. However, marriage is as much a matter of class positioning as anything else. In this sense, characters from a working-class background accommodate more traditionalist understandings of manhood, womanhood and especially marriage, as in the case of the domestic maid in *Medico de Familia* and the men in *Manos a la obra*.

This section has examined the ways in which gender inequality is lived through, with Britain, Greece, Spain and Sweden as type cases, by offering a textual analysis of a number of situation comedies in these countries. It has looked closely into the representation of stereotypical and alternative myths of femininity and masculinity in these texts, reading them in terms of female participation in paid work (the myth of the career woman), the domestic division of labour (the 'sensitive' man), and the institutions of marriage and family (the single parent within and outside wedlock). It is now necessary to provide an explanation for these readings by looking into different national experiences by way of their existing gender cultures.

8.3 Explanations: gender cultures and sitcom representation

Earlier in this chapter, it was argued that the social processes of gender disparity do not happen in a vacuum but, instead, happen in spatially organised socio-cultural contexts where they interact with already established norms and values. This is what Duncan has called 'the spatial contingency effect' (1998: 121), whereby gender relations are differentially developed over space, at both national and regional levels. What this also means is that people will develop different understandings and different attitudes in different places, and that, in fact, the same values and relationship structures will be interpreted differently in each place (Duncan, op. cit.). For example, the expectations on what 'good mothering' involves will be different from country to country (and *within* each country as well). What lies in the background is a complicated set of 'gender contracts', which differ significantly across space. The term contextualises gender expectations and roles – that is 'the subjective, lived understanding of what women and men are' (Forsberg 1998: 193) – without, however, implying gender equality. Therefore, the gendered coding of society is still in effect, although within it women's space has now been enlarged. These contracts are not inflexible but evolve over time, as Yvonne Hirdman details for Sweden, where a 'housewife contract', prevalent in the 1930s, was replaced by an 'equality contract' from the late 1960s onwards (Hirdman 1990 cited in Duncan, op. cit.). However, gender contracts within a given society evolve not only over time but also across space differentially, affecting the lives and routines of men and women on a regional level as well. Gender contracts thereby form regionally differentiated gender identities (see Forsberg 1998). This is a feature which should not escape analysis, although it is not possible to provide a regional dimension of how different comedy texts are perceived at this point.

In Chapter 9 Rosemarie Sackmann examines prevailing attitudes towards women's roles in the European Union and compares these with existing employment rates for mothers (see also Sackmann 1988). In this way, Sackmann aims to assess the extent to which the *ideal* of gender equality matches the *reality* of gender employment patterns across different spatio-cultural contexts. Her findings are rather interesting.

Greece, for example, belongs to the group where the equality ideal is most pronounced and where employment rates for mothers are above average. Although Sweden is not examined (as the study looked into the twelve member states before 1995), we could perhaps venture a projection of a Swedish profile premised on the Danish example which shows characteristics similar to Greece. What is striking here, though, is the positive motherhood effect (that is the impact motherhood has on female employment) which at +2 indicates that motherhood in Denmark, following the Scandinavian model where childhood is a 'public issue', does not stop women from going to work. Greece and Spain are seen to belong in a 'southern' or 'Mediterranean' model (although in Spain the full-time employment rate for mothers is below the European average). In Greece, in particular, the motherhood effect is quite negative, at –22, which in itself can be explained by the late and weak development of the Greek welfare state, and prevailing traditional values and family perceptions. Having said that, employment data in Greece need to be handled with caution as they stand for registered employment only and do not include the family economy and informal economy.

In Britain, there is a marked difference between the level of agreement with the equality model (among the highest in Sackmann's grouping for both men and women) and the rate of full-time employment for mothers (among the lowest in the group, coupled with a very negative motherhood effect at

−34). The reason behind these trends lies in the British tradition of a liberal welfare state wherein the increased penetration of women in paid work is market driven. However, although women were seen as a 'reserve army', the dominant perceptions of motherhood revolve around a housewife mother rather than a working one – and the lack of publicly funded childcare testifies to that. Mothers in Britain are expected to give up full-time work, and resume it later on a part-time basis. This has largely been the rationale informing the practice of the British state, a practice that goes back to the inter-war years and even earlier than that, in the nineteenth century, and places women at home raising their children. Despite the gradually increasing participation of women in the British labour market in recent times, the central state has not encouraged women's entry to employment by providing adequate levels of childcare. As a result, the case for working parents in 1990s Britain is that they have to make provision for caring responsibilities through either their social networks or the private sector (Crompton 1998).

This is in stark contrast to what is practised in the social democratic Scandinavian regimes, where the state actively helps both parents with caring responsibilities. Under the influence of 'second-wave feminism', different regimes in Scandinavia compensate the male or female carer (with maternity and paternity leave for instance), and provide childcare facilities so that both parents can remain in paid employment.

However, welfare states are informed by pre-existing moral codings, and form manifestations of 'gendered moral rationalities' – that is 'collective negotiations and understandings about what is morally right and socially acceptable' (Duncan and Edwards 1997: 30). It is the latter that primarily shape men's and women's attitudes to work and parenthood, with state caring provision being a corollary of the gendered moral rationalities. For example, attitudes towards paid work by mothers can best be interpreted on the basis of gendered moral rationalities rather than on existing welfare regimes: the extent to which mothers will enter employment will ultimately be determined by the 'right' behaviour expected from a mother in a given socio-cultural context. On a more general level, welfare support will reflect what has been described as 'gender culture' (Pfau-Effinger 1998: 150), a concept which allows for the inclusion of cultural and societal actors in the understanding of differentiated gender regimes.

Diversity in the conceptualisation of gendered moral rationalities is also found at the regional level, as research has shown in the Swedish case. Contrary to the widespread belief that welfare policies in Sweden have managed to eradicate inequality and that the country is a homogeneous state where regional differences are unimportant, there is a spatially differentiated gender culture, due to different traditions and political ideologies (Forsberg 1988). Overall, gender segregation and the 'glass ceiling' in the Swedish labour market follows a regional pattern, being most pronounced in the industrial and forestry areas, and least in the metropolitan areas, Jämtland, Gotland, and the Norrland coast (ibid.: 195–206).

Research has also shown that there is a definite pattern of regional variations between the north and the south of Europe when it comes to household structures. Most countries in northern Europe have entered a later (third) phase of demographic transition from the mid-1980s onward (its main features being a stabilisation of divorce rates in countries which had already reached high levels; the emergence of post-marital cohabitation and 'living apart together' relationships; the recuperation of childbirth after the age of 30). Mediterranean countries, on the other hand, are still experiencing what has been called 'the second demographic transition', with pre-marital cohabitation, and a rise in fertility after the age of 25 (despite the increase in extramarital births) as its principal characteristics (Solsona 1998: 212–213; see also Chapter 3, this volume).

Within this context, Europe can be split into four regions: the southern region (comprising Greece, Italy, Portugal and Spain) with low fertility, divorce, cohabitation and birth outside marriage; the northern region (Sweden and Denmark) with high levels of fertility, divorce and cohabitation, and a high or medium level of births outside marriage; the western region (Britain, France, Norway, the Netherlands) with low fertility, low level of cohabitation, high divorce rates, and high rate of births outside marriage; and the central region (Austria, Belgium, Germany, Luxembourg, Switzerland) with high divorce levels, medium cohabitation, few births outside marriage and very low fertility (Roussel 1992 in Solsona 1998: 213).

The pattern of diversity in the experience of family forms and gender relations is also entrenched *within* countries, not only across them, as the Catalan case illustrates. The position of Catalan women is superior to that in the rest of Spain, as women in Catalonia have more approval in combining family and career than in other Spanish regions (Solsona 1998). Nevertheless, although Catalonia has a lot in common with other European countries (such as declining marriage and fertility rates coupled with increasing divorce, separation, cohabitation and birth outside marriage rates), the family still plays a crucial support role, unlike in the north of Europe (Solsona 1998: 221–223).

Greece is also characterised by a gender culture that is oriented towards strong family relations and support networks, and forms an interesting example of the way structural changes are taking place not so much in response to embedded social values and gender contracts but rather as a result of political changes endogenously and exogenously brought forward. A high proportion of women in Greece are in non-paid work. The reasons for this can be found in the Greek economic structure, the significance the family plays in Greek society, and the traditional attitudes concerning women's roles (the prevailing 'gender contract' in other words) (Kyriazis 1995). In fact, the importance of the family lies in the fact that it was the basic agricultural production unit for a long time. Its centrality within Greek society is marked by the significance attached to the role of the mother: although the father was the public representative of the family, it was the mother who was the organiser of the household and the guardian of its cohesiveness. The public profile of the family rested heavily on the ability of the woman to carry out the household duties properly. This was reflected in the capacity of the woman as *nikokyra* – a term which means much more than 'housewife', and can be best interpreted as 'mistress of the house'. Being a good nikokyra was deemed extremely important for the social status of the family, and the self-esteem of the woman of the house, taking pride in the proper performance of household duties. In that respect, Kyriazis suggests caution in the application of Western models of analysis of gender relations as the latter are premised on the assumption that the domestic role is inferior and/or subordinate in the Greek case (ibid.: 274).

Another interesting dimension within the Greek context is the way the feminist movement developed. The various women's organisations were formed during a period of political turmoil, during which participation in feminist movements was an acceptable means for the mobilisation of women, with the additional advantage of not threatening the position of men. However, underlying this structure was the fact that, although the Greek society was ready to accept a policy that led to role equity, any attempts to change the gender contracts of men and women were met with serious resistance, which 'suggests that traditional values regarding the respective roles of men and women remained well entrenched' (Kyriazis 1995: 277). In that respect, despite various legislative changes with the aim of institutionalising gender parity, gender contracts and attitudes did not shift accordingly, as the occupational gender segregation in Greece indicates. This suggests that legislative equality cannot immediately erode attitudes and behaviour which remain tied to tradition. More likely, an ongoing process of modernisation is under way, which goes hand in hand with a tendency to cling to the past.

The above analysis presents the national experiences of existing gender cultures for each one of the four type case countries. The question to ask now is how do these relate to the televisual representations of gendered myths as illustrated in various sitcoms?

In Britain, the situation comedy offers a variety of women in professional occupations. In defiance of stereotypical gender norms, which call for a 'homebound' mother, there are women in British comedy who are career rather than family oriented. Eddie's character, for example, goes against entrenched 'gendered moral rationalities' with the intention to shock and to satirise the difficulties of modern womanhood. The sitcom as a genre puts the complexities and contradictions of the everyday lives of modern women on the agenda by going against the dominant gender culture which requires that mothers should not be in full-time employment (Crompton 1998). Furthermore, the institutions of marriage and family are largely demystified within the British sitcom, in accordance with the high divorce rates that characterise the country. Having said that, attitudes towards marriage and family life are also influenced by class culture, with working-class characters exhibiting more 'traditional' gender behaviour (as in the case of *Men Behaving Badly*).

In Sweden, the situation comedy offers an array of strong women professionals, most of whom are also mothers (*Svennson, Svennson*). This is in line with the existing gender culture in Sweden – and across most Scandinavian countries for that matter – according to which women (and men) can practise their careers. This kind of gender expectation and moral coding has informed and shaped state care provision for children, further ensuring opportunities for career development for both sexes. There are also characters in Swedish comedy who live outside the confines of the 'traditional' nuclear family (*Papas flicka*), thus representing a slice of real life where childrearing takes place increasingly outside marriage and the rates of divorce and cohabitation are constantly rising. At the same time, nevertheless, there is a variety of attitudes towards participation in the labour market, family life and the domestic sphere on Swedish television which demonstrates the existence of a spatially differentiated gender culture (Forsberg 1998) that is influenced by class orientation as well (*Rena rama Rolf*).

The situation comedy in Greece portrays a more 'progressive' televisual reality than the one suggested by a 'southern Mediterranean' model. Women are not only career oriented, but they seem to be above men (*The Mess*). They also seem to be ahead of them in the sense that women on television take the initiative to break away from the conformity of marriage (*Making the same mistake twice...*). Even when sitcom action revolves around more 'conventional' settings where married couples are involved, dominant gender myths are inverted and ridiculed, and they are replaced by new ones which defy the prevailing gender contracts (*The Top Floor*; *The Unacceptables*). That said, though, there is a limit regarding the extent to which traditional gender contracts and expectations will be resisted (Kyriazis 1995), as Greece is as much tied to its past as it tries to break away from it. The interplay between tradition and modernity, characteristic of a country and a culture in transition, is prevalent within the Greek television comedy and is also encoded in real life.

Spanish televisual experience shares the same transitional status with its Greek counterpart. Spain, also part of the Mediterranean model, conforms partially to the features of the 'second demographic transition', while exhibiting at the same time characteristics of the 'third demographic transition' (see above, Solsona 1998). Thus, we see on screen a number of powerful career women, who are also mothers, either within or outside wedlock (*Medico de Familia, Querido Maestro*), and a number of men in reconstituted or surrogate families (*A las 11 en casa, Todos los hombres son iguales*). Attitudes towards marriage and family, and the domestic division of labour, are a matter of the prevalent gender culture, which, in the case of Spain, struggles between modernising and traditional tendencies. However, an important variant differentiating gendered norms and attitudes is class culture, as representatives of the working class hang on to more 'traditional' understandings of domestic and family life (*Manos a la obra, Querido Maestro*). This further demonstrates the pattern of diversity in the experience of family structures and gender relations that takes place not only across countries but also within them.

8.4 Afterword

This chapter has analysed the differences in the ways in which gender inequalities are represented in situation comedies. It has done this by taking into consideration both the geographical differences in patriarchal culture (i.e. the notion of 'differentiated patriarchy') and the mechanisms which encode gender roles (i.e. 'gender contracts'). Based on the premise that processes of gender inequality are formed in particular places, within particular cultural contexts, and always in constant interaction with prevailing social norms, the chapter focused on the national experience in situation comedy of four type case countries, Britain, Greece, Spain and Sweden. Each one of these countries represents a different model of social policy. Britain stands for the liberal welfare state and the homemaker gender contract, while Sweden stands for the social democratic welfare state and the 'dual role' gender contract. Greece and Spain, each with its own specific characteristics, belong to a south Mediterranean model which has more 'traditional' gender contracts.

The question then emerged of to what extent televisual representations of gender relations within the situation comedy verify the above categorisation. The answer to this question was that differences in the pre-existing gender contracts, and gender cultures in general, lead to different interpretations of masculinity and femininity, and to different representations of gendered myths in different countries, as illustrated in Figure 8.1. What needs to be emphasised, though, is that this figure should be read as a rough guide towards the depiction of gender inequalities across Europe, as it offers only an *indication* of gendered identities at a national level. Further research that breaks away from the national model needs to be done so that regional differentiation can be studied.

Another issue that needs to be addressed is that although all four type cases offer a combination of traditional and progressive myths, this is, in effect, an illusory degree of similarity. The notion of 'traditional' and 'progressive' or of 'role maintenance' and 'role renewal' differs according to the cultural and spatial context. In this respect, 'role maintenance' in Sweden refers to a more or less established context of gender equality, whereas the same term in Greece or Spain refers to the prevalence of more 'traditional' gender mores and values. Apparent similarities in the televisual representation of gender myths come as a result of the generic conventions of the sitcom, rather than of similarities between the four countries. The sitcom has often been accused of being a conventional and conservative form – after all, it works towards the normalisation of heterosexual love, marriage and family. In cases where there is a deviation from the 'average family' towards situations of disrupted and dysfunctional family structures, normative

	Traditional	Borderline	Progressive
Role maintenance	Simply Rolf (Sw) Manos (Sp)		Svensson (Sw)* Papas Fl. (Sw)*
Borderline	TopFloor (Gr)		Unacceptables (Gr)
Role renewal		Medico (Sp) Men BB (GB)	Mess (Gr) Mistake (Gr) A las 11 (sp) Querido (Sp) Hombres (sp) AbFab (GB)

Figure 8.1 Sitcoms and gender myths. *Note*: Borderline cases stand for series which show both traditional and progressive elements and/or features of role maintenance and role renewal. The asterisks indicate that in these Swedish comedies 'role maintenance' refers to a more or less already established gender parity model, whereas in other cases 'role maintenance' refers to more 'traditional' gender roles.

conceptions of the family function as a point of reference: 'surrogate' families are evoked where the principles of unity, allegiance, obligation and conflict are prevalent (Neale and Krutnik 1990).

The interplay with dominant norms (heterosexual love leading to marriage, children and a structured sexual division of labour) and marginality is another integral part of the situation comedy as the genre depicts and reworks the social transformations which have become resonant in the wider culture. At the same time, though, the sitcom seeks the middle ground audience, without alienating the more liberally minded, 'quality' demographic categories (Feuer 1992). This ambivalence between the dominant and the 'deviant' problematises the potential of the situation comedy for subversiveness: any sign of progressiveness within the television comedy can be a mere 'token' of liberalism rather than anything more (Feuer 1984). Having said that, the institutional position of television broadcasting as one of the mechanisms towards the construction of collective identities and the notion of a community needs to be stressed. As such, there is a limit as to how shocking television can be at peak viewing times.

Finally, attention needs to be drawn to the fact that more systematic research is needed that focuses on existing gender cultures and on regional patterns of gender inequality, and the way these are portrayed in situation comedies. This type of cross-national comparative research should, at best, be the result of a single project, instead of being based on work done for other research purposes, by different authors.

Acknowledgements

Thanks to Gunnel Forsberg in Sweden and Marta Ortega and Marian Vilarrias in Spain for their invaluable help in providing me with information about, and insight into, their domestic programmes.

References

Barthes, R. 1973. *Mythologies*. Paladin, London.

Blumler, J. 1992. *Television and the Public Interest*. Sage, London.

Brants, K. and Siune, K. 1992. Public broadcasting in a state of flux. In Siune, K. and Truetzschler, W. (eds) *Dynamics of Media Politics: Broadcast and Electronic Media in Western Europe*, pp. 101–115. The Euromedia Research Group. Sage, London.

Crompton, R. 1998. Women's employment and state politicies. *Innovation: the European Journal of the Social Sciences*, 11, 2, 129–146.

Duncan, S. 1995. Theorizing European gender systems. *Journal of European Social Policy*, 5, 4, 263–284.

Duncan, S. 1998. Introduction: The spatiality of gender. *Innovation: the European Journal of the Social Sciences*, 11, 2, 119–128.

Duncan, S. and Edwards, R. 1997. Lone mothers and paid work – rational economic man or gendered moral rationalities? *Feminist Economics*, 3, 2, 29–61.

Eaton, M. 1985. Television situation comedy. In Bennett, T., Boyd-Bowman, S., Mercer, C. and Woollacott, J. (eds) *Popular Television and Film*, pp. 117–136. British Film Institute, London.

Elefteriotis, D. 1995. Questioning totalities: constructions of masculinity in the popular Greek cinema of the 1960s. *Sczeey*, 36, 3, 233–242.

Esping-Andersen, G. 1990. *The Three Worlds of Welfare Capitalism*. Polity Press, London.

Feuer, J. 1984. Melodrama, serial form and television today. *Screen*, 25, 4–16.

Feuer, J. 1992. Genre study and television. In Allen, R.C. (ed.) *Channels of Discourse, Reassembled*, pp. 138–161. Routledge, London.

Fiske, J. 1990. *Introduction to Communication Studies*, 2nd edn. Routledge, London.

Forsberg, G. 1998. Regional variations in the gender contract: gendered relations in labour markets, local politics and everyday life in Swedish regions. *Innovation: the European Journal of the Social Sciences*, 11, 2, 191–210.

Hester, M., Pearson, C. and Harwin, N. 1998. *Making an Impact: Children and Domestic Violence*. Barnardo's, Barkingside.

Hirdman, Y. 1990. *Genussystemet, in Statens Offentliga Utredningar*. Demokrati och Makt i Sverige. SOU, Stockholm.

Humphreys, P.J. 1996. *Mass Media and Media Policy in Western Europe*. European Policy Research Unit Series. Manchester University Press, Manchester.

Kyriazis, N. 1995. Feminism and the status of women in Greece. In Constas, D. and Stavrou, T.G. (eds) *Greece Prepares for the Twenty-first Century*, pp. 267–302. Johns Hopkins University Press, Baltimore.

Lewis, J. 1992. Gender and the development of welfare regimes. *Journal of European Social Policy*, 2, 3, 159–173.

Lovell, T. 1986. Television situation comedy. In Punter, D. (ed.) *Introduction to Contemporary Cultural Studies*, pp. 149–168. Longman, London.

McDonald, M. 1995. *Representing Women: Myths of Femininity in the Popular Media*. Edward Arnold, London.

Medhurst, A. and Tuck, L. 1982. The gender game. In *Television Sitcom*, BFI Dossier No. 17, pp. 38–49. British Film Institute, London.

Neale, S. 1980. *Genre*. British Film Institute, London.

Neale, S. and Krutnik, F. 1990. *Popular Film and Television Comedy*. Routledge, London.

Pfau-Effinger, B. 1998. Gender cultures and the gender arrangement – a theoretical framework for cross-national gender research. *Innovation: the European Journal of the Social Sciences*, 11, 2, 147–166.

Roussel, L. 1992. La famille en Europe occidentale: divergences et convergences. *Population*, 1, 133–152.

Rowe, K. 1995. Studying *Roseanne*. In Skeggs, B. (ed.) *Feminist Cultural Theory Process and Production*, pp. 78–102. Manchester University Press, Manchester.

Sackmann, R. 1998. European gender roles: public discourses and regional practices. *Innovation: the European Journal of the Social Sciences*, 11, 2, 167–190.

Silverstone, R. 1994. *Television and Everyday Life*. Routledge, London.

Solsona, M. 1998. The second demographic transition from a gender perspective. *Innovation: the European Journal of the Social Sciences*, 11, 2, 211–225.

Spigel, L. 1992. *Make Room for TV: Television and the Family Ideal in Postwar America*. University of Chicago Press, Chicago.

Taylor, E. 1989. *Prime-time Families: Television Culture in Postwar America*. University of California Press, Berkeley, California.

Tsaliki, L. 1995. *The role of Greek television in the construction of national identity since broadcast deregulation*. Unpublished DPhil thesis, Brighton, University of Sussex.

9 Living through the myths

Gender, values, attitudes and practices

Rosemarie Sackmann

9.1 Issues: the relation between values and practices

Looking at the theoretical discussion of the 'women question' in the last thirty years we can broadly distinguish between three perspectives: liberal feminism, 'social feminism' and an approach influenced by post-modern theory (Farganis 1994). The proponents of liberal feminism were concerned with gender equity. Rejecting the notion that inequalities are established by nature, they struggled to desanctify the family and motherhood and to deconstruct ideas of essential gender differences (for example Mitchell 1971). Proponents of 'social feminism' want to rescue certain values connected with 'maternal thinking' from deconstruction (Ruddick 1980; Elsthain 1982). Social feminism tries to transplant ideals and habits of caring to the public sphere, and to implement them in the political and popular consciousness of our societies.

Both perspectives have been criticised. Liberal feminism not only risks assimilating women into a male model, there is also the quandary that with equity women would be subject to all the problems of liberalism, for example the abstract idea of the individual, the primacy of rights over responsibility and the artificial separation of the public and the private sphere (Farganis 1994). The critique of social feminism is twofold. First, social feminism tends to essentialise women *as* woman. Second, it attempts to ground public (democratic, and therefore inclusive) politics on values and principles that belong to the sphere of intimate, and therefore exclusive, relations (Dietz 1985; Mouffe 1992). The critique at first glance seems convincing, but it depends on the narrowness of the concept of 'maternal thinking' being used. If it is possible to expand the perspective of a caring morality beyond mothering and the sphere of intimate relationships, things may look different. The result could be a picture of humans as carers (see for example Bubeck 1995). This view would include the perspective that basic principles should be designed less according to the logic of rights, which is primarily a logic of personal freedom and is often accompanied by attitudes of indifference towards others, but instead according to a logic of involvement.[1] 'Maternal thinking' would therefore be understood not as an ultimate goal, but as a preliminary model that helps prefigure the desired direction. In my opinion it is an open question whether we ground our societies on broad principles of

234 Gendered understandings

involvement or not. However, this discussion, and others that search for principles that can guide social and political transformations towards more just social relations (for example the contributions to Squires 1993), indicates a need for debates around concepts of the 'good life'. Finally, the third perspective, that is feminist theory from a post-modern viewpoint, has offered much critique of the two other perspectives, and has opened horizons by the deconstruction of reifications and oppositions such as male–female or subject–object (see Farganis 1994). But while post-modernism shows sympathy with experience as well as with action, it cannot (and does not want to) establish principles for a better life that could be institutionalised in our societies.

Here, I will not pursue such a theoretical discussion about the principles of democracy. And for the moment I leave aside the question of which concept of the good life might be the best one to guide our attempts to reach greater justice in gender relations. Rather, I aim in this chapter to examine the attitudes that Europeans hold about gender and equality, and how these link – or do not link – to gendered practices in families. Certainly, the values 'freedom' and 'equality' can be regarded as central values in Western democracies. In this broad sense European states are equal, but between and within different countries there is seldom much agreement about the meaning of these values. Values such as these may be shared by most people, while the same people disagree about the proper interpretation and institutionalisation of these values. This can be seen, for example, in the discussions around affirmative action (Rosenfeld 1991). We can find different beliefs about the hierarchy and ordering of given values. These are for example expressed in opinion polls in which individuals are asked which principle they find more important, 'equality' or 'freedom'. And there also exist differences concerning the strictness of social norms that are related to values (Harding *et al.* 1986).

Values are involved in a wide range of human activity, but where do they come from? Usually social sciences differentiate between 'traditional' and 'modern' societies. For all traditional societies values stemming from religious beliefs have been important. The perspective of social scientists on the influence of such religious beliefs on societies varies widely. At one pole we find Emile Durkheim, who stressed the influence of religion on social cohesion, and at the other pole Max Weber, who stressed the influence of religious beliefs and norms on social change (see Giddens 1997).

However, during the course of modernisation religion has lost its central role as world interpreter. Instead secular ideals from philosophies, and social and psychological theories, were installed in and together with new social organisations. Since the nineteenth century relations between 'structure' and 'culture' have usually been conceptualised as a matter of determination (see Robertson 1988). The question was whether structure determines culture or vice versa (for example, idealism versus materialism). Today, most social scientists would reject the idea of a direct influence of values on behaviour. Both Bordieu with his concept of 'habitus' (Hahn 1995) and Giddens with his notion of 'structuration' (Giddens 1992), two particularly influential social theorists, take this position. Rather social relations are seen as a source of normative orientations. This means thinking of social interaction as the basic experience of humans which underlies all constructions of meaning (for example social feminism). Others think of structured social relations as the basis for, more or less legitimising, interpretations of these structures (catchwords here are hegemony and ideology).

Overall, the understanding of culture as a reflection of social relations has been common in sociology (Robertson 1988; Friedland and Alford 1991). Since the 1980s social scientists have shown a growing interest in culture. In different scientific fields and from different perspectives we find many attempts to develop concepts that assure culture an independent status (which implies that cultural factors can have explanatory power). In these concepts the relation between structure and culture is seen not as determination but as interaction and transformation; this implies that what we call 'structural' at one point in time and from a certain perspective can be called 'cultural' at another point in time and from another perspective (Elkins and Simeon 1979; Jepperson and Swidler 1994). This understanding is mainly a way of separating structure and culture, especially where they are deeply interwoven, as for example in institutional analysis. Institutions can be understood as socially constructed rules which structure human behaviour in specific settings or contexts. Routine reproductive procedures support and sustain institutions. But this definition gives only a reductive understanding of institutions. At two points we have to add culture (see Fuchs 1997). First, institutions are not only constituted by rules, but these rules are part of a selective implementation of values. Second, these values must be socially acknowledged (or internalised, see Parsons 1969) because otherwise individuals would not reproduce the institutionally specific behaviour.

While institutions (like culture) are often identified with stability, institutions can change and they can be sources for change (Friedland and Alford 1991; Jepperson 1991). Besides institutional development, which is best understood as continuation rather than change, we can find processes of de-institutionalisation and re-institutionalisation. De-institutionalisation represents exit from institutionalisation, for example towards non-reproductive patterns. Re-institutionalisation represents exit from one institutionalisation and entry into another (Jepperson 1991). Such changes can be induced from the environments of an institution, for example through contradictions with other institutions. One institution that is of special interest for this chapter is the family. Clearly, 'the family' is institutionalised in different forms and to different degrees (compared over time as well as between states). An institution is more institutionalised if it is more embedded in a framework, which implies that it has been long in place or more centrally located within a framework. Thus, if the family as an institution is embedded in laws that, for example, protect a certain family form, and if financial transfers from state to family are also shaped in accordance with that certain family form, then this family form is highly institutionalised. And if a family form is a cultural pattern but not embedded in a framework, then this form is not institutionalised, or only to a low degree. Lone parenting, for example, is in many countries not institutionalised, and in some countries it is institutionalised not as a family form but as a form of poverty.

The face of research on the family has altered during the last twenty years. The new approaches, and how they are different from older ones, are of significance for this paper. To summarise the main trends I follow Sgritta (1988). With regard to structures and functions of the family, theory and research turned from assumptions about linear development to an interest in cyclical developments. Former theories were connected with functional theories about the effects of industrialisation and urbanisation, which were thought to bring about the nuclear family as the standard family form. Nowadays, empirical research stresses the diversity of family forms, where family cycles are just one example. With regard to production and reproduction, or the spheres of economy and family, it has been recognised that both are not separated but exist in a reciprocal relation. Two research fields have been especially important in this context, the analysis of female careers and the analysis of caring activities within the family. With regard to ideas about modernisation and progress, another linearity assumption has lost its influence, namely the idea of an ongoing process of differentiation. Now, growing interest is paid to processes of de-differentiation. An example here is again the taking up of caring responsibilities by families. Sometimes these activities are clearly induced by economic crisis (self-help is cheaper than any other version), but often decisions to take up caring responsibilities within the home are at least interwoven with values, if not primarily driven by value orientations.

To summarise, we can now answer the questions about value transmittance and change. Early socialisation and ongoing socialisation during the life course must be regarded as crucial mechanisms of cultural reproduction. Processes of reproduction occur at different levels: practices in everyday life, institutional reproduction and public discourse. Values and ideals are leading principles in a society. They are used to define the appropriate way of living and to exclude some forms as inappropriate. That does not mean that other forms of living, different from those propagated in public discourse, do not exist. They do. Sometimes an existing alternative form is propagated as a counter-ideal (the ideal of 'maternal thinking' is one example). But the leading ideal remains the point of reference until a new one is widely shared and accepted as the leading principle. In this way an ideal is not the average of real forms, nor is it always the representation of the most widespread form of living. However, translated into leading principles, ideals influence the frame for practices, for example by opening and closing opportunities.

For individuals values and ideals exist in two ways: first as a pool of common-sense knowledge and understandings, and models of life shared (or believed to be shared) in a society, and second as versions of these models which an individual conceptualises and invokes in everyday perception, thought and interaction (Keesing 1987). As interpretations play such an important role for the reproduction or change of ideals, it is possible that practices differ widely. Which interpretations, of the meaning of family roles for example, are seen as proper can be influenced by other differentiations, for example by ethnicity (Glenn 1994; Segura 1994; Duncan and Edwards 1997), social class (Rosenbaum 1982) or regional socio-historical settings (Sieder 1987; Sackmann 1997). Usually we know – more or less – about such differences in our own society. The fact of differing practices does not in itself lead to a change of publicly propagated ideals; indeed, in public discourses some alternatives are regarded as deviant rather than as alternative life forms, for example, in many countries, the lone parent family. To a certain degree, the kind of institutionalisation of relations is a mirror of public opinions and a change of institutions is likewise a mirror of a change in public opinions.

In the following sections I will first give an overview of differences in the distribution of an equality ideal with regard to gender roles in the member states of the European Union (section 9.2). I make use of the survey 'Women and Men in Europe' and of the European Values Survey (EVS). As ideals and realities should be regarded together I discuss the survey findings in relation to employment data published by the European Commission's Network of Experts on the Situation of Women in the Labour Market (Bulletin 1994, 1995a,b). These data are not strictly comparable, or easy to interpret, but nevertheless, together with information from more detailed studies, it is possible to draw some provisional conclusions. Using these results, I turn to a regional approach in the attempt to understand more fully the interrelation between culture and practice (section 9.3). On the basis of apparent diversity I return to the question of which principles might be the best to guide the transformation of our societies towards greater justice with regard to gender relations (section 9.4).

9.2 Patterns: gender values and practices in the European Union

In the following discussion I assume that people act in accordance with their attitudes or, if they do not, that they have good reasons to act against their attitudes. For example there may be subject constraints, or other attitudes, connected with values that range higher in their value system, may take precedence. If we accept this assumption it follows that every divergence between attitudes and practices needs explanation. For divergence must therefore be a result of constraints or of competing value orientations.

I will describe the dispersion of gender equality as an ideal, as it is expressed in individual attitudes, and as a reality, as expressed in female employment rates, in twelve European Union countries for which data were available (the EU 12). First, I want to look at attitudes. One question, usually asked in

Eurobarometer surveys (Women and Men in Europe 1983, 1987), combines two aspects of modern gender roles: the division of labour in, and between, the spheres of the household and paid employment. Respondents were asked to choose one ideal family model out of three. The family models were: (1) both husband and wife have an equally absorbing job and share housework and care of the children equally (the equality model); (2) the wife has a less demanding job and does the larger share of housework and caring for the children (the part-time model); and (3) the husband has a full-time job and the wife runs the home and cares for the children (the housewife model).

This comparison of expressed attitudes with actual practices has already been taken up by other research on gender roles (Alwin *et al*. 1992; Ellingsaeter 1996). In these publications the authors were able to combine not only aggregated data (what I am going to do here) but also individual data files. Their research findings are revealing. Alwin, Brown and Scott, who used data from the International Social Survey Programme in which the questions were directly about whether women should work part-time, full-time or not at all, have shown that generally attitudes and practices do not differ. For example, in their study of West Germany, Great Britain and the United States, it was found that women who preferred part-time employment (rather than full-time employment or full-time household work) indeed usually worked part-time. Among the influences on attitudes and practices that were discussed in that study I want to emphasise one: the importance of life-cycle stages. This influence is twofold: first, couples with and without children differ in their attitudes (the majority of the former – with the exception of the German respondents – favoured an employment involvement of women). Second, the age of children is important for the question of whether parents think that the mother should work at all, work part-time or full-time. Many parents with older children think that the woman should take up paid work, at least on a part-time basis.

Ellingsaeter, using data from a Scandinavian survey in which some questions were similar to the question I will be using from the EVS, has shown that we can find great divergence between the perception of the dominance of a specific national 'provider model' on the one hand and personal preferences on the other. This is in accordance with the theoretical difference between 'common' values – those which characterise the representation of the society as united – and 'shared' values – those expressed by many or all (see Jepperson and Swidler 1994). But Ellingsaeter's study additionally offers empirical evidence for differences between countries with regard to the convergence or divergence between 'common' and 'shared' values. For example, the divergence between norm perception and individual preference is much higher in Norway than in Sweden. The shared ideal of Norwegian parents is the equality model (to a degree very similar to Sweden), but Norwegian parents tend to believe that other people are more in favour of the housewife model (that is clearly not the case in Sweden). Ellingsaeter speaks of a situation of fluid norms and of an ongoing change in Norway in particular as one example of this. Thus, we can hypothesise that divergence is indicative of societies in transition. However, while this is a very interesting point, the kinds of data that are available does not allow me to follow this direction of research for the EU as a whole. Instead the following analysis deals, mostly, with shared values, where 'shared' means held by a number of individuals (that is, percentages of respondents).

The three ideal models in the EVS that are offered to the respondents suffer from additional problems because they are formulated in a way that does not fit well with the social science discussion of gender roles around household and employment. For example, the formulation for the second model, which demands 'less absorbing' jobs for wives, offers more and other possibilities of interpretation than just 'part-time job'. While we can interpret the formulation in this direction, we cannot be sure about the meaning that respondents gave to these formulations. And, if the respondents did indeed translate 'absorbing' into working hours, we do not know what they would call a 'less absorbing' job (10 hours a week or 30 hours?). Despite these objections, I use only full-time employment rates of mothers as an indicator of the realisation of the equality model. I do this despite the fact that in some countries, as in the Scandinavian countries, part-time work often means 'long part-time' of 20 hours a week or more (Bulletin 1995a). For there is still a difference between part-time and full-time employment even in these countries and, as men are mostly working full-time, I suspect that even long part-time hours do not meet the equality model, where this demands 'equally absorbing jobs'. However, we should remember that one of the standard models of employment, the model of life-long full-time employment, may be changing towards a new employment model. This new model would integrate household and caring work (and other socially valuable work outside the labour market) by a reduction in hours in gainful employment. It may be that respondents have these ideas, rather than full-time employment, in mind when they agree with the equality model. As we will see, there is some evidence for this reading of the equality model in the analysis that follows.

I will not look here at all possible answers about preferred types of the distribution of work and responsibility between household and employment. As this is not a report about survey findings the analysis presents as much data as necessary for the argument and no more, and I will use only the percentage of agreement with the equality model in the year 1987. This means that some interesting differences that emerge from the data will not be followed up. For example, it is interesting that the housewife model finds few proponents in Denmark (just 12 per cent). Even more interesting is the fact that in three countries (Ireland, Luxembourg, West Germany) respondents agree in higher percentages with the housewife model than with the equality model (equality: West Germany 26 per cent, Ireland 34 per cent, Luxembourg 20 per cent; housewife: West Germany 32 per cent, Ireland 39 per cent, Luxembourg 39 per cent). In the same three countries the percentage agreeing with the part-time model (the wife has a less absorbing job and is the primary household and family carer) is less than that agreeing with the equality model. In all other countries the equality model is the one that received the highest level of agreement (Women and Men in Europe 1987: 16).

The data for values used in the following analysis are from 1987 and 1990, while the employment data are from 1991. There is a possibility that values might change appreciably even within the narrow timespan of four years. Thus attitudes held in 1983 and 1987 on the ideal family model in the Eurobarometer survey do show some remarkable changes (Women and Men in Europe 1987: 14). For example, agreement with the equality model in the United Kingdom and Denmark is significantly higher in 1987 than in 1983 (UK: 48 per cent versus 37 per cent; Denmark: 53 per cent versus 46 per cent), whereas in Greece agreement is actually lower in 1987 than in 1983 (43 per cent versus 51 per cent).[2] Thus, rather like the possibility of a 'fluidity of norms' in societies in transition, we have also to remember that values may change over the period of analysis and that what appears as divergence between attitudes and practices in the analysis might in reality be partially an effect of change over time. We will have to keep this in mind when we interpret the findings.

Table 9.1 shows the percentage of agreement with the equality model for twelve EU countries in 1987 compared with the full-time employment rates for mothers – defined as women with dependent children (women aged 20 to 39 with at least one child aged 14 or less). In addition Table 9.1 presents an index of the 'motherhood effect'. This provides a standardised measure of the difference between the full-time employment rate of women without children and the full-time employment rate of mothers (Bulletin 1995a). For some purposes this index can be very useful, but it must also be handled with care. For example, in a country with a low female employment rate, the motherhood effect may also be low. This is because, where women are strongly orientated towards household and caring responsibilities, they may also show low employment orientation even if they are not actually mothers. In such a case (as for example Greece), or where women generally (not only as mothers) are severely constrained from participating in paid labour, the motherhood effect itself can be small. Where all women have low participation in the labour market, the low participation of mothers will not be particularly obvious with this measure.

Looking at Table 9.1, we can first distinguish countries with an above average agreement rate with the equality model from those with a below average agreement rate. On average 41 per cent of all respondents chose the equality model as their family ideal. The range is large, between 20 per cent and 53 per cent, but only four countries show a below average agreement rate to the equality model: Belgium, Ireland, West Germany and Luxembourg. The full-time employment rate for women with children is used as a second source of differentiation and for this index half of all countries show above or below average readings respectively. The twelve countries can thus be grouped in four categories (Table 9.2).

Table 9.1 The equality model in the European Union: ideal and reality

	Agreement with the equality model*	Employment rates: women with children†			
	Total (women/men)	Full-time (%)	Part-time (%)	Total (%)	Motherhood effect‡
Denmark	53 (55/51)	49	27	76	+2
United Kingdom	48 (46/51)	18	35	53	−34
Greece	47 (48/38)	39	3	42	−22
Spain	47 (48/46)	30	5	35	−37
France	45 (47/43)	44	17	61	−17
Portugal	43 (46/40)	66	5	71	−6
The Netherlands	43 (44/42)	5	36	41	−43
Italy	42 (47/36)	38	5	43	−30
Belgium	34 (39/28)	39	23	62	−16
Ireland	34 (36/31)	23	9	32	−51
West Germany	26 (27/25)	20	28	48	−39
Luxembourg	20 (21/19)	27	13	40	−48
EU 12	41 (41/38)	31	20	51	−31

Sources and definitions:

*Women and Men in Europe (1987: 16, 60).

†Bulletin (1995a: 4); data relate to women aged 20 to 39 in 1991 who were household heads, either individually or as part of a couple; women with children were defined as women with a dependent child aged 14 or less.

‡Calculated as (Activity rate of women without dependent children − Activity rate of women with dependent children) / Activity rate of women without dependent children × 100; for women aged 20 to 39 in 1991. *Source*: Bulletin (1995a: 8). *Note*: The motherhood effect is calculated from a database that differs from that for the employment rates in the table. Only women who have finished their education, training etc. are included here.

Table 9.2 Ideal and actual divisions of labour, EU 12*

		Agreement with the equality ideal	
		Above average	Below average
Full-time employment of women with children	Above average	P, Dk, F, Gr, I	Belg
	Below average	UK, Sp, Neths	WG, L, Irl

*Belg, Belgium; Dk, Denmark; F, France; I, Iceland; Irl, Ireland; Gr, Greece; L, Luxembourg; Neths, the Netherlands; P, Portugal; Sp, Spain; UK, United Kingdom; WG, West Germany.

As the grouping of the countries is somewhat surprising it is necessary to keep the purpose of the differentiation in mind: I am looking for convergence and divergence between ideal and reality. We will shortly see how far this somewhat artificial grouping can lead us to real findings about the compared countries.

To get more information on gender roles I have presented in Table 9.3 additional data from the European Values Survey (Zulehner and Denz 1993). From a wide range of questions, of which many have some connection with attitudes towards gender roles, I chose six as most indicative:

1   'both man and woman should contribute to the income of the household';
2   'employment is the best way for a woman to gain independence';
3   'a profession is good, but what women really want is a home and children';
4   'a small child will suffer if the mother is working';
5   'being a housewife is as fulfilling as having a job';
6   'a woman needs children in order to have a fulfilling life'.

The pattern of relative agreement with the six statements is somewhat puzzling and obviously needs more analysis. However, in the following I will point only to some of these data in order to highlight possible connections between the equality ideal of the family and gender attitudes and gender practices. Additionally I will use detailed information for some countries to take the discussion further.

Now, to begin with let us look at the countries in which the equality ideal is most pronounced and in which the employment rates for mothers stand above the European average: Denmark, Portugal, France, Greece and Italy (Group I). In Table 9.1 the positive motherhood effect in Denmark is striking. One explanation is that in this age group (20–39) not all women have completed their training, but that at the same time the combination 'mother in training' is rare. We also know that motherhood in Denmark, as in the other Scandinavian countries, does not in general form a hindrance to female employment (see Duncan 1995).[3] The extent of agreement with the equality model is large. We can add here that public childcare is widespread in Denmark compared with the other countries investigated. Children are a

Table 9.3 Attitudes to women's roles in the European Union, 1990, percentage of full agreement with the six statements

	Both should contribute to the household income	Employment is the best way for a woman to gain independence	What women really want is a home and children	A small child will suffer if the mother is working	Being a housewife is as fulfilling as having a job	A woman needs children in order to have a fulfilling life
Group I						
Denmark	34	36	51	10	7	72
France	35	36	40	21	21	68
Iceland	22	22	19	18	18	63
Portugal	42	81	47	37	29	57
Group II						
West Germany	19	11	8	31	9	34
Ireland	10	14	17	12	10	24
Group III						
Spain	26	26	29	12	15	46
United Kingdom	11	16	20	11	8	19
Netherlands	14	8	28	22	10	11
Group IV						
Belgium	24	26	40	18	18	41

Source: Zulehner and Denz 1993: 59ff. No data available for Greece and Luxembourg.

'public issue' (Women of Europe 1990). Against this background it at first seems astonishing that Danish respondents in the EVS agree, at such a high level, with the statements that 'what women really want is a home and children' and 'a woman needs children in order to have a fulfilling life' (see Table 9.3). The agreement with the last statement is extremely high at 72 per cent compared with just 34 per cent in West Germany and 24 per cent in Ireland, even though the latter are usually seen as much more traditional in terms of gender relations (Duncan 1995). In my opinion the Danish answers reflect positive attitudes towards parenthood (the upbringing of children as a central social issue), not traditional family values (the family as the basic institution of coherence in an otherwise interest-driven society). Unfortunately, the EVS and other surveys do not ask about parenthood or even about the importance of children for men, so I am unable to pursue this question further here.

Among the countries compared here Portugal shows the highest integration of women with dependent children in the workforce, at 66 per cent, although agreement with the equality model is small by comparison, at 43 per cent. On the other hand, respondents to the EVS show comparatively high agreement with the statements listed in Table 9.3, which would seem to indicate traditional female roles. We should note here that agriculture is still an important field of employment in Portugal (20 per cent of female full-time employees, and 32 per cent of female part-time employees). Among the countries compared only Greece shows an even higher importance of agriculture for female employment (30 per cent of female full-timers, 39 per cent of female part-timers) (Bulletin 1994: 8). But even taking the importance of agriculture into account, the employment rate of women with children in Portugal must still be regarded as high. Perhaps employment in agriculture can partly explain how traditional gender roles and high employment rates come together. However, truly outstanding is the very high agreement with the statement 'employment is the best way for a woman to gain independence'. Combined with the high agreement with the statement 'both the man and the woman should contribute to the income of the household' this can be taken as an indicator for an 'economic' rationality as motor for the integration of women into the workforce.

In European comparisons of female employment (or of welfare states, or the level of economic development) we usually find a category of 'southern' or 'Mediterranean' states, comprising Greece, Italy, Spain and Portugal. The comparatively low female employment rate in the first three of these countries is usually explained, on the one hand, by the late and weak development of their welfare states and/or by their retarded or peripheral economic development. On the other hand the same phenomenon is explained by the predominance of traditional values and family perceptions, in turn resulting from a particular religious moulding plus the persistence of rural economies. According to the data in Table 9.1 it would be possible to combine Greece and Italy as a sub-group within Group I: the level of agreement with the equality model, as well as the differences between the sexes regarding the equality ideal, are similar for both countries. In contrast, employment rates for women without children show considerable differences, with Greece at 61 per cent and Italy at 74 per cent (Bulletin 1995a).

So, are Greece and Italy similar cases with regard to women's roles and employment? More detailed analysis for these countries might offer more information. In Italy, for example, we find a clear change of behaviour and attitudes towards the family that differentiates younger age cohorts clearly from older ones (see Pinnelli and De Rose 1995). In addition, to understand gender roles in Italy we have to take considerable regional differences into account with regard to opportunity structures (jobs, childcare facilities) as well as cultural influences (Addabbo 1997).

A different complex of effects is cited for Greece, consisting on the one hand of the inflexible formal labour market, combined with the possibility of income and work from the family economy and the informal economy, and on the other hand of the influence of traditional values. One important factor in this complex is the inflexible labour market, which increases the costs of leaving employment for family reasons considerably, because re-entering is very difficult. Women are forced to decide whether ultimately to remain in employment after the birth of their children, or to give up employment altogether (Symeonidou 1997). There are indications that this alternative is anticipated; women already decide in their early years for or (more usually) against an employment orientation. And employment is often already given up at the point of marriage and not upon the birth of the first child (Symeonidou 1997). In Greece family economy and informal employment can be seen as alternatives to formal employment (Bulletin 1994). Where, as in Greece, the family widely provides the economic basis of relationships, family coherence and dependence is strengthened.

The data for France in Tables 9.1 and 9.3 show a situation where attitudes and practices are in accordance. For a long time France was seen as a mixed case or even a 'miracle' with regard to female roles in family and employment (Lefaucheur and Martin 1997). The well-known stress on pronatalist policies and high rates of female employment participation are ingredients in this picture. Jane Lewis (1992) has clarified the case by classifying France as a welfare state that developed a 'parental model' concentrating more on the child than on women (Lechaufeur and Martin 1997). I would alter the stress a bit. What makes France special is a concentration on the de facto family. The specificity is obvious if we compare France and West Germany (Schultheis 1998). In West Germany the family is an institution or, in other words, a traditional, normative ideal of the family has been the framework for welfare state regulations as well as – until 1974 – for family law. Indicative of the differences between the two countries are the birth rates outside marriage, which in France currently amount to 40 per cent, but in West Germany to only 10 per cent, of total births.

West Germany is representative of a second group of countries in Table

9.2 – those with both below average agreement with the equality ideal and below average full-time employment of mothers. Here we can distinguish two groups of working mothers, those with and those without a strong employment orientation. What is remarkable is that the dividing line between the two groups does not follow qualification levels, and that the influence of motherhood on the employment behaviour of women with high qualifications is high, certainly in comparison with the European average. This also applies to Ireland, Luxembourg and the Netherlands, albeit being clearly less pronounced in the last. For women between 20 and 39 years of age, with a child aged 14 or below, and with qualifications at a graduate level, the employment rate in West Germany is just 62 per cent (Ireland and Luxembourg 68 per cent; the Netherlands 70 per cent) compared with the EU average of 76 per cent (Bulletin 1995a). That is the lowest rate of all the countries we compare.

The results of an event history analysis carried out by Blossfeld and Rohwer (1997) allow us to complete the picture. The expansion of part-time employment among German women meant first of all an increase in transitions from full-time to part-time work. This started with the birth cohort 1934–1938, increased with the following cohorts and was not ended by the economic crisis of the 1980s. Up to the 1970s transitions from full-time employment to housewife status were not influenced by the supply of part-time work. The re-entry of a housewife into the labour market thus became virtually equivalent to taking on a part-time job. Part-time work is only slowly becoming a transitional status to full-time work. Only for women with high qualifications was there an indication in the 1980s that part-time work was becoming a bridge between housewife status and full-time work. And, in accordance with the findings from the employment survey cited above (Bulletin 1995a), transitions from employment to housewife status are not influenced by the level of education.

Thus, to characterise the case of West Germany, I would emphasise the differentiation between women with high work commitment and women with lower work commitment. Among women with higher work commitment there are some who are working mothers. But very often mothering and employment participation are seen as mutually exclusive. In West Germany 60 per cent of women working full-time do not have children, whereas in France, for example, this was only 27 per cent (Schultheis 1998).

We turn now to Group III (high agreement with the equality ideal, below average full-time employment of women with dependent children: UK, Spain, the Netherlands). The UK shows a pronounced difference between agreement with the equality model and its realisation in the form of full-time employment of women with dependent children. The full-time employment rates are the second lowest among the countries compared, while the agreement with the equality model is the second highest (see Table 9.1). Men agree with the model even more strongly than women. A slightly confusing picture! I will attempt to clarify it.

The UK is the European example of a liberal welfare state, in which the increased employment participation of women is described as an effect of demand from the private economy. 'Women', meaning here married women and mothers, were seen as 'reserve army' (Burchell *et al.* 1997). They were included in the labour market when the increasing demand could no longer be met from other sources (for example immigrants). The post-war ideology remained nonetheless clearly committed to the ideal of the woman as housewife. Today there is still hardly any publicly organised childcare for pre-school children, nor much after-school or holiday childcare for older children. One way of combining family and employment orientations that is favoured by British women is the interruption of employment upon the birth of a child and the subsequent return to employment on a part-time basis. Apart from this influence on the supply-side, an influence of the demand-side is visible: since the 1980s, under the influence of the economic crisis, the proportion of part-time jobs on re-entering employment has risen (see the transition rates from full-time to part-time employment in Burchell *et al.* 1997).

The development of the labour market might therefore provide an explanation for the divergence between the high agreement with the equality model of the family and its low realisation in the UK. This explanation implies that individuals hold on to their ideal despite the low likelihood of its realisation. In this case, we could expect that women work part-time only involuntarily. But in 1990 79 per cent of married women in part-time employment in Britain said that they did not want full-time employment (Women of Europe undated). Another possible explanation for the divergence between high agreement with the equality ideal and a low rate of realisation could be that most of those respondents who favour the equality model – usually the young generation – are actually not in a family situation and their attitudes will change once they are in that situation (see Rost and Schneider 1995). Only longitudinal studies can clear up this point. However, this seems unlikely where an analysis of attitudes on gender roles in different stages of the life course reports high rates of convergence between attitudes and practices (Alwin *et al.* 1992). A third explanation takes a highly developed sense of individual life into account (Finch 1997; Le Bras 1997). A highly developed individualism may remain untouched by opportunity constraints when the respective value areas are not interrelated. Research findings on the attitudes of lone mothers, for example, show that most White respondents see good motherhood and employment as dichotomous (Duncan and Edwards 1997). But the personal commitment to motherhood may not hinder a woman from agreeing with a general model of equality for women and men.

Let us look at another country from Group III, the Netherlands. Despite a high agreement with the equality model, the motherhood effect on female employment is high and only 5 per cent of women with dependent children are in full-time employment (Table 9.1). The Dutch hardly agree with statements that women primarily want children, that household work can be as satisfying as gainful employment and that small children will suffer from the mother's employment (see Table 9.3). Again we have the problem of divergence between ideal and reality. Let us first turn to history.

Up to 1960 the following view was valid for the Netherlands: only unmarried women worked, married women at the most casually assisted. While in 1960 only one in five women were gainfully employed, by 1990 this had increased to one in two. Thus, the development of female employment participation was delayed in the Netherlands. This has been explained by a mix of economic and cultural factors (de Graaf and Vermeulen 1997; Pfau-Effinger 1998). In the Netherlands the reaction to the rise in labour demand in the 1960s was such that Dutch men switched to service occupations, while manual occupations were taken over by immigrants.

During the 1960s the value system of Dutch society was strongly tied to religion. From the 1970s onwards the demand for labour (especially in the service sector) could no longer be satisfied as it had been. Religious commitments had been weakened in this period, and the integration of married women into the labour market began. It was then, and still is, an integration on a part-time basis. Dutch women clearly favour part-time employment, mostly short-time with few hours (de Graaf and Vermeulen 1997). de Graaf and Vermeulen see two possible explanations for the low employment orientation of Dutch women: lack of childcare facilities and the after-effects of the religious commitment of earlier times. Thus, either a structural or a cultural lag is the source of the divergence between egalitarian attitudes and female employment participation in the Netherlands (see de Jong Gierveld and Liefbroer 1995 and Knijn 1994 for the structural lag explanation).

A cultural lag is not an explanation in itself, but a symptom that needs explanation. If there really is a divergence between ideal and reality, how did it come about? The structural lag hypothesis seems to offer an answer. But what about the fact that Dutch women prefer part-time work while at the same time the agreement with the equality model is high? Trude Knijn (1994), despite her adherence to the structural lag explanation, has analysed images of motherhood in the Netherlands. The predominant image of motherhood of the 1980s presented motherhood as a source of self-realisation. A free choice of lifestyles was socially advocated, which also implied that the individual burden increases, as various models are not generally binding. This in turn implies that there is a consistent and great danger of making wrong decisions. At the same time the idea of the 'real mother' was still present. A 'real mother' does not leave the care of her children to others. Knijn sees the main dilemma of Dutch women in the perception of the choice between motherhood and paid work, or in combining them, as an individual problem and not as a social one. While this is a general problem in the re-organisation of modern gender roles, in my opinion it is not specific enough to explain the Dutch situation. I argue that there are two other relevant factors – one is connected to a general value change in Dutch society and one is the absence of alternative models. To start with the latter: in the situation of Dutch women as it is described by Knijn, there still exists only one model of motherhood, the model of the 'real mother'. Very few women live alternative lifestyles. However, in a situation of choice, alternatives that can influence a change of behaviour must be lived (realised) and socially recognised alternatives. Realised alternatives do not only work as examples, they also make visible what is involved in one way of living or another. The real lived alternative is also important in allowing identification with a role. Otherwise, cultural changes can occur only very slowly as a stepwise change of routines and habits.[4] If we look at the answers to the questions with high relevance for gender roles shown in Table 9.3, we see that Dutch respondents are the least likely to believe that employment is the best way for women to gain independence.[5] This was an important way in which women and women's movements tried to change traditional gender roles. Obviously, this way has not found much acceptance in the Netherlands.

Let us now have a look at the second issue of value change. During the last two decades researchers have observed a 'value change' in Western societies towards a predominance of the value 'freedom' over that of 'equality' (Felling *et al.* 1983; Meulemann 1993; Peters *et al.* 1993; Inglehart 1997). For a long time, 'equality' has been characterised as a value of the political left, 'freedom' as a value of the right. In this understanding 'freedom' was closely linked with the market rationality of free competition and individual success. 'Equality', by contrast, expressed the importance of equal chances and pointed thereby to social and structural constraints on equality. Possibly a new connection of these two values has now occurred, transcending these old left and right positions. I would call this a value change, that is a change in the meaning of 'freedom' and in the meaning of 'equality'. Freedom with its new meaning is 'the freedom to be different'[6] and it is closely linked to equal rights for different social groups (Young 1990), for the right to be treated as equal, the right to be recognised, or even for the right not to be categorised at all (see Fraser 1995).

For the Netherlands it has been shown that an ongoing process of individualisation was accompanied by a decrease in the Calvinistic work ethos (Fellings *et al.* 1983; Peters *et al.* 1993). Whether linked with Calvinism or not, this value pattern – which has come to be termed the 'work ethic' (see Ashford and Timms 1992) – was built on central principles of which at least two have become less important, namely individualistic success and deferred gratification (that is, a willingness to postpone immediate pleasure in order to build up a store of virtue as well as money). While subordination of life to the demands of work is a less important driving force in the work commitment of individuals, values connected with self-realisation have become more important (see Meulemann 1998). At the same time people in Western industrialised countries give more importance to 'well-being values' (see Inglehart 1997). Given this, I interpret the situation of high levels of part-time work by women in the Netherlands as an example of an alternative work orientation. Catherine Hakim (1997) sees this as the main characteristic of the combination of orientations expressed in the decision to work part-time. The growing number of part-timers among Dutch men might in addition be an indication of a move towards an alternative understanding of instrumental work. But until now this has not meant new definitions of female roles.

The first approximation to an analysis of the role of women in the European Union attempted here can be summarised as follows. First, I have differentiated the EU 12 countries using two indicators to obtain a picture of the national dispersion of ideal and real equality models in gender relations (the average of the agreement with an equality model of the family, and the average of full-time employment participation of mothers). Second, I examined possible social mechanisms explaining this convergence or divergence between the ideal of an equality model and its realisation. Thus Denmark, as an example of a social democratic welfare state,[7] not only integrates women in the workforce, but also defines childcare as a public issue. In Denmark the modern family form (what is usually called 'traditional') of father–mother–child has clearly lost its influence. In France, former divergences between pronatalist policies, strong traditional family relations and high female employment rates have disappeared. The developments can be summarised as the re-institutionalisation of the family. The image of reconstituted families (step-parent families) as a new type of large family relationship founded not on blood ties but on the fact of living together (Le Gall and Martin 1997) indicates this change. In contrast, Greece is deeply influenced by the prevalence of traditional family relations. Here, alternative lifestyles for women exist only to a very low degree, and alternative family models hardly exist at all. While in Portugal the transformation process is primarily driven by economic development and expressed in high female employment rates, backed by an idea of emancipation through economic participation, women in Italy, especially more highly educated women, began to change female roles by postponing or avoiding marriage. West Germany gives an example of the differentiation between women that follows from the perception of a severe dichotomy between motherhood and employment participation. The female population is roughly divided in three parts, namely those who choose motherhood as prime focus (including part-time work), those who decide for a career in employment and those (a small proportion) who integrate the two spheres. Finally, while trying to find explanations for the divergence of the equality ideal and reality in the Netherlands, I found evidence for a value change that probably has also changed the meaning of the equality model. I assumed that in the Netherlands the equality ideal is connected with a specific meaning of freedom that fosters alternative work orientations and alternative orientations besides work orientation.

One underlying structure is common to all the examples: family practices, economic practices and attitudes towards gender roles are interconnected. But the connection between the family sphere and the employment sphere shows both different forms and different kinds of changes in different countries. How, and how closely, are family forms and economic structures interconnected? This question is of some importance as the Greek example above shows. Additionally, we know other regions in Europe where social and economic structures are closely linked together. For example in Italy, three types of regions – North, South and the 'Third Italy' in between – can be differentiated according to the economic structure and in relation to family forms (Mingione 1993; Addabbo 1997). However, for many European regions the connection between economic structures and social forms is more complex.

All too often, the connections of gender roles with family forms on the one hand and employment structures on the other have been analysed as two sides of the same phenomenon. But the relationship between women's family orientation and their employment orientation is not an inverse one. Family practices do not simply just follow on from economic structures, or vice versa. In this sense both are autonomous from one another. Thus it is necessary to analyse not only employment orientations but also family orientations (see Born *et al.* 1996).

9.3 Explanations: connecting values and practices

In analysing cultural differences such as those shown in the last section, regions rather than nation states will often be the more appropriate unit of analysis. This is because what appears today as 'cultural difference' stems from former social practices that have developed regionally. In this section I will follow this up using examples of different connections between family and work spheres in Germany (see Sackmann and Häussermann 1994; Sackmann 1997). First, I start with differences in the degree of familiarisation. Second, I turn to different forms of labour organisation that have hindered or enabled women to participate in paid employment, and also to different kinds of labour allocation and their possible determinants and outcomes. Finally, I argue that some arrangements that evolved at a regional level create cultural milieus that are more supportive for 'individualism' than others.

There are two main regional family forms in Germany in the north and south, and these have their origins in the process of industrialisation, which was contemporaneous with a process of 'familiarisation' (Tenfelde 1992). By 'familiarisation' I mean the process where for every adult it became the rule to form a family. This was a new development because up to around 1,800 marriage restrictions, as well as lack of money and especially lack of land, hindered large parts of the population from marrying. By 1900 the idea of women as housewives and mothers (not as workers) was institutionalised and thus became the common framework (see Sackmann 1997). Laws were formed to protect the father–mother–children family with its dualised gender roles. Practised forms, however, varied according to class (Rosenbaum 1982) and to region (Sieder 1987).

Pre-existing family forms have been important factors for regional differentiation. The two main regional forms have been influenced by different structures of agricultural production (large scale in the north, small scale in the south) that were a result of former differing inheritance laws. In the north, only one son inherited the whole farm. In the south (especially Bavaria and Baden-Wurtemberg) the land was divided between all sons. (I leave aside here differences concerning the inheritance law with regard to women. These regulations varied locally and over time.) Thus, in the south farms became smaller over time and many farmers searched for additional income as craftsmen, workers in manufacturing or homeworkers in the production of linen. Often, women ran the farm while men were working elsewhere. In the northern system all but one son had to leave the farm or work as labourers for the heir. In north-eastern regions (Prussia) the situation was even more severe for most of the population because the bulk of the land was in the hands of the aristocracy.

The varying organisation of agriculture had deep influences on the life courses of women and men. In regions with small-scale agriculture, as in the south, status transitions in family relations were connected with status transitions in economic relations for both women and men. In contrast many agricultural workers in the north (especially in Prussia) did not have the opportunity to form families. Many went to cities and/or into service occupations in households, which are well known as usually incompatible with marriage (Gottlieb 1993). As a result of these situations southern regions had higher marriage rates than northern ones, and birth rates outside marriage were (and still are) higher in northern regions (especially in the east) than in southern regions.

Towards the end of the nineteenth century some regions in Germany underwent new processes of familiarisation, which were attributable not to the organisational forms of agriculture but rather to industrialisation. The Ruhr area in Nordrhin-Westphalia was first: here the dominance of wage earning in manufacturing radically altered the former connection between land ownership and marriage. In the Ruhr, and soon after also in Saarland as another emerging industrial region, the preferred labour allocation strategies excluded women from the work sphere. It has been shown that this was not an inevitable result of the economic structure (Schmidt 1983; Lüsebrink 1993), which was dominated by mining and heavy industry. Nevertheless, women were simply not employed in these heavy industries, not even in clerical work, and the logic of industrialised, large-scale production was transferred to other industries, such as the garment industry. Thus, homeworking (which allowed combining of waged work and childcare) and small-scale production were rare in these regions. Given the very low wages and bad working conditions, and the further problem of combining these kinds of employment with the care of children, only those women who were deeply in need of money took up paid work.

The Ruhr area is one example of the influence of strategies of labour allocation on the employment participation of women. There are other examples. Cigar production, for example, had in different regions different forms of labour allocation, preferring men to women in the north and women to men in the south. In the north, where women were employed it was only for poorly paid work and usually as assistants to their husbands. In the south, women had better-paid and skilled work and they were employed as individuals and not as assistants to their husbands. The German garment industry is another example of different strategies of labour allocation. In some regions women were trained and could mainly work under their own responsibility, while in others they were clearly subordinated to men. Where the production was industrialised, as in the Ruhr area, this usually meant low wages (cheap products) as well as few possibilities to combine employment participation with childcare. In other regions, such as in Bielefeed, the production system was more flexible (more varied products). Women could change to homeworking and later again to work in the factory, and some (for example women of higher social strata) might work continuously in homeworking. Two important factors appear in this diversity: flexibility in labour organisation fitting in with the needs of women as mothers (promoting high rates of employment participation), and qualification (vertical integration, which strengthens the employment orientation of women).

Today, there are two broad regional differences in Germany. First, there is an east–west divide of different employment orientations, attributable to the differentiations following the separation of the two Germanys, with high employment participation of women in the East and a much lower participation in the West. This reflects the different positioning of women under quite different welfare state regimes and political systems. (There is another divide between regions with regard to employment orientation, namely a divide between northern and southern regions based on the historical conditions referred to above. But compared with the present-day differences between eastern and western regions the effects of the older divide between south and north with regard to the employment orientation of women are small.) Second, there is a north–south divide of different family forms that dates back to the nineteenth century. It seems reasonable to speak of regional cultures regarding family forms, whereby northern Germany (particularly in the east and to a lesser degree in the west) follows the pattern of strong separation between marriage and family. This is why there are higher numbers of children born outside marriage. In contrast southern Germany (especially in the west and to a lesser degree in the east) follows a pattern with high consistency between marriage and family formation (Nauck 1995).

The smaller or larger connection between marriage and parenthood has important consequences. Both concepts are linked with basic cultural norms through inter-generative relations. For the individualistic strategy of family formation the basic condition for parenthood lies in opportunity structures (employment opportunities and the social security system), while the familialistic strategy of family formation depends much more on the stability of the socio-cultural milieu than on changes in the opportunity structure (Nauck 1995). Thus the decision for parenthood is taken in different contexts, that is in different regional milieus, and is influenced by different factors. And the same is true for many other decisions, such as the decision of a mother to take up gainful employment and partially to give up the care of her children into the hands of others (relatives, household employees, professional childcarers).

What can we learn from the analysis of regional family milieus in Germany? First, the example shows how blind research that uses only national boundaries as points of reference can be (see Duncan 1995). Social and cultural differences do not simply equate with nation states. Similarly, the differentiation of cultural milieus happens slowly. The development of cultural milieus can be influenced by changes in the opportunity structure, but if and how such influences occur depends on the kind of connection of different factors and contexts in a given milieu. Lifestyles are embedded in social milieus and are thus complex constructs in which orientations for all spheres of life are institutionalised via basic norms. A new model is connected to the structure of the old one.

9.4 Afterword: gender difference and equality

If the above argument is correct, one can draw the conclusion that even if the gender equalisation between life situations in the European Union is a declared goal the paths towards it will have to be different. This is particularly the case because there is no integrated model, at the EU level, of employment and family spheres which takes the structures of different lifestyles and their different connections to the values of freedom and equality into account. The analytical differentiation of women according to employment orientation is common in sociological writing, but this has rarely been complemented by an analysis of family orientation (but see Born *et al.* 1996; Duncan and Edwards 1997). Family orientation cannot, however, be deduced from employment orientation: the relationship between the two is not an inverse one.

Many feminist researchers have turned to the analysis of workplaces (and other institutions such as the state) in order to criticise conservative ideologies, according to which female gender roles belong to the family sphere. The analysis in this chapter shows that this critique is not sufficient: we also need to analyse more closely family and cultural practices. However, where feminist-inspired scientists have been interested in the complexity of families, they have wanted to show that family relations are in many different ways interwoven with institutional repression on the one hand and with practices by which husbands directly subordinate women on the other (see for example Connell 1994). Despite the fact of repression or subordination, it is also important to develop analytical concepts that allow us to see women as actors. But what does this mean? In my view it is necessary to appreciate that women not only reproduce gender roles by practices, but also act as interpreters of situations, roles and needs. We find this view in the writings of Nancy Fraser, for example, who develops a perspective on change that centres on the interpretation of needs, and that emphasises the influence of non-institutionalised discourses on institutionalised ones (Fraser 1994, especially chapter 8).

If we take seriously differentiation as an expression of cultural differences, we have to consider the possibility that different life models exist that deserve equal recognition. At first sight a 'freedom model' would be the suitable point of reference for the institutionalisation of the recognition of differences. A 'freedom model' works on the premise that all act according to their preferences. On this basis the attention of politics is limited to the securing of certain framework conditions (for example absence of discrimination). A realised freedom model would show a random distribution of men and women in paid employment and family work. While the allocation between the sexes and spheres would probably not be equal, it would not – in this view – be structured in the gendered sense.

The argument against the implementation of an equality model as the basic principle for the recognition of differences is, however, that we cannot assume equality of opportunity. Rather we are dealing with several overlapping situations of inequality. First, there is opportunity inequality between men and women (see Duncan 1996). In order to work on the premise that women freely choose their life, opportunity inequality would have to be eliminated. From this perspective, only the path of consistent equality policies which includes employment and family spheres can be seen as promising success (Bubeck 1995). This implies integration of women into the labour market and integration of men in the area of unpaid caring responsibilities. While this model of reform seems convincing, its application, however, depends on certain conditions, especially on the predominance of a formalised labour market with both a high degree of economic development and a favourable situation. These conditions do not exist everywhere in the EU to the same degree. Even from a perspective of equal opportunities it is therefore necessary to consider, together with universal goals, context-specific regulations which will enable their achievement. But programmes for the improvement of equality will hardly have the desired effects if we do not take their dependence on interpretation and the cultural embeddedness of structures into account. Life orientations of women differ in different cultural milieus. So, we have to listen to different voices. The universal principle of equality can be a guide for politics, as well as for discourses of self-interpretation and need interpretation by women from different cultural backgrounds.

Such a discourse must avoid two pitfalls. First, we should be aware that the goal is not to promote one and the same lifestyle for all women. While it is important to foster greater individual freedom for women, we have to take into account that employment participation is only one way of social participation. While it can be a means towards freedom and equality it is not the only means. Second, we should not believe that we know enough about social relations and culture. Recent research on social and cultural diversity has been especially useful in uncovering the connection between social forms and cultural concepts. What is missing is a deeper analysis of world-views, everyday concepts of the nature and fate of humans and of society. For example, terms like commitment and belonging, or a desire for continuation in time, the wish to behave as a moral person, all relate to cultural concepts which are deeply linked to gender questions and to social questions in general. While I agree with the critique of Dietz (1985) and Mouffe (1992) of theories of 'social feminism', I have the impression that these theories do nevertheless point to the importance of general concepts and cultural codes that are covered by gender relations (both hidden and mediated). What does it mean to live a good life? What do we want to transfer to future generations? These questions remain.

Acknowledgement

I thank Simon Duncan for useful comments on earlier drafts of this paper, and for patient help with the English.

Notes

1 We should note that there have been other concepts, like those of use value and exchange value, in which more 'material' values are constructed in opposition to abstract ones (see Friedland and Alford 1991).
2 Some of these findings may be due to errors in data analysis and presentation and/or errors from the process of data collection. I tried to eliminate the first kind of error by comparing and using different sources (for example Ashford and Timms 1992 and Zulehner and Denz 1993).
3 Perhaps we should be more careful here. Anne-Lise Ellingsaeter (1996) pointed out that the Danish system with high work incentives and, compared with for example Sweden, small possibilities for parental leave may cause stress for Danish women. Ellingsaeter sees the high unemployment rate of women with small children as indicative of problems for mothers in combining caring and work.
4 Behavioural change can occur very quickly, even without a pre-existence of alternative roles in a given culture, if there are strong incentives. But such change must be integrated in the value system. 'Integration' does not mean that there cannot be contradictions between cultural standards. As long as contradictory demands are limited to different groups or situations, or if they are set into a hierarchy, they may cause no difficulties (see Landecker 1950).
5 I have used only the percentage of full agreement with the statements analysed here. Sometimes, differences might be more a matter of degree (and Dutch respondents especially are well known for avoiding extremes). But if we look at the total percentage of agreement, the Dutch rate remains at a very low level. Only 29 per cent agree with the statement that having a job is the best way for a woman to be an independent person. In all other countries the rate of agreement is higher (EU 12 average: 73 per cent; Zulehner and Denz 1993). Note that these data for the Netherlands are different from those in Ashford and Timms (1992), where 29 per cent agree with the statement that both the husband and wife

should contribute to household income. In this case the agreement of Dutch respondents with the statement concerning the contribution to household income is extremely low. It would appear that the tabulation lines either in the publication of Zulehner and Denz or in that of Ashford and Timms have been mixed up. Anyway, with regard to both a widespread idea about the best way towards female independence and the distribution of responsibilities between men and women, Dutch respondents show an extremely low agreement and differ clearly from others.

6 This change is followed by new problems. For example, 'the right to be different', that is the right to reject 'sameness' as an underlying principle of equality, has been taken by some as the right to deny equality, for example in campaigns of extremist right parties in France (Hargreaves 1995).

7 Social democratic welfare states (or 'Scandinavian' welfare states) have some features in common, especially the high integration of women into the labour force and a high level of childcare facilities. However, during the 1990s divergences between them have attracted more attention (Leira 1989; Ellingsaeter 1996).

References

Addabbo, T. 1997. Part-time work in Italy. In Blossfeld, H.-P. and Hakim, C. (eds) *Between Equalization and Marginalization: Women Working Part-time in Europe and the United States of America*, pp. 113–132. Oxford University Press, Oxford.

Alwin, D.F., Braun, M. and Scott, J. 1992. The separation of work and the family: attitudes towards women's labour-force participation in Germany, Great Britain, and the United States. *European Sociological Review*, 8, 13–37.

Ashford, S. and Timms, N. 1992. *What Europe Thinks: a Study of Western European Values*. Dartmouth, Aldershot.

Blossfeld, H.-P. and Rohwer, G. 1997. Part-time work in West Germany. In Blossfeld, H.-P. and Hakim, C. (eds) *Between Equalization and Marginalization: Women Working Part-time in Europe and the United States of America*, pp. 164–190. Oxford University Press, Oxford.

Born, C., Krüger, H. and Lorenz-Meyer, D. 1996. *Der unentdeckte Wandel: Annäherung an das Verhältnis von Struktur und Norm im weiblichen Lebenslauf*. Sigma, Berlin.

Bubeck, D. 1995. *Gender, Work and Citizenship: Between Social Realities and Utopian Visions*. European University Institute (Florence), European Forum, Working Paper 95/7.

Bulletin 1994. *Bulletin on Women and Employment in the EU*, 4, April 1994.

Bulletin 1995a. *Bulletin on Women and Employment in the EU*, 6, April 1995.

Bulletin 1995b. *Bulletin on Women and Employment in the EU*, 7, October 1995.

Burchell, B.J., Dale, A. and Joshi, H. 1997. Part-time work among British women. In Blossfeld, H.-P. and Hakim, C. (eds) *Between Equalization and Marginalization: Women Working Part-time in Europe and the United States of America*, pp. 210–246. Oxford University Press, Oxford.

Connell, R.W. 1994. Gender regimes and the gender order. In *The Polity Reader in Gender Studies*, pp. 29–40. Polity Press, Cambridge.

Dietz, M. 1985. Citizenship with a feminist face: the problem with maternal thinking. *Political Theory*, 13, 19–37.

Duncan, S. 1995. Theorizing European gender systems. *Journal of European Social Policy*, 5, 4, 263–284.

Duncan, S. 1996. Obstacles to a successful equal opportunity policy in the European Union. *European Journal of Women's Studies*, 3, 4, 399–422.

Duncan, S. and Edwards, R. 1997. Lone mothers and paid work – rational economic man or gendered moral rationalities? *Feminist Economics*, 3, 2, 29–61.

Elkins, D.J. and Simeon, R.E.B. 1979. A cause in search of its effect, or what does political culture explain? *Comparative Politics*, 11 (1978/1979), 127–145.

Ellingsaeter, A. 1996. *Dual breadwinner societies – provider models in the Scandinavian welfare states.* Paper presented at the conference Analysing European Welfare States and Gender Inequality, European Science Foundation GIER, Mekrijävi, September.

Elsthain, J.B. 1982. Feminism, family and community. *Dissent*, 29, 4, 442–449.

Farganis, S. 1994. Postmodernism and feminism. In Dickens, D.R. and Fontana, A. (eds) *Postmodernism and Social Inquiry*, pp. 101–126. Guilford Press, London.

Felling, A., Peters, J. and Schreuder, O. 1983. Bürgerliche und alternative Wertorientierungen in den Niederlanden. *Kölner Zeitschrift für Soziologie und Sozialpsychologie*, 35, 83–107.

Finch, J. 1997. Individuality and adaptability in English kinship. In Gullestad, M. and Segalen, M. (eds) *Family and Kinship in Europe*, pp. 129–145. Pinter, London.

Fraser, N. 1994. *Widerspenstige Praktiken, Macht, Diskurs, Geschlecht*. Suhrkamp, Frankfurt am Main. (Translation of: *Unruly Practices: Power, Discourse and Gender in Contemporary Social Theory*. Oxford, 1989.)

Fraser, N. 1995. From redistribution to recognition? Dilemmas of justice in a 'post-socialist' age. *New Left Review*, 212, 68–93.

Friedland, R. and Alford, R.R. 1991. Bringing society back in: symbols, practices, and institutional contradictions. In Powell, W.W. and DiMaggio, P.J. (eds) *The New Institutionalism in Organizational Analysis*, pp. 232–263. University of Chicago Press, Chicago.

Fuchs, D. 1997. Wohin geht der Wandel der demokratischen Institutionen in Deutschland? Die Entwicklung der Demokratievorstellungen der Deutschen seit ihrer Vereinigung. In Göhler, G. (ed.) *Leviathan*, Sonderheft 16, Institutionen-wandel, pp. 253–284. Westdeutscher Verlag, Opladen.

Giddens, A. 1992. *Die Konstituition der Gesellschaft: Grundzüge einer Theorie der Strukturierung*. Suhrkamp, Frankfurt am Main. (Translation of: *The Constitution of Society: Outline of the Theory of Structuration*. Polity Press, Cambridge, 1984.)

Giddens, A. 1997. *Sociology*, 3rd edn. Polity Press, Cambridge.

Glenn, E.N. 1994. Social constructions of mothering: a thematic overview. In Glenn, E.N., Chang, G. and Forcey, L.R. (eds) *Mothering: Ideology, Experience, and Agency*, pp. 1–29. Routledge, London.

Gottlieb, B. 1993. *The Family in the Western World from the Black Death to the Industrial Age*. Oxford University Press, Oxford.

de Graaf, P. and Vermeulen, H. 1997. Female labour market participation in the Netherlands: developments in the relationship between family cycle and employment. In Blossfeld, H.-P. and Hakim, C. (eds) *Between Equalization and Marginalization: Women Working Part-time in Europe and the United States of America*, pp. 191–209. Oxford University Press, Oxford.

Hahn, C. 1995. *Soziale Kontrolle und Individualisierung: Zur Theorie moderner Ordnungsbildung*. Leske und Budrich, Opladen.

Hakim, C. 1997. A sociological perspective on part-time work. In Blossfeld, H.-P. and Hakim, C. (eds) *Between Equalization and Marginalization: Women Working Part-time in Europe and the United States of America*, pp. 22–70. Oxford University Press, Oxford.

Harding, S., Phillips, D. and Fogarty, M. 1986. *Contrasting Values in Western Europe: Unity, Diversity, and Change*. Macmillan, London.

Hargreaves, A.G. 1995. *Immigration, 'Race' and Ethnicity in Contemporary France.* Routledge, London.

Inglehart, R. 1997. *Modernization and Postmodernization: Cultural Economic and Political Change in 43 Societies.* Princeton University Press, Princeton.

Jepperson, R.L. 1991. Institutions, institutional effects, and institutionalism. In Powell, W.W. and DiMaggio, P.J. (eds) *The New Institutionalism in Organizational Analysis,* pp. 143–163. University of Chicago Press, Chicago.

Jepperson, R.L. and Swidler, A. 1994. What properties of culture should we measure? *Poetics,* 22, 359–371.

de Jong Gierveld, J. and Liefbroer, A.C. 1995. The Netherlands. In Blossfeld, H.P. (ed.) *The New Role of Women: Family Formation in Modern Societies,* pp. 102–125. Westview Press, Boulder.

Keesing, R.M. 1987. Models, 'folk' and 'cultural': paradigms regained? In Holland, D. and Quinn, N. (eds) *Cultural Models in Language and Thought,* pp. 369–393. Cambridge University Press, Cambridge.

Knijn, T. 1994. Social dilemmas in images of motherhood in the Netherlands. *European Journal of Women's Studies,* 1, 183–205.

Landecker, W. 1950. Types of integration and their measurement. *American Journal of Sociology,* 56, 332–340.

Le Bras, H. 1997. Fertility: the condition of self-perpetuation: differing trends in Europe. In Gullestad, M. and Segalen, M. (eds) *Family and Kinship in Europe,* pp. 14–32. Pinter, London.

Lefaucheur, N. and Martin, C. 1997. Single mothers in France: supported mothers and workers. In Duncan, S. and Edwards, R. (eds) *Single Mothers in an International Context: Mothers or Workers?,* pp. 217–240. UCL Press, London.

Le Gall, D. and Martin, C. 1997. Fashioning a new family tie: step-parents and step-grandparents. In Gullestad, M. and Segalen, M. (eds) *Family and Kinship in Europe,* pp. 183–201. Pinter, London.

Leira, A. 1989. *Models of Motherhood. Welfare State Policies and Everyday Practices: the Scandinavian Experience.* Institute for Social Research, Rapport 89:7. Oslo.

Lewis, J. 1992. Gender and the development of welfare regimes. *Journal of European Social Policy,* 2, 3, 159–173.

Lüsebrink, K. 1993. *Büro via Fabrik: Entstehung und Allokationsbedingungen weiblicher Büroarbeit 1850 bis 1933.* Sigma, Berlin.

Meulemann, H. 1993. Säkularisierung und Werte: Eine systematische Übersicht über Ergebnisse aus Bevölkerungsumfragen in westeuropäischen Gesellschaften. In Schäfers, B. (ed.) *Lebensverhältnisse und soziale Konflikte im neuen Europa,* pp. 627–635. Verhandlungen des 26, Deutschen Soziologentages in Düsseldorf 1992. Campus, Frankfurt am Main/New York.

Meulemann, H. 1998. Arbeit und Selbstverwirklichung in Balance: Warum ist den Franzosen die Arbeit, den Deutschen die Freizeit wichtiger? In Köcher, R. and Schild, J. (eds) *Wertewandel in Deutschland und Frankreich,* pp. 133–150. Leske und Budrich, Opladen.

Mingione, E. 1993. Fragmented societies, regional inequalities and social identities: the lesson of the Italian case. In Schäfers, B. (ed.) *Lebensverhältnisse und soziale Konflikte im neuen Europa,* pp. 350–368. Verhandlungen des 26, Deutschen Soziologentages in Düsseldorf 1992. Campus, Frankfurt am Main/New York.

Mitchell, J. 1971. *Woman's Estate.* Bantam Books, New York.

Mouffe, C. 1992. Feminism, citizenship, and radical democratic politics. In Butler, J. and Scott, J.W. (eds) *Feminists Theorize the Political*, pp. 369–384. Routledge, London.

Nauck, B. 1995. Regionale Milieus von Familien in Deutschland nach der politischen Vereinigung. In Nauck, B. and Onnen-Isemann, C. (eds) *Familie im Brennpunkt von Wissenschaft und Forschung*, pp. 91–121. Luchterhand, Neuwied.

Parsons, T. 1969. *Politics and Social Structure*. Free Press, New York.

Peters, J., Felling, A. and Scheepers, P. 1993. Individualisierung und Säkularisierung in den Niederlanden in den achtziger Jahren. In Schäfers, B. (ed.) *Lebensverhältnisse und soziale Konflikte im neuen Europa*, pp. 636–645. Verhandlungen des 26, Deutschen Soziologentages in Düsseldorf 1992. Campus, Frankfurt am Main/New York.

Pfau-Effinger, B. 1998. Gender cultures and the gender arrangement – a theoretical framework for cross-national gender research. *Innovation*, 11, 2, 147–166.

Pinelli, A. and De Rose, A. 1995. Italy. The new role of women. In Blossfeld, H.-P. (ed.) *Family Formation in Modern Societies*. Westview Press, Boulder, CO.

Robertson, R. 1988. The sociological significance of culture: some general considerations. *Theory, Culture and Society*, 5, 3–23.

Rosenbaum, H. 1982. *Formen der Familie: Untersuchungen zum Zusammenhang von Familienverhältnissen, Sozialstruktur und sozialem Wandel in der deutschen Gesellschaft des 19. Jahrhunderts*. Suhrkamp, Frankfurt am Main.

Rosenfeld, M. 1991. *Affirmative Action and Justice: a Philosophical and Constitutional Inquiry*. Yale University Press, New Haven.

Rost, H. and Schneider, N.F. 1995. Differentielle Elternschaft: Auswirkungen der ersten Geburt für Männer und Frauen. In Nauck, B. and Onnen-Isemann, C. (eds) *Familie im Brennpunkt von Wissenschaft und Forschung*, pp. 177–194. Luchterhand, Neuwied.

Ruddick, S. 1980. Maternal thinking. *Feminist Studies*, 6, 2, 342–367.

Sackmann, R. 1997. *Regionale Kultur und Frauenerwerbsbeteiligung*. Centaurus, Pfaffenweiler.

Sackmann, R. and Häussermann, H. 1994. Do regions matter? Regional differences in female labour market participation in Germany. *Environment and Planning A*, 26, 9, 1377–1396.

Schmidt, M. 1983. Krieg der Männer – Chance der Frauen? Der Einzug von Frauen in die Büros der Thyssen AG. In Niethmammer, L. (ed.) *'Die Jahre weiß man nicht, wo man die heute hinsetzen soll'. Faschismuserfahrungen im Ruhrgebiet. Lebensgeschichte und Sozialkultur im Ruhrgebiet 1930 bis 1960*, Bd. 1, pp. 133–162. Berlin.

Schultheis, F. 1998. Familiale Lebensformen, Geschlechterbeziehungen und Familienwerte im deutsch-französischen Gesellschaftsvergleich. In Köcher, R. and Schild, J. (eds) *Wertewandel in Deutschland und Frankreich*, pp. 207–225. Leske und Budrich, Opladen.

Segura, D.A. 1994. Working at motherhood: Chicana and Mexican immigrant mothers and employment. In Glenn, E.N., Chang, G. and Forcey, L.R. (eds) *Mothering: Ideology, Experience, and Agency*, pp. 211–233. Routledge, London.

Sgritta, G.B. 1988. Wege der Familienanalyse: Ein Überblick über das letzte Jahrzehnt. In Lüscher, K., Schultheis, F. and Wehrspaun, M. (eds) *Die „postmoderne" Familie: Familiale Strategien und Familienpolitik in einer Übergangszeit*, pp. 329–345. Universitätsverlag, Konstanz.

Sieder, R. 1987. *Sozialgeschichte der Familie*. Suhrkamp, Frankfurt am Main.

Squires, J. (ed.) 1993. *Principled Positions: Postmodernism and the Rediscovery of Value*. Lawrence & Wishart, London.

Symeonidou, H. 1997. Full- and part-time employment of women in Greece: trends and relationships with life-cycle events. In Blossfeld, H.-P. and Hakim, C. (eds) *Between Equalization and Marginalization: Women Working Part-time in Europe and the United States of America*, pp. 90–112. Oxford University Press, Oxford.

Tenfelde, K. 1992. Arbeiterfamilie und Geschlechterbeziehungen im Deutschen Kaiserreich. *Geschichte und Gesellschaft*, 18, 179–203.

Women and Men in Europe 1983. *Frauen Europas*. Nachtrag 16. Kommission der Europäischen Gemeinschaften, Generaldirektion Information, Information der Frauenverbände und der Frauenpresse, Brüssel.

Women and Men in Europe 1987. *Frauen Europas*. Nachtrag 26. Kommission der Europäischen Gemeinschaften, Generaldirektion Information, Kommunikation, Kultur, Fraueninformation, Brüssel.

Women of Europe 1990. Kinderbetreuung in der Europäischen Gemeinschaft 1985–1990. *Women of Europe*, Special issue 31. Kommission der Europäischen Gemeinschaften, Generaldirektion Information, Kommunikation, Kultur, Fraueninformation, Brüssel.

Women of Europe undated. Die Lage der Frauen auf dem Arbeitsmarkt: Entwicklungstendenzen in den zwölf Ländern der Europäischen Gemeinschaft 1983–1990. *Women of Europe*, Special issue 36. Generaldirektion Audiovisuelle Medien, Information, Kommunikation, Kultur, Fraueninformation, Brüssel.

Young, I.M. 1990. *Justice and the Politics of Difference*. Princeton University Press, Princeton.

Zulehner, P.M. and Denz, H. 1993. *Wie Europa lebt und glaubt. Europäische Wertestudie. Tabellenband*. Patmos, Wien.

10 Conclusion

Gender cultures, gender arrangements and social change in the European context

Birgit Pfau-Effinger

10.1 Introduction

Those recent changes in Western European countries which can be characterised (perhaps caricatured) as a change from Fordist industrial to post-Fordist service societies have also been accompanied by changes in the overall division of labour and in processes of democratisation. These processes have therefore also created new spaces for change in gender relations. Traditional forms of gender inequality have been weakened or restructured, although, as this book has shown, there were considerable differences between European countries. This comparative difference in change in gender structures over the last few decades provides the main focus of this chapter. The central question is how such change, and how differences in these changes, can be explained. I distinguish here between three gender structures: (1) the gender division of labour, (2) power relations between women and men, and (3) sexual and emotional relations between women and men (Connell 1987). The three gender structures are mutually interrelated, but at the same time are also relatively autonomous. For instance, a specific form of the gender division of labour is not automatically connected with a specific kind of power relations between women and men. Similarly, it seems that the degree to which men are violent against women in any country is in part independent of the gender division of labour (Chapter 7, this volume). These social structures are also reproduced by the social practices of individuals and, under certain conditions, are thus subject to change, as we have experienced over the last few decades.

Within these structures, and in their interrelation, a broad variety of forms of gendered social inequality can exist.[1] These forms have been the subject of this book:

- forms of the gendered division of labour in employment, based on hierarchical differentiation (Chapter 2);
- forms of the gendered division of labour and power within families, based on the hierarchical differentiation and supremacy of men (Chapters 3 and 7);

- forms of the gendered division of labour based on the different position of women and men in relation to unpaid family work and paid employment (Chapter 4);
- the gendering of the quality and range of social rights, connected to the different positions of women and men in employment and families (Chapters 5 and 6);
- the gendered structures of images, values and attitudes (Chapters 8 and 9).

10.2 Main changes in Western European gender structures

In this section I will describe some basic features of change which have characterised many Western European countries over the last few decades. It should be borne in mind, however, that this change has not always been linear – there have been substantial time lags and even retreats.

1   Everywhere central features of the gender division of labour have changed. Women have increasingly been integrated into the employment system, including professional and management jobs, while the employment to population ratio of men has decreased nearly everywhere, mainly due to processes of de-industrialisation. Consequently, the employment to population ratios of women and men have converged everywhere (Chapters 2 and 4). Similarly the balance between unpaid and paid work in the biographies of women in most countries has changed in favour of paid work. However, social inequality within the employment system has partly just been reproduced in a new form; in several countries, for example the UK, more women than men are working in peripheral forms of 'atypical' employment or in the informal sector (Chapter 2).

2   Gender structures within households and families have also changed, and in this women have been the main driving force (Chapter 3). In countries and regions where family structures were strongly patriarchal they have been at least weakened, mainly because of general processes of democratisation. Nonetheless, nowhere – even today – do men share equally in housework and caring tasks (Chapter 3, this volume), even though the primary responsibility of women for these tasks in the family can be seen as the main factor which prevents gender equality in the employment system (Fagan *et al.* 1999). It is moreover problematic that power relations within marriage and partnerships in which men control and suppress those women with whom they are closely related have survived (Chapter 7).

In general marriage is less dominant in the life of women than it was before. On average women have postponed marriage and the birth of a first child until later in their life course, and in many countries they have fewer children overall. Moreover, new forms of family life have

264 *Gendered understandings*

developed which are increasingly accepted within Western European societies, and which in part are not based on the traditional idea of the unity through marriage of affectional relationship and reproduction. These include lone parenthood and cohabitation (Chapter 3).

3   In addition, women are more integrated into political processes and decision-making institutions at the local, national and European levels. This is only a rather limited change, however; in many parliaments and political institutions women are still heavily under-represented (Hoecker 1998).

Different social groups of women have been involved in this development to a differing degree. Women of the urban middle classes, who have been best able to use the extended space for action in the educational and employment systems, seem to be the main winners. It seems as if female migrants in particular have participated to a disproportionately low degree in women's improved educational and career chances, and in many Western European countries they are often excluded from access to central resources and privileges. Indeed, some groups of female migrants, for example those from Southeast Asia and the Eastern European countries, seem to represent a group of cheap workers in private households who fill the gaps which an inadequate welfare state provision leaves in several countries. In turn this gives women of the indigenous middle classes the opportunity to seize new career chances (Chapter 6).

10.3 The integration of 'culture' into cross-national analysis of change

The empirical research presented in this book shows that, beyond these basic and common changes in social practices and gender structures, there were also considerable differences between different Western European countries and regions within them. How can these differences be explained?

Differences in the institutional framework play an important role in explaining such variations, combined with differences in the overall division of labour as reflected by the varying economic structures of different countries and regions. Differences in welfare state policies seem to be particularly relevant. Thus comparative research on European welfare states has shown that their gender policies (often implicit) differ considerably in the degree to which they promote the integration of women into the employment system (Lewis 1992; see also Chapters 2 and 5, this volume). Moreover, the social rights of women as mothers, workers and citizens differ considerably across countries with regard to their quality and range (Chapter 5). Different welfare states have also, again to a differing degree, created variable opportunities for women to reject marriage as the only context for reproduction, as for example through their policies towards divorce and lone motherhood. The Scandinavian welfare states in particular are seen as the most progressive with regard to the quality of women's social rights (Chapters 3 and 5).

However, the overall division of labour, and the way this is restructured by institutions, also contributes to the explanation of cross-national differences in gender inequality. Thus, for instance, the service sector, especially social services, has been particularly important for the integration of women into employment, and this sector varies considerably in size and structure between European countries. It should be remembered, however, that the size of this sector is itself heavily influenced by the development of paid work overall for women, for the private demand for services by households increases with the employment of women (Häußermann and Siebel 1995; Meyer 1999). Economic differences are thus important both in causing and as an outcome of cross-national differences in gender structures. But while the economy can contribute to the explanation of gender differences, this is only in its interrelationship with other, more 'cultural', explanatory factors (Chapters 2 and 9; Pfau-Effinger 2000a).

Institutional and economic factors together are therefore not sufficient to explain cross-national variations in gender. They do not simply determine the behaviour of individuals and social groups, even if they set a context for this behaviour (Pfau-Effinger 1993, 1999a,b,d; Duncan 1998). For cultural values and ideals are crucial in explaining differences (see also Chapters 5 and 9). This is because those social practices through which individuals reproduce, or change, the existing gender structures emerge within the complex interrelations of cultural, institutional and economic contexts. For example, in West Germany the high rate of part-time work for mothers with pre-school children is sometimes explained by reference to limited opening hours of public day care institutions. However, an at least equally good explanation lies in the particular, and widespread, cultural ideals of the family in West Germany, according to which many people think that it is detrimental for pre-school children to be away from home and mother the whole day. In turn, these ideals interact in specific ways with the way in which the institutional framework develops, for example the nature and availability of daycare (Pfau-Effinger and Geissler 1992). Or to take another example, in those countries or regions where male violence against close female partners is an important problem, one central explanation seems to be that violence is part of the cultural construction of masculinity (see Chapter 7). Similarly, Duncan and Edwards (1996, 1999) have stressed the central role of culture for individual action in their research on how lone mothers combine employment and paid work. It was 'gendered moral rationalities', that is cultural ideas about 'the proper thing to do' in being a good mother, which was dominant, not institutional or economic factors.

How, then, can 'culture' be integrated into a theoretical framework in explaining gender differences cross-nationally? This undertaking requires a more concrete definition of 'culture', and of the relation of culture to other theoretical levels.

In recent comparative sociology, the role of culture in explanatory frameworks was more or less neglected for a long time. Culture is often still seen as something specific or particular in a society which cannot otherwise be specified, and as a sort of 'dustbin term' which in itself cannot be analysed (see also Pfau-Effinger 1994; O'Reilly 1996; Fagan and O'Reilly 1997). However, in the 1990s 'culture' has experienced something of a revival in sociological thinking, and at the same time it has become important in feminist thinking (although ideas about precisely how culture actually relates to social structures and institutions differ considerably in different sociological theories: Wimmer 1996; Pfau-Effinger 2000b).

My own theoretical development of these interrelations is encapsulated in the concept of a 'gender arrangement'. This was developed as an explanatory framework for cross-national analyses of social practices in gender relations, drawing on the theories of Max Weber, David Lockwood and Margaret Archer. This approach is a further development of the gender contract approach (see Chapter 1). However, the term 'contract' is not used here, for this term is based on the liberal history of ideas according to which a contract is based on equal rights and free will of all citizens. This precondition does not exist in all modern societies – for instance, migrants are partly excluded from this contract (see Chapter 6). The analytical concept of an 'arrangement' is in contrast more open.

The central ideas on which this approach is based will now be briefly described (see also Figure 10.1, and Pfau-Effinger 1998, 2000a for further details). The way culture is embedded in society is conceptualised by differentiating between three theoretical levels: the cultural system, the social system, and the level of social actors (see also Archer 1995, 1996). Culture is defined here after Friedhelm Neidhard (1986: 11) as 'the system of collective constructions of sense by which men [*sic*] define reality, that complex of general imaginations by which they distinguish between important and unimportant, true and false, good and bad as well as beautiful and ugly'. For this construction of sense, cultural stocks of knowledge, values and ideals are available, and together these can be called 'ideas'. The cultural system is not necessarily a coherent unity where dominant and more marginalised ideas can coexist (Archer 1996). Thus dominant ideas in any particular context of time and space are the result of conflicts and compromises between social actors with different powers in former historical periods. They can be logically consistent, or contradictory, and coexist with more marginalised ideas prevalent in other social groups (Pfau-Effinger 2000a). I argue that the gender culture is a particular part of the cultural system. Cultural ideals and values exist in relation to the gender division of labour, the power relations between women and men and the relations between generations and extend to the sexual and emotional relations between women and men. These then form a central basis for the social agency of individuals although they are not causal in a deterministic sense.

Social actors, individuals, political parties, associations and social movements act in any historical phase on the basis of the historical context of ideas. They refer to this context by their discourses, social interactions, negotiation processes, conflicts and compromises, and reproduce, modify or

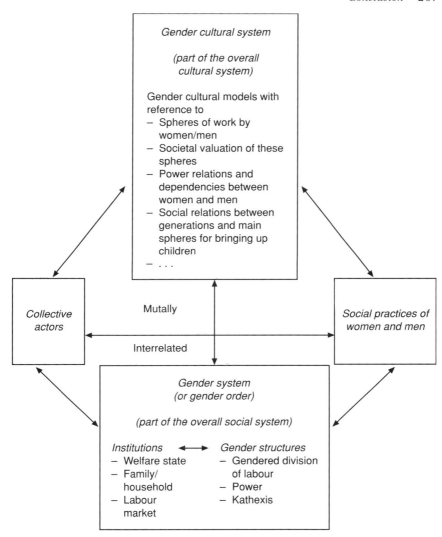

Figure 10.1 Culture, institutions, social structures and social action within the gender arrangement.

change the cultural stock, or add innovative ideas which can stem from inside or outside the society. In order to compare cultural constructions of sense cross-nationally, it is necessary to identify more central dimensions by which cultural ideas or values can be identified and classified (see also Chapter 9). Moreover, it is important to analyse the range of the dominant ideals in relation to class, ethnicity and region (Pfau-Effinger 2000a).

Social agency is based not only on ideas, but also on the interests of the relevant actors (Lepsius 1990). The social system is important for the development of interests. This is made up of the mutual interrelations of institutions, and of social structures within these institutions (Archer 1996). These include the structures of the division of labour, of power relations and hierarchies, and of sexual and emotional relations. Thus the gender structures and the interrelations between central institutions, which form the main framework for the social practices of women and men, are an important part of the social system. Together they form the 'gender system' or, according to Connell (1987), the 'gender order'. The dominant ideas and values in society are a central reference point for the institutions and are, in part, integrated into the institutions as norms. They function as 'expectations of normality' to which welfare state institutions, among other things, refer in their regulation. The social system, including the gender system as part of it, can also be changed by conflicts and negotiations between social actors (Pfau-Effinger 2000a,b). Change at the level of the central institutions and social structures itself, on the other hand, can contribute to changes in the dominant gender cultural ideals, though only as mediated by social agency. The social system and the cultural system thus are mutually interrelated but at the same time also relatively autonomous (see also Archer 1996).

My own 'gender arrangement' approach (Pfau-Effinger 1998, 2000a) refers to the specific interrelations between the institutional and cultural framework, and with social actors, by which gender structures are reproduced or, under certain circumstances, changed. It is based on the assumption that gender cultural ideals and values form an important basis for the behaviour of women and men, as well as the institutional framework and the overall structural context, and that the basic institutions of society – like the welfare state, the labour market and the family – also function on the basis of such ideas. According to empirical research, forms of hierarchical differentiation within gender structures can be explained by the fact that central institutions of society, and the behaviour of women and men, are heavily influenced by cultural values, ideals and norms which are in turn connected to differential cultural constructions of 'femininity' and 'masculinity', and differing expectations and ideas about the 'normal' behaviour of women and men, which connect the main privileges in society to the male norm in particular.

This approach is based on the assumption that such theoretical differentiation between the cultural level, the structural level, and the levels of institutions and of social actors is useful, and in this way is different from structuration theory as developed by Giddens (1984). For these levels form a coherent unity only under particular conditions of time and space. Otherwise, tensions and contradictions, as well as time lags, can develop within this field (see also Lockwood 1964; Archer 1995, 1996). Such discrepancies are also a central precondition for change in gender structures (Pfau-Effinger 1998, 2000a).

I argue, therefore, that the interrelations of gender culture, institutions, gender structures and social agency are not necessarily coherent within the gender arrangement, but rather that they can be characterised by contradictions or time lags. Social change can be the result if some groups of social actors act against such contradictions or time lags and try to establish a new gender arrangement through conflicts and/or negotiation. Such processes can lead to an overall change of the gender arrangement or, if the effort fails, to a reproduction of the old one – perhaps in a 'modernised' form. The question of which power resources can be mobilised by social groups with innovative ideals then becomes important.

Social change in gender structures over the last few decades can therefore be explained by the manifold interrelations between institutional, structural and cultural frameworks, and by social agency within this context. In many Western European countries, women have become increasingly oriented towards paid work, and the mother–worker role has more than ever become socially acceptable, particularly in those countries in which the housewife model of the male breadwinner family was dominant some decades ago. Also important for this kind of change were the new, and in part contradicting, public discourses on the injustice of gender inequality and the necessity of equalisation. These cultural processes can also be interpreted as part of general processes of 'reflexive modernity' (Beck 1986). They contributed in part to an erosion of the male breadwinner norm to which in many countries the privileges of the employment system and the welfare state are still directed (Crompton 1998, 1999). The result of this change, which is still in part contradictory and characterised by time lags, also reveals itself in innovative ideals about gender relations in the media (Chapter 8).

Institutional change, and change in the overall structures of the division of labour – as interrelated with cultural change – has been another important precondition for the integration of a higher proportion of women into the employment and political systems. This includes the extension of the educational system, the transition to a service society and political democratisation processes. Many welfare states also recognised gender equality as an important aim, although the political objectives of this aim differed considerably. Some welfare states, especially those in Scandinavia (Siim 1994), paved the way for an improvement of the situation of women as workers, mothers and citizens (although note that there are considerable differences in gender policies between these countries; see Ellingsaeter 1999). Other Western European welfare states in general, and to an increasing degree, have also promoted the employment of women and increased public or publicly financed day care provision (Knijn and Kremer 1997). Welfare states in part also changed the basis for power inequality within marriage and partnerships by the improvement of divorce and cohabitation laws, some easing of the situation of lone mothers, and the definition of male violence within marriage as a criminal act (see Chapters 3 and 7).

Such change was promoted by new social movements, particularly feminist movements, who have tried to alter the central social institutions, and dominant cultural ideals, according to innovative ideas of gender equality. In most cases these movements referred to contradictions which had developed within gender arrangements, often caused by general social change. For instance, in many countries the general processes of democratisation and modernisation in the two or three decades after World War II exacerbated the contradiction between the cultural construction of inequality and dependency within marriage and the idea of free and equal citizens entering the 'social contract' (see also Pateman 1988). Another contradiction which was relevant here was that, even though the chances of a relatively good education for women were increased considerably by the expansion of the educational system in many countries, the chances of women finding a professional job and making a career did not improve to a similar degree.

Change itself led to new contradictions, discrepancies and time lags. Thus the relationship between those cultural ideals to which welfare state policies referred, and the innovative cultural ideals to which women oriented their social practices, were sometimes at variance (Pfau-Effinger 1999c, 2000a). A good example is the Netherlands, where at the beginning of the 1970s women started to direct their employment behaviour to a modernised ideal of the male breadwinner family, that is the 'male breadwinner/female part-time carer model'. In contrast welfare state policies continued to promote the housewife model of the family, which had been culturally dominant previously, until the middle of the 1980s (Pfau-Effinger 1996, 1998). Similarly those cultural ideals and values to which individuals orient their behaviour, and the social practices of individuals, can deviate from each other (Chapter 9, and Knijn 1994; Geissler and Oechsle 1996; Pfau-Effinger 1998, 2000a). Such discrepancies can often be explained, as in the Dutch example, by time lags at the level of institutions, which do not promote the realisation of innovative cultural ideals in practice.

The gender cultural basis of Western European countries, as well as the way it has changed, differ (see Chapter 5). Because the dominant ideal(s) in the respective gender arrangement(s) which are mediated by institutions and social agency have a strongly structuring impact for gender arrangements, it is useful to classify these arrangements according to the gender cultural models on which they are based (see Chapters 1 and 5). Development paths of gender arrangements can then be classified according to the differing gender cultural models which are dominant in different periods of their development.

Cross-national research suggests that the gender cultural foundation of different gender arrangements has strong explanatory power in accounting for cross-national differences in the social practices of women and men, in the gender structures which are reproduced by these, as well as for the direction of change of gender arrangements (Jensen 1996; Pfau-Effinger 1998, 2000a; Chapter 9, this volume). These interact in specific ways with welfare state policies, economic structures and employment structures which in turn also play an important role for the explanation of these differences. Gender policies of welfare states are based on specific gender cultural models which have often tended to lag behind cultural change in the last few decades in

Western European countries (see Chapter 5). As a result the social practices of women in many countries are embedded in a contradictory field of tensions between cultural and institutional influences (see Geissler and Oechsle 1996).

Variations in gender cultures within countries are also important in explaining regional differences in gender structures. Thus Gunnel Forsberg (1998) has shown how 'traditional', 'modernising' and 'non-traditional' regional gender cultures, within Sweden's overall equality gender contract, can have important effects on the way in which women and men live their lives. Such differences may lie behind regional variations in gender divisions of labour and family practices (see, for example, Duncan 1991).

A 'quasi-national' example is Germany after re-unification in 1989, where two different gender arrangements exist, with distinctly different gender cultural foundations and social practices of women (Nickel 1995; Schenk 1995). Gender cultures can also reach beyond national borders. According to the findings of a cross-regional study by Elisabeth Bühler for Switzerland, differences in the dominant gender cultural models match the language borders within the country, so that within the Italian-speaking, German-speaking and French-speaking regions people orient their behaviour to different gender cultures. It can however be expected that, even though there are commonalities concerning the dominant gender culture in the German-speaking part of Switzerland and West Germany as its neighbour, the gender arrangements and in part also the gender structures will still differ because of the different policies of the two national welfare states. This is because the social practices of individuals are not directly caused by the cultural system, but rather embedded within the complex interrelations of institutional, structural and cultural conditions.

The different ways in which the field of collective actors was structured during change in earlier decades, and the power relations between them, is another explanatory factor in accounting for cross-national differences between European gender arrangements, and for the ways in which they have changed. The role of the feminist movements is important in this context, especially the way in which they were able to insert innovative gender cultural ideals into public discourses, the media and welfare state policies. There were considerable variations in this, and in how these movements connected to different social groups of women. Important in this context are the resources they were able to mobilise, the coalitions they formed, and how far the political culture and the structures of political decision making were open to the demands of new social movements (Pfau-Effinger 2000a).

10.4 'Gender equality' as a relational concept

In order to undertake cross-national comparison of gender structures some kind of scale is often used which ranges from 'traditional' to more 'innovative', 'modern' or 'progressive' structures. One central problem here is that the concrete context of the societies which are included in the analysis is often not adequately respected. This refers to (1) the concept of what are 'traditional' gender structures, and (2) the concept of what is 'gender equality'.

1   Traditional gender structures are often equated with the housewife model of the male breadwinner family and the forms of gender inequality which are connected to it. It is often presupposed that this characterises the historical starting point of the post-war development in all European societies. The problem here is that this assumption is based on the specific social and cultural historical context of the researchers involved who have generalised the experiences of their own social context to other countries and societies. However, 'traditional' gender structures, which were the starting point for change in the last decades and have affected the way change has proceeded since then, have been very different. For instance, in Finland an agrarian family economic model (in a relatively egalitarian version) was dominant up to the post-war period, and this model can be seen to be the 'traditional' starting point in many European countries up to the Industrial Revolution.

In this sense, the 'traditional' male breadwinner/female carer model can be a relatively 'non-traditional' model. In Finland, this was never a dominant model to which women oriented their behaviour (Pfau-Effinger 1998, 2000a). In addition, the extent to which this model was based on the assumption of gender inequality also varied in time and space. This can also vary regionally. For example, in the old textile area of Lancashire and Yorkshire in Britain, a 'dual role' of women in employment as well as working as homemakers and carers has been dominant over at least the last 200 years. In such areas it is not at all 'traditional' for wives and mothers to withdraw from the labour market (Duncan 1991). The concept of 'tradition' therefore has to be filled with content by empirical analyses for particular times and spaces.

2   A normative measure of 'gender equality' has often been used as the main measure for change. This usually derives from abstract theoretical reflections which do not consider the respective social context in which the idea of equality has emerged. Often integration of women into full-time waged work and full-time public day care provision is used as the central measure for gender equality. The idea of such a unique model might also emerge by using cross-national attitude data such as the ISSP, Eurobarometer, 'Women and Men in Europe' or the European Values Survey, which – even though each asks different questions about gender, families and waged work – all relate to this particular conceptualisation of gender equality. The problem of such an essentialist approach is that the concrete development of ideas about gender equality in different countries is often ignored (see Chapter 5). Thus problems of an ethnocentric and sociocentric reduction exist in relation not only to 'exotic' and unfamiliar regions of the world but also to those just outside our own front door. As Chapter 5 suggests, it is therefore necessary to

treat the concept of 'gender equality' as a relational concept and to contextualise it. Instead of using an abstract idea of 'what is good for women', this means analysing for each country, even for particular regions or localities, which kind of cultural concept of 'gender equality' has emerged, distinguishing also between dominant, peripheral and deviant concepts for instance by social class and ethnicity. This can be a more adequate basis on which to find out what is beneficial for women, and can better contribute to promoting gender equality on the ground (see also Pfau-Effinger 2000a).

Certainly empirical research shows that there is no one unique 'equality' model in Europe. Instead at least three different ideas about equality can be distinguished. Besides a 'dual breadwinner/dual carer model' (as adumbrated in the Netherlands) and a 'dual breadwinner/ state carer model' (as developed in Scandinavia) (Pfau-Effinger 1998), there is also a 'dual breadwinner/marketised carer model' (as increasingly promoted in Britain and the USA) (Crompton 1999; Yeandle 1999) as well as intermediate forms. What all of these models have in common is the aim of integrating women and men into waged work on equal terms, currently also an explicit aim of the European Union. Beyond this idea cultural values and ideals vary, particularly in relation to ideas about the central sphere of care for children and elderly people. Should this be mainly a task of the state or, and to what degree, should this be shared by the state and the family? Should women and men share the tasks equally, or should the market mainly provide care? Connected with these ideas about care are differing ideas about the amount of time which women and men – as carers – should spend in employment.

10.5 Afterword

Cross-national analyses of gender relations are confronted with the problem that comparative statistics which refer to central aspects of this issue are still incomplete or even missing altogether. For example, differentiated data on the development of gender relations in agriculture and the informal sector are missing (see Chapter 2). Similarly, cross-national statistics on the development of households and family structures are often not very differentiated and do not provide an adequate statistical basis for deeper comparative analysis (Chapter 3). There have been only very few representative surveys on male violence, as well as data on the development of shelters for women and information on welfare state policies in relation to this problem (Chapter 7). Moreover, data which are differentiated at the level of regions are rare in relation to all of these subjects.

Nor are data from cross-national attitude surveys usually adequate for differentiated comparative analysis of cultural ideals and values in relation to gender relations and gender equality in European countries and regions. The concepts of surveys such as the ISSP or Eurobarometer need further development, or perhaps new kinds of attitude surveys are required. Comparative qualitative research in this field also needs to be further developed, particularly so as to include the dimension of 'culture' systematically into cross-national and cross-regional analyses. The contributions to this volume can be seen as a basis for the further development of representative and qualitative cross-national and cross-regional investigations of gender inequality.

Acknowledgement

I thank Simon Duncan for comments on an earlier draft and help with the English.

Note

1 For an elaborate discussion on theoretical approaches to gender inequality see Gottschall (2000).

References

Archer, M.S. 1995. *Realist Social Theory: the Morphogenetic Approach*. Cambridge University Press, Cambridge.

Archer, M.S. 1996. *Culture and Agency: the Place of Culture in Social Theory*. Cambridge University Press, Cambridge.

Beck, U. 1986. *Risikogesellschaft: Auf dem Weg in eine andere Moderne*. Frankfurt am Main.

Connell, R. 1987. *Gender and Power: Society, the Person and Sexual Politics*. Polity Press, Cambridge.

Crompton, R. 1998. The equality agenda, employment, and welfare. In Geissler, B., Maier, F. and Pfau-Effinger, B. (eds) *Der Beitrag der Frauenforschung zur sozioökonomischen Theorieentwicklung*, pp. 154–176. Sigma, Berlin.

Crompton, R. 1999. The decline of the male breadwinner: explanations and interpretations. In Crompton, R. (ed.) *Restructuring Gender Relations and Employment: the Decline of the Male Breadwinner*, pp. 1–25. Oxford University Press, Oxford.

Duncan, S.S. 1991. The geography of gender divisions of labour in Britain. *Transactions of the Institute of British Geographers*, 16, 420–439.

Duncan, S. 1998. Theorising gender systems in Europe. In Geissler, B., Maier, F. and Pfau-Effinger, B. (eds) *FrauenArbeitsMarkt: Der Beitrag der Frauenforschung zur sozioökonomischen Theorieentwicklung*, pp. 195–227. Sigma, Berlin.

Duncan, S.S. and Edwards, R. 1996. Lone mothers and paid work: neighbourhoods, local labour markets and welfare state regimes. *Social Politics*, 3, 2, 195–222.

Duncan, S. and Edwards, R. 1999. *Lone Mothers, Paid Work and Gendered Moral Rationalities*. Macmillan, London.

Ellingsaeter, A.L. 1999. Dual breadwinners between state and market. In Crompton, R. (ed.) *Restructuring Gender Relations and Employment: the Decline of the Male Breadwinner*, pp. 40–60. Oxford University Press, Oxford.

Fagan, C. and O'Reilly, J. 1997. Conceptualising part-time work: the value of an integrated comparative perspective. In Fagan, C. and O'Reilly, J. (eds) *Part-time Perspectives*, pp. 1–32. Routledge, London.

Fagan, C., Rubery, J. and Smith, M. 1999. *Women's Employment in Europe: Trends and Prospects*. Routledge, London.

Forsberg, G. 1998. Regional variations in the gender contract: gendered relations in labour markets, local politics and everyday life in Swedish regions. *Innovation: the European Journal of the Social Sciences*, 11, 2, 147–166.

Geissler, B. and Oechsle, M. 1996. *Lebensplanung junger Frauen: Die widersprüchliche Modernisierung weiblicher Lebensläufe*. Deutscher Studien-Verlag, Weinheim.

Giddens, A. 1984. *The Constitution of Society*. Polity Press, Cambridge.

Gottschall, K. 2000. *Soziale Ungleichheit und Geschlecht*. Leske und Budrich, Opladen.

Häußermann, H. and Siebel, W. 1995. *Dienstleistungsgesellschaften*. Suhrkamp, Frankfurt am Main.

Hoecker, B. 1998. *Handbuch Politische Partizipation von Frauen in Europa*. Leske und Budrich, Opladen.

Jensen, P.H. 1996. *Komparative Velfaerdssystemer: Kvinders reproduktionsstrategier mellem familien, velfaerdsstaten og arbejdsmarkedet*. Nyt fra Samfundsvidenskaberne, Kopenhagen.

Knijn, T. 1994. Social dilemmas in images of motherhood in the Netherlands. *European Journal of Women's Studies*, 1, 183–206.

Knijn, T. and Kremer, M. 1997. Gender and the caring dimension of welfare states: toward inclusive citizenship. *Social Politics*, 5, 3, 328–361.

Lepsius, R.M. 1990. *Interessen, Ideen und Institutionen*. Westdeutscher Verlag, Opladen.

Lewis, J. 1992. Gender and the development of welfare regimes. *Journal of European Social Policy*, 2, 3, 159–173.

Lockwood, D. 1964. Social integration and system integration. In Zollschan, G.K. and Hirsch, W. (eds) *Explorations in Social Change*. Houghton Mifflin, Boston.

Meyer, T. 1999. Mehr Beschäftigung durch einfache Dienstleistungen? Eine Einführung. *WSI-Mitteilungen*, 25, 4, 217–222.

Neidhard, F. 1986. "Kultur und Gesellschaft": Einige Anmerkungen zum Sonderheft. In Neidhard, F., Lepsius, R.M. and Weiss, J. (eds) *Kultur und Gesellschaft*, pp. 10–19. Special volume 27 of the Kölner Zeitschrift für Soziologie und Sozialpsychologie. Westdeutscher Verlag, Opladen.

Nickel, H. 1995. Frauen im Umbruch der Gesellschaft: Die zweifache Transformation in Deutschland und ihre ambivalenten Folgen. *Aus Politik und Zeitgeschichte: Beilage zur Wochenzeitung das Parlament*, B 36–37/95, 1, September, 23–33.

O'Reilly, J. 1996. Theoretical considerations in cross-national employment research. *Sociological Review Online*, 1, 1 (http:\\www.soc.surrey.ac.uk).

Pateman, C. 1988. *The Sexual Contract*. Stanford University Press, Stanford.

Pfau-Effinger, B. 1993. Modernisation, culture and part-time work. *Work, Employment and Society*, 7, 3, 383–410.

Pfau-Effinger, B. 1994. The gender contract and part-time paid work by women – a comparative perspective. *Environment and Planning A*, 26, 8, 1355–1376.

Pfau-Effinger, B. 1996. Analyse internationaler Differenzen in der Erwerbsbeteiligung von Frauen – theoretischer Rahmen und empirische Ergebnisse. *Kölner Zeitschrift für Soziologie und Sozialpsychologie*, 48, 3, 462–492.

Pfau-Effinger, B. 1998. Gender cultures and the gender arrangement – a theoretical framework for cross-national comparisons on gender. *Innovation: the European Journal of the Social Sciences*, 11, 2, 147–166.

Pfau-Effinger, B. 1999a. Defizite der Theoriebildung zu den Grenzen wohlfahrts-staatlicher Geschlechterpolitik. In Hradil, S. (ed.) *Verhandlungen des 29. Kongresses der Deutschen Gesellschaft für Soziologie, des 16. Österreichischen Kongresses für Soziologie und des 11. Schweizerischen Kongresses für Soziologie "Grenzenlose Gesellschaft?"*, Vol. 1, pp. 203–218. Centaurus, Plenumsveranstaltungen, Freiburg.

Pfau-Effinger, B. 1999b. Welfare regimes and the gender division of labour in cross-national perspective – theoretical framework and empirical results. In Christiansen, J., Kovalainen, A. and Koistinen, P. (eds) *Working Europe – Reshaping European Employment Systems*. Ashgate, Aldershot.

Pfau-Effinger, B. 1999c. The modernisation of motherhood in Western Europe in cross-national perspective. In Crompton, R. (ed.) *Restructuring Gender Relations and Employment: the Decline of the Male Breadwinner?*, pp. 60–79. Oxford University Press, Oxford.

Pfau-Effinger, B. 1999d. Change of family policies in the socio-cultural context of European Societies. In Leira, A. (ed.) *Family Policies Yearbook: Comparative Social Research*, pp. 135–159. JAI Press, Stamford.

Pfau-Effinger, B. 2000a. *Kultur und Frauenerwerbstätigkeit im europäischen Vergleich*. Leske und Budrich, Opladen.

Pfau-Effinger, B. 2000b. Kontextualisierung der international vergleichenden Analyse von Arbeitsmarktwandel. In Berger, P.A. and Konietzka, D. (eds) *Neue Ungleichheiten der Erwerbsgesellschaft*. Leske und Budrich, Opladen, in press.

Pfau-Effinger, B. and Geissler, B. 1992. Institutionelle und sozio-kulturelle Kontextbedingungen der Entscheidung verheirateter Frauen für Teilzeitarbeit: Ein Beitrag zu einer Soziologie der Erwerbsbeteiligung. *Mitteilungen aus der Arbeitsmarkt- und Berufsforschung*, 31, 3.

Schenk, S. 1995. Neu-oder Restrukturierung des Geschlechterverhältnisses in Ostdeutschland? *Berliner Journal für Soziologie*, 5, 4, 475–488.

Siim, B. 1994. Engendering democracy – the interplay between citizenship and political participation. *Social Politics*, 1, 3, 286–306.

Wimmer, A. 1996. Kultur: Zur Reformulierung eines sozialanthropologischen Grundbegriffs. *Kölner Zeitschrift für Soziologie und Sozialpsychologie*, 49, 3, 401–425.

Yeandle, S. 1999. Gender contracts, welfare systems and "non-standard working": diversity and change in Denmark, France, Germany, Italy and the U.K. In Felstead, A. and Jewson, N. (eds) *Global Trends in Flexible Labour*, pp. 95–118. Macmillan, Basingstoke.

Index

actor–structure dichotomy in welfare 134–7
Addabbo, T. 245, 251
ageing and citizenship 160–1
AGISRA (Arbeitsgemeinschaft gegen
   internationale sexuelle und rassistische
   Ausbeutung) 157
alienation in paid work 44–5
alternative living arrangements 49, 50, 51,
   79–81
alternative scenarios on divisions of labour
   109–10
Alwin, *et al.* 238, 247
ambiguity of 'change' in families 51
Anderson, B. and Phizacklea, A. 159, 160,
   161
anthropology, explaining gender inequalities
   102
anti-essentialism in gender analysis 115–16,
   130–2
Anttonen, A. 126
Apitzsch, U. 162
Archer, J. 173
Archer, M.S. 144, 266, 268
Das Argument 147
Ashford, S. and Timms, N. 249, 256, 257
attitudes and practices compared 237–51
attitudes to women's roles: analysis of 242–
   51; summary of analysis 250–1
Australian Labour Force Survey (1996) 156
authority: order and stability 134; welfare
   and political 130–2, 133–4, 138
autonomy of women and intervention 199–
   201

Bader, V. 145
Bagguley, *et al.* 17
Balibar, E. 149
Bang, *et al.* 130
Bang, H.P. 131
Bang, H.P. and Dyrberg, T.B. 131, 137
Bang, H.P. and Sørensen, E. 130
Barbalet, J.M. 163
Barlow, A. and Duncan, S. 70, 71, 76

Barret, M. and MacIntosh, M. 49
Barthes, R. 215
Baxter, J. 108
Baylina, M. and Garcia-Ramon, D. 29, 45
Beck, U. 63, 128, 269
Becker, G.S. 49, 63, 102, 103, 119
Bellaagh, K. and Gonäs, L. 43
Benard, C. 174
Benard, C. and Schlaffer, E. 176
Benard, *et al.* 177, 188
Benhabib, *et al.* 148
Berg, A.M. 117
Bernard, J. 49
Best, D.L. and Williams, J.E. 194
Bettio, F. and Villa, P. 66
Bhabha, J. and Shutter, S. 151
Bimbi, F. 60
biosocial explanations of violence 173
birth outside marriage, social meaning of
   76–8
Björnberg, U. 106
Blau, F.D. and Ferber, M.S. 119
Blossfeld, *et al.* 64
Blossfeld, H.-P. and Rohwer, G. 246
Blumler, J. 212
Bobbio, N. 165
Boehnisch, L. and Winter, R. 173, 174
Boh, *et al.* 61, 69, 73, 76
Born, *et al.* 251, 254
Bourdieu, *et al.* 115
Bourdieu, P. 131, 135, 138
Bourdieu, P. and Passeron, J.-C. 132
Bradshaw, *et al.* 57
Brah, A. 149
Brannen, J. and Moss, P. 105
Brants, K. and Siune, K. 213
Britain: comedy and career-oriented women
   227; comedy and professional women
   216–17; deconstruction of nuptiality in
   221–2; families and society in 54–5;
   gendered class attitudes 219–20; liberal
   welfare tradition in 224–5; post-war
   migration to 150–1, 152

British Nationality Act (1981) 150
broadcasting systems, differences in 212–13
Brooks, A. 115
Bruegel, I. 46
Bruegel, I. and Perrons, D. 34
Bühler, E. 20, 44, 271
Bubeck, D.E. 104, 233, 255
Bulletin (EC Network of Experts on Situation of Women in Labour Market) 237, 239–41, 244–6
Burchell, *et al.* 247
Bussemaker, J. and van Kersbergen, K. 124, 125
Butler, J. and Scott, J.W. 131, 136

Calloni, M. 163
Campani, G. 160
Canada, Census data (1991) 156
care for the elderly (and other adults) 101
Catalunya, Generalitat de 83
challenges to violence 181, 188–91
Champion, A.G. 155
childcare 97, 100–1
Childcare, EC Network on 118, 120
Chodorow, N. 101, 102
'choices' of women, negative effects of 87
Christiansen, E. and Koch-Nielsen, I. 183
citizenship, migration and social inequalities: ageing 160–1; Britain, post-war migration to 150–1, 152; changing migrant profiles 155; citizenship, dynamic form of 165; citizenship, grounding principles of traditional form 163–4; communist regimes, fall of 162; cooperation and collaboration 163; cosmopolitanism 161–5; de-colonialisation 152; demand for domestic work 161; democratic balance, fairness and 165; differentiated universalism 164–5; domestic workers, migration of 158–61; education, devaluation of 161; feminisation of migration 155–7; gender balance of old migration 154; gender contracts and migration 144–6, 148; gender contracts and multiculturalism 143–4, 145; gender, contracts and 143–9; Germany, post-war migration to 152–3; globalisation 161–5; Holland, post-war migration to 151–2; interconnected levels of discussion on 148; interpretation of statistics, difficulties with 157–8; migration, European perspectives on 146–7; migration, feminised 158–61; migration, interconnected human rights and 164; migration, multifaceted nature of female 162; migration, reconceptualisation of

144–5; migration, the 'new' and a 'new Europe' 154–8; migration, the old and its aftermath 149–54; multiculturalism 161–5; new migration, distinguishing features of 155; politics of borders 147; public–private divide, domestic employment and the 160; spousal egalitarianism, myth of 160–1; traditional citizenship and cultural variables 147–8
Clarke, L. and Henwood, M. 55
Cockburn, C. 103
Codagnone, C. 155
cohabitation: pattern of increase in 75; proneness to 70; stability of 68–9
Cohen, J.L. and Arato, A. 132
cohesion policies and paid work 45–6
Collinson, *et al.* 103
Coltrane, S. 105
Commonwealth Immigrants Acts (1962 and 1968) 150
communist regimes, fall of 162
connection of values 251–4
Connell, R.W. 175, 202, 254, 262, 268
Connolly, W.E. 133, 135
Conservative Welfare Regime 5, 6
contingent foundationalism 132
control by violence *see* violence, men towards women
Cooke, P. 17
Cornelius, *et al.* 155
cosmopolitanism 161–5
Cottar, A. and Willems, W. 151
Council of Europe 76, 77, 157, 193
couples with children 53–5
couples without children 55–6
Crompton, R. 128, 212, 225, 227, 269, 273
cross-national comparisons: differences in welfare regimes 121–3, 126, 129; integration of culture into 264–71; lack of research on 171
Crouch, C. 62
Cruz, P. 76
CTS (Conflict Tactics Scale) 182–5
culture: classification of models of 126–30; concrete definition of 265–6; cultural theories of violence 175; foundation of gender arrangements, explanatory power of 270–1; growth of interest in 235; integration of cross-national analyses 264–71; mixes in models of 128–9; myths and specificity of sitcom content 212; paid work and cultural traditions 43–5; social action and gender arrangement 266–9; variation in models of 124–5; violence and 'feminine' 193–4; violence and 'masculine' 193–4; violence and meanings of actions 177–8

Dahlström, M. 44
Dal Lago, A. 163
Daly, M. and Wilson, M. 173
Davidoff, L. 109
De Certeau, M. 132
De Santis, G. 68, 83
de-colonialisation 152
de-institutionalisation of families 50–1, 62–3, 75–6
Deacon, *et al.* 5
definition: of culture 265–6; of violence (and measurement of) 177–80
Della Costa, M. and James, S. 104
Delphy, C. 189, 197
Delphy, C. and Leonard, D. 27, 64, 103–4, 105
democratic balance, fairness and 165
demographic pattern changes 50, 54
demographic research, implications for 81
Denmark, telephone survey of violence 183–4, 187
Dietz, M. 233, 256
differentiated: family orientation 254–5; patriarchy 8–11, 212; universalism 164–5; vulnerability to violence 174–5, 194–6
diversity: complexity converging to 61–2, 80; in 'equality' models 273
divisions of labour, reconciliation of: anthropology, explaining gender inequalities 102; care for the elderly (and other adults) 101; childcare 97, 100–1; complexity of 'atypical' working arrangements 96; domestic 219–21; 'economic activity', measurement of 88–94; 'economic activity', rates of 89–90; education 98–9; familial exploitation 104–5; family workers 93–4; fatherhood, changing masculinities and the role of 106; Folbre's alternative scenarios on 109–10; full-time employment 90–2; gendered nature of part-time employment 92; homeworking 94–5; households and 99–101; housewives, 'economically inactive' 97–9; human capital theory, explaining gender inequalities 102–3; ideal and actual 240, 242; labour markets and 88–99, 107; marriage and housework 104–5; married women, part-time employment of 92; Marxist feminist debate, explaining gender inequalities 103–4; negative effects of women's 'choices' 87; paid work, female participation in 88–99, 107; part-time employment 90–3; patriarchy, paid work and the household 87–8; patriarchy, state welfare and 99;

patriarchy, structures of 87; patriarchy, working arrangements and 105; psychoanalytic theory, explaining gender inequalities 101–2; reasons for part-time working 92–3; role sharing 108–9; Saturday/Sunday working 94–5; scoiological theory, explaining gender inequalities 103; shift working 95–6; social change and 263, 265; socialisation of housework 104; spatial differences in inequality, gendered states of welfare 106–8; temporary working 94; traditional measures of labour market activity 88–9; weekend working 94–5; welfare states and housework 107–8; working arrangements, female/male differences 96–7, 99
divorce 71–3
Dobash, *et al.* 177
Dobash, R.E. and Dobash, R.P. 173, 176
domestic work, demand for 161
domestic work, migration for 158–61
domestic work, public–private divide and 160; see also employment
Drew, E. 92, 99
Drew, *et al.* 97, 108
Duncan, S.: differentiated patriarchy 212; divergence, women's relationships with men 211; 'dual role' of women in British textile industry areas 272; gender contracts, transition in 13; gender cultures, variations in 271; gender relations in Ireland 244; gender, cross-national variations in gender inequalities 265; gendering welfare regimes 8, 21, 106–7, 199; geography of gender 18; independence of women 19; male as norm 144; motherhood in Scandinavia 242, 244; national boundaries, research deficiencies of using only 254; opportunity inequality 255; patriarchy 9; spatial contingency 3, 223–4
Duncan, S. and Edwards, R.: culture, central role of 265; family orientation 254; gender, welfare state classification and 6; gendered moral rationalities 225; 'genderfare' in developed countries 15–16, 126; interpretation and differentiation 237; lone parenthood 56–7, 247; patriarchy, escape from 78; social behaviour 129, 139; women's work, locality and tradition 18
Duncan, S. and Savage, M. 3
Duncan, S. and Smith, D. 271
Durkheim, E. 234
dynamic citizenship 165

Easton, D. 131, 134, 135, 138
Eaton, M. 213
ECHP (European Community Household
  Panel) 93, 97–8, 100
economic: 'activity', measurement of 88–94;
  dependency 73; determinism,
  prolongation of 18–20; equality, progress
  towards and violence 191–3; factors in
  social change 265; inactivity, housewives,
  of 97–9; inactivity, demarcation of 29;
  restructuring and female participation
  37–9; transformation and gender
  relations 45–6
Eduards, M. 190
education: devaluation of 161; divisions of
  labour and 98–9
efficacy of violence 180–81
egalitarian gender relationships 49
Egger, *et al.* 189, 190, 199
Elkins, D.J. and Simeon, R.E.B. 235
Ellingsaeter, A.-L. 238, 256, 257, 269
Elman, R.A. 198
Elman, R.A. and Eduards, M. 177
Elsthain, J.B. 233
Emerek, R. 104, 105
employment: activity by gender and age 29–
  36; attitudes towards female 216–19;
  female participation in paid work 28, 88–
  99, 107, 116–19, 120, 130; full time 90–2;
  gendered nature of part-time 92; part-
  time 90–3, 117–19; part-time working,
  reasons for 92–3; relative wages of
  women 119; self-employment 41; shift-
  working 95–6; temporary working 94;
  unemployment levels 35–6; weekend
  working 94–5; working arrangements in
  96–7, 99; *see also* domestic work
empowerment and promotion of equality
  125–6
epistemology and theory, relationship
  between 135–6
equality: central nature of value 234;
  contract for 13; difference and 254–6;
  ideal and reality of 240–1; normative
  measure of 272–3; relational concept of
  gender 271–3; *see also* gender inequality,
  inequality
Ercomer (1999) 162
Ermisch, J.F. and Wright, R.E. 57
escalation of violence 177
Esping-Andersen, G.: comparative approach
  to welfare state regimes 144, 211;
  gendering welfare capitalism 4, 28, 106–
  7; integration of gender differences 135;
  variations in welfare state regimes 116,
  126
essentialism in gender analysis 116, 130–2

Etzioni, A. 132
European citizenship *see* citizenship
European Commission 37, 46, 55, 69, 76, 97
European surveys of violence 185–6
European Urban and Regional Studies 21
European Women's Lobby 176
Eurostat: divorce 71–2; employment 91;
  families, both parents working 100;
  female activity rates 90; fertility rates
  61; household size 59; housewives and
  education levels 99, 100; inactive women
  98; labour force participation 120, 156;
  labour force survey data from 28–41;
  lone-parent families 56, 83; male activity
  rates 83; migration, report on 157; part-
  time working 92, 93; remarriage 79;
  unemployment rates 156
evolutionary explanations of violence 173
EVS (European Values Survey) 237–9, 244

Fagan, C. and O'Reilly, J. 266
Fagan, *et al.* 263
families and households, changing
  arrangements: alternative living
  arrangements 49, 50, 51, 79–81;
  ambiguity of term 'change' 51; birth
  outside marriage, social meaning of 76–
  8; British society and 54–5; cohabitation,
  pattern of increase in 75; cohabitation,
  proneness to 70; cohabitation, stability of
  68–9; complexity, 'converging to
  diversity' 61–2, 80; concept of 'family' 52;
  concept of 'household' 52; contextual
  considerations 51–2; couples with
  children 53–5; couples without children
  55–6; de-institutionalisation 50–1, 62–3,
  75–6; demographic pattern changes 50,
  54; demographic research, implications
  for 81; divorce 71–3; dynamics of, and
  explanations of violence 173–4; economic
  model of 14, 127; egalitarian gender
  relationships 49; familial exploitation
  104–5; family workers 93–4; female
  economic dependency 73; feminisation of
  childhood 56; feminisation of poverty 57;
  fertility 54, 61; gender difference 61;
  gender relations and living
  arrangements 49–52; gender
  relationships, reformulation of 80–2;
  household forms 52–3; household size
  58–62; household structures, regional
  variations in 226; households and
  divisions of labour 99–101; housewife
  marriage model 49, 63, 79–81;
  independence within family 66; LAT
  (living-apart-together) 49, 50, 66; lone
  living, one person living alone 57–8; lone

motherhood, societal perceptions of 78–9; lone parenthood 56–7; marriage, rejection as only form for relationships 63–75, 82; Mediterranean societies and 54, 66; national and regional differences 81–2; parental home, prolongation of stay in 66–7; partnership, durational differences in 68–9; patterns of new and old households 52–62; Portugal, case study on sub-national differences 73–5; postponement of marriage and fertility 64–5; radical feminist theory on 63–4; reproduction, rejection of family union as only context for 75–9, 82; Scandinavian society and 54, 55; sex bias in marriage 79; social change and 263–4; theoretical explanations 62–3; transformation in family life 51; unpaid work, unequal distribution of 60; welfare state and family function 70–5; women's individual strategies 50–1; women's role in inducement of change 50–1, 62–79

Farganis, S. 233, 234

Fassmann, H. and Münz, R. 155

fatherhood, changing masculinities and the role of 106

Federkeil, G. 71

Felling, *et al.* 249

Felson, R.B. and Tedeschi, J.T. 193

feminisation: of caring 217; of childhood 56; of migration 155–7; of poverty 57

Ferrara, M. 5

fertility 54, 61, 64–5

Feuer, J. 214, 230

FFS (Fertility and Family Survey) 56, 58, 66, 75

Finch, J. 247

Fiske, J. 216

Folbre, N. 109, 110

Forsberg, G. 20, 27, 36, 224, 228, 271

Foucault, M. 130–31

Fox-Harding, L. 70

Fraser, N. 148, 249, 254–5

Frauenforschung, Zentrum für interdisziplinäre (ZiF) 184

freedom: central nature of value 234; models of and recognition of differences 255–6; power and 137–8

Friedland, R. and Alford, R.R. 235, 256

Friese, M. 161

Fuchs, D. 235

Gardiner, J. 104

Geissler, B. and Oechsle, M. 270, 271

Gelles, R.J. and Loseke, D.R. 179

gender arrangement: culture, social interaction and 266–9; welfare and 124–5

gender balance of old migration 154

gender blindness of welfare regime classification 6

gender coding of society (and gender system) 12

gender contracts: citizenship, migration and 143–9; multiculturalism and 143–4, 145; myths and 212; national models of 42–3; nature of 12–15; paid work and perceptions of 41–2; paid work and social relations 46; sub-national scales of 20

gender cultures: differentiated in sitcoms 211–15; dual breadwinner/dual carer model 128; dual breadwinner/state carer model 128; dual earner/marketised female carer model 128; male breadwinner/female home carer model 14, 127; male breadwinner/female part-time carer model 14, 127; sitcoms and 223–9; three worlds of 12–21; values in the EU 237–51

gender differences: in families 61; in paid work 28–36; in socio-cultural contexts 212, 223–4, 229; in violence 177

'genderfare' 15–16

gender inequality (comparison of theories of): comparative categorisation of gender inequality 9–11; Conservative Welfare Regime 5, 6; differentiated patriarchy 8–11, 212; divisions of labour and space 17; economic determinism, prolongation of 18–20; equality, contract for 13; family economic model 14; gender blindness of welfare regime classification 6; gender coding of society (and gender system) 12; gender contracts, nature of 12–15; gender cultures, three worlds of 12–21; gender variations in welfare regimes 15; gender-sensitive welfare regime classification 6–8, 211–12; 'genderfare' 15–16; geography of gender 17–18; housewife contract 13; inequality, variations in 1; Japanese style welfare state 5; Liberal Welfare Regime 4; male breadwinner/female home carer model 14; male breadwinner/female part-time carer model 14; Mediterranean Welfare State Regime 5; national assumptions in social policy 16–17; outcomes, space and gender 2; patriarchy, geographical differences in 10–11; patriarchy, structures of 9–11, 87; regional traditions of social integration 19; research, need for further 20–1; scale effect of 2; social constitution of spatial differences 3; Social Democratic Welfare Regime 4–5; social processes and space

2, 3; socio-economic position of women 8; spatial determinism 3; spatiality and 1–21; spatiality, neglect of 1–3; sub-national scales of gender contracts 20; welfare regimes, classification of 4–8

gender-neutral societies and violence 192–3

gender relations: families and reformulation of 80–2; living arrangements and 49–52; paid work and 36–41

gender representations and the sitcom 215–23

gender segregation by economic sector 39–40, 41

gender-sensitive welfare regime classification 6–8, 211–12

gender structures: main changes in 263–4; mutual interrelationship of 262; regional differences in 271: social change in 269

geography of gender 17–18

Germany: crime survey of violence in 184, 187–8; family forms and female employment in 251–4; post-war migration to 152–3

Giddens, A. 131, 134, 135, 234, 268

Gilbert, P. 174

Gillioz, *et al.* 174, 178, 183, 185–7

Ginn, J. and Arber, S. 125

Giovannini, D. 97, 106

Gislason, I.A. 174, 183

Glendon, M.A. 197

Glenn, E.N. 237

globalisation and citizenship 161–5

Godenzi, A. 175, 176, 180

Gonäs, L. 32

Gonäs, L. and Spånt, A. 29

Gottlieb, B. 252

Gottschall, K. 274

Graaf, de, P. and Vermeulen, H. 248

Greece: 'progressive' reality in 228; development of feminism in 227; equality ideals in 224; gender culture in 226–7; segregation of domestic roles in 220–1; tradition and modernity in 222; women's power in sitcoms 218–19

Gregory, D. and Urry, J. 3

Gregory, J. and Lees, S. 189

Gregson, N. and Lowe, M. 161

Gunnell, J.D. 132

Gustafsson, S. and Jacobsson, R. 119

Gutmann, A. and Thompson, D. 145

Häussermann, H. 18

Häussermann, H. and Siebel, W. 265

Haavio-Mannila, E. 126

Habermas, J. 134, 135

Hagemann-White, C. 176, 178

Hagemann-White, *et al.* 176, 177

Hahn, C. 234

Hakim, C 249–50

Haller, M. and Höllinger, F. 125

Hancock, L. 73

Hanetseder, C. 176

Hanmer, J. 172, 178, 196–7

Hanmer, J. and Sanders, S. 176

Harding, *et al.* 234

Hargreaves, A.G. 257

Harris, C. 150

Hartmann, H. 49

Hearn, J. 172, 175, 176, 187, 202

Heath, S. and Miret, P. 66

Heiligers, P. 124

Heimer, G. 186

Heise, L.L. 173

Heiskanen, M. and Piispa, M. 174, 180, 183, 185, 186

Held, D. 132

Held, *et al.* 161, 164

Hernes, H.M. 83, 115

Hester, *et al.* 174, 176

Hirdman, Y.: differential patriarchy 11; gender contracts 12–13, 27, 99, 124, 145, 224; gender system 12, 124, 144

Hirdman, Y. and Åström, G. 42

Hirst, P. 132

Höpflinger, F. 109

Hobson, B. 5

Hoecker, B. 264

Hoffman-Nowotny, H.J. and Fux, B. 103

Hofstede, G. 193, 202

Holland, post-war migration to 151–2

Holmes, C. 150

Holst, E. 123

homeworking: and divisions of labour 94–5; and paid work 45

Honnegger, C. and Heintz, B. 127

Hoppe, M. 193

households *see* families and households, changing arrangements

housewife: contract 13; designation as 'economically inactive' 97–9; marriage model 49, 63, 79–81

human capital theory 102–3

Humphreys, *et al.* 109

Humphreys, P.J. 213

independence and family 66

individuals and values 236–7

Industrial Revolution 19

INE Demographic Statistics 74

inequality: forms of gendered social 262–3; gender regimes, cultures and contracts 41–6; mapping and explaining in paid work 27–8; patterns in paid work 28–41; variations in gender 1; *see also* equality; gender inequality

Inglehart, R. 249

Innovation: the European Journal of the Social Sciences 21
institutional change 235–6, 264, 265, 269
institutionalism, new 136
Instuitut für Praxisorientierte Sozialforschung 184
intervention strategies on violence 189–90, 199–201
Ishwaran, K. 124

Japanese style welfare state 5
Jarvis, H. 18
Jaspard, M. 186
Jensen, A.M. 51, 55, 56
Jensen, P.H. 119, 270
Jepperson, R.L. 235
Jepperson, R.L. and Swidler, A. 235, 238
Johnson, H. 185
Jong Gierveld, de, J. and Liefbroer, A.C. 248
Jonung, C. and Persson, I. 29
Jukes, A.E. 175, 176
Jurado, T. and Naldini, M. 54, 75

Kamerman, S.B. and Kahn, A.J. 119
Kandiyoti, D. 175, 195
Kaufmann, *et al.* 60
Kaufmann, F.X. 122
Kauppinen, K. and Kandolin, I. 38
Kay, D. and Miles, R. 150
Keane, J. 132
Keesing, R.M. 237
Kelleher, *et al.* 184, 185, 186
Kelly, L. 176, 177, 181
Kennedy, F. and McCormack, K. 78
Kiernan, K. 65, 69, 70
King, M. 155
Klijzing, E. and Macura, M. 78
Knijn, T. 124, 125, 248–9, 270
Knijn, T. and Kremer, M. 269
Knudsen, L.B. 60
Kofman (1996) 155
Koser, K. 155
Koser, K. and Lutz, H. 154, 155
Kovalainen, A. 144
Kuijsten, A. 61–62
Kyriazis, N. 43, 221, 226–7, 228

Labour Force Surveys (EU) 97
labour markets and divisions of labour 88–99, 107
Laclau, E. 135
Landecker, W. 256
Langan, M. and Ostner, I. 6, 7
LAT (living-apart-together) 49, 50, 66
Le Bras, H. 247
Le Gall, D. and Martin, C. 250
Lees, S. 189

Lefaucheur, N. and Martin, C. 245
Leibfried, S. 6
Leira, A. 55, 119, 257
Lepsius, R.M. 267
Lesthaeghe, R. 72
Lewis, J.: breadwinner states 7, 8, 107, 211; childcare 100; France, 'parental model' welfare state 245; gender blindness of analysis 6; gender welfare regimes approach 27; integration and employment 264
liberal feminism 233
Liberal Welfare Regime 4
liberalism, third way between socialism and 134–7
Liddington, X. 19–20
life, violence in everyday 186–8
Lister, R. 115, 145, 164
Little, J. 19
Lockwood, D. 266, 268
Logar, R. 200
lone living 57–8
lone motherhood 78–9
lone parenthood 56–7
Lorentzen, J. and Løkke, P.A. 173
Lorini, M. 121
Lourenço, *et al.* 182, 183, 185
Lovell, T. 213
Lüsebrink, K. 252
Lundgren, E. 175, 177, 202
Lutz, *et al.* 149
Lutz, H. 151, 152, 166
Lutz, H. and Huth-Hildebrandt, C. 162

Maastricht Treaty 144, 146, 149, 153
McDonald, P. 61, 217
McDowell, L. 46
McDowell, L. and Massey, D. 18
Mahon, E. 76, 78
mapping of violence 180–1
March, J.G. and Olsen, J.P. 131
Margalit, A. 165
Mark-Lawson *et al.* 19
Mark-Lawson, J. 19
marriage: family life and 221–3; housework and 104–5; part-time employment of married women 92; postponement of 64–5; rejection as only form for relationships 63–75, 82; sex bias in 79; social meaning of birth outside 97
Marshall, T.H. 163
marxist feminist debate, explaining gender inequalities 103–4
Massey, D. 17
Medhurst, A. and Tuck, L. 213, 229
Mediterranean societies and families 54, 66
Mediterranean Welfare State Regime 5, 43

Meil, G. 57
Meisaari-Polsa, T. 68
Meulemann, H. 249
Meyer, T. 265
migration: changing migrant profiles 155;
European perspectives on 146–7;
feminised 158–61; interconnected
human rights and 164; multifaceted
nature of female 162; 'new' (and
distinguishing features of) 155; 'new' and
the 'new Europe' 154–8; 'old' and
aftermath 149–54; reconceptualisation of
144–5
Miles, R. 150
Millar, J. 78
Millar, J. and Warman, A. 120, 121
Mincer, J. 119
Mingione, E. 60, 66, 251
Minssen, A. and Müller, U. 173
misfits and interpretation 121
Mitchell, E. 105, 108
Mitchell, J. 233
Mósesdóttir, L. 139
'modernist' feminism and welfare 115
Morokvasic, M. 153, 155, 160
Moss, P. 121
mothers and violence 196–9
Mouffe, C. 133, 233, 256
Münz, R. 153, 155
Mujer, Instituto de la 203
Mullender, A. 174
multiculturalism and citizenship 161–5
myths, sitcoms illustrative of: Barthes on
myths 215–16; British comedy and
women professionals 216–17; British
comedy, career-oriented women in 227;
British deconstruction of nuptiality 221–
2; British gendered class attitudes 219–
20; British liberal welfare tradition
224–5; differentiated broadcasting
systems 212–13; differentiated gender
cultures and the sitcom 211–15;
differentiated patriarchy 212; domestic
division of labour 219–21; female
employment, attitudes towards 216–19;
femininity and caring 217; gender
contracts 212; gender disparity, socio-
cultural contexts of 212, 223–4, 229;
gender representations and the sitcom
215–23; gendered welfare modelling
211–12; Greek 'progressive' reality 228;
Greek comedy, power of women in 218–
19; Greek equality ideals 224; Greek
feminism, development of 227; Greek
gender culture 226–7; Greek interplay of
tradition and modernity 222; Greek
segregation of domestic roles 220–1;

household structures, regional variations
in 226; marriage and family life 221–3;
naturalisation of history 216; progressive
myths 229–31; sitcom development 214–
5; sitcom representation and gender
culture 223–9; sitcom as tool for
examination of gender inequality 213;
Spanish 'demographic transitions' 228;
Spanish comedy and social reality 219;
Spanish cultural transition in division of
domestic labour 221; Spanish family
structures, wide variety of 222–3;
specificity of cultural context 212;
spousal egalitarianism 160–1;
stereotyping 213–14; Swedish division of
domestic labour 220; Swedish gender
culture 228; Swedish masculine
domesticity 222; Swedish positivism on
women in employment 217–18; Swedish
social democratic welfare regime 225;
traditional myths 229–31

Nätti, J. 117
national and regional differences in family
life 81–2
national assumptions in social policy 16–17
naturalisation of history 216
Nauck, B. 253, 254
Neale, S. 213
Neale, S. and Krutnik, F. 214, 230
Neidhard, F. 266
Newell, S. 105
Nickel, H. 128, 271
Nilsson, A. 51
Nini, *et al.* 176
Nussbaum, M. and Glover, J. 165
Nussbaum, M. and Sen, A. 165

Oberlies, D. 181
OECD 120, 125, 126, 154, 155, 157
Olsen, J.P. 136
Oppenheimer, V.K. 65
O'Reilly, J. 266
Orloff, A.S. 115, 144
Ortner, S. 102
Ostner, I. 7, 8, 87, 104
outcomes, space and gender 2

paid work: active/inactive, demarcation line
between 29; activity by gender and age
29–36; alienation 44–5; cohesion policies
and 45–6; culture and traditions 43–5;
economic restructuring and female
participation 37–9; economic
transformation and gender relations 45–
6; gender contracts, national models of
42–3; gender contracts, perceptions of

41–2; gender contracts, social relations and 46; gender differences and 28–36; gender relations in 36–41; gender segregation by economic sector 39–40, 41; homeworking 45; inequality in, gender regimes, cultures and contracts 41–6; inequality in, mapping and explaining 27–8; inequality in, patterns of 28–41; Mediterranean welfare model 43; occupational segregation 41; participation in 28; regional dimensions, weighting gender differences 36; Scandinavian welfare model 43; self-employment 41; spatial scales and 28; unemployment levels 35–6

Palidda, S. 163

parental home, prolongation of stay in 66–7

parental leave arrangements 122–3

Parsons, T. 49, 133, 235

Parsons, T. and Bales, R.F. 49, 103

partnership, durational differences in 68–9

Pateman, C. 145, 270

patriarchy: geographical differences in 10–11; intervention in violence and 199–201; paid work and the household 87–8; state welfare and 99; structures of 9–11, 87; working arrangements and 105

patterns of old and new households 52–62

Peng, I. 5

perceptions and explanations of violence 201–2

Perrons, D. 27, 32, 36, 45, 46

Perrons, D. and Gonäs, L. 27

Peters, *et al.* 249

Pfau-Effinger, B.: change, gender arrangements and 270; childcare 122; classification of gender cultural models 126–7; comparison of welfare regimes 119, 125; cross-national differences, gender arrangements 271; culture, social structures and institutions 266; dominant ideals 267; female employment participation 248; 'gender arrangement' approach of 268; gender contracts 27, 124; gender cultural models, complexity of interrelationships 128–30; gender culture 14, 225, 265; gender equality as relational concept 271–3; gender inequality, dynamic nature of social processes of 212; gender, contracts and citizenship 144, 145; heterogeneity in marital behaviour 65; part-time working 126; violence, differential vulnerability 174

Pfau-Effinger, B. and Geissler, B. 123, 265

Phillips, A. 165

Phizacklea, A. 155, 157, 159, 160

Pilkington, H. 155

Pinnelli, A. and De Rose, A. 245

Plantenga, J. 125, 126

politics: borders and 147; decision making 264; European institutions 146; political community and welfare 135; political content of research into violence 176; practices of governance 136–7; solidarity in welfare 131; violence and progress to equality in 191–3

Portugal, case study on sub-national differences 73–5

Posse, B. and Heimer, G. 198

post-modernist theory 233, 234

power and freedom 137–8

power and the state 130–31

Praxisorientierte Sozialforschung, Institut für (IPOS) 184

prevalence surveys on violence 181–6

Pringle, K. 119

progressive myths 229–31

psychoanalytic theory, explaining gender inequalities 101–2

public–private divide, domestic employment and the 160

Putman, R.D. 133

quality of welfare schemes 122

Qvortrup, J. 51

Räthzel, N. 149

radical feminist theory on families 63–4

Rantzinger, *et al.* 160

Rawls, J. 137, 145

regional traditions of social integration 19

relationship between values 233–7

religious beliefs 234

reproduction, rejection of family as sole context for 75–9, 82

Rerrich, M. 160

research: design to map indicators of violence 181; methodological problems of surveys on violence 178–80; need for further on gender inequality 20–1

Römkens, R. 183, 185, 186

Robertson, R. 234, 235

Rogers, B. 102

role sharing 108–9

Roll, J. 57

Rosenbaum, H. 237, 251

Rosenfeld, M. 234

Rost, H. and Schneider, N.F. 247

Roussel, L. 226

Rowbotham, S. and Tate, J. 89

Rowe, K. 218

Rubery, *et al.* 28, 32, 41

Ruddick, S. 233

Rudolph, H. 153, 155
Rudolph, H. and Hillmann, F. 155
Rudolph, H. and Hübner, S. 153
Ruggie, M. 106
Russell, S.T. 56

Sackmann, R. 199, 212, 224, 237, 251
Sackmann, R. and Haüssermann, H. 18, 19, 251
Sainsbury, D. 5, 8, 27, 28, 196
Saraceno, C. 59
Sayad, A. 146
Sayer, A. 3, 9
scale effect of gender inequality 2
Scandinavian: society and families 54, 55; welfare model 43
Schama, S. 129
Schengen Treaty 147, 165
Schenk, S. 271
Schmidt, M. 252
Schröttle, M. 183, 192
Schultheis, F. 245, 246
Schuster, J. 151, 152
Schwartz, M.D. 177
Scully, D. 203
Segal, L. 87, 97, 106
segregation, occupational 41
Segura, D.A. 237
Seidler, V.J. 175
sexuality and violence 202–3
Sgritta, G.B. 236
Siaroff, A. 6, 21
Sieder, R. 237, 251
Siim, B. 115, 116, 269
Silva, E. and Smart, C. 55
Silverstone, R. 215
sitcoms: development of 214–15; gender culture represented by 223–9; gender representations in 215–23; toll for examination of gender inequality 213
skandalon (stumbling block) in explanations of violence 175
Sørensen, A. 70
Sørensen, B.W. 176, 180, 188
social change and gender cultures: class and change 264; comparative statistics, problem of 273–4; cultural foundation of gender arrangements, explanatory power of 270–1; culture, definition of 265–6; culture, integration into cross-national analyses 264–71; culture, social action and gender arrangement 266–9; diversity of 'equality' models 273; divisions of labour 263, 265; economic factors 265; families and households 263–4

social forms of gendered social inequalities 262–3; 'gender arrangement' 266, 268; gender structures, main changes in 263–4; gender structures, mutual interrelationship of 262; gender structures, regional differences in 271; gender structures, social change in 269; institutional change 269; institutional factors 265; institutional frameworks 264; normative measure of 'gender equality' 272–3; political decision making 264; relational concept of 'gender equality' 271–3; social agency 267–8; social movements, promotion of change by 269–70; time lags and contradictions 270; traditional gender structures 272
social agency 267–8
social capital 133–4
social change and violence 192
social constitution of spatial differences 3
Social Democratic Welfare Regime 4–5
social feminism 233–4
Social Justice, Commission on 165
social movements, promotion of change by 269–70
social processes and space 2, 3
socialisation: and change 236; of housework 104; and interaction 234–5
socialism, third way between liberalism and 134–7
socio-economic position of women 8
socio-structural explanations of violence 174
sociological theory, explaining gender inequalities 103
Solsona, *et al.* 57, 73
Solsona, M. 67, 70, 80, 83, 226, 228
Solsona, M. and Treviño, R. 60
SOPEMI: *Trends in International Migration* 154, 155, 157
Soros Foundation 162
Soysal, Y.N. 164
spatiality: divisions of labour and 17; gender inequalities and 1–21; links to violence 173–5; neglect of 1–3; paid work and scales of 28; social construction of differences 3; spatial determinism 3; spatial differences in inequality 106–8; violence and patterns of 171–2
Spain: comedy and social reality in 219; cultural tradition in divisions of domestic labour 221; demographic transitions in 228; family structures, wide variety of 222–3
Specialists, Group of (1997) 178
Spigel, L. 213, 214, 215, 222

Squires, J. 234
Starling, R. 155
Stasilius, D. and Bakan Abigail, B. 165
statistics, problem of comparing 273–4
stereotyping 213–14; *see also* myths, sitcoms illustrative of
Stets, J.E. and Straus, M.A. 177
Stolk, B. van and Wouters, C. 176, 195
Stratigaki, M. and Vaiou, D. 29, 41, 43
Straus, M.A. 179
Straus, M.A. and Gelles, R.J. 177, 182
Strong, T.B. 137
structural efforts to address violence 190–1
structure (of this book) xiii
subjective nature of violence 172
Sundin, E. 18
Swartz, D. 131, 132, 135, 138
Sweden: divisions of domestic labour in 220; gender culture in 228; masculine domesticity in 222; positivism in women's employment in 217–18; social democratic welfare regime in 225
Symeonidou, H. 245

Taylor, E. 215
Tenfelde, K. 251
Teubner, *et al.* 176
Theorising Patriarchy (Walby, S.) 9
theory and epistemology, relationship between 135–6
time lags and contradictions in social change 270
traditional: citizenship 147–8, 163–4; gender structures 272; measures of labour market activity 88–9; myths 229–31
transformation in family life 51
Trifiletti, R. 5
trivialisation of violence 178
Tsaliki, L. 218

under-recording of violence 178
under-reporting of violence 176
UN-ECE 155
unemployed *see* employment 50–1
UNHCR 162
United Nations 162, 166
Unwin, T. 41
US National Family Violence Survey 179

Vaiou, D. 43
values and practices; attitudes and practices compared 237–51; attitudes to women's roles, analysis of 242–51; attitudes to women's roles, summary of analysis 250–1; connection of 251–4; culture, growing interest in 235; difference and equality 254–6; differentiation according to family orientation 254–5; divisions of labour, ideal and actual 240, 242; equality model, ideal and reality 240–1; equality, central nature of value 234; 'freedom models' and recognition of differences 255–6; freedom, central nature of value 234; gender in the EU 237–51; Germany, family forms and female employment in 251–4; indicative questions on attitudes towards gender roles 242; individuals and 236–7; institutions and change 235–6; liberal feminism 233; post-modernist theory 233, 234; relationship between 233–7; religious beliefs 234; social feminism 233–4; socialisation and change 236; socialisation and social interaction 234–5; women's roles, analysis of attitudes to 242–51
Van de Vliert, E. 194
Veil, M. 125
violence, men towards women: autonomy of women and intervention 199–201; biosocial explanations 173; challenges to 181, 188–91; control by means of 180–1; cross-national comparisons, lack of research on 171; cultural meanings of actions 177–8; cultural theories of 175; Danish telephone survey 183–4, 187; definition and measurement of 177–80; differential vulnerability and 174–5, 194–6; economic equality, progress towards, and 191–3; efficacy of 180–1; escalation of 177; European representative surveys 185–6; evolutionary explanations 173; family dynamics explanations 173–4; 'feminine' cultures and 193–4; gender disparity, women's violence to men 177; gender-neutral societies and 192–3; German crime survey 184, 187–8; interrelation of forms and sites of 176–7; intervention strategies 189–90, 199–201; mapping of 180–1; 'masculine' cultures and 193–4; men's propensity to encounter violence 188; mothers and the address of 196–9; patriarchy and intervention 199–201; patterns in everyday life 186–8; perceptions and explanations of 201–2; political content of research into 176; political equality, progress towards, and 191–3; prevalence surveys 181–6; research design to map indicators of 181
violence research surveys, methodological problems for 178–80; sexuality and 202–3; skandalon (stumbling block) in theoretical explanations of 175; social

change and 192; socio-structural explanations 174; spatiality, links to 173–5; spatial patterns, difficulty in identification of 171–2; structural efforts to address 190–1; subjective nature of 172; theories of 173–5; trivialisation of 178; under-recording of 178; under-reporting of 176; visibility, identification and documentation of the problem 175–7; visibility, increase in 171–3; vulnerability, levels of 195–6; wives and the address of 196–9

visibility of violence 171–3, 175–7

vulnerability to violence, levels of 195–6

Wajcman, J. 103

Walby, S.: choice and options 103; differentiated patriarchy 27; economic transformation and gender relations 45; familial exploitation 104; gender wage gap 73; jobs and gender 17; patriarchy 9–11, 42, 115; private patriarchy and state dependency 78; structures of patriarchy 87–8

Wallace, *et al.* 155

Weber, M. 234, 266

weekend working 94–5

Weinert, P. 157

Welch, M.R. and Martin, L.L. 79

welfare states, gender in context of: actor–structure dichotomy 134–7; anti-essentialism in gender analysis 115–16, 130–2; comparison of regimes 119–23; contingent foundationalism 132; cross-national differences in regimes 121–3, 126, 129; cultural models, classification of 126–30; cultural models, mixes in 128–9; dual breadwinner/dual carer model 128; dual breadwinner/state carer model 128; dual earner/marketised female carer model 128; empowerment and promotion of equality 125–6; essentialism in gender analysis 116, 130–2; family economic gender model 127; freedom, power and 137–8; gender arrangement and 124–5; liberalism, third way between socialism and 134–7; male breadwinner/female part-time carer model 127; male breadwinner/female home carer model 127; misfits and interpretation 121; 'modernist' feminism and 115; new institutionalism 136; order and stability, the problem of

authority 134; parental leave arrangements 122–3; part-time working 117–19; participation, female in labour force 116–19, 120, 130; policies, contextualisation of 115–16; policies, gender arrangements and 123–30; policies, interrelations with cultures, institutions and social agency 123–6; policies, interrelations with social practices 129–30; policies, variations and interpretation of 116–23; political authority 130–2, 133–4, 138; political community 135; political solidarity and 131; power and freedom 137–8; power and the state 130–1; practices of governance 136–7; quality of schemes 122; social capital 133–4; socialism, third way between liberalism and 134–7; theory and epistemology, relationship between 135–6; variation in cultural models 124–5; women, relative wages of 119

welfare capitalism 4–15

Welfare Capitalism, The Three Worlds of (Esping-Andersen, G.) 4, 211

welfare regimes: classification of 4–8; comparison of 119–23; family function and 70–5; gender variations in 15; housework and 107–8

Wetzels, *et al.* 174, 180, 182–4, 188

Wetzels, P. 174, 176, 187

Whatmore, S. 19

Williams, F. 16, 144, 145

Wimmer, A. 266

wives and violence 196–9

Women and Men in Europe 237, 240, 241, 272

Women of Europe 242, 247

women's roles: analysis of attitudes to 242–51; change and 50–1, 62–79

work, participation in *see* paid work

work, unequal distribution of unpaid 60

working arrangements, complexity of 96

Yeandle, S. 128, 273

Young, I.M. 249

Zentrum für interdisziplinäre Frauenforschung 184

Zincone, G. 163

Zugic, J. 162

Zulehner, P.M. and Denz, H. 242, 243, 256, 257